# To Build a Castle

# VLADIMIR BUKOVSKY

# To Build a Castle
## *My life as a dissenter*

*Translated from the Russian by*
MICHAEL SCAMMELL

ANDRE DEUTSCH

First published 1978 by
André Deutsch Limited
105 Great Russell Street London WC1

Printed in Great Britain by
Ebenezer Baylis and Son Ltd
The Trinity Press, Worcester, and London

ISBN 0 233 97023 1

# To Build a Castle

They say that if you bring a deep-sea diver too quickly to the surface he may die, or at the very least feel the blood boiling in his veins and everything bursting inside. That is rather how I felt one dark December morning in Vladimir prison.

It was the start of an ordinary prison day, a perfectly normal day in the endless monotonous round of life under lock and key. At six o'clock, as usual, the prison guard made his way from cell to cell, hammering on the doors with his keys and squawking hoarsely: 'Wake up! Wake up!' The convicts stirred in the cold grey light of dawn and crawled reluctantly out of their sacks, disentangling themselves from the blankets, reefer jackets and jerkins in which they had been wrapped up for the night: GET STUFFED!

The radio loudspeakers blared, booming out the solemn swelling chords of the national anthem, just as if it were parade time on Red Square. Jesus, somebody forgot to turn them off again last night! 'This is Moscow calling! Good morning, comrades. We shall begin our morning exercises with jogging on the spot.' For Christ's sake, turn the damn thing off! Every day in this country begins with jogging on the spot.

Even to a free man a gloomy winter's morning is like a hangover, but here in jail there is nothing more depressing. You haven't the least desire to live and the day ahead hangs over you like a curse. Not for nothing did the cons sing:

> You wake at dawn when the town still sleeps,
> In the jail, no sleep – the time for that's long gone,
> But your poor heart shudders and beats
> As if scorched by a passing flame.

The 'jail buggy' – the cart full of urns in which they brought breakfast to

7

the various blocks – came rumbling across the snowy yard. You could hear the urns being unloaded below and dragged heavily upstairs, their bottoms banging on the floor. Then came the sound of food flaps clicking open and shut, the tinny scrape of basins and mugs. The gruel came runny but hot. And hot water, the con's faithful companion. People were kicking up a racket, blinding and cursing – short measure, probably. They pounded the door with their basins. Too late. Missed the boat. You had to shove your basin out while the food flap was still open. Breakfast, clanking and rumbling like a medieval battle, passed on down the corridor to the far end. Who was there to check it, who could prove that they had lost out on the gruel?

My usual occupation in the mornings, after breakfast, was to run through the English words I had copied out the previous day. Twice a day I would practise them – in the morning and just before lights out. These were my exercises, rather than jogging on the spot, to stir my sleepy brain. Later in the day, after lunch, I would tackle something harder. I had just settled down on my bunk, with my legs tucked under me, when the food flap opened: 'Cell number ten! Grab your things and get ready to leave!' That was all I needed. By the time you got ready, dragged all your gear off to another cell and settled in, there went another day of your studies. Where to, this time? Those bastards never tell you a thing – top secret.

'Hey, chief! Do we need to take our mattress covers? What about the mattresses? What about our basins?'

This was reconnaissance. Taking mattresses meant we'd be staying in the same block. Leaving them meant a different block. Mattress covers meant blocks 1 or 3 – block 2 issued its own, and basins too.

'Take the lot,' said the prison officer vaguely, keeping us in the dark.

Where are they taking us? To the box, maybe. Or block 1, to work. Then we'll have to strike again, and they'll drag us off to strict-regime cells and put us on punishment rations. But maybe it's just a frisk? God forbid, that'd be even worse. I've got books stashed away all over the cell in case we get searched, and a whole collection of valuables – a pen-knife, several razor-blades, a home-made awl. They'll clean out the lot in no time.

There was a general commotion. Every one of us had his particular hoard, his treasures.

Quick, put it in your jacket, shove it in among the padding, maybe they won't find it. Or your boot – oh no, they've started X-raying boots lately. For yourself you can't get an X-ray for love or money, but for boots it's okay. My God, my boots! I've handed them in for repair.

'Boss! Ring up and see about my boots, they're in the repair shop. Boss, I won't go without my boots!' I had worked and struggled for two months to get that repair done, writing complaints, putting in demands. They had finally taken them, and damned if I didn't need them again. Now I'd be glad to have them back as they were – everything had gone to hell. Thank God we'd had our breakfast – who knew where we'd be by lunchtime?

I seemed to have accumulated stacks of gear – a whole mattress-cover full. You wouldn't think a man would have much stuff in prison, but you just never noticed how it piled up. Your comrades, let out slowly one by one, went back to the camps, and managed to leave their priceless treasures as a legacy for those left behind. It would be a sin to take things out that had been smuggled in through the searches with so much difficulty. Every knick-knack had its value. Take those three foreign razor-blades – any single one would clinch a deal with the gruel deliverer to slip some hot food to one of our boys in the box. That meant three weeks' extra life for somebody, maybe me. Those notebooks were also worth a mint; just try to lay your hands on one. Three ballpoint pens, extra refills, above all, books – God help me if we were searched! I had a dangerous amount of these riches and I never seemed to have a chance of slipping them to somebody who was staying on. I just never got into the same cell with them; I was unlucky.

But basically it looked as if we were simply being transferred to another cell, so we took along our soap and rags and various bits of string. Everything would come in handy in our new cell, especially if it had been occupied by criminal cons before us. They always left the place looking as if it had been ransacked: the cell would be filthy, everything in it battered and broken, and it invariably took a couple of days to clean it up and repair everything, to scrape the walls clean and wash the floors. They usually left no soap and no rags, so we took our floorcloth with us as well.

Whew! It looks as though we've got everything together.

'Ready?' yelled the prison officer through the door.

The door opened, and the block officer pointed a finger in my direction. 'Come with me,' he said curtly.

Christ. Where was he taking me? It must be the box. Groping helplessly for possible reasons, I asked, 'Shall I take my mattress with me?'

'Drop it in the corridor!'

That's it, the box. But what for? What have I done? Nothing. I'll go on hunger strike!

We went down the steps to the ground floor and turned away from the exit and along the corridor – the box! No, we passed it and went straight on down the hall. They were going to frisk me; the frisking room was straight ahead. Bloody hell, they'd take everything I'd got. How could I draw them off? I said the first thing that came into my head: 'Boss, get me my boots, my boots are in the repair shop!'

'They've been sent for already.' Sent for? Why did they send for my boots if I was only going to be frisked? Maybe I was being shipped out?

We went into the frisking room.

Petukhov's team was already there, waiting for me, like jackals. Now they'd pick me clean. 'All right, put your sack down here and get undressed.' They made me strip, as per regulations. Then they fingered the seams of every item of clothing. One razor-blade was hidden in my padded jacket – they didn't find it, thank God – one week's life for somebody. 'Get dressed!' I was led out into the corridor and locked in the departure cell.

I was being shipped out after all! But how the hell was I going to manage all that gear on a prison transport? I hardly had the strength to walk. And now I would lose the lot – every transit prison meant a new search. I was flabbergasted. What's this? You bloody fool, you've taken the soap and the floorcloth. And my boots! If they're swiped, I've had it. 'Boss, get me my boots, they're in the repair shop!' 'They've been sent for already.'

I had to let the other boys know, but how? I was in the end cell. There was no one above me, no lavatory pan in the cell and no mug, blast it! With a stub of pencil I wrote on the wall in English: 'Shipped out to an unknown destination.' Then my name and the date. But that wasn't enough. How long would it be before anyone noticed it? I had to try to yell out. Maybe they'd take me to the bathhouse first? But the door was already opening. A bath? No, we headed for the exit. Outside we turned the corner of the building and made for the guardhouse. Quick, now was the time to yell. Cell number 15 was right above me. Suddenly I let out such a bellow that Kiselev, beside me, literally leapt back in fright.

'Nu – u – umber fif – teen, Yego – o – or, I'm being shipped out! They're shipping me out, fifteen!'

At that point the guards recovered their wits and shoved me through the guardhouse door. 'Be quiet, what are you yelling for? Want the box?' Don't give me that one, chief, where are you going to find a box on a prison transport?

In the guardhouse, we went into a spacious room that was a sort of cross between a recreation room and a changing-room for the guards. I was made to sit on a chair. 'Sit here!' At this point our political instructor came into the room, Captain Doinikov, looking somewhat ill at ease and with an air of melancholy solemnity. Softly, so that no one else could hear me, I said to him, 'Where are they sending me, sir?'

He squirmed and looked away. 'I don't know, no, really I don't, I don't know. You're being shipped out.'

'Come off it, stop beating about the bush and making mysteries – where to?'

*'I honestly don't know, it's nothing to do with me. They said you were being shipped out – to Moscow, most probably.'*

*He knew everything, the swine, I could tell by his face. 'What about my things?'*

*'They're already loaded.'*

*Well, beat that! And who's been carrying my gear for me, the armed guards? Oh, my boots. 'Tell them to bring my boots, they're in the repair shop.'*

*'They'll bring them.'*

*'What do you mean, they'll bring them? We're in the guardhouse, I'm already on my way!'*

*Then suddenly he said, ever so softly: 'You won't be needing your boots any more.'*

*What the hell was this? What did he mean, I wouldn't be needing my boots any more? I replied, just as softly: 'How do you know I won't need my boots if you don't know where I'm going?' He turned red.*

*I shouldn't have asked. It was clear enough anyway that something extra-ordinary was afoot: prisoners were never shipped out from the guardhouse; the prison van drove right inside the yard and was loaded there. But they had carried my gear themselves and I didn't need my boots any more, so maybe I was getting out, maybe they were letting me go? Or there could be other reasons for not needing any boots.*

*'Oh well, goodbye,' said the captain.*

*They led me straight towards the exit, as if letting me go. But I wasn't allowed to look to the sides – men in civilian clothes were standing about. Ah, the KGB! Of course, they weren't letting me go at all. 'This way, please, get in.' Right by the gate stood a minibus and a number of cars. The snow was all trampled and dark. Where was the prison van? No, I was being asked to get into the minibus, a miracle! Inside, on the back seat, I found my sack in the prison mattress cover. The windows were sealed off with blinds, and KGB men in plain clothes surrounded me. They warned me not to touch the blinds or try to look out of the windows. Some blinds had also been lowered over the partition between us and the driver, but they weren't secured at the bottom and fluttered slightly. That meant they would flap when we drove and I would get a chance to see a little bit. We were waiting for some senior officer or another. He got in the front, beside the driver, slammed the door, the blinds fluttered – and we were off. We swung round, turned the corner and drove away.*

*Christ, I wonder if the boys heard me? I yelled loudly enough. But where the hell are they taking me? To Moscow? Doinikov said Moscow. But he might have been lying. Where could they be taking me? And why in a* minibus instead of a prison van? And why didn't I need my boots any more? *Well, there was every likelihood they might do it. All they had to do was turn into the woods outside the town and – 'while attempting to escape'* . . .

The minibus was travelling at breakneck speed. *The blinds trembled and flapped, and all of a sudden, to my great astonishment, I caught sight of a police car in front of us with a flashing light on its roof. Inside were two police officers, one with his hand thrust out of the window, holding a thin cane and gesturing at other vehicles to get out of our way. Was this a coincidence? No, five minutes later the blinds jerked again, and again I caught sight of the police car with its flashing light. Glancing furtively over my shoulder I saw the regular flashing of a light reflected on the blinds behind us. So there was a police car behind as well. Meanwhile we were speeding along and I began to worry in case we skidded and turned over – after all, it was winter and the roads were slippery. At the next bend the blinds flapped again and I saw the police car ahead of us. And the light behind us continued to blink. Only members of the government travelled like this. Certainly I had never been transported in this way before. Where were they taking me?*

The goons with me in the minibus were talking among themselves, glancing only rarely in my direction. *Only the two sitting on either side of me were on their guard. And no matter how hard I looked at their faces, or at the road ahead through the gap in the blinds, I couldn't learn anything new. Oh well, if it was to the woods, so be it, and if to Moscow, so be it, there was absolutely nothing I could do. There was no point in thinking about it any more. Che sarà, sarà.*

# 1

Iᴛ was December 1976, and I really had very little time left to do – five months or so in Vladimir prison,* before returning to my old camp, number 35, in Perm Province, for about ten more months. That was tantamount to going on holiday, or even home. I was already wondering which of the boys I would find back at the camp and who would be gone by then. Vague snippets of news were brought in by new arrivals at the prison – something was being done in the camp compound, some new regulations had come into force, there were new bosses. In March 1978, I was due to go into internal exile. And those benighted five years of exile infuriated me more than the whole of my prison sentence, like a useless appendage, neither one thing nor the other, neither prison nor freedom. And everything depended on where you were sent, what work you got and who your bosses were. Sometimes it was worse than the camp. It was well-known that from the Perm camps they used to send you to Tomsk, and then you knew you were in for felling timber, swamps, the back of beyond, where it was the law of the wild and Bruin was king. But from Vladimir you went to Komi, and although Komi was no bed of roses either, and also meant logging and swamps, still it was closer to Moscow – still Europe. Therefore I was calculating how I might get myself sent back from the camp to Vladimir again. But I hadn't much hope. There were rumours that, according to a new ordinance, prisoners with less than a year to do would not be sent to prison but be reformed on the spot, using camp methods.

* A high-security prison with especially severe conditions in the town of Vladimir, 100 miles north-east of Moscow. (*All notes are by the translator.*)

I had planned out my remaining five months in prison very carefully – which books I would read and when. In camp there was no hope of getting any reading done, you were kept too much on the run. And in exile I probably wouldn't have time. Where else would there be a better opportunity to study, if not in prison? There was plenty of time to spare, and it would only be wasted otherwise.

No matter how I looked at it, it was clear there could be no other university for me but Vladimir prison. Even if they didn't stick a new stretch on me, I'd be in exile until 1983, when I would be forty-one and that was no age for studying. And there was nothing good to be expected when I was let out. Only greenhorns, when they come in for their first stretch, look forward to their release and count the days. Life outside appears to them as some bright, sunny, unattainable shore. But I was in for the fourth time, I knew that there is nothing more disillusioning in life than to be released from jail. I also knew that I had never managed to last longer than a single damned year outside – and never would. Because the reasons that had landed me in jail in the first place would land me there again and again. These reasons were immutable, just as Soviet life itself was immutable, just as you yourself could never change. You would never be allowed to be yourself, and you would never agree to lie and dissimulate. And there was no other way out.

That was why, every time I was released, my only thought was how to get as much done as possible, so that afterwards, back in prison again, I wouldn't have to spend sleepless nights dwelling on lost opportunities, punishing myself and making myself sick with rage over my own indecision. These nights of sleeplessness were my greatest torture, and therefore my brief spells of liberty couldn't by any stretch of the imagination be described as normal living. They were a feverish race against time, in the constant expectation of arrest, with the KGB breathing down my neck, and meetings with people, people, people – so many, I had no time even to check them properly. If you met someone once and he didn't squeal on you, you treated him as an acquaintance, twice and he was your friend, three times and he was the closest of blood-brothers, as if you had spent half a lifetime shoulder to shoulder with him.

But when you met a person for the first time, you invariably thought of him as a witness at your future trial. Which interrogation would he crack at – the first or the second? Which of his weaknesses would the KGB seize upon? If he was timid, they would try to frighten him; if he was vain, humiliate him; if he loved his children, they would threaten to put them in a children's home. And you looked searchingly into his eyes – would he crack when they threatened him with the lunatic asylum? Few can hold out then. Therefore, don't burden your neighbour with information he doesn't need, don't place him in a position where he will later be stricken with a guilty conscience. You are a leper, you have no right to a normal human life, everyone who comes into contact with you runs the risk of being infected, and if you truly care for someone, avoid him, steer clear, pretend you didn't recognise him and didn't see him. Otherwise, the full weight of the State will descend on his head tomorrow.

And that is why, cramming twenty-five hours into twenty-four, stretching every week into a month, you have got to accomplish the maximum of what is possible and even impossible, because tomorrow you will be back in Lefortovo jail and it will be a long, long time, or perhaps never, before you get the chance to do anything again. And again you will agonise over the things you omitted to do, or could have done better and more effectively, and you will punish yourself for dawdling. Just think of all those decades when people were helpless to do anything at all – even to spit in the faces of their murderers. Millions went to their graves, dreaming of some way to avenge their agonies. And you – you had the chance to broadcast it to the whole world, you had friends you could rely on, and time, and what did you do? Millions of dead eyes will scorch your soul with their reproachful, questioning look.

In Siberia I once heard of a method of catching bears. Somewhere near their usual track you place some bait in a pine tree, usually a piece of carrion. Then you suspend a good, solid, heavy block of wood from the nearest suitable stout branch, blocking the bear's path to the bait but swinging freely at the end of its rope. Sniffing the bait, Bruin shins up the trunk and comes face to face with the block of wood. Being what he is, he doesn't even attempt to bypass the block, but simply shoves it aside and crawls on. The block of wood swings away and comes back, thumping the bear in the ribs. Bruin loses his temper and gives the block a harder shove, and naturally the block also comes back harder, and so on, harder and harder. Eventually the block of wood knocks him unconscious and out of the tree. This is an approximate description of my relations with the powers that be: the longer the stretch they gave me, the more I tried to do when I was let out; and the more I did, the longer the next stretch they gave me. However, times were changing and my possibilities were growing, and it was difficult to say which of us was the bear and which the wooden block, and how it would all end. I, at any rate, had no thought of retreating.

It followed from this that I had planned out not only the next five months but my whole life: ten months in the camp, five years in exile, and then, at best, a year of the fever called freedom, and then ten more years of jail and five more in exile. By that time I would be fifty-seven. All right, time for one more turn of the wheel and back in prison in time to die. This was why I hadn't been looking forward to my release, hadn't been counting the days and months. I reminded myself of that genie in the bottle in the 'Arabian Nights', who spent the first five million years vowing to make a rich man of the person who let him out, and the second five million vowing to murder the person who let him out. Let us say that I understood the genie's feelings.

There was, however, another reason why I felt obliged to plan out my prison time in advance and see that I spent every minute studying, and that reason was prison life itself.

Anyone who didn't discipline himself, who didn't concentrate his attention on some steady object of study, was in danger of losing his reason, or at the very least of losing control of himself. When subjected to such total isolation and absence of daylight, given the monotony and the constant cold and constant hunger of prison life, a man tended to fall into a kind of half-conscious trance. For hours and maybe even days on end he would sit there, gazing with unseeing eyes at a photograph of his wife and children, or leafing through the pages of a book, taking in and remembering nothing, or else he would suddenly start an endless, senseless altercation with one of his neighbours over some totally trivial issue, bogging down repeatedly in the same arguments, not bothering to listen to what his opponent was saying and in fact not answering his objections at all. He would find it absolutely impossible to concentrate on anything definite or follow the thread of an argument.

Strange things happened to time. On the one hand it seemed to pass with preternatural speed, beggaring belief. The entire daily routine with its ordinary, monotonously repetitive events – reveille, breakfast, exercise, dinner, supper, lights out, reveille, breakfast – fused into a sort of yellowish-brown blur, leaving behind nothing memorable, nothing for the mind to cling to. And lying down at night, a man would be at a loss to remember what he had been doing all day, what he had eaten for breakfast and what for dinner. Worse still, the days would become indistinguishable from one another and be completely erased from your memory, so that when you woke one day, as if someone had jogged you, you would realise: Christ, it's bath day again! That meant that seven or sometimes even ten days had flown by. And so you lived with the sensation that you were getting a bath every day. On the other hand, this same time could crawl with agonising slowness: it would seem as if a whole year must have gone by, but no, it was still the same old month, and no end was in sight.

Then again, a man could go into paroxysms of rage if something interrupted his monotonous routine. One day, for example, at the start of a new month, they would suddenly take you out for exercise, not after breakfast but after dinner instead. What difference, you might ask, would such a little thing make? But this was enough to drive men into frenzies. Or you had a row with one of the guards, or were called out by the instructor and lost your temper with him – and now you couldn't read and couldn't sleep and couldn't think of anything else. The book swam before your eyes, you couldn't keep your mind on anything and you would be trembling all over. So what, you might say. Nothing new about any of this. How many of these arguments and quarrels, how many rows with the guards had you had in your time? Too many to count. Still, for days and nights afterwards you would continue to relive it all in your mind – what he said, what you said, what you might have said but didn't because you couldn't think quickly enough. And how you might have found a particular way of getting under his skin or stopping him dead in his tracks or finding answers that were more cutting and convincing. Like a scratched gramophone record this dialogue would go round and round in your head, and there was no way of stopping it. Or else you would get a picture postcard from home and sit there staring at it like an idiot, the bright colours so exotic and enticing that you couldn't tear your eyes away.

I can't say that prison hunger was particularly agonising – it wasn't a biting hunger but, rather, a prolonged process of chronic undernourishment. You very quickly stopped feeling it badly and were left with a kind of gnawing pain, rather like a quietly throbbing toothache. You even lost awareness that it was hunger, and only after several months did you notice that it hurt to sit on a wooden bench, and at night, no matter which way you turned, something hard seemed to be pressing into you or against you – you would get up several times in the night and shake the mattress, toss and turn from side to side, and still it hurt. Only then did you realise that your bones were sticking out. But by then you didn't care any longer. Nevertheless, you didn't get out of your bunk too quickly in the mornings, otherwise your head would spin.

The most unpleasant thing of all was the sensation of having lost your personality. It was as if your soul, with all its intricacies, convolutions, hidden nooks and crannies, had been pressed by a giant flat-iron, so that it was now as smooth and flat as a starched shirt-front. Prison makes you anonymous. As a result, every man strives to stand out from the crowd, to stress his individuality, to appear superior and better than the rest. There used to be constant fights in the criminals' cells, constant struggles for leadership, culminating even in murder. Among the political prisoners, of course, there was none of that, but after four or five months of sitting in the same cell with the same people, you got to know them so well that you came to detest them, and they you. At any moment of the day you knew what they were going to do next, what they were thinking, what question they were about to ask you. And it usually ended up with nobody saying anything to anybody, because they already knew all there was to know about one another. You wondered at the paucity of man's resources, if after six months we have nothing left to say to each other.

It was particularly irritating when one of your cell mates had an unconscious tic – sniffing his nose, say, or tapping his foot. After a couple of months you couldn't bear it any longer and were ready to kill him. Yet if you were separated and put in different cells, or if you did a spell in the box, and met again after some time apart, you were like bosom pals – you smothered one another with questions, stories, bits of news, reminiscences, and celebrated for a whole week. There are cases, of course, of total psychological incompatibility, when men can't bear to live two days in the same cell with one another, yet are destined to spend years. In general it is possible to divide mankind into two categories – those you could share a cell with and those you couldn't. But then *your* opinion is never asked. You are obliged to be extraordinarily tolerant of your cell mates and to suppress your own habits and peculiarities: you have to adapt yourself to everybody and get along with everybody, otherwise life becomes unbearable.

Now multiply all these burdens by years and years, square them, add all the years you've served in other camps and investigation prisons, and you will understand why it is essential to fill every spare minute of your time with activity – best of all with studying some complex subject that demands enormous concentration. From the unremitting electric light, your eyelids start to itch and become inflamed. You read the same phrase dozens and dozens of times and still you can't grasp it.

With a superhuman effort you master a page, but no sooner have you turned it than you've forgotten it again. Go back. Read it twenty, thirty times. Don't allow yourself a cigarette until you've finished the chapter, don't allow yourself to think of anything else, don't dream, don't get distracted, don't even allow yourself to go to the toilet – nothing in the world is more important than to finish what you have set yourself for that day. And if, by the next day, you've forgotten it all, go back and read it again. And if you've finished a whole book, you can allow yourself the luxury of a day off – but only one, because after the first day your memory starts to slacken again, your attention wanders, and you slowly begin to go under, like a drowning man – down, down until there's a roaring in your ears and you see spots before your eyes, and it's touch-and-go whether you will ever come up again.

This is particularly noticeable when you are alone in the punishment cell, in the box. There you get no paper, no pencil and no books. They don't take you out for exercise or to the bathhouse, you get fed only every other day, the only window is blocked, and the one electric light-bulb is set in a niche right at the top of the wall, where it meets the ceiling, so that its feeble light barely illuminates the ceiling. A ledge jutting out from the wall is your table, another your chair – ten minutes is as long as you can sit on it. At night they issue you a bare wooden duckboard for a bed, and blankets or warm clothes are forbidden. In the corner there is usually a latrine bucket, or else simply a hole in the floor that stinks to high heaven all day. In short, it's a concrete box. Smoking is forbidden. The place is indescribably filthy. Gobs of bloody saliva adorn the walls from the TB sufferers who have been incarcerated here before you. And right here is where you start to go under, to slip down to the very bottom, into the ooze and the slime. The words they have for it in jail express it exactly – you 'go down' to the box, and you 'come up' again.

You spend your first two or three days down there groping round the entire cell – maybe somebody has managed to smuggle some tobacco in and has left a bit behind, or has tucked a fag-end away somewhere. You poke into every little hollow and crack. Day and night still mean something to you. You spend most of the day walking up and down, and at night you try to sleep. But the cold and hunger and boredom wear you down. You can doze off for only ten to fifteen minutes at a time before leaping up again and running for three-quarters of an hour to get yourself warm. Then you doze off for fifteen minutes again, huddled either on your duckboard (at night) or on the concrete floor (by day), with one knee drawn up under you and your back to the wall, until it's time to jump up again and start running.

Gradually you lose all sense of reality. Your body stiffens, your movements become mechanical, and the more time passes the more you turn into some sort of inanimate object. Three times a day they bring you a drink of hot water, and that water affords you indescribable pleasure, melting your insides, as it were, and bringing you temporarily to life. For about twenty minutes or so, an exquisite ache permeates your entire being. Twice a day, before you use the latrine, they give you a scrap of old newspaper and you read it greedily, devouring every word, several times over. In your mind's eye you run over every book you have ever read, everyone you have ever met, every song you have ever heard. You begin doing additions and multiplications in your head. You remember snatches of tunes and conversations. Time comes to a halt. You fall into a stupor, starting up and running about the cell for a while, then lapsing into a daze again, but it doesn't help the time to pass. Gradually the patches on the walls start to weave themselves into faces, as if the entire cell were adorned with the portraits of prisoners who have been here before you – it is a picture gallery of all your predecessors.

You can spend hours making them out, questioning them, arguing with them, quarrelling and making up again. But after a while they don't help to pass the time either. You know everything there is to know about them, as if you've been cell mates for half a lifetime. Some of them irritate you, while others are still bearable. There are some that need to be cut short right at the beginning, otherwise you can't get rid of them. They will bore you to tears with miserable, stupid stories about their miserable, stupid lives. They will spin yarns and invent things about themselves if they detect that you're not listening to them. They are disgustingly fidgety and servile. Others stay silent and glower at you – with them you have to keep a sharp eye open: the moment you drop off they'll pinch your rations. There are also friendly, sociable lads, usually the younger ones – with them it's possible to swap a joke. They are easygoing, never downhearted, and will do anything just to keep you company. They are usually in for hooliganism, gang rape, or a gang robbery. The corner place, over the latrine bucket, belongs to a veteran crook who knows all the ropes. Before you know where you are he is scheming, setting groups on to one another, and all of them on to you. He whispers in the corners with them, exchanges meaningful glances. Underlining his own importance and authority and addressing no one in particular, he tells tall stories about the old days, reminiscing about transit prisons, labour camps, murdered prisoners. He is clearly out to start a fight, to set it up the way he wants it. He knows who should get what and who not. There is no way of avoiding a serious confrontation with him, and the sooner you get it over with the better, before he forms his little gang and consolidates his authority. But then all this too recedes, disappears, and leaves you alone with eternity, alone with the abyss.

It is hard to understand where you yourself end and infinity begins. Your body is no longer you, your thoughts are no longer yours, they come and go of their own accord, independently of your wishes. But do you have any wishes? I am absolutely convinced that death is not a cosmic void, not a blissful zero. No, that would be too comforting, too simple. Death must be an agonising repetition, an unbearable sameness. And that is why you fall prey to a monotonous, obsessive state somewhere between a waking dream and meditating in your sleep. And this agonising sense of emptiness festers in your consciousness like an open wound, and it is a long, long time before the scar tissue forms in your soul. Nothing at all remains in your memory from this period – it is a total blank.

On one occasion I had a fabulous piece of luck – I found about half a packet of shag neatly hidden in a crack in the wall. Half a packet of damp shag . . . but it would have been better for me if I hadn't found it at all! I hadn't the slightest hope of getting any matches, but I had a fiendish craving to smoke. Hundreds of times I felt round the cell to see if I could find some matches, but without success. The only course left open to me, if I wanted to smoke, was to climb the wall until I could reach the ceiling, push a scrap of clothing into the niche there, between the bars, with some sort of stick, and then balance it on the light-bulb. After a couple of minutes the rag would start to smoulder and from that it would be possible to get a light. But how could a starving, exhausted man climb ten feet up a bare wall without a single toehold to support him? Judging by certain spots and scratches, it was clear that a number of my predecessors had somehow managed it. And this made my craving insuperable. It took me half the next night to break a splinter off my bed-boards with my fingernails – it had to be a long one, of course, to reach from the grille covering the niche to the light-bulb. Then, the next morning, I began my assault on the wall. What a hope-less, idiotic occupation – to try and scramble up a bare wall, whether from a running or a standing start, scrabbling at it with your fingernails and literally snarling with helplessness and rage. Perhaps my predecessors had been taller, stronger or better-trained. Perhaps they had been mountaineers. But it was too late, I could think of nothing else, I grew savage with frustration and rage.

The first day ended in failure. But in the night I leaned my bed-boards against the wall, scrambled up until I could reach the ceiling and succeeded in getting a light from the bulb. But that couldn't satisfy me – it only tantalised me with its apparent accessibility – and the next morning I commenced the assault again. In this way another day passed, and another night, and yet another day and a night. I had completely ceased to exist. All that was left was an all-consuming desire to climb that wall. My nails were broken and bleeding, my fingers were swollen, and by night-time I was usually so exhausted that it took me several attempts to clamber up the boards. I used to slip off, fall down, get up again and again lunge for the light, like an insect drawn to a lamp. I could no longer feel anything, neither cold, nor pain, nor hunger – there was nothing left but desire, a desire that was outside of me and apart from me: an overwhelming desire to climb that damned wall and reach that blasted light-bulb. I no longer knew why I needed it any more, so that when, during the fourth day, after a series of unimaginable exertions – leaping, elbowing and grabbing – I suddenly found myself under the ceiling, with my fist fastened vice-like on the grille, I discovered that the splinter with the rag fastened to the end of it had long since slipped from my teeth and was lying on the floor. And there I was, dangling, hanging on to the grille for dear life, within six inches of that light-bulb, with tears pouring down my cheeks.

It goes without saying that I had forgotten what exact combination of moves had got me up to the bulb in the first place, but the main thing was that I now knew it could be done. It could be done even by me, with my lack of height, strength and knowledge of climbing. I spent two more days on the assault. By the end of the fifth day I had achieved victory. Never in my life have I had a greater achievement or a bigger victory, or one of which I was prouder. After that I used to clamber up three times a day just to light a tiny fag-end. And it became such a normal part of my everyday life that it no longer even broke the monotony, or averted the usual gradual descent into the agonising blankness of an endlessly repeating void.

Knowing all this in advance, I would try, when sent to the box, to smuggle in a fragment of pencil lead, usually by hiding it in my cheek. Then I could spend my time drawing castles – on scraps of newspaper or directly on the floor and walls. I set myself the task of constructing a castle in every detail: from the foundations, floors, walls, staircases and secret passages right up to the pointed roofs and turrets. I carefully cut each individual stone, covered the floor with parquet or stone flags, filled the apartments with furniture, decorated the walls with tapestries and paintings, lit candles in the chandeliers and smoking torches in the endless corridors. I decked the tables and invited guests, listened to music with them, drank wine from goblets, and lit up a pipe to accompany my coffee. We climbed the stairs together, walked from chamber to chamber, gazed at the lake from the open verandah, went down to the stables to examine the horses, walked round the garden – which also had to be laid out and planted. We returned to the library by way of the outside staircase, and there I kindled a fire in the open hearth before settling back in a comfortable armchair. I browsed through old books with worn leather bindings and heavy brass clasps. I even knew what was inside those books. I could even read them.

This was enough to occupy me for my entire spell in the 'box', and still there were plenty of problems left over to solve the next time; it was not unknown for me to spend several days trying to decide on the answer to a single question, such as what picture to hang in the drawing room, what cabinets to put in the library, what table to have in the dining room. Even now, with my eyes closed, I can retrace that castle, in every detail. Some day I shall find it – or build it.

Yes, some day I shall invite my friends and we shall cross the drawbridge over the moat, enter these chambers and sit at the table. Candles will be burning and music will be playing, and the sun will gradually set behind the lake. I lived for hundreds of years in that castle and shaped every stone with my own hands. I built it between interrogations in Lefortovo, in the camp lock-up and in the Vladimir punishment cells. It saved me from apathy, from indifference to living. It saved my life. Because one must not let oneself be paralysed; one cannot afford to be apathetic – that is precisely when they put you to the test. It's only in sport that referees and competitors wait for you to reach your best form – records achieved that way are not worth a damn. In real life they make a point of testing you – to the limit – when you are sick, when you are tired, when you are most in need of a respite. At that point they take you and try to break you like a stick across their knees! And that's the very moment, whilst you are still groggy, when the godfather,*

---

* Camp slang for the KGB or MVD security officer, whose task is to carry out intelligence work among the prisoners.

the fisher of men, hauls you out of your cellar, or the political instructor invites you in for a chat.

Oh no, they won't put it to you pointblank, suggesting that you collaborate. They need much less than that for now – just some trivial concessions. They simply want to accustom you to making concessions, to the idea of compromise. They carefully feel you out, to see if you're ripe for it. Not yet? Okay, go back to your cellar, there's still plenty of time to ripen, they've got decades ahead of them.

Idiots! They didn't know that I was returning to my friends, to our interrupted conversation before the fire. How were they to know that I was talking to them from my castle battlements, looking down on them, preoccupied more with how to fix the stables than with answering their stupid questions? What could they do against my thick walls, my crenellated towers and embrasures? Laughingly I returned to my guests, firmly closing the massive oak doors behind me.

It is at moments when you lapse into apathy, when your mind grows numb and can think of nothing better to do than gloomily count the days till your release – it is precisely then that someone in the next cell is taken ill, loses consciousness and collapses on the floor. You ought to hammer on the door and demand that a doctor be sent. In return for that hammering and commotion the enraged prison governor will undoubtedly prolong your stay in the punishment cell. So keep your mouth shut, shove your head between your knees, tell yourself you were asleep and heard nothing. What business is it of yours? You don't know the man, he doesn't know you, you will never meet. And you might very well not have heard. But can a castle-dweller permit himself such behaviour?

I lay my book aside, pick up a candlestick and go to the gate to admit a traveller who has been overtaken by bad weather. What does it matter who he is? Even if he's an outlaw, he must warm himself at my hearth and spend the night under my roof. Let the storm rage outside the castle – it can never tear off the roof, penetrate the thick walls or extinguish my fire. What can it do, the storm? Only howl and sob down my chimney.

Prison as a social institution has been known to man since time immemorial, and it is safe to say that the moment society came into being, prison came with it. Evidently the literary genre of prison memoirs, diaries, notes and observations has been flourishing for just as long. Not that jailbirds are particularly garrulous. On the contrary. A man just released from jail is more inclined to avoid company and conversation, and likes nothing better than to sit in quiet solitude, staring motionlessly at a single spot. But he is pestered to death by the people around him, who inundate him with what are usually outlandish questions and demand ever new stories; he begins to feel that he will never have a quiet life until he writes his reminiscences. In the course of world history, millions have been in jail and thousands have written their impressions. But this has not slaked mankind's eternal burning curiosity about prison. Since ancient times, man has been accustomed to regard three things as the most terrifying on earth: *death, madness* and *imprisonment*. This terror fascinates and attracts – terror always means the unknown. Let someone return from the next world – what a mountain of questions he'd have to answer!

These three things, outside our control and dependent on fate, are in a sense interrelated. Madness is spiritual death or spiritual imprisonment; imprisonment is a kind of death, and often enough drives a man to madness or death. An imprisoned man is mourned like a dead one and remembered as one who has gone to his grave – remembered more and more rarely with the passage of time, as if he truly existed no longer. And these three terrors that reside in every one of us are exploited by society to punish the disobedient. Or rather, to deter the remainder, for who nowadays speaks seriously of punishment?

It is understandable that every member of society takes a lively interest in what there is to frighten him, and what may be done to him. This deterrent function of imprisonment has become so firmly fixed in the minds of people – from legislator to prison guard – that they take it for granted that prison must be made nasty and degrading. Tough luck on you! Neither air nor light, neither warmth nor food should you expect in there: this is no holiday camp, you're not at home now, you know! Otherwise you'll never want to leave, wild horses won't drag you back to freedom. And society is particularly upset if prisoners start to stammer something about rights and human dignity. Well, I ask you, what would it be like if the sinners in hell suddenly started shouting for their rights – what sort of situation would that be?

Somewhere along the line it seems to have been forgotten that the original aim of prison was to frighten, not the prisoners but those who remained at liberty, that is to say, society itself. The more society tortures the prisoner, the more it is able to frighten itself. Consequently it craves the prisoner's fear. Of course, the prison population, too, like any respectable society, has its own internal prison – the punishment cells, and also a variety of different prison regimes, ranging from the ordinary to the strict and to the especially strict. Even in prison, a man is not supposed to be indifferent to his fate. There is always something he can be deprived of. A man who has nothing to lose, of course, is mortally dangerous for society and constitutes a colossal temptation for honest people – provided, that is, that he isn't a corpse. And so that the rest of mankind shall not come to envy him and righteous souls shall not be tempted from the true path, all these regimes and internal punishments are calculated in such a way that the last stage, when a man truly has nothing to lose, is brought as close as possible to the state of actual death. That is why the experienced con doesn't judge a jail by its appearance or its general cells, but by its box. Similarly it is more just to judge a country by its prisons than by its monuments.

For centuries prisons have been organised along more or less the same lines, and the average tourist who visits, say, the Peter and Paul Fortress of Tsarist times hasn't the least idea what it was that made that prison so special. Look, the bunks are like bunks, the walls are like walls. And bars across the windows, of course. But that's what prison is for – to stop people running away. And the prisoners were allowed to read – what more did they want? The average tourist hasn't the remotest idea what today's 'prison regime' means.

Well, what difference does it make whether you get a half-hour or a full-hour exercise period, 12 or $13\frac{1}{2}$ ounces of bread a day, $2\frac{1}{4}$ or $1\frac{3}{4}$ ounces of fish? You have to be a bookkeeper or a cook to keep track of such figures. The average tourist asks only one question: did the prisoners die on that regime or didn't they? They didn't? Ah well then, what more is there to say? The thing that impresses them most of all is the vaulted ceilings and the thick walls. How gloomy, how oppressive! Look at that for a prison, eh!

No matter how many prison memoirs they might have read, they will never be able to understand these trivial and minor details. Take this bedstead, for instance, made of welded metal rods. It's got a kapok mattress on it and looks completely normal. But it seems that cons sleeping on beds like these have been going on hunger strike to get the gaps between the rods reduced. How peculiar – those beds have been in use for twenty years at least, and it never occurred to anyone before to complain about the gaps between the rods. What's the matter with those cons? Have they gone mad, don't they want to eat any more, are they cocking a snook? The painstaking researcher might perhaps ransack the prison archives and come up with the fact that at about the same time the prison governor ordered the prisoners to give up all their old newspapers and magazines. A perfectly reasonable regulation, obviously designed to prevent the prisoners from cluttering up their cells with trashy literature. Very commendable. But not even the conscientious researcher would see any connection between these two events, and only a con would perceive the vital link – what if, for instance, you were able to sleep on the bed only by stuffing magazines and newspapers between the mattress and the rods? And the moment they were taken away the bedstead became an instrument of torture? During the night the mattress would sink between the rods and you ended up sleeping on an iron grille.

In the punishment cell, for example, you are supposed to have a stool or another kind of seat, and every punishment cell has some such, usually a ledge sticking out from the wall: go ahead, sit on it all day long if you like. But say they've placed the ledge a fraction higher than it should be, and made it a fraction narrower and shorter, so that you can't quite sit on it properly and your feet don't quite reach the floor. All it comes down to is an inch or two either way.

Or take those $1\frac{1}{2}$ ounces of bread or $\frac{1}{2}$ ounce of fish – how petty, one is almost ashamed to mention them. But you forget that it took only a straw to break the camel's back. You forget that the difference between life and death is just as petty, just as trivial: you need only alter the body's temperature by a degree or two and behold, it's a corpse. Ever since prisons began, ever since this social institution came into being, this battle has been going on, this feverish war between convicts and society. For ounces, inches, degrees, minutes. And victory goes first to one side, then the other. One moment the cons advance – $1\frac{1}{2}$ ounces here, 2 inches there, 5° more, and before you know it, life is bearable! But society cannot allow life to be bearable in prison. Prison has to be oppressive and brutal, not a holiday camp. Society starts to press forward: $1\frac{1}{2}$ ounces is lopped off here, 4 inches there, 5° less, and the cons start dropping like flies. Gnawing hunger, starvation, exhaustion, despair. And you get self-cannibalism, insanity, suicides, murders, escapes.

For many years I contemplated that war, so muffled and incomprehensible to outsiders. It has its own laws, its own great dates, battles, victories and defeats, its heroes and military leaders. The front line in this war, as in most wars, is constantly moving. Here it is known as the prison regime. Where the front is depends on the willingness of the cons to risk all for a single ounce, inch, degree or minute. The moment they relax their defences the squadrons with the red epaulettes or blue piping* will dash forward with the cry of victory on their lips. They

* Officers of the MVD (Ministry of Internal Affairs) and KGB (Committee of State Security), respectively.

will break through the front, form a pincer movement, attack from the rear. And woe to the vanquished! The victors are never put on trial.

A new generation of prisoners will never succeed in winning back lost ground – they will accept the new situation as normal, time-honoured and inevitable. They may win their own battles dozens of times, but each time they lose only once. That is why cons who go on hunger strike and then call it off without achieving anything have not only lost their own war but have worsened life for many generations to come. This is another reason why you mustn't lapse into apathy or fall into a stupor. Apathy will whisper in your ear: the main thing is to survive, think only of today, thank God you're still alive. But that means the hooves are already drumming, the trumpet is sounding, and the squadrons are on the attack.

And so I was sitting quietly in Vladimir, reading books. Apart from my proper subject, biology, I was also learning English. Most of the prisoners used to learn some language or other: the Jews as a rule studied Hebrew, while the rest studied English, German or Spanish. The method we used was the simplest possible, namely to read as many books as we could with the help of a dictionary, write down the new vocabulary, and sit and learn it. For the sake of convenience, we'd take a scrap of paper and write the word on one side and the Russian equivalent on the other. And so as not to mix them up or lose them, we made tiny chests of drawers out of empty matchboxes. They were extremely convenient, these miniature chests with five or six banks of drawers. You could group them in various categories in the different drawers. In this way, given a certain amount of concentration, you could learn up to two and even three thousand words in a month. The guards got so used to matchbox drawers that they even stopped confiscating them during their routine searches.

With books, and especially with dictionaries, the situation was much more difficult. We were not allowed to receive books from home, the library was poor, and we could only order books from bookshops if we paid a surcharge. Even then, not all books were allowed. The authorities were particularly down on any books not published in the USSR, even dictionaries, even if they were published in Warsaw or Prague. As a result, the cons contrived to get hold of books illegally.

I myself was lucky in this respect. While I was under investigation in Lefortovo prison, my mother had started bringing me three or four books every month, together with food parcels. Furthermore, among the Soviet books would be some others published abroad, in England or the United States. The Lefortovo administration never passed them on to me, of course, but put them in the prison store. They were hoping I didn't know about the books and wouldn't demand them when I left. About thirty books thus accumulated. When I was dispatched from Lefortovo to Vladimir it was at night, and no senior officials were on duty. Naturally I kicked up a fuss, demanded my books, and threatened to inform my armed escort that the prison was refusing to give me my belongings. The escorts were subordinate neither to the prison administration nor to the KGB: indeed, like all Interior Ministry employees, they hated the KGB's guts. So I calculated that they might well take umbrage and refuse to convoy me as someone 'having a material claim against the prison', as they used to put it in their jargon. And that, apparently, was what the Lefortovo guards feared as well. For the sake of appearances the duty officer swore at me for half an hour or so and tried to force me to back down, but they knew me well by now. (This was my third time in Lefortovo.) They realised I wouldn't budge, and they gave me the books. So I dragged a whole sack of books to Vladimir with me – I could hardly lift them off the ground.

Later I had constant headaches with those books. Sometimes the guards would take them away for inspection and not give them back; at other times, on the contrary, they said they had no one to inspect them and for that reason couldn't give them back; and on one or two occasions they introduced a limit of five books and confiscated the rest. Each time, I wrote complaints or went on hunger strike. Once when I was in camp, I even stole my books from the store, replacing them with others. In a word, it was a whole saga. What is interesting, however, is that no one ever looked at them, and nobody knew that they included non-Soviet editions; if they had, no amount of hunger striking would have helped me. It was simply that my sack irritated the prison officers. 'This isn't a university, you can study when you get out of here.' And that was all.

One way or another, we all had our sacks of books. What is more, they were usually passed on as a legacy from one generation of prisoners to another, and therefore were a sort of public property. That was another reason why we waged this constant book war with the administration. The books had to be concealed so that they weren't seen by the guards, especially when the cells were cased. And this was no easy matter. A book isn't a needle – where can you hide it? But no matter how hard it was, you always managed to find somewhere. There was absolutely nothing worse than suddenly hearing the food

29

flap open and the block officer saying: 'Pack up your things and get going.' You were bound to be frisked. What the hell could you do with all those books?

It was a great help if you ripped off a book's covers, the title page and occasionally the preface too. Then you could argue that it wasn't a book at all, but toilet paper. That way you could get away with a couple of books. The boys also had the bright idea of forging a rubber stamp – see, it's a library book, not mine. But in time they got on to that one, too. Or you might tear the cover off and glue a magazine cover on in its place, so that you could pass it off as a literary journal – *Oktyabr* or *Novy Mir*. But then they started confiscating literary journals as well. The safest thing was simply to read the book fast and copy as much as you could into your notebook. Such notes were considered a con's private property, though they were taken in from time to time by the KGB and checked in case we were writing anti-Soviet novels or prison diaries. In brief, it was the Hundred Years' War – in books.

Our bosses quickly tumbled to the fact that unlike the criminal prisoners, we political prisoners suffered much more from being deprived of books, visits or correspondence with our families than from the loss of parcels or being put on strict regime or reduced rations, and therefore they deliberately concentrated on these psychological punishments. But of course, striking at the stomach, as the criminals used to say, still remained our re-educators' favourite weapon. On our side we had our own weapons: official complaints, hunger strikes, stubbornness and resourcefulness. Our main instruments, without which no amount of resourcefulness would have helped us, were undoubtedly solidarity and publicity.

It is an astonishing fact that no more than thirty years ago, millions of political prisoners in Russia were rounded up and driven out to work on the great construction projects of communism. Hundreds of thousands of them died of scurvy and malnutrition. Meanwhile, large numbers of people, overcome with admiration, lauded the Soviet regime. It wasn't that they lacked the necessary information, simply that they didn't want to know, didn't want to believe it. People need their beautiful dream of justice and happiness somewhere on this earth. And even the most serious Western observers were astounded by the grandiosity of Soviet achievements, the sweep of their schemes, the enthusiasm of the Soviet people – and not a word was said about the prisoners.

In my day there were no more than 10–20,000 of us political prisoners in the entire country, about the same number as used to die in Norilsk in the course of a single winter. But the West had long since got wind of the fact that its own fate and its own future were in some part being decided within the walls of Vladimir prison. The Western press started paying us attention and even began to investigate our battles over food and living conditions – all those ounces, inches and degrees. The world became interested in the question of whether you could have a prison with a human face. This for us was highly topical – prison we had known for ages, but the human face was exactly what was missing. And so it came about sometimes that we had barely finished one of our regular hunger strikes when the guards whispered to us the contents of some broadcast by the BBC or Radio Liberty on the subject of that very same strike; even they were intrigued by this radio war.

Our Kremlin leaders were also agitated by this new development – they were worried lest the façade of their grandiose structure should be tarnished. And always at just the wrong moment! Just when the proletarians of the world were at last ready to unite and embody the centuries-old dream of mankind, just when it was necessary to direct the world's energies into the struggle against the dictatorship in Chile or apartheid in South Africa, suddenly these cons would emerge from nowhere with their ridiculous hunger strikes, rations, ounces and inches. And this distracted the workers, aided world imperialism and postponed the bright future.

On the other hand, the nature of the state machine was also changing: that early revolutionary zeal and fervour had been wiped out by Stalin in the 1930s and 1940s, and the apparatus was growing more and more sclerotic, overtaken by bureaucratic inertia – fear of responsibility, fear of superiors – and by respectable bureaucratic indifference. It was overgrown with a tangle of laws, regulations and decrees, and it wasn't always clear how to interpret them. It was much better just to pass the buck to your superiors and wait for instructions. At the top they were in no hurry to issue instructions. They much preferred to punish their subordinates for negligence, or to hand down new regulations and decrees, which all had somehow to be interpreted and have their contradictions reconciled.

And the prison governor's head was simply bursting. It was crystal clear to him that every new regulation was designed to be deployed against the cons, but the question was where to draw the line. If you overdid it a fraction, or put a bit too much pressure on, you had a hunger strike on your hands. And then you had London, Munich, Washington kicking up a stink again, which meant a Moscow commission on your backs within a few weeks. 'What's going on here,

comrades? Falling for the provocations of world imperialism again?!'
And of course, these commissions were bound to find blemishes and
blunders, note them down, draw attention to them, reprimand you,
and sometimes even sack you for them – every bureaucrat had a horde
of enemies just waiting to scheme against him, take his place, snatch
the bread out of his mouth. For that reason the prison guards and
officers also listened to the Western radio stations, twiddling the knobs
of their receivers at night, asking one another the next morning: did
you hear anything? And if they had, a commission was bound to come.

The old jailers used to sigh: you're hopelessly spoiled. Now twenty
years ago. . . . But we too were nothing like the rabbits who died
without a murmur. We had grasped the great truth that it was not
rifles, not tanks and not atom bombs that created power, nor upon
them that power rested. Power depended upon public obedience,
upon a willingness to submit. Therefore each individual who refused
to submit to force reduced that force by one 250-millionth of its sum.
We had been schooled by our participation in the civil rights movement,
we had received an excellent education in the camps, and we knew of
the implacable force of one man's refusal to submit. The authorities
knew it too. They had long since abandoned any idea of basing their
calculations on communist dogma. They no longer demanded of people
a belief in the radiant future – all they needed was submission. And
when they tried to starve us into it in the camps, or threw us into the
punishment cells to rot, they were demanding not a belief in communism, but simply submission, or at least a willingness to compromise.

We in Vladimir prison had been culled from the camps as the most
recalcitrant and obstinate cases – hunger strikers, sit-down strikers,
trouble-makers. Almost none of us was there by accident, and the few
who were took their places willy-nilly in our line of defence.

The cons around us were on the same special regime and had been
convicted under the same articles of the criminal code as we had been.★
But the majority of them were here by chance – they were mainly
crooks who had reneged on gambling debts or had in some other way
sinned against their cell-mates according to the underworld code. Then,

★ Corrective labour camps and prisons in the USSR are divided into four types according to their regime: 'normal', 'reinforced', 'strict', and 'special' or 'specially strict', in
ascending order of severity. The degree of severity defines the type and quantity of
rations the prisoner receives, the number of privileges (letters, food parcels, visits) he is
allowed and the scale of punishments he can be subjected to. The type of regime is
usually specified in his sentence, but it can be altered during his term of imprisonment.

to escape retribution, they had put up political posters or tattooed themselves with anti-Soviet slogans – thus getting their sentences increased but enabling them to get transferred as 'political recidivists' to this special regime. Of course, psychologically they had remained crooks. And the wonder is that in their case, special regime was an exact replica of the regime in Stalin's camps. The same officers, the same guards treated them completely differently from the way they treated us: they were beaten and humiliated, they fought over crusts of bread, betrayed one another to the guards – and there was no question of solidarity!

Until 1975, politicals in Vladimir prison were not obliged to work – the prison authorities regarded it as inexpedient: they knew the majority simply wouldn't do it, and even those that did never met the quotas. It was too much of a loss for the prison to maintain the workshops, hire skilled foremen from outside and work out additional targets for us without getting any real income from it. In the spring of 1975, however, Moscow decreed otherwise. It was decided to force us to work.

Forced labour is always degrading. But in prison conditions, where sixty per cent of your earnings is deducted to pay for the armed guards, where further deductions are made to cover the cost of your food, clothing and maintenance, where work is said to be one of the means of your re-education, where it robs you of eight hours a day, six days out of every seven, and where the productivity quotas are artificially raised to a point where you can't possibly meet them – working under such conditions is intolerable to a man with any self-respect.

Naturally we refused. And the long siege started. The whole lot of us were treated as vicious malingerers and repeatedly subjected to every imaginable form of punishment. I, for instance, spent eighteen months (out of a total of less than two years) on strict regime, while others saw more of the punishment cells, some spending as many as sixty and even seventy-five full days in them. Our letters home were cut off, and we were deprived of visits and food parcels. It was a war without quarter, a war of attrition. We all understood that we dare not lose. Therefore, besides the normal defence tactics – hunger strikes, the smuggling out of information about the violations taking place in the prison – we resorted to a weapon that took the authorities completely by surprise: we overwhelmed official channels with a veritable avalanche of complaints.

You need to know the Soviet system of bureaucracy to understand how effective this was. Under Soviet law, every prisoner has the right to petition any state or public institution and any public official with a complaint. Every complaint has to be forwarded by the prison administration within three days of its receipt. In the interim, the administration has to write an explanation to accompany the complaint, add relevant details from the prisoner's dossier, and put everything into the same envelope for further dispatch. The public official or institution that receives the complaint records it in a daily register of incoming documents and must answer within a month. If the official or institution is not competent to deal with the matter complained of, they have to pass it on to someone who is. Repeated complaints set the whole machinery in motion each time they are made. The order in which complaints are scrutinised is regulated by a battery of laws and ordinances. In practice, it is never very effective to write just one complaint. Your complaint is invariably sent to the 'competent official', in other words to the person you are complaining of, and he quite naturally finds the complaint unfounded. It is even more likely, however, that nobody reads it at all, and it is simply sent back down the chain, from office to office. This is why most people have no faith in the system of complaints.

However, complaints can be decidedly effective, even in prison, provided that certain rules are observed. All you need is to know the law and the system under which complaints are examined; have a detailed knowledge of all the regulations pertaining to the prison regime; and compose your complaint so that it is brief and to the point, preferably on not more than a single page, otherwise no one will read it. The complaint should merely state the fact that a law or regulation has been infringed, the date when the infringement occurred, the names of the people responsible, and the nature of the law or regulation in question. It should be written in large clear letters, with generous margins. If you want your complaint to be examined by a high official, complain about his immediate subordinate. In other words, if you want an answer from the Ministry of the Interior, complain not about the prison governor, but about the head of the regional Ministry office. And to get to that point you need to progress patiently up the bureaucratic ladder, complaining one rung higher each time about the reply received from the person immediately below. You should never complain about two different matters in the same letter. You should always send complaints by registered post, with confirmation of delivery. And most importantly of all, you should write enormous numbers of complaints and send them to the officials least equipped to deal with them.

At the height of our war, each of us wrote from ten to thirty complaints a day. Composing thirty complaints in one day is not easy, so we usually divided up the subjects among ourselves and each of us wrote on his own subject before handing it round for copying by all the others. If there are five men in a cell and each man takes six subjects, each of them has the chance to write thirty complaints while making up only six himself. And copying out thirty lines of text in large letters takes about one-and-a-half to two hours.

It is best to address your complaints not to run-of-the-mill bureaucrats, but to the most unpredictable individuals and organisations, for instance to all the Deputies of the Supreme Soviet, or of the Soviets at republican, regional or city levels, to newspapers and magazines, to astronauts, writers, artists, actors, ballerinas, to all the secretaries of the Central Committee, all generals, admirals, productivity champions, shepherds, deer-breeders, milkmaids, sportsmen, and so on and so forth. In the Soviet Union all well-known individuals are state functionaries.

The next thing that happens is that the prison office, inundated with complaints, is unable to dispatch them within the three-day deadline. For overrunning the deadline they are bound to be reprimanded and to lose any bonuses they might have won. When our war was at its hottest the prison governor summoned every last man to help out at the office with this work – librarians, bookkeepers, censors, political instructors, security officers. And it went even further. All the students at the next-door Ministry of the Interior training college were pressed into helping out as well.

All answers to and dispatches of complaints have to be registered in a special book, and strict attention has to be paid to observing the correct deadlines. Since complaints follow a complex route and have to be registered every step of the way, they spawn dossiers and records of their own. In the end they all land up in one of two places: the local prosecutor's office or the local department of the Ministry of the Interior. These offices can't keep up with the flood either and also break their deadlines, for which they too are reprimanded and lose their bonuses. The bureaucratic machine is thus obliged to work at full stretch, and you transfer the paper avalanche from one office to another, sowing panic in the ranks of the enemy. Bureaucrats are bureaucrats, always at loggerheads with one another, and often enough your complaints become weapons in internecine wars between bureaucrat and bureaucrat, department and department. This goes on for months and months, until, at last, the most powerful factor of all in Soviet life enters the fray – statistics.

It is reported to some senior functionary – along with other figures, tables, reports and memoranda on the progress of communism – that, say, Vladimir prison or maybe Vladimir region has been the recipient over a given period of 75,000 complaints. No one has read these complaints, but it's an unheard-of figure. It immediately spoils the entire statistical record and the various indicators of socialist competition between collectives, departments and even regions. Everybody suffers. The entire region drops from its leading place in the tables and becomes one of the worst, losing its red markers, pennants and prize-cups. The workers start seething with discontent, there is panic at the regional party headquarters, and a senior commission of inquiry is dispatched to the prison.

This commission won't help the prisoner personally – at the most it will resolve a few minor points raised in the complaints. But it is bound to find a mass of shortcomings and defects in the work of the prison administration. That's why it has been sent here, its members paid travelling allowances, expenses and bonuses. Admin is taken to pieces. Individuals are fired, demoted, bawled out. The commission reports back to its superiors and with a sigh of relief goes home. Meanwhile, to the extent that you have petitioned sundry milkmaids, deputies, ballerinas and deer-breeders, they too are obliged to respond, investigate and comply with protocol, informing you of the commission's decisions and the measures taken.

You go on writing and writing, spoiling the statistics for the next period under review and drumming up a new commission, and so on for years. Add to this the commissions and reprimands provoked by the leaking of information abroad, the directives, circulars and counter-orders, the petitions of relatives, the campaigns and petitions abroad, and you will have some idea of what our prison administration endured in warring with us to make us go out to work. What prison governor, what prosecutor, what regional party secretary would relish such a life? If it had depended only on them, the blockade would soon have been lifted. But the orders had come from Moscow.

My God, what didn't they do with our complaints! They confiscated them by the sackful, they refused to give us paper or sell us envelopes and stamps, they forbade us to send them by registered post with recorded delivery (so as to make it easier to steal them), they issued a special order making it an offence to petition anyone other than the Public Prosecutor and the Ministry of the Interior, they threw us into the punishment cells. And the answers – you should have seen the answers we got! It was fantastic. The bemused bureaucrats, having no time to read our complaints properly, answered completely at sixes

36

and sevens, mixing up the complainants and confusing their complaints. They so twisted and garbled our poor laws that they could have been jailed for it themselves. A colonel in the local branch of the Ministry of the Interior, for example, overwhelmed by this paper hurricane, wrote to me that the Congress of the Communist Party was not a social organisation and therefore could not be the recipient of complaints. Naturally I followed this up with a whole gamut of complaints against the colonel, and he sank in the ensuing whirlpool. Meanwhile the Vladimir judges, driven berserk by the mountains of suits and demands for criminal investigation pressed by us, replied that officers of the Ministry of the Interior do not come under the jurisdiction of Soviet judges. Sometimes two different offices gave diametrically opposed answers to the same complaint, and then we would set them at one another's throats. Finally, they washed their hands of the whole business and instead of answers started to send us receipts, which ran approximately as follows: 'During the past month 187 complaints have been received from you and refused', followed by the signature. The entire bureaucratic system of the Soviet Union found itself drawn into this war. There was virtually no government department or institution, no region or republic, from which we weren't getting answers. Eventually we even drew the criminal cons into our game, and the complaints disease began to spread throughout the prison – in which there were 1,200 men altogether.

I think that if the business had continued a little longer and involved everyone in the prison, the Soviet bureaucratic machine would simply have ground to a halt: all Soviet institutions would have had to stop work and busy themselves with writing replies to us. But they surrendered. In 1977 the siege was lifted after two years of struggle. The governor of our prison was removed and pensioned off, some transfers were made within the administration, and everything died down. Moscow had retreated from its orders. Our poor Colonel Zavyalkin! He suffered for nothing, the victim of an administrative injustice. As a matter of fact, he wasn't a bad man, merely a bureaucrat who carried out orders. He had barely understood what was going on. Faced with the innumerable commissions and contradictory instructions that had rained down on his head, he had evolved a most original line of defence: he pretended to be a simpleton, a mere simpleton who did as he was told and wanted all to be for the best, though somehow or other things always seemed to go wrong. He was hauled over the coals, but he took it all with the air of an innocent down on his luck.

★　★　★

Our victory cost us dear. The prisoners were all gaunt and skinny, at death's door in some cases, and every single one was suffering from some disease or other – a stomach ulcer, TB. Prison is hard even on the fit – for the sick it's curtains. Sickness was simply a pretext for blackmail – be cooperative and we'll treat you, put you on a diet, transfer you to hospital. If a man has an ulcer or a kidney disease, he can't stomach all that rotten herring and mouldy sauerkraut which accounts for sixty per cent of his diet, so what can he do? If he's got TB or, say, is suffering from hunger spasms because of an ulcer, they love to send him to the punishment cells. Then on one of the starvation days, when no food is forthcoming, they contrive to call him out for a cosy chat.

In fact, no one gets proper medical treatment in the clink. They might just slow the progress of an illness a bit, give you some superficial treatment or keep you from dying. Which means, as a rule, that your illness becomes chronic and you are stuck with it for ever, so that you can spend the rest of your life working to pay for the medicines. This is regarded as quite normal. 'What? Did you come here for a rest cure? We didn't ask you, you know. You shouldn't have come in the first place,' the doctors would say. In any case, the prison hospital hardly differed from the regular cells: the same concrete floors, the same shutters on the windows, no light and no air. The only thing was that they fed you a bit better. But they had no water closets – twice a day you were taken out to the latrines. Such a hospital was hardly missed.

Generally speaking, medical treatment was regarded as a reward for good conduct. In the neighbouring cell to some crooks there was an epileptic. Every day the cons used to hammer on the door and call for a doctor. Some hope! After four hours or so, a medical orderly might peep in through the food flap: 'What is it? The epileptic? Don't worry, he won't die, stop your yelling.' And he would slam the flap shut again. When Gunnar Rode was taken ill in our cell, we spent half the night pounding on the door and roaring through the window. We wrenched a bench free of the floor and ran it at the door, using it as a battering ram. We knocked out the food flap and the door was starting to split. Afterwards they threw us all in the punishment cells, but at least they took Gunnar Rode to the hospital. On another occasion they put Suslensky in the punishment cells. He had a heart complaint, and whenever they put him in the box, after a couple of days he would have a heart attack. This time it happened again. Then the entire block, every single cell, including the crooks, started battering at the doors – the noise was like an artillery barrage, and the block was shaken to its foundations. Suslensky was carried out on a stretcher and put in the box in another block, and that was all.

Yes, it was a hard-earned victory. On the other hand, who knows how many generations of political prisoners were assured of their right not to work as a result of our action? And we obtained many other improvements too. The most important result of all was that our prison bosses now feared us like the devil! And when the new prison governor made an attempt to restrict our book privileges again, it took only a handful of days on hunger strike to make him give in. After that they didn't dare lift a finger to us. As for the crooks, not an evening passed without one of them being dragged into the toilets and beaten up. Sometimes they would be hustled in in handcuffs and kicked into a pulp. Every night there were yells and groans. Particularly notorious for this sort of thing was Major Kiselev. Permanently drunk and bleary-eyed, he couldn't bear his shift to pass without somebody getting thrashed. But he gave us a wide berth, afraid even to breathe in case we caught a whiff of the alcohol on his breath.

We came down on him especially hard at the end of 1974, when a crook nicknamed Savage was killed in the box during Kiselev's shift. Nobody knew this poor fellow's proper name, and we didn't know how to describe him in our statements – in the end we simply wrote 'the criminal prisoner nicknamed Savage'. They beat him for ages, all night long probably, because he was moaning all night. Several times we summoned the duty guard and asked him what was going on. 'I've no idea,' he replied. 'He's probably off his head.' The following morning the crooks told us what had happened. For the next two years poor Savage figured constantly in all our complaints (we wrote about 1,500 altogether, demanding that Kiselev be put on trial). We didn't get our way, of course. The prosecutor's office replied: 'There are no grounds for implicating the prison administration in the death of the convict Gavrilin.' Only in this way did we find out his real name.

Kiselev drew in his horns after that and became really frightened of us. At the same time he hated us passionately and always tried to get us into trouble. His entire shift was exactly like him, as if specially picked for it: old Forty-One was a prize example! Sergeant-Major Sarafanov, our diminutive block guard, was always on duty in block number 1 during Kiselev's shifts. He had been given his nickname by the cons several years ago for having reported forty-one of them in the course of a single shift. How he had found the time for so many was a mystery, especially since he could hardly read or write. He was a really vicious bastard! He and a block guard called Gipsy used to give us hell and openly hated our guts. But Gipsy was more direct and honest about it. He used to yell after us quite unabashed: 'It's a pity Hitler didn't roast the lot of you in his ovens!' He regarded us all as Jews. Needless to say, we gave as good as we got.

The rest of the guards, especially the younger ones, treated us reasonably well and sometimes with open sympathy. Just like us, they hated Captain Obrubov of the KGB, who was attached to the prison as security chief. They used to call him Admiral Canaris, a nickname the crooks had given him. In appearance Obrubov really did resemble Canaris, though I think he must have been a lot stupider. He was always sending kitchen helps, errand-boys and other trusties to offer to take messages and letters out of the jail for us. In return he used to slip them some tea on the quiet (tea was banned in jail). Naturally the trusties told us all this, regarding it as the easiest way out, and begged us to supply them with fake messages. We also profited from the system, since in return the trusties agreed to smuggle tobacco or sometimes even bread into the punishment cells. So we regularly supplied Obrubov with fake messages for the outside, and even occasional petitions to the UN, all of which he sent up the line to prove his usefulness. The tea the kitchen help earned was subsequently sold to the crooks in the cells, and everyone was satisfied. It was said that years ago Obrubov had been far more arrogant and obstinate and had regularly summoned all the cons in turn and proposed that they work for him or write denunciations. As a reward, some had been promised food, others vodka, and yet others parole. Finally the men got sick and tired of it. They were particularly incensed after Obrubov summoned Boris Borisovich Zalivako, a former priest, and in return for his cooperation offered to help him get a parish after his release. It took a while to set it up, particularly to get the different blocks to agree, but on the appointed day everyone joined a unanimous hunger strike, demanding that these brazen attempts at enlistment be stopped and Obrubov removed from his post. To everyone's surprise, the hunger strike was met with jubilation on the part of the administration and even in the prosecutor's office. In no time at all the prison governor and the local prosecutor made personal appearances and asked if it was true that Obrubov had been using such crude recruiting methods. After that Obrubov ceased to appear around the prison, didn't dare to do any more recruiting, summoned hardly anyone to his office and simply skulked in the background. The crooks told us that he was often seen to spend hours standing and listening at our cell doors.

★ ★ ★

It must be said that the attitude of the crooks to us politicals had completely changed. They say that only twenty years ago the crooks used to call us fascists, rob us on prisoner transports and in transit cells, terrorise us in the camps, and so on. But now these same crooks used to volunteer to help me with my sacks of books on convoys and share their food and tobacco with me. They used to ask us to tell them what we were in jail for and what we wanted. They read the text of my sentence with enormous interest, and the only thing they couldn't believe was that we did all this for nothing, and not for money. They were absolutely astonished that people could go to prison just like that, deliberately and not for gain. In Vladimir prison our relations with them were those of good neighbours: they constantly turned to us for answers to their questions, advice and even help. We were the ultimate arbiters of all their quarrels, and we would help them to write complaints and explain the laws to them. And of course, they used to question us endlessly about politics.

In prison even crooks read the newspapers, listen to the radio and – perhaps for the first time in their lives – get to thinking: why is life such a mess in the Soviet Union? The overwhelming majority of them are violently anti-Soviet, and the word 'communist' is virtually an insult. Because of their lack of solidarity and their illiteracy, they are incapable of sticking up for their rights. The administration takes advantage of their feuds and sets them against one another. Whenever a prison officer wants to break one of them, he does it by transferring him to a cell where the inmates hate his guts. Then it is merely a question of who will kill whom, and whoever does the murder will be sentenced to be shot.

It was well known that our new governor, Lieutenant-Colonel Ugodin, had once transferred a crook named Tikhonov to a cell full of his enemies. They took a long time to polish him off – for almost two days they kicked him slowly to death. He screamed so much that the whole block could hear him, but nobody intervened. They say that Ugodin repeatedly went to the door of the cell, looked through the peephole, listened to Tikhonov's screams, and then moved off with a satisfied expression on his face. He was caught at this by the cons from the cell next door, who were being led out for exercise, and the prisoners in the cell opposite could see him through the crack in the door. Only on the third day did the guards enter the cell to remove the corpse. The culprits were later sentenced to death, but nothing at all happened to Ugodin. When we learned about it we wrote to the Public Prosecutor's office. The answer, as usual, came from the local prosecutor:

41

'The involvement of prison personnel in the murder of Tikhonov has not been confirmed by our investigation.' And with this the affair ended.

Given the circumstances of our permanent war over prison conditions, the need to synchronise our actions and exchange information required us to have reliable methods of communication among the cells with politicals in them, which were scattered about the prison. And it was here that our criminal pals proved to be extraordinarily useful – for them, particularly if they were members of regular gangs, the whole prison was honeycombed with channels through which they could circulate messages. Invisible threads stretched from window to window, from exercise yard to exercise yard, linking all blocks and floors, and all we did was simply plug into this system.

The crooks in this respect were scrupulously honest: our messages never once fell into the hands of the guards and invariably arrived sealed and sewn round the edges exactly as we had sent them. In return, we had to cooperate in forwarding their post too, and I must say we took more pains over theirs than over our own. It would have been terrible to let down friends who heroically went to the punishment cells for us or swallowed notes rather than surrender them to the authorities.

Given our complete isolation and the strict regime in the prison, it was astonishing how many means of communication existed – it turned out that you could connect any two points in the jail at will. All of this, of course, was strictly forbidden, and people caught breaking the rules were severely punished for 'inter-cell communication', as it was called.

I remember the day I arrived in Vladimir prison for the first time, still green. After frisking me they put me temporarily in the transit cell, which was dark, dirty and cold. Instead of a lavatory pan there was a sort of throne – a hump about two feet off the floor, with steps leading up to it and a hole in the middle. It stank to high heaven. Above the hole was a tap – in lieu of a washbasin. I perched on my cot somewhat baffled by this cell. Was this where I was destined to spend the next three years? Suddenly I heard a noise: 'Ahem!' Was I imagining things, or had somebody coughed right by my ear? I looked all round me – nobody there. And then again: 'Ahem! Brother!' What the devil? To be on the safe side, I answered: 'What do you want?' 'Come closer to the pan, brother, I can hardly hear you!' This was my first introduction to the prison telephone.

In other cells, where they had real lavatory pans, they used to siphon the water out with a rag or a broom and then talk down the pan just like a telephone. Particularly in the evenings you would often hear someone shouting from one cell window to another – say to cell 31: 'Hey, thirty-one! Thirty-one! Pump!' Or: 'Pump out!' Or else simply: 'Thirty-one, telephone!'

However, not all the cells were connected to this telephone. Not all the cells had lavatory pans. Usually you could only phone up and down, although occasionally you could phone across as well, depending upon which way the drains went. But the cells were linked by central heating. Thus, if you took the aluminium mug that everyone in the prison was issued with, pressed the bottom hard against the heating pipes and your mouth hard against the open top and gave a loud shout, the sound would be efficiently carried by the pipes in all directions. In the receiving cell you needed to press your mug just as carefully against the pipes and put your ear to it instead of your mouth. This was a terribly overloaded line, and all day the pipes hummed with voices. But it had a number of drawbacks. You had to wait your turn, since it couldn't be used by several people at once. Secondly, it was very hard to hear when you were several cells away, and then you had to ask others to pass the message on from cell to cell. Thirdly, not every message was suit- able for open transmission. It was for these that the post office existed.

Such messages were usually passed on by 'knight'*, the method also used for bulky objects such as food, books and so on. The method was to unravel a number of socks and plait a stout cord out of the threads. The packet would be secured to the end of this cord. Then it would be eased through the crack in the shutters – which in most cases was barely a finger's breadth – and swung sideways to the adjoining cell or lowered to the cell below. The receiving cell would then fish for the 'knight' with an 'arm', a stick with a hook on the end or else simply a tightly rolled newspaper which they would push through the crack in the shutters. Having captured the 'knight' in this way, they would haul it into the cell and tie whatever it was that they themselves wanted to send on to the end of the cord. And in this way your packet swung through the prison from window to window. Of course, if the guards caught you at it you were guaranteed fifteen days in the box.

Another method was to pass things on during your daily walk. This cheerful word 'walk' was applied to what was in fact an abysmally boring procedure. Long gone are the times when prisoners used to stroll sedately round the prison yard in pairs. Now the exercise yards are concrete rectangles barely larger than a cell. The walls are covered

* Derived from the knight in chess, whose movements across the board recalled the passage of the parcels from cell to cell.

43

with a rough cement rendering or 'fur coat' – to prevent you from writing messages on them – are ten feet high and instead of a ceiling have an iron grating over the top. The doors are just like cell doors, clad in sheet steel with a peephole in the middle. We were led out for our walk cell by cell, so that we got no variety. There were usually about ten to twelve of these rectangles built in a cluster – five or six on each side of a central gangway. Above the gangway, on a raised catwalk, the guard could walk up and down and peer to right and left. The moment he turned his back the cons would try to toss notes or small packets over the walls. Any cell caught doing this was usually deprived of its walk.

Later, in an attempt to stop this form of communication, they stretched fine-gauge wire netting over the gratings, so that when it snowed heavily in winter, the snow settled on the top. Not even this did the trick, however, for the cons managed to prise the netting loose and push their messages underneath and into the next box. In places they also tried to tear holes, so that one of them could stand on another's shoulders, push his arm through and toss whatever was necessary into the yard next door or opposite.

Having plugged into the general communications system in the jail, we politicals had to form links in the chain. The things we had to toss at our neighbours' request! On one occasion it was a bag of tobacco – we could hardly get it through the gap under the wire. Another time it was fifteen bars of soap; and for each bar we had to find a moment when the guard's back was turned. One day, before we had even had time to discover who our neighbours to left and right were (our usual procedure), the men on our right – with enormous difficulty – shoved a big fat book through the wire, quickly followed by another. These turned out to be the memoirs of Marshal Zhukov. We managed to pass on one of the books, but the other stuck in the wire, and neither we nor our neighbours could force it through.

And then there was what you might think was the most primitive method of all – writing on the walls – but it turned out to be extremely effective. You found tiny pencilled messages absolutely everywhere you were taken: in the bathhouse, exercise yards, transit cell – people would simply write down their names or lists of their cell occupants, and sometimes a brief message. Practice showed that these inscriptions would invariably come to the notice of whomever they were meant for. We usually wrote in English so that the guards couldn't understand us. They guessed, of course, that politicals were doing the writing. English quickly became a form of code or special lingo for us – we could even shout from the windows in English or talk along the pipes, because nobody else understood us.

In this way I had five months to go in Vladimir prison before returning to a labour camp. The three months before December 1976 had witnessed a lull. The prison administration no longer tried to chase us out to work or put us on strict regime. This lull struck me as suspicious. On top of that they had gathered almost the whole lot of us politicals on the second floor of block 4, at the same time making sure that no two of us occupied adjacent cells. Until then they had always tried to scatter our cells about the prison, as far away from one another as possible, in order to hinder communication. Now there were three of us in cell 21, eight in cell 15, two in cell 12, and four in cell 10. I was in number 10. There had also been four in cell 17, but two had just gone off to the labour camps and the other two into exile. There were about ten more politicals in block 1, but they weren't sent out to work with the others. Our bosses said that by the end of the year we would all be together. It was difficult to say whether admin had some design in all this or had simply decided to leave us in peace. If you didn't count the routine attacks on our books, there seemed to be no signs of preparations for any sort of assault. On the other hand, we had all been deprived of the right to correspond with home and that was always a bad sign.

Since the beginning of 1976 the authorities had made it a rule to confiscate all our letters. When we asked why, they replied that they were not obliged to say, and told us to write fresh letters. But when we did so, these too were confiscated. This stalemate went on for almost a year. I couldn't work out whom they were trying to punish – me or my mother? It was the same with the others – one of them had to go six months without letters, another eight. We had no alternative but to use illegal channels.

News trickled through from outside with great difficulty, and what there was of it was not cheerful. Some people were being arrested, others driven abroad. Some went East, others West, and they were all my friends, people I had known for many years. No matter how sorry I felt for those who went to jail, at least there was some hope of seeing them again, they weren't disappearing for ever. But it was like watching the funerals of those who were sent to the West – you would never see them again. Moscow was emptying, and somehow I found myself thinking less and less about life outside. It was particularly painful when someone I knew recanted or confessed – it was like having to forget a part of your body for ever. And long afterwards memories of meetings and snatches of conversation with them would float into your mind and refuse to go away, as if you yourself were to blame for their betrayal.

Once upon a time I had been a very sociable fellow, had got on easily with people and after a few days' acquaintance regarded them as friends. But as time went on, one after another of them was carried off, and I gradually came to avoid new acquaintances. I could no longer face the pain and turmoil when a person you had relied on and loved suddenly turned coward and betrayed you, and you had to excise him from your mind for ever. Old cons who used to stand by the guardhouse when new arrivals were led into the compound had an almost infallible eye for who would turn out to be a nark, a queer, a scavenger or a good man. As time went by I too began to measure everyone I met for convict's clothing and this further reduced the number of my friends. Gradually I was left with a small circle of especially dear friends: the only riches I had accumulated over all these years, and if one of them broke down it was pure torture to me. Then there would be even fewer of us in the castle, one more place would be empty by the fire, our conversation would subside, the music cease and the candles go out. And night would cover the earth.

Vague bits of news about some of these dear ones going off to the West would reach us in the jail, mainly via the Soviet press – like voices from the next world. And then suddenly the Soviet press remembered my existence too. For more than five years, true to character, they had been silent about me, but now there was a whole page in the *Literary Gazette* – an interview with A. Y. Sukharev, the Deputy Minister of Justice. In 1972, immediately after my third trial, a Moscow paper had published a scurrilous article about me headlined 'A Life of Ignominy'. But with all its lies and abundant abuse, quite normal for Soviet propaganda, it hadn't gone beyond the bounds of my court verdict, that is to say it hadn't added any fresh lies. According to the Deputy Minister of Justice, however, I had been convicted of virtually plotting with Hitler and of incitement to armed revolution. It was ironic to read all this, printed in millions of copies and dispatched to the farthest ends of the country, and meanwhile hold in my hand a copy of the sentence with the Soviet court's seal on it. Who was this patent rubbish aimed at? At such a time, when almost everybody listened to foreign radio stations and when even the armed guards on my transport knew me, what was to be gained by such idiocy?

Naturally I tried to protest legally: I wrote letters to the editor of the *Literary Gazette*, the Procurator General and the Ministry of Justice. I was anxious to receive some sort of official answer, no matter how ridiculous. The amusing part of the whole thing was that under Soviet law any verdict by a court (unless it is revoked) is binding on all public officials and organisations. I wanted to know how Sukharev would wriggle out of that one, and so I wrote my letters in an extremely calm and restrained manner, eschewing any conclusions or opinions and merely pointing to the discrepancy between the published words and my sentence. However, the prison let nothing through. Not one complaint was I allowed to send over this business, not even a request for an official court action for libel. That's how they always operate: one lot can broadcast lies over the whole country, while another gags those who could expose the lies. There's communist division of labour for you.

The political instructor, Captain Doinikov, called me in for a chat and tried to persuade me to give it all up. 'Don't write any more, why do you insist? It's nonsense, of no importance.' 'How so?' I replied. 'I was sentenced in the name of the Russian Federation and it's binding upon everybody. You are keeping me in this jail according to the terms of that sentence, and now all of a sudden it turns out to be wrong.' 'Come now,' he said, 'pay no attention, the newspapers are full of rubbish, it's not worth worrying about.' 'But it's the Deputy Minister of Justice writing! Maybe he knows better what I was charged with? Maybe they've re-examined my sentence and changed it? And I'm sitting here in complete ignorance.' 'No, no, your sentence is correct, don't worry, they would have told us otherwise.'

Our political instructor was not a spiteful man and wouldn't himself play any dirty tricks. In fact, his duties were very light, since nobody seriously expected him to re-educate us. His job was to call us in for a chat from time to time. With anyone else we would have absolutely refused. We had had three or four different instructors, and at first they were delighted to be transferred to such easy work: the men were quiet, didn't swear, brawl or play cards, just sat about quietly reading books. It wasn't work, it was a rest cure! But before three months were out they would beg to get away and were willing to take on even the most hardened gangsters and cut-throats. For on the one hand they were leaned on by admin, who demanded incriminating evidence about us and insisted they tighten the screws; when we resisted, it was the instructor who got the blame and was hauled over the coals. On the other hand, we also put the pressure on, and our complaints alone were enough to drive them out of their minds. On top of this, they could not strike up any sort of relationship with us or adjust to our ways. They were used to crooks and the criminal psychology – a stream of curses here, a cuff on the ear there, and order was restored in no time – but with us they needed a different approach, and they never could figure out what it should be, until at last we got Captain Doinikov.

He had been sent to us as a sacrificial lamb, to be tortured for a while before being pensioned off after three to four months for incompetence. In the prison he was regarded as the most gormless officer of them all. He was a hopeless speaker, and not very handy at reading and writing either. To everyone's surprise, however, he settled down with us. He suited us perfectly and we never complained about him. His skinny, clumsy frame in its absurd dirty uniform provoked more sympathy than scorn. And in his incoherent and completely disconnected torrent of speech, constantly jumping from one subject to another, he blurted out a great deal that was useful to us. He understood that we were tolerant of him, and when he called us in for a chat, he would talk about everything under the sun – fishing, football, and so on – for a solid hour or more, and occasionally, with a guilty rush, throwing in a few words about the policy of the Party before switching back to his endless twaddle, hurrying to smoothe over his tactlessness. Thus he would chatter away and then note in his book that he had carried out the interview. On closer examination he was not at all stupid, and on occasion even suspiciously shrewd, and it seemed that this feigned dim-wittedness of his had been acquired like the zebra's stripes – as a result of natural selection. What he needed was to reconcile his cruel functions with his by no means cruel character.

It is amazing how these disparities are reconciled in the Russian character. I have rarely met prison guards who were sadists – even the percentage of cruel people among them is very small. Usually they are simple Russian peasants who have fled from their collective farms to the towns. Yet if this Doinikov had been ordered to shoot us, he'd have done it without turning a hair. Of course, he'd have done his best to see to it that he was considered too gormless to be given such a job, and he would try to soothe us so that we wouldn't be too angry with him. But he would shoot us all the same!

I am ashamed to say that he was often successful in persuading us not to send complaints. He would come into the cell, stand there pathetically with the complaints in his hand and start his endless maunderings and meanderings. His whole expression begged us to take the complaints back. 'Why bother? You know the complaining will get you nowhere. What's the point of suddenly making all these complaints? Take them back, it's a bitch of a life anyway!' Hell! Here we were deep in a war to the death, we'd been practically ground into the dust and crushed, and yet we would take our complaints back. We were helpless and disarmed – we felt sorry for Doinikov.

When I was at the Serbsky Institute for observation,* there were women working there as orderlies – simple village bodies, almost all of them believers, with crucifixes hidden under their dresses – who used to feel sorry for us, especially for any of us who had come from jail or the labour camps all skinny and emaciated. They used to bring us things to eat on the quiet, slipping an apple unnoticed under the pillow, or cheap sweets, or a tomato. It was amusing to watch how they behaved with the true madmen, the ones whose minds had already gone blank and who spent the whole time staring at the same spot or aimlessly wandering about. They used to shout at them exactly like village girls herding cows, without the least malice or rancour: 'Come on! Gee up, I said, gee up. Where do you think you're going? Gee up, old thing!' You expected them to flourish a switch at any moment. And yet these same village women used to rat on us without mercy. They would pick up the slightest little word we said, and squeal to the nurses, who wrote everything down. At times when escapes were planned, or somebody tried to feign madness (especially if he faced the death penalty), these women would notice everything and report it immediately. If you asked them: 'Why do you do it? You're supposed to be Christians!', they replied: 'We can't help it, it's our job.' And it was useless to argue with them. Maybe Brezhnev's not such a bad fellow either, it's just that he's got a lousy job.

It is interesting that despite the huge variety of books, research projects and monographs on socialism – political, economic, sociological and so on – no one has thought to write on 'man's soul under socialism'. And yet, without such a guide to the labyrinths of the Soviet soul, all the other studies are absolutely useless or, worse, actually obscure the issue. My God, how difficult it must be to understand this confounded Russia from outside! Such an enigmatic country, and the enigmatic Russian soul!

Judging by their newspapers, books and films – and by what else is one to judge Soviet life? – the Soviet people are satisfied. True, they

* The Serbsky Institute of Forensic Psychiatry in Moscow, though nominally under the jurisdiction of the Ministry of Health, is at least partly controlled by the Ministry of the Interior, and many of its senior staff are officers of the KGB. The Serbsky Institute is the place to which the KGB habitually sends dissidents that it wishes to have pronounced insane (to avoid the unwelcome publicity of a trial).

don't have political freedom or a variety of parties, but they like it that way – the people and the Party are at one. Then they have elections that are not elections – God only knows what they are: only one candidate and there's nobody else to choose from – yet 99·9 per cent of the population takes part and 99.8 per cent votes in favour. Then again they have a low standard of living and there are food shortages – but no strikes! It is said that people are being hounded and starved in jails and camps there, although they have done nothing wrong, and are prevented from going abroad. But look at their factory and village meetings: the Soviet people unanimously endorse the policies of the Party and the government. They will repay the Party's concern for them with a new rise in productivity! The vote is over-whelming, all hands go up – what the hell's going on? Foreign correspondents attend the meetings and see for themselves: it's absolutely true, everybody supports the Party's policies, there aren't even any abstentions. It is said that the country is economically backward, with much of the work still hand-labour and so on, yet they launched the sputnik, put the first man into space, overtook the United States. More than that, they have a massive arms industry, powerful enough to keep the whole world trembling in fear. How is that? They have great scientific discoveries to their credit. And the Bolshoi Theatre, and the ballet! Do you mean to say that all this is done by slaves, people who are unfree?

True, Soviet literature is pretty boring – all about factories and production and meetings, but the people nonetheless read it and buy the books, so they must like it. There are a few isolated shortcomings, but they recognise and criticise them. And there was something in the past, unjust repressions and so on, but that's all over now – they got to the bottom of it, condemned the mistakes and released the innocent. And now they let their people go abroad: tourists, sportsmen, performers and delegations of all kinds, and they're perfectly satisfied and always go back. Well, the odd few occasionally defect, but perhaps they're the only ones who don't like it, and the others are all happy and content?

Ask any Soviet man in the street whether he has a good life or a bad one and he will answer like a gramophone record: 'A good one – much better than yours in the West.' And maybe it really is better? Free education, free medical care, cheap rents, no unemployment, no inflation. Maybe Western propaganda is spouting rubbish and their life is wonderful?

Or there's another explanation: maybe their life is better *for them*, because they're different and special, that's the only kind of life that suits them and they don't need Western comforts and freedoms?

And these blasted dissidents are so confusing. If everything's as bad as they say it is, with such injustice and tyranny, why are they still alive – some of them aren't even in jail! So there must be some freedom and some rights. Or is it all a cunning plot by the Soviet authorities? Or maybe the CIA? Anyway, how many dissidents are there? That last protest petition had only ten signatures on it. What a laugh in a country of 250 millions! If everybody is really having such a lousy time of it, why are there no uprisings, mass protests, demonstrations or strikes? The mass terror is over, isn't it? Well, they jail about ten to fifteen people a year – it's not like Chile or South Korea.

There are hundreds of similar perplexed questions that can't be answered. The Western observer, after what seems to him to be an exhaustive analysis of the situation, comes to one of two conclusions. He may decide that the USSR is a wonderful country with the most wonderful and progressive social system. Its people are happy, and despite individual shortcomings, are building a shining future, though bourgeois propaganda, of course, tries to latch on to these individual shortcomings in order to distort, slander and defame the shining essence. The other viewpoint is that the Russians are peculiar people. They like what we hate. They are such fanatics and are so determined to build that socialism of theirs that they are prepared to go without our accustomed comfort and way of life. In both cases the conclusion is the same: don't interfere, you mustn't stop people suffering if that's what they want, you can't save them against their own will. That's Russians for you!

It is hard to understand this country from outside, but is it any easier from within? Is it any easier for the Russians themselves (the West calls us all 'Russians', from Moldavians to Eskimoes) to grasp and appreciate what is going on?

And so he has just been born, this future Soviet man, this new type of man. To begin with there is no way in which he can be considered a dissident: he demands no special freedoms, reads no forbidden books, doesn't ask to go abroad, doesn't protest against his date and place of birth. He doesn't yet know, of course, how much he is already in debt to the Soviet State and his beloved Party. He wouldn't be lying there so peacefully in his pram and sucking away so peacefully on his dummy were it not for the Party's tireless efforts on his behalf. But it won't be long now before his debts are called in.

His parents, being terribly busy, will hand him over first to a creche and then to a nursery school, and if the first words he learns are *mama* and *papa*, the next is bound to be *Lenin*. On his days off he will astonish his parents by coming home and reciting:

> November seventh, it is clear,
> the reddest day in all the year.
> Through the window look ahead,
> Everything outside is red!

After that, in school, his horizons are broadened. Gradually he finds out that God doesn't exist and never did, that mankind's entire history consists of a journey from darkness to light, from injustice and oppression to freedom and socialism. That men have dreamed throughout the ages of living in a country such as the Soviet Union and that that is why they have rebelled, laid down their lives and endured tortures and suffering for thousands of years. That all the great men of the past were striving for exactly the sort of society we have at last built – even when they didn't realise it. Who was Leo Tolstoy, for instance? The mirror of the Russian revolution. And now the world is divided in half: on one side stand the forces of light, happiness and progress; on the other, reaction, capitalism and imperialism, whose one dream is to destroy our happiness and enslave us, as it has enslaved the people of its own countries. In order to prevent this happening, you have to study diligently and later be inspired in the way you work.

The further you go – first at school, then at college, then in the army and then at work – the more detailed and precise are the ways in which these concepts are instilled into you. Explicitly in the teaching of the history of the USSR and the Communist Party, political economics, scientific communism, scientific atheism, the foundations of Marxism–Leninism, dialectical materialism, historical materialism, and so on and so forth. Implicitly and almost in a whisper, like hypnosis, in films and books, in paintings and sculpture, in radio and television, in newspapers and lectures, in textbooks on mathematics, physics, logic and foreign languages, in posters and placards, and even in works translated from foreign languages.

Or take the news they offer you in the press or in a cinema newsreel. A new holiday resort is being opened in Bulgaria; a typhoon hits Japan; workers in the Urals have surpassed their targets; thousands of workers are on strike in France; a rich harvest is being gathered in the Ukraine; statistics about car accidents in the USA are monstrous; a new residential district is completed in Tashkent; student demonstrations are being broken up in Italy. Abroad, one long procession of natural disasters, catastrophes, demonstrations, strikes, police truncheons, slums and a constant decline in the standard of living; whilst here it's all new holiday resorts, factories, harvests, boundless fields, beaming smiles, new homes and the growth of prosperity. *There* the black forces of reaction and imperialism are grinding the faces of the workers and threatening us with war; *here* the bright forces of progress and socialism are building a radiant future and battling for a stable peace. And the forces of peace, socialism and progress are bound to prevail. And all this is pumped out every hour of every day, in thousands of newspapers, magazines, books, films, concerts, radio programmes, songs, poems, operas, ballets and paintings. There is nothing else *at all* – nothing against. Even when you are travelling by train and gazing absentmindedly at the landscape speeding past, your eyes unconsciously scan – and your brain assimilates – the slogans spelled out in stones and broken bricks on either side of the track: 'Peace to the world!', 'Lenin lives!', 'Forward to the victory of communism!'

What should parents do? Try to explain to their children from the outset that they are being deceived? But that is dangerous – the children will tell their friends, and the friends their parents or the teachers. And what advice are you to give your children? Should they speak up and say they disagree? Or keep quiet, conceal their views, lie and lead a double life? And will the children believe *you*, rather than what they are taught at school and by propaganda? Furthermore, this ideology not only exists in its pure form, but is embedded in every subject in school: history, literature, botany, geography, etc., and the pupil has to be able to answer with what is written in the textbooks. More often than not the parents simply wash their hands of the whole matter: 'Oh well, to the devil with it, he'll understand when he grows up.'

Sooner or later the moment of illumination comes for almost every inhabitant of the Soviet Union, and he does understand. There is a joke about this. The teacher at nursery school is giving the children a little talk. She hangs a map of the world on the wall and explains: 'Look, children, here is America. The people there are very badly off. They have no money, therefore they never buy their children any sweets or ice-cream and never take them to the cinema. And here, children, is the Soviet Union. Everybody here is happy and well off, and they buy their children sweets and ice-cream every day and take them to the pictures.' Suddenly one of the little girls bursts into tears. 'What's the matter, Tania, why are you crying?' 'I want to go to the Soviet Union,' sobs the little girl.

But that's only the first impulse, the first misunderstanding. Gradually it dawns on people that in real life not everything is as smooth as it's depicted in the newspapers. Except for the big shots, everybody lives from payday to payday. And for days beforehand people can barely make ends meet, so that they are always trying to borrow from one another. To buy clothes, or furniture, or a television set, you have to beat the system, go without, or work on the side. And then there are the constant shortages – no meat, butter has disappeared, the potato crop has failed. There are queues for everything – you no longer even notice them, but just stand there for hours.

Take the first time the roof in your apartment house springs a leak: this is a major catastrophe, because getting a roof repaired is practically impossible. Whole delegations of residents troop off to see the district council, the city council, their deputies to the Supreme Soviet; they write complaints, compose petitions; commissions come to inspect it – they conduct an examination of the roof and confirm that it does indeed leak. But there is no money for repairs, they weren't foreseen in the plan. And so it goes on, sometimes for years. Meanwhile the residents muster their old wash-tubs, basins and buckets, put them in the attic to collect the drips and anxiously scan the sky each morning to see if it is going to rain.

All these details accumulate, of course, and cloud Soviet man's happiness, his belief in the radiant future. But the gargantuan chorus of newspapers and magazines, films and radio programmes, lectures and instructors, is standing by, ready to explain everything to him: 'Why rush to generalise, comrades? Yes, we do suffer from isolated shortcomings and temporary difficulties. The local authorities are still insufficiently careful in the way they work. We criticise them and try to set them straight. You mustn't forget that the path we are following is, so to speak, untravelled, we are the first to build a new type of society, there is no one to give advice, and occasionally we do indeed make mistakes. But look at how much we've achieved and how much has been done in comparison with 1913! Of course, in order to create the perfect society of the future we do have to steel ourselves sometimes to make certain sacrifices. If it's not always easy now, nevertheless our children will thank us for it. After all, no matter how many mistakes we make in individual cases, we are generally following the right road and our ideas are bright. Nor must you forget the capitalist encirclement, which is out to wreck us and will keep on trying. All they are waiting for is for us to weaken and start doubting our correctness. The enemy is not sleeping! And in order to win the struggle with him we must also make certain sacrifices,' and so on and so forth, etcetera, etcetera.

The years go by, nothing changes, and doubt begins to creep in: are we really building communism? Maybe we haven't begun yet? After all, it's quite clear what was happening from 1917 to 1922 – there was no Soviet power yet, it was civil war. Then up to 1930 we had the New Economic Policy (NEP), and everybody knows that that was a retreat. After that, up till 1953, we had the personality cult – again no Soviet power. Then, up to 1964, it turns out that Khrushchev got it all wrong, but luckily they tumbled to him too and kicked him out. And so it emerges, apparently, that we didn't even begin to live properly until 1965. But who knows – maybe this one will also be kicked out, or after he's dead they'll tell us that he, too, got everything wrong.

This wavering state of uncertainty soon gives way to a conviction that all the propaganda is totally false. No matter how hard it is to get information, one is still not completely isolated. And it becomes apparent that in other districts and regions the situation is not a whit better – and in some cases is even worse – than at home, that other branches of the economy are also in a shambles, that space is a red herring, while the biggest factories and dams were built by convict labour for a crust of bread. The only thing that can't be explained away is that ballet – how come the ballet doesn't fall apart? But to hell with the ballet, we can't live by ballet.

More than that, it percolates through to us that not everything (in fact nothing) in the West is as it's painted. The unemployed, it turns out, get paid for not working! What a dream. Here they'd be sent to Siberia, in the West they're paid. Everybody has his own car, there is every sort of sausage and salami in the shops and no queues. Paradise! Fairyland! And bang goes the belief in a radiant future.

One day in the 1950s a friend of mine carried out an experiment. He was queuing for milk in a shop. The queue was enormous, the sales girls were working slowly and lackadaisically. The people in the queue began to mutter, the way they always do, that there wasn't going to be enough to go round and the service was too slow. During one of the pauses between these outbursts of popular discontent, my friend piped up and said in a loud, distinct voice: 'This is absolutely disgraceful. We've been queuing all morning, just like in America!' And he was engulfed by a wave of popular indignation: 'What are you saying, citizen? Like in America! This could only happen here!' And for a long time afterwards they looked at him with pity and scorn.

And the further it goes, the worse it gets. It transpires, for instance, that while we are having our temporary difficulties, our bosses in the district and regional party committees and in the Kremlin have long ago built communism for themselves. They divide up the caviare, salami and imported goods among themselves in secret. They've built villas for themselves, with high fences and armed guards so that nobody can see them guzzling their caviare. They couldn't give a tinker's cuss for us, whether we live or die.

This represents the longest possible path of reflection and of progress towards insight, covered by a man in the very best situation in society. For most of us it is much shorter and quicker. Sooner or later you encounter such a glaring injustice or falsehood that you can no longer remain silent. Almost anything can set it off – anything that brings you into direct conflict with the regime. It is particularly useful when a working man has dealings with the workers' and peasants' regime in the capacity of a supplicant or protester.

At first the working man tries to get at the truth, searches high and low, writes complaints and petitions, goes for interviews, and gets answers that are progressively more insolent – or no answers at all. 'How can this be, in my workers' and peasants' state?' he fumes. 'Let's try *Pravda*, let's try the Central Committee!' And again nothing. And at interviews, if he gets them, he is confronted by a blockhead in specs who simply smacks his lips – and again nothing. That does it for our working man! He goes into a fury of writing: to the Committee of Soviet Women, to the Society for the Protection of Animals, to the spacemen, and even to the UN. As things proceed he gets wilder and wilder. And he ends up by writing things about the Soviet regime that make him amazed by his own thoughts.

Some of the cons even conceived the idea of sending their complaints to Lenin in his mausoleum! You say Lenin lives, okay let Lenin sort it out for me. And that's nothing. For the Kremlin commandant replies punctiliously that the complaint has been forwarded to the proper quarter! Usually, however, the answer comes from the district prosecutor's office. And the answer usually says that everything has been done according to the law and there are no grounds for complaint.

Generally speaking, all complaints converge in the office of that bespectacled blockhead of whose callousness you are complaining. And you get the most soothing reply back again: we sympathise, we understand, but unfortunately we cannot help. The working man brightens up. It is astounding how quickly he recalls everything he was taught in school, the entire history of the Soviet Union, all its literature and geo-graphy, all the propaganda that since childhood has been haranguing him about individual shortcomings and temporary difficulties, about the radiant future and capitalist encirclement; and even all that stuff about the mirror of the Russian revolution and the verses he learned about Lenin in his nursery school.

And the propaganda blares merrily on as though nothing is wrong – about that typhoon in Japan, that strike in England, about the radiance in the distance and the forces of peace and progress. And so on, day and night, day and night from all sides. Until suddenly our working man goes berserk. People all around him, millions of people, are meeting the targets, accepting new labour tasks, repaying the Party's solicitude with increased productivity – and *they don't know a thing*. The moment they find out, the moment he explains it to them they will stop, every-thing will change and the whole situation will be different. Hey, people, stop! Give me the microphones. Let me get at the microphones! *This is Moscow calling – and all the radio stations of the Soviet Union!*

But why only Moscow? The whole world, the whole planet should know!

While he is in this state our working man performs certain standard actions. He attempts to make a speech at a meeting exposing the whole situation, or to distribute leaflets, or, with the help of foreigners, to send a message to the UN or the American president. Or at the very least airs his opinions frankly among a wide circle of acquaintances. He experiences an extraordinary sense of freedom and omnipotence. Simple human words now appear to him as mighty weapons capable of moving mountains and damming rivers. But at the same time our working man notices that no one is very eager to listen to his words. On the contrary, he finds himself in a sort of vacuum, or rather he feels stifled. At meetings he is not allowed to speak, friends avert their eyes or try to make a joke of it, then hastily remember some urgent business. His wife is in tears all day and scolds him for being a selfish egotist who is ruining her life. And suddenly his mother-in-law, whom he hasn't heard of or seen for five years or more, materialises from Kaluga to persuade her daughter to return home with her.

At work one day, just before lunchtime, he gets an urgent message to go to the personnel office. There a polite but firm gentleman of about forty, neatly combed, wearing a well-cut grey suit, going by the name of Nikolai Ivanovich, Vladimir Fyodorovich or, at the outside, Sergei Petrovich invites our working man to take a short trip with him to his office not far away. No, no, he doesn't need to take anything with him, no, there's no need to phone the wife and there's no point in calling home either – it won't take long. After that Nikolai Ivanovich, Vladimir Fyodorovich or, at the least, Pyotr Sergeyevich escorts him to his car and they ride in it together, indeed not for long. They climb the stairs of an absolutely normal block of flats and enter a door, which opens into a corridor with lots of other doors. One of them leads into an office where a man is sitting behind a desk, greying and wearing a grey suit, whose name is Nikolai Petrovich, Sergei Ivanovich or, at worst, Vladimir Fyodorovich.

'Take a seat,' they say to him politely. 'How's work?' Beyond the window it's high summer or, on the contrary, a bright frosty morning, or maybe ripe, rosy autumn. How nice it would be to go for a walk now in the woods – somewhere far, far off, remote from civilisation.

The working man begins to expound his new discoveries, still with vigour but without his former ardour. He tries to work himself up into a lather, but somehow he no longer has that sense of world tragedy, the seething passion and the urge to get at the microphones. His turns of phrase and conclusions seem automatically to become softened and toned down, and evasive formulations and deprecating epithets leap to his lips. Meanwhile Vladimir Nikolayevich, Sergei Petrovich or maybe Ivan Ivanovich listens in silence, like a father, shaking his head from time to time and jotting notes in his notebook. Then, waiting for a pause in the disjointed narrative, he says:

'And who else did you tell this to? Aha. And who else was present? Yes–yes. And who else saw your letter to the UN? And you were thinking of fleeing abroad? Yes–yes–yes, I see! Do you know what you've done? Your country nursed you, sparing no effort, raised you, educated you, refused you nothing. And you? And at a time when our enemies are frantically searching for ways to injure us! And what would have happened if you'd gone abroad? You'd have been interrogated by counter-intelligence; where did you work, where did you serve in the army, what was the number of your unit, what weapons? . . .'

At the mention of this proposition the working man breaks into a cold sweat – no, no, not that! At this point Vladimir Ivanovich, Nikolai Petrovich or Sergei Mikhailovich takes a bulky file from his desk and opens it, and to his horror, the working man catches sight of all his complaints, declarations and protests, including his letter to the UN, lying there with blue-pencilled comments in the margins.

Lord in heaven, a man doesn't need much in this life. All right, so there's no meat, but you can still buy potatoes – or anyway sour milk. All right, so the roof's leaking – put a bucket under it, what's the problem? All right, some things are not quite as they should be, or maybe even wrong, but you can't set the world to rights in a day, can you? Bad pay? At least you can work a bit extra in the evenings or something. As for the claptrap, well, it's the same everywhere, isn't it – always claptrap. Always was and always will be. It's not my fault, is it, and there's nothing I can do to change it.

The telephone rings and Vladimir Nikolayevich or God-knows-who picks up the receiver: 'Yes?' And suddenly he straightens in his chair and sits to attention: 'Yes, comrade general. Yes, he's here. We were just having a little chat. No, not for the time being, comrade general. No, I don't think it's necessary. You know how it is, a man's work starts to get him down a bit, of course. Yes. At your service, sir. Yes, sir!'

'All right, now then, sign here and here. And over here. You may go . . . home. If we need you again we'll phone. Goodbye.'

And if our working man hasn't actually got up to much, he won't be arrested, oh no. If they were to jail everyone like him they'd have to jug half the country, and that's no longer necessary. It's enough to put away one out of every 10,000 of those who have seen the light – the most uppity one – to frighten all the others. It's not like in the old days. Then you only had to open your mouth to find yourself on a prison transport. Times have changed. Nobody insists that you like this regime or even believe in it – it's sufficient for you to fear it, submit to it, meet your production targets, raise your hand at meetings, unanimously approve and wrathfully condemn.

Our working man scampers through the spring, autumn or winter streets as fast as his legs can carry him – home to his wife and his Kaluga mother-in-law. A heavy door has opened a crack in front of him, he has caught a whiff of crypt-like dankness, putrefaction and despair, but thank God he has got away. A week or two later all the men at his place of work are called to a general meeting, speeches are made by the party organiser, the Komsomol organiser and a representative of the local party committee. They wrathfully condemn him and hold him up to shame, and the elderly foreman, Petrovich, declares that in his opinion there is no room for such people in their collective. Then our working man speaks up himself, expressing repentance and promising to reform. Somewhere on the outer fringes of the meeting, unnoticed, sits Nikolai Ivanovich, Petrovich or Sergeyevich. No, no, he doesn't want to sit on the platform, nor is he planning to speak. He just wants to sit in and listen to the comrades' speeches. Just before the meeting ends the workers' collective resolves to take responsibility for its prodigal son and votes to reform him collectively. Some time later that evening, in the bar, the elderly foreman Petrovich, who has been loudest of all in his denunciations earlier that day, says confidentially to our working man over a mug of beer: 'That's the way it is, me old mate: no man can flay a stone.'

Take a good look, my friend, look closely into the eyes of your workmates, look at the crowds of people thronging the streets, going to the pictures, at football matches or even in the Palace of Congresses, and you will see that almost all of them know all about flaying the stone. So what could you have told them? Every one of them has experienced, or is destined to experience, the spasms of this revelation. And every one of them writhes for a while and then calms down; there is no way you can jolt them out of their lethargy again. What can you tell them in a skimpy leaflet, or even via all the radio stations of the Soviet Union? They know, my friend. They still remember those evil times when the prison vans used to cruise the streets every night collecting their human tribute. And they remember the war. Just think of the colossal force that crashed into us then, but not even that could flay the stone. They keep quiet because they know, not because they don't know. Can you blame them?

Once when I joined a geological expedition in Siberia, at one of our camp sites I caught three ants and put them into a mug – I wanted to see to what degree ants were better than people. Naturally they tried to climb out, but I shook them down to the bottom again. They tried again, and again I shook them down. Overall they made about 180 attempts to climb out of the mug and every time, of course, were unsuccessful. Then they gave up, crawled towards one another and settled in a circle. I watched them for a long time, but they made no more attempts to get away. The mug with the three ants in it stood there in the grass for almost three days. Several times it drizzled, the sun set and rose, but they simply stayed there in the mug, twitching their whiskers – probably telling one another jokes.

What else could they do? They had grasped the situation, they needed nothing more. They would have been happy to narrow their world to the confines of family and home, to live for their quiet antlike joys, to bask in the sun on warm spring days and have a drink together. And to savour the moment while it was still sunny, while it was still so cosy sitting there over their drinks in the ale-house, while every minute consisted of sixty blissful seconds, each of which could be stretched still further by the booze. But a man can't be left alone, can't be allowed to live inside his own little world. He is pursued everywhere by propaganda, by that ubiquitous bawling that drowns out the spring chirruping of the birds. Like a mountain echo, this voice bears down on us from all sides, spawning a strange creation that travels from person to person – the joke. And as he drinks away in his cosy nook, it isn't sufficient for Soviet man simply to relish the moment. The things he has been holding back all day are bursting to come out. Peering over his shoulder is that ever-present companion, the joke. And nibbling on a morsel of processed cheese he says: 'What's the best way to have plenty of everything? Plug your refrigerator into the radio network – it will always be full.'

Because, whether he wishes it or not, inside himself Soviet man is engaged in a permanent dialogue with Soviet propaganda.

Look at them, those Soviet people, streaming silently down the underground passages of the Metro or along the main streets, past the newspaper stands, where they just pick out the headlines and gnash their teeth. Everyone is silent, each conducting his inner dialogue. And in the course of a lifetime he builds up such a store of rage that the whole world turns black for him.

An intelligent-looking little old man wanders down the Arbat and into the Prague to do some shopping, a quiet, subdued little man bothering nobody. 'Aha,' he says to himself, 'the sun's shining, the bloody sun's grinning its head off again. They'll be calling that a socialist achievement next.' He hates the sight of that sky, that Soviet sky. Even the green leaves look as if they've come off a Mayday poster. There's a fresh newspaper pinned to the wall – what claptrap are they blathering now? He knows it's claptrap and it sickens him to read it, but still he stops and scans it, if only to feed his rage. 'Aha, the harvest! Unprecedented, as usual, in record time, as usual. So we'll be importing grain from Canada again. Students helping on the collective farms. Oh yes, the usual thing: collective farmers, help the students to fill the nation's granaries! A strike in France. Go on, strike away, you'll strike once too often one of these days. Student demonstrations dispersed. Send them here to help with the potato picking, they'll soon forget about demonstrating.' Comrade Pinochet is the only one to warm the cockles of his heart: 'Are our dear chaps squawking now you've put the squeeze on those communists of yours? Squeeze away, my friend, you're our only hope. Should do the same everywhere.' No, Soviet man is so created that he can't possibly walk away from this stuff and shut himself away – like an addict he needs to feed his rage with this poison.

This same old man worked for that newspaper all his life, until he retired, and all his life wrote about those fantastic harvests. Or perhaps didn't write about them, but was a compositor or a printer, a factory foreman or a schoolteacher. And why not? If it isn't a crime to manufacture barbed wire, why is it to be a prison guard? One way or another everyone is implicated in the crimes of the regime, everyone works for government enterprises, reinforcing the system and creating its wealth. Everyone raises his hand at meetings, votes at elections and, most important of all, omits to protest. Whatever you do is proclaimed to be the achievement of the system. A scientific discovery, a new symphony, a win in the Olympic Games – everything is a new victory for socialism and proof of its progressiveness. So why is it all right to make discoveries, write music, play hockey and beat production targets, but not to make Soviet propaganda?

Why is it wrong to be a member of the Party or the Komsomol? They do nothing special there, and nothing is required of the average member other than to pay his dues. Beyond that nobody asks you for your opinion – what difference does it make whether they send you to work for the police or the KGB? If I don't do it, someone else will. Work's the same everywhere – carrying out orders. After all, everybody in our country is a functionary, everybody works for the government. And the people *there* are no worse than anyone else, it's their job, that's all. And as for the ones at the top who give the orders, they are just functionaries too, slaves of the system, of the internal struggle for power. If a sort of Nuremberg trial were held in Moscow today, the judges and prosecutors would find no one guilty. From top to bottom no one believes in Marxist dogma any more, even though they continue to measure their actions by it, refer to it and use it as a stick to beat one another with: it is both a proof of loyalty and a meal ticket.

But how can this mysterious being reconcile all these things? Thinking one thing, saying another and doing a third? Jokes alone are not enough to explain it, and even the ants need elaborate theories to justify their submission:

No man can flay a stone.

What can I do alone? (If everyone acted, so would I.)

If I didn't, someone else would. (And better me because I'll do less harm.)

You must make compromises, concessions and sacrifices for the sake of the main cause. (Thus the Church holds that it must make concessions for the sake of self-preservation, yet there is no end to these concessions, so that priests are now nominated by the KGB, and Soviet power is celebrated from the pulpit. Thus the writer, eager to publish the work his readers are waiting for, agrees to cross out a line here, add a paragraph there, change the ending, remove one of the characters, revise the title and hey presto, the whole point of the work has gone. Nevertheless, boasts the writer, on page so-and-so there is an innuendo and the villain says almost *everything* – though it's true that he's later reformed and says quite the opposite.)

We must live for Russia, the communists will one day disappear of themselves. (This argument is a favourite with scientists and the military.)

We must live for posterity, create the eternal values of science and culture; a trivial preoccupation with protests merely distracts us from the main thing.

Never ever protest openly; that is a provocation which merely enrages the authorities and brings suffering on the innocent.

Open protests play into the hands of the hardliners in the Politburo and prevent the doves from carrying out a liberalisation.

Open protests hinder liberalisation, which can only succeed by means of power politics and secret diplomacy.

To protest about details is merely to expose oneself. The thing to do is to lie low. Then, when the decisive moment comes, okay. But in the meantime we'll disguise ourselves.

Yes, but not now, this is the worst possible time: my wife's pregnant, my children are ill, I have to defend my thesis first, my son's about to go to university . . . (and so on till the end of a lifetime).

The worse things get, the better. We must deliberately take all the system's idiocies to their logical and ridiculous conclusion, until the people's patience runs out and they understand what is happening.

Russia is a land of slaves. The Russians have never had democracy and never will. They don't have the aptitudes for it, it's no use trying. There's no other way for our people.

The people are silent. What gives a handful of malcontents the right to speak out – whom do they represent, whose opinion are they expressing?

I have even heard the following argument:

Your protests are misleading world public opinion: people in the West will think that we are allowed to speak openly here and change things. Therefore you are helping Soviet propaganda.

You have to get on quietly with your career, get to the top and try to change things from there; you won't achieve anything from the bottom.

You have to gain the trust of the leaders' advisers and teach and educate them on the quiet, there's no other way of influencing the government's course.

You protest, I'll stay out of it. Someone has to survive to bear witness. (I heard this in the labour camp just before a hunger strike.)

If only there were a new theory to replace Marxism and carry people away; you can't build anything on sheer negation.

Communism has been visited upon Russia in retribution for her sins; to resist God's retribution is equally sinful.

And so everyone, from members of the Politburo, academicians and writers down to collective farm labourers and factory workers, manages to find a justification. Moreover, most people sincerely believe that these are their true feelings. Very few realise that they are pretexts and excuses. And hardly anybody will admit openly and honestly that he is simply afraid of reprisals. Only one person in my entire life has said that he actually likes living in a Communist state – because it allows him to earn a good salary by publishing all sorts of demagogic rubbish in the newspapers. 'In a normal country,' he said, 'they wouldn't let me within a mile of the press! What would I be doing? Working as a navvy.'

In point of fact, only the so-called true Orthodox believers – the sect that has cut itself off from the Russian Church and does not recognise the Soviet State, considering it the work of the devil – only they are not supporting this tyrannical system. But there are very few of them, and they are all in jail because they refuse to work for the state. They don't read newspapers, don't listen to the radio, don't touch official documents, and in the presence of all functionaries, including investigators, they make the sign of the cross – out of my sight, Beelzebub! When released from jail they live off what they can earn from private individuals.

And maybe the tramps living off handouts can be said to exist outside the Soviet system (although in the camps they have to work). All the rest, whether they wish it or not, are building Communism. The State doesn't give a tinker's damn what theories they use to justify their participation, or what they think or feel. So long as they don't resist, protest or publicly disagree, they suit the Soviet State. Nobody says they have to like it, everything is quite simple and cynical. Do you want a new flat? Make a speech at the meeting. Do you want to earn an extra twenty or thirty roubles, or get a responsible job? Join the Party. Do you want to keep your privileges and avoid unpleasantness? Vote at meetings, keep your nose to the grindstone and your mouth shut. Everyone does it. Who wants to spit into the wind? These are the foundations that allow this State to hound its people from prison to prison, to hold everyone in a state of terror, enslave other nations and threaten the entire world.

So what could be expected of Captain Doinikov? One day he said to me: 'When you get out of here I expect you will remember me with hatred.' 'What for?' I asked. 'Well, I'm your jailer, aren't I, keeping you in jail, starving you, confiscating your letters.'

No, in all the years I spent in various camps and jails, I never came to hate the guards, especially not those who didn't go out of their way to harm us. The last people you envy in jail are the guards. Most of their time they are stuck in the jail themselves, are themselves prisoners. And just try patrolling those corridors all round the clock – at night it's enough to make you scream. Never-ending obscenities, brutality, hatred. The cons give you such an earful through the food flap in one day that it's enough to last a lifetime. Some guards get so used to a steady stream of abuse that they don't feel at home until one of the cells lets fly at them. They walk about deliberately trying to pick a quarrel and get themselves cursed, their hearts actively aching for it. One senior guard, quite an old man, used to be driven so crazy by the boredom of the night shift that he would miaow, bark and bray like an ass – he couldn't bear to think that the cons were all sleeping, while he had to stay awake. Another used to walk up and down the corridors and bellow at the top of his voice: 'Who's the boss here, eh? I'm asking you, who's the boss here?' 'You're the boss here, so screw you!' yelled back the cons from the cells. 'Up yours!' After a pause of two or three minutes, off he would go again: 'Who's the boss here, eh? I'm asking you, who's the boss?'

The young guards were at the very least curious about us, and sometimes sympathetic. Whenever they frisked us they would examine our books with great curiosity, leafing through them and even furtively asking us what the books were about and what was in them. After Sukharev's article about me in the *Literary Gazette*, for instance, during one of their routine searches they took the opportunity to read through my sentence and then passed it round behind the officer's back, grinning as they read it. If only the Deputy Minister of Justice could have seen those grins!

Why should I hate them? If anyone was to be hated it was the people at the top, scrapping over the plum jobs and forgetting about everything else in the world; the big shots who pontificated in the name of the people from their platforms; and those who, for fat salaries, hymned them in prose and verse. The people on whose orders the country had been drowned in a welter of blood for sixty years. But even these I could not hate. I could despise them, and the entire society they had created, just as I despised their ideology and their self-justifications – the psychology of slave and tyrant at the same time. I despised Soviet man – not the one depicted on the posters or in Soviet literature, but the one who existed in reality, who had neither honour, nor pride, nor a sense of personal responsibility, who was capable of tackling a bear alone with a pitchfork but who shrank away and broke into a cold sweat at the sight of a policeman, who would betray and sell his own father to avoid the boss thumping his fist on the desk at him. The tragedy was that he existed inside every one of us, and until we could overcome this Soviet man within, nothing in our life would change. It was he who kept me in jail. And so from this point of view it was clear that I was destined to spend a very long time in prison – perhaps the rest of my life.

*But where were they taking me? The goon on my left had dozed off and even let out a snore. Then suddenly, as if jolted by something, he woke up and looked about with alarm. We were still careering along at breakneck speed, with police cars back and front, their lights still blinking. But one could sense that we were approaching a city – probably Moscow. Now we began turning, corner after corner, and slowed down. Yes, it must be Moscow. But where? Lefortovo prison? Of course. Within twenty minutes we were gliding through the familiar Lefortovo gates.*

*Arriving at a familiar prison is like coming home. I got out of the minibus and was taken to the 'boxes' to be frisked. But what about my things? 'Don't worry.' Walking to meet me was my old friend Lieutenant-Colonel Stepanov. Laughing, the rat. 'Did you have a good journey?' He still had the same provincial accent as ten years before. Everything was now more or less clear to me and I calmed down. They had probably brought me here to persuade me to renounce my views and come to terms with the powers that be. Maybe they would even take me for a ride around Moscow.*

*Last winter they had taken Gunnar Rode to Riga in just the same way. They had driven him round town, even taken him to see his mother, trying to persuade him all the while what a lovely life everyone was having. 'While*

66

*you've been inside these last fifteen years, life has moved on, we've built socialism and everybody's happy. Ask for a pardon and we'll let you go.' But they chose the wrong man. Rode drove around town, visited his mother, inspected his Riga and then dug his heels in: 'Take me back to Vladimir.' And so they took him back, having gained nothing.*

*They might, of course, be bringing me here as part of some investigation. Perhaps they had arrested one of my friends in Moscow, and the threads had led them to me. I had already been questioned in connexion with four other cases, but the KGB had long since concluded that they would never get anything out of me and had stopped summoning me. Usually it was the other way round – a KGB investigator came to me in the jail, asked me some formal questions, got no replies and went away again. They had got so used to this that the last time, in connexion with Superfin, the investigator had even begun by saying: 'All right, I know you won't tell us anything, and anyway we don't need you, these are purely formal questions. We'll fill out the record of the interrogation and leave.' But you never knew if they wouldn't make a fresh attempt – they had the patience of the devil. Still, what could I lose? I would feed up a bit, have a rest, give the fuzz the run around, and maybe even wangle a visit. Then back to my own Vladimir. The only thing was that I wouldn't be able to study here.*

*Meanwhile they were frisking me as usual – I had to take off all my clothes while they pinched and patted them.*

*'Hey, what's up? How long do I have to stand here in my birthday suit?'*

*'Just a minute.' Then they brought me some quite different clothes, new ones. Some sort of black suit, shoes and a silk shirt. What the bloody hell was going on now?*

*'What about mine?' I said. 'Give me my own clothes back.' I was particularly worried about my padded jacket – I had that razor-blade in the lining and I also liked to sleep under it. What did I need their clobber for?*

*'Later, later,' they said. 'Your clothes have to be disinfected, it's the rules.'*

*'What disinfection, what rules, what line are you shooting me, you sap? I was in this jail when you were still wearing short trousers. I know the Lefortovo rules, and disinfection was never one of them!'*

*Something was in the wind, I could tell. Then there was that unctuous smile spread all over his face. Suddenly I thought of the forest again, of attempted escape – 'you won't be needing your boots any more.' And I let out a roar: 'I don't want fresh gear, I want my own! Damn disinfection! I've come from another jail, not from outside. We're not in quarantine and we have medical inspections!'*

*That got the bastards and they ran for help. Some officers came charging in. 'We've got new rules, disinfection is compulsory, you can't possibly avoid* disinfection. Go and take a bath.' No matter how much of a fuss I created, it was all a waste of time. Damn and blast you! Shoot me in my own clothes if that's what your orders are.

'But where are my things?'

'Don't worry, we'll give them to you tomorrow.'

'Can I at least have my toothbrush, toothpowder, soap and tobacco?'

'Yes, you can,' they said. And with that they led me to a cell.

It felt very strange to be wearing civilian gear. I hadn't worn any for six years, I'd got out of the way of it and felt awkward. Now it was almost supper-time – which was typical with these transfers. It was all very well, but if they forgot to feed you you could never make up for it afterwards – too late. Cell number 40. I had been here before. I knew all the block officers and all the guards. It really was like coming home. Laughs all round: 'So they've brought you back again!'

There were two others in the cell. Both under investigation. Strange. They shouldn't be holding me with investigation prisoners. That meant I too was under investigation. They were smoking cigarettes and offered me one. It was ages since I'd had one – they didn't satisfy me any more, I was too used to shag. We introduced ourselves and started talking. I let them do most of the talking – who knew what sort of people they were? I wouldn't be put in with good people. One had a gold ring on his finger, which stuck out a mile. He saw me looking at it and explained that they hadn't been able to take it away because it wouldn't come off. Tell me another one! Do you think I don't know the fuzz? They'd take the finger off with it! Okay, forget it.

I asked whether it was true that they disinfected everybody's clothes now – after all, I hadn't been here for three-and-a-half years, maybe the rules had changed.

'Did they do yours?' I asked.

'Yes, they did.'

'And what did they give you instead?'

'Suits as well, but plain ones, not like yours. Jesus, what an outfit they gave you! Undo the jacket. Look at it, it's French!'

And it really was, there was a picture of the Eiffel Tower on the lining. My cell-mates started examining me with great curiosity – what sort of big wheel are you, why the smart suit? To me they were practically free men, they had only been in for two months, so there was plenty to ask about. Lights out. We lay down on our bunks. The other two tossed and turned a bit and fell asleep. But I couldn't.

Something strange was happening to me. All my prison experience told me that this couldn't happen, that it was all wrong – they were setting some sort of trap for me. Perhaps they would let me out for a walk through Moscow and *take photographs of me: you see, he's not in prison at all, he's strolling down Gorky Street in a brand-new suit. Perhaps they were even preparing to show me to Western correspondents from a distance – see, he's alive! Perhaps someone from abroad had got permission to visit me? I made endless conjectures.*

*Lefortovo prison was, in any case, as always full of memories for me. I had been here before – in 1963, 1967, 1971 and 1973, for a total of over two-and-a-half years, under different regimes and even different governors. An investigation prison has the remarkable capacity to squeeze reminiscences out of a prisoner. Gradually your reminiscences reach further back, and your mind begins to dwell on scenes from your childhood. Just as sinners in purgatory are tormented by their former sins, so your memory is haunted by all those nasty things that you wanted to forget and haven't thought about for years, and they are so persistent and inescapable that it is enough to make you gnash your teeth. It is as if all the sediment is stirred up from the bottom and rises to the surface of your consciousness – it is absolute torture, and it is slow to pass. So you feel guilty and ashamed, you want to escape, to disperse those phantoms, but all in vain. And therefore, no matter how often I found myself back in Lefortovo, I inevitably found myself recalling my childhood, our yard, where I grew up, and the witch.*

USUALLY I can't remember a thing about my childhood. It is all clouded, like an ancient film, and doesn't resemble my life in the least. There are isolated scenes and flashes. I know about it mostly from what my parents told me.

I was born in 1942 in the Urals, in the Autonomous Republic of Bashkiria, where all our family had moved from Moscow at the time of the German advance. The little town where I was born was to cause me no end of trouble, although I never went back there. In the first place, nobody could spell it, and I constantly had to dictate it to bureaucrats letter by letter: B–e–l–e–b–e–i. Not Pelepei and not Belidei, but Belebei, damn and blast them, they didn't know the first thing about our geography. On my last identity card they had written Belebel.

And then I had only to mention this benighted Belebei in conjunction with the Autonomous Republic of Bashkiria to receive an answering stare of curiosity and interrogation, like an aviation call-sign: ours or theirs, Bashkirian or Russian? And I would have to explain that I am not a Bashkir but a Russian, that I was simply born there during my evacuation, that both I and my parents have lived all our lives in Moscow. Because it makes a difference to people whether you are Bashkirian or Russian, and it makes a difference to you what people think of you: how damned annoying – why couldn't they have had me in Moscow? It is the peculiarity of prison to flush out all your skeletons from the cupboard. 'Aha,' says prison, 'you've spent your whole life pretending you think everybody equal – both Russians and Bashkirs.' And the very thought tears at you, as if you had condemned all those Bashkirs to the gas chambers.

I found out later that I was born at the very height of the war, when

70

millions of men were slaughtering one another to decide what colour the concentration camps of the future were going to be – brown or red. But I myself remember nothing of that period. My earliest memory is of the victory salute in Moscow. Someone lifted me to the window and said: 'Look, remember this for the rest of your life. That is the victory salute.' And it seems that I did remember. As for the salute, it consisted of a series of coloured spots, like those you see when you screw your eyes up tight.

I am told that I spent my early life in a suitcase. During the war there was no chance of getting a pram or a cot, and it was quite a time before I began to speak – at the age of two-and-a-half. My parents were worried, but a doctor friend set their minds at rest by blaming it all on shortage of food, especially sugar. Where they then managed to lay hands on some sugar for me I don't know. On the other hand, I started to read very early, at the age of about five, mainly from newspapers. I was very fond of the cartoons, which I used to copy out before reading the captions. Tall, skinny, ungainly Uncle Sam, with his striped trousers, top hat and goatee, together with a portly John Bull wearing boots and a tail-coat, never left the pages of the Soviet press in those days. And the things that used to happen to them: one day they would tumble into a puddle, another day they were being kicked out of somewhere by a couple of hefty fellows, and sometimes they simply fought one another. If an inordinately fat capitalist was shown wearing a top hat, he was absolutely certain to be holding a bulging bag with a number and lots of zeros printed on it – the more zeros the better. Occasionally there were holes in the bag with coins and notes dropping out of them. If the British lion appeared in the arena, he was inevitably shown with a patch on his behind or the imprint of somebody's boot. I was so captivated by the adventures of these characters that I began thinking up new disasters for them on my own. My parents weren't over-impressed with this recreation of mine – at any rate they tried to distract me with some old German books, printed in Gothic type and illustrated with lithographs, which had been left behind by my grandfather. The prison seemed to have been gloatingly waiting for me, to overwhelm me with these recollections.

In those days we lived not far from Pushkin Square, in an old stuccoed wooden house with two storeys that was very typical for Moscow. There were three of them in a row in our street, and while I was still a child they were inspected by some commission and adjudged unfit for human habitation. On the corner of each one they painted the big

71

blue letters T.B.D. – 'To Be Demolished'. They remained standing, however, until 1970, and people continued to live there all that time.

There were four families living in our flat on the first floor, one of them being our relatives. The kitchen, corridor, bathroom and lavatory were communal. We were regarded as damned lucky, for other flats had up to twelve families in them, and some people lived in what amounted to barrack huts, where families were separated only by curtains or plywood partitions. Also, our neighbours were comparatively quiet.

During the war practically all the inhabitants of Moscow were evacuated to the interior, while families who had been driven out of the frontline zone landed up in Moscow and occupied the abandoned homes. After the war, when the old inhabitants returned, Moscow was bulging at the seams. Nobody wanted to leave, since the capital was better supplied with food than the provinces. People lived in cellars, barns, barrack huts, and every flat had several families crammed into it. Even before the war, communal flats had been cramped, but now the situation was far worse. And it stayed that way till the 1960s. To this day over a third of Moscow's flats are communal.

Such a way of life gave rise to endless feuds, quarrels and brawls. People were unable to conceal even the tiniest details of their lives from one another, and everyone knew what was cooking in the neighbour's pot. A carelessly dropped word could become a weapon in this kitchen warfare, to be used for a political denunciation, particularly if it offered the hope of moving into a vacated room. It was the hardest of all for cultivated people, members of the old Moscow families who had been brought up in the old-fashioned way. They were unable to descend to the kitchen quarrels, to the daily struggle for room to breathe, and they had no aptitude for it. Their upbringing demanded deference, compromise, courtesy, whereas daily life demanded aggression. This problem, in its generalised form, seems to have become one of the central problems of our age. Cultivation and courtesy have turned out to be impracticable when confronted with uncouthness, baseness and brute force. How can one oppose these things? By using the same methods? But this leads to spiritual degeneration, the two sides become indistinguishable from one another. By remaining the same? But then you face physical extermination.

Isn't this the same problem that dogs Western societies seeking to oppose communism or urban terrorism? My grandmother, unaware, perhaps, of the universal nature of this problem, was ashamed to enter the kitchen when the neighbours were drying sheets that they had stolen from her. Carelessly forgotten crockery disappeared in the same way. Fortunately – and probably thanks to our accommodating ways – our family got by without scandals and brawls, which couldn't be said of other houses in the district. It was not unusual to find a drunken husband chasing his wife round the yard with a knife, or to hear a brawl taking place in one of the flats, with panes of glass tinkling to the floor, or a gang of women having a go at one another and turning the air blue for hours on end.

There were five of us living in two rooms. My parents spent most of the day at work, my sister was at school and I stayed at home with my grandmother. The two of us used to go for paraffin (we had no gas in those days and used to cook on paraffin stoves) and stand in mile-long queues for flour. To get to the front you had to queue for several days, and in order not to lose track, they used to scribble your queue number on your palm with indelible pencil. In the mornings and evenings people used to come to have their numbers checked. Whole families used to come – with the children – since the amount of flour per person was rationed. In the evenings grandmother used to read to me aloud – mainly Pushkin, Zhukovsky, Nekrasov, and tales by Hans Christian Andersen or the Brothers Grimm. She was extremely old by then and used to fall asleep while reading. Her glasses would slip down her nose and she would begin to snore, while I prodded her: 'Grandma, what comes next? Grandma, don't go to sleep.'

Sometimes grandmother and I used to go for long walks. We would walk at a leisurely pace along the river embankment, across Red Square and into the Alexandrovsky Gardens, which girdled the walls of the Kremlin. Dusty green trucks used to rattle over the cobblestones of Red Square. Grandmother told me that they were camouflaged. The mysterious fortress of the Kremlin loomed in front of us – it was forbidden to go in. All we could see behind the walls were inviting cupolas and towers. Grandmother told me lots of stories about our history: about the Tartars and Ivan the Terrible, and the emperor-bell and the emperor-cannon. She told me about the tsars and the boyars, about the Kremlin bells, and how the bells used to ring out over Moscow in the mornings, and the people in festive apparel would flock to the Kremlin. Whenever we passed the Spassky Tower she invariably recited:

> Who the emperor-bell durst raise,
> And swing the emperor-cannon?
> What gallant doffs not his cap
> At the holy gates of the Kremlin?

73

I always imagined that gallant standing by the Spassky Gate, arms akimbo and gazing upwards, his head thrown so far back that his cap almost fell off. A devil-may-care fellow!

Otherwise I spent most of my day in the yard. Surrounded by all the usual scandals, swearing and knife-fights, we boys paid little attention to what went on around us. Attics, cellars and staircases comprised our private world. Naturally we were constantly playing at war, in which one side was always *ours* and the other invariably the *Germans*. Given that nobody wanted to be the Germans, each side considered itself ours and the others the Germans. Our yard also had an abundance of sheds and outbuildings which were ideal for setting up ambushes.

The older boys raced pigeons, swapped them, trapped other people's and secretly swigged vodka in their pigeon lofts. In the evenings they used to gather by the gate, sometimes with guitars. Almost all of them, one way or another, indulged in stealing, and the whole atmosphere reeked of the underworld. So far as I am able to judge, this was typical of Moscow in those years.

The idol of us small boys was a powerfully built, permanently drunk fellow named Yurka, an ex-wrestler and ringleader in all the fights. He loved going into the yard stripped to the waist, so that you could see his powerful muscles, and he patronised a bar in the neighbourhood. There he would get drunk and start a fight with someone, invariably emerging the victor. And he would stand at the gate for hours, taunting the passers-by. We used to whisper legends about his strength and exploits.

The largest and most quarrelsome families lived in the basements. They often got involved in genuine pitched battles, and sometimes the whole yard would take one side or the other and join in the punch-ups. When the weather was nice, some of the old grannies would come out and sun themselves, while their grandchildren crawled in the dust and the laundry hung out on the lines to dry. Meanwhile, somewhere in the depths of the yard, in a semi-basement room, skulked our witch. She was a genuine, ugly old witch, with a hairy wart on her cheek and a hooked nose. It was said she never spoke to anyone and never went to the kitchen, but cooked on a paraffin stove in her room. She didn't even use the communal electric light, but sat with a paraffin lamp. It was also said that at night she used to pore over ancient, occult books, which nobody but she could read, and mutter over them.

It is true that when we crept up to her window in the evenings, as we often did, we could make her out through the grubby panes as she sat there by the light of the paraffin lamp, reading her eerie books. Her appearances outside her room were very rare, but whenever she did

74

appear in her invariable mangy fur coat and old-fashioned hat, we got very excited. In winter we would throw snowballs at her, and sometimes icicles, and run after her and scream hysterically: 'Witch! Witch! Witch!' She would halt at her door, turn her hooked nose to face us and say in a plaintive voice: 'Children, why are you so unkind, children? What have I done to you?' And naturally that provoked us to even greater rage.

One early summer evening there was a sudden scurrying of women about the yard, and the older ones whispered in alarm: 'The witch is dying! The witch is dying!' A large crowd of them, overcoming their apprehension, tore the door down and stampeded into her room, pushing and shoving one another and stumbling over the threshold.

'She's dead, the old witch is dead!'

I couldn't see a thing from behind them, so I inspected the ceiling and walls. The place smelt all mouldy and dusty, like an attic. On one wall hung a large photograph behind framed glass: it showed a young officer with a jaunty moustache and a bashfully smiling girl wearing a white wedding dress.

It was very late that evening before the excitement died down in the yard. People stood around in little groups, talking about the witch. One crone was saying: 'She was a very educated lady. They say she knew ten languages. Her bridegroom ran away to the south in 1918, to join the Whites. He was an officer. But he never came back. They said he was killed. But she never believed it and kept on waiting.' Other groups were more interested in the fact that a room had become free and in who might get it.

This story of the witch came back to haunt me every time I was in Lefortovo. The memory of her drove me crazy and no excuses could help. I would see her as plainly as if she was flesh and blood, turning in her doorway in her tattered fur coat and saying in her plaintive voice: 'Children, why are you so unkind, children!'

Our school was at the far end of the street, on a small hill, a grey, four-storey building built like a barracks. The very sight of it used to plunge me into irreversible gloom.

I especially hated the humanities – history, literature, and even geography, for they were so saturated with ideology that nothing else was left. Not that this ideology provoked any serious objections on my part at the time, it simply made every subject deadly boring. What interest is there in history if everything is reduced to the class struggle and nothing more, to the gradual march to socialism? Nothing but the dates of various battles and uprisings, and the births and deaths of outstanding revolutionaries.

And literature? It was only as a grown-up, in prison, that I re-read Tolstoy and discovered that he was fantastically interesting. Yet during my school years I had been obliged to write essays on his works and analyse his 'types' – positive and negative – with the result that I fiercely hated him. I mechanically memorised all the facts, mechanically repeated them, and just as mechanically forgot them, like the majority of my fellows.

Soviet children are not supposed to exhibit any independence, they have to do only what they are told. Playfulness, mischievousness, restlessness, the natural attributes of a normal child, are rooted out at all costs. Soviet school authorities, who dish out tedious reprimands and punishments and set the parents on to the children, won't allow anyone simply to be himself, they have to try to change everyone and re-educate everyone, as in an institution for young criminals. This refusal to recognise their individuality evokes a desperate resistance from young people.

It should be added that, like doctors, teachers are the lowest-paid of all professionals in the Soviet Union. Most people, therefore, go into it only out of necessity, when they can't get a job elsewhere, or if they are failures, incapable of doing highly skilled work. Of course, there are also a small number of truly inspired teachers, honest and talented men and women, but they are so few that they do not alter the overall picture in any way. School for them is not life but forced labour – they are in permanent conflict with the administration. The children's instinctive love of them is quite understandable: it is not so boring in their classes, and more importantly, these teachers are the victimised, not the victimisers.

But education is compulsory. Children who don't want to learn at all are obliged to trail to school every day and sit through their lessons. They are given low marks, punished, kept down for an extra year, but they know perfectly well that in the end they will be given satisfactory marks and will get their leaver's certificate when they finish school. And no matter how often they are punished or what is done to them, they will still be rowdy and misbehave – it's too boring otherwise! Those that are kept down are older and stronger than the rest of the class and soon establish their own order.

I am ashamed to recall the tricks that we got up to with our teachers. We had a history teacher, for instance, nicknamed the Walrus by many generations of schoolchildren because of her prominent moustache. She was not at all an unpleasant person, but alas, she was deaf in one ear and we used to spend the whole of her classes letting off percussion caps by her deaf ear. She never turned a hair, which we found hilarious. Another teacher, the unfortunate woman who taught us natural history, once told us that she had been on an expedition where everyone was bitten by an encephalitis-carrying tick. 'Encephalitis,' she told us, 'is the sort of illness from which you either die or go mad. Everyone else on the expedition died, but I, as you see, survived.' Her lessons were general scrimmages, and nobody paid the slightest attention to her.

We had quite a different approach to our elderly teacher of Russian. She was a very old and sentimental lady, and she adored birds. As soon as class started, one of us would begin whistling in passable imitation of a bird. 'Aha,' she would cry delightedly, 'listen children, it will soon be spring, the birds are singing.' Spring, the old crackpot, when we were still in December! But this was only the beginning. Someone else would immediately announce, as the birdsong continued: 'I'm going to make a catapult and shoot those birds.' And there the Russian language ended and a lecture on bird life began: they are so useful, it's a crime to kill them. The amazing thing was that we never got tired of hearing about those birds every day. Especially as the lesson went by without her asking anybody to answer questions or inspecting our homework.

Most of our teachers, however, were cruel and heartless machines who terrorised us ruthlessly. The best example was our headmaster, a hefty giant of six-foot-six. Even the senior boys, aged sixteen to seventeen, he used publicly to strike in the face, while the younger ones would get dragged back to his study and beaten mercilessly. One day, when he had beaten someone in our class, a dozen or so of us stayed on after lessons and went to see him in his study. We were about fourteen years old, though a few were older; we didn't know what fear was, and we looked as if we meant business. We swiftly disconnected the telephone when he tried to call the police, and explained that we would disconnect him too if he touched any of us again. He didn't take much convincing. After that he pulled in his horns and left us alone.

The only man whom all the boys more or less respected was our English teacher. He was a short man with a scar on his forehead and an amazing capacity for instilling fear. He was always extremely badly dressed and apparently lived in penury. It was said that he had been wounded at the front and had even been a prisoner-of-war. At any

77

rate, his eyesight was damaged in the most unusual way: he could see things close up, when he held the page literally against the end of his nose, or else at a distance. But he couldn't see the middle distance at all, and we had occasion to confirm this many times, although nobody dared take advantage of this defect. He used to sweep into the classroom sideways, opening the class register while still on the move. 'Whom shall I ask, whom shall I ask, whom shall I ask first?' he would say ominously, poking his nose into the pages of the register, and a deathly silence ensued. 'Oh mother, please not me!' we all prayed. He never beat anybody, yet we all studied hard, even the laziest among us, even those who were repeating the year. He was something of a mystery to us, and awe-inspiring.

Later on, when I had moved to another school, I went to visit him several times. I was astonished by his ability to treat me as an equal, knowing how unapproachable and awesome he was in the classroom, and considering I was then fifteen and he was forty-five. One day I found him listening to the radio, but he quickly switched it off and I realised that it wasn't Radio Moscow. But we didn't talk about it. Another time he asked me to copy a photograph for him. At that time I was interested in photography, but my cheap camera was not equipped for such tasks. I worked at it for a whole month, improved my camera, studied optics out of a senior-class textbook, calculated the necessary aperture, broke the stop, unscrewed the lens too far, but made a copy better than any studio could have done. I didn't even consider the possibility of not doing what he asked me.

After that we lost touch with one another. Many years went by, the KGB was already collecting information about me, and I knew it, when suddenly he found me through some of my former schoolfellows. We met in the street and he informed me that the KGB had been to the school to collect evidence against me. 'I don't know what it's about and I don't want to know,' he said, 'I simply wanted to warn you so that you knew.' We parted and I never saw him again, for which I was sorry. He was obviously somebody very rare.

Two particularly painful and shameful episodes from my school life I now recalled most often of all.

The bulk of our class was taken into the Pioneers when we were eight years old, and nobody asked our permission. They simply announced that on such and such a date there would be a ceremony for entry into the Pioneers and they would accept the ones who were fittest for it. On the appointed day we were taken to the Museum of the

Revolution, which fortunately was just round the corner, on Gorky Street, and lined up in one of the big rooms. A banner was solemnly carried in and each of us had to swear an oath before it: 'I, a Young Pioneer, solemnly swear before my comrades that I shall stand fast for the cause of Lenin and Stalin and the victory of Communism,' etc. Then you had a red tie put around your neck and the master of ceremonies, standing by the banner, declaimed: 'Young Pioneers, be prepared to struggle for the cause of Lenin and Stalin!' 'We shall always be prepared!' we replied in unison.

In fact, I had nothing against being a Young Pioneer. When you were old enough you became a Young Pioneer, then a member of the Komsomol and then a member of the Party.* It was as simple as that. That was what happened to everybody, just as you moved regularly from class to class. But things turned out worse than I had expected. There were regular Pioneer assemblies, marching sessions and parades, and while the fortunate non-Pioneers made their way home to amuse themselves and kick their heels, we had to sweat it out at exercises, discuss such topics as our classmates' study performance and behaviour, attend political information sessions and so on and so forth. Our instructors took every opportunity to reproach us: you are a Pioneer, you're supposed to be more obedient and not to do this and that. And we were all given social tasks to perform: issuing wall newspapers, preparing reports, keeping stragglers up to the mark, and above all, educating others and one another, and admonishing classmates who got low marks or misbehaved. All of us were obliged to censure wrong-doers. Thus we found ourselves arrayed on the side of the teachers, which seemed unnatural and even ignoble. From the point of view of our classmates it was a betrayal.

The result was a kind of schizophrenia. Some of us turned into sneaks and were heartily hated as a result. But most of us simply lied and feigned ignorance, saying that we had seen and heard nothing.

All of this became crystal-clear to me a year or two later, when I was ten and, as one of the best students, was made chairman of the Pioneers in my class. I was the one who had to call the confounded assemblies, make sure all the other Pioneers carried out their instructions, attend meetings of the Pioneer leadership of the whole school,

* The Young Pioneers and the Komsomol (League of Communist Youth) are a kind of Soviet equivalent of the cubs and brownies or scouts and girl guides, except that they come under the direct control of the Communist Party and are openly manipulative in their practices.

and so on. The teachers would tell me quite bluntly who was to be discussed at the next assembly, who should be expelled from the Pioneers or punished in some other way. And then I personally had to participate in reprimanding the stragglers and mischief-makers.

One day a teacher summoned me to carry out one of these reprimands. I was supposed to give my erring classmate a dressing down in the teacher's presence. I started off with the standard arguments and said that he was letting the side down, that he would have to reform himself in order to help the country build Communism. Then, suddenly, I had a bright idea: this boy's name was Ulyanov, the same as Lenin's, and I began telling him that he was bringing disgrace to our leader's name, that with a name like that he ought to be studying the way Lenin studied, and I added something to the effect that Lenin himself would have been most upset if he knew of this boy's behaviour. I must have been very eloquent and convincing, and also offensive, because all of a sudden he turned red, twisted his face up and burst into tears.

'You bastard!' he said. 'You swine!'

The teacher was delighted with this result but I really did feel like a swine. I didn't at all feel that the boy was bringing disgrace on anybody, and I wasn't in the least angry with him. But I had grown used to parroting the words expected of me, and everyone I had spoken to before had realised I didn't mean what I said and merely did it to get it over with. Nobody had taken offence and I was on friendly terms with everybody; more than that, I was respected, because I never ratted on anyone and always pretended I hadn't seen anything. Now I had caused this boy real distress and I was stunned.

I realised I couldn't and wouldn't play this idiotic role any longer. I resigned. They tried talking me round, upbraided me, censured me, but I stuck to my guns. I didn't explain the reason for my resignation – I don't think I could have done so, but from then on I stopped even wearing the red tie. (Lots of others didn't either: you carried it in your pocket, and if a grown-up noticed, you simply slipped into the lavatory and put it on. You could always say it had got dirty and your parents hadn't had time to wash it.)

I was ten years old at that time. When I was fourteen, which is when they started taking everyone into the Komsomol, I refused to join. 'What's the matter? Do you believe in God?' they asked me curiously, but I refused to give any explanation. They pressed me for a very long time, because I was a good student and it was the accepted thing for all the good ones to be in the Komsomol, but they didn't get anywhere and in the end gave up. 'Watch out,' said my friends, 'you'll find it harder to get into the university.'

The other, equally shameful episode occurred during my Pioneer years. In 1952 we heard about the 'doctors' plot', which coincided with a wave of anti-semitism.* Hatred of the Jews was growing all the time, and now there was a lot of talk about all the Jews being deported because they were enemies who had wanted to kill Stalin. For every single one of us, Stalin was greater than God, a reality in which it was impossible not to believe; he thought for us, he was our saviour, he was responsible for our happy childhood. There could be nothing higher in the scale of human values. It was impossible to imagine an act of greater barbarism than killing Stalin.

I took these developments extremely hard. Several times I dreamed the same persistent dream: I was sitting in an enormous auditorium, full of people who were clapping and shouting; Stalin was on the platform, giving a speech and being interrupted by the applause. He reached for a pitcher of water, poured some into a glass and was about to drink it. I was the only one there who knew that the water was poisoned, but I could do nothing. I cried out: 'Don't drink it, don't drink it!' But my voice was drowned by the ovations and shouting. I wanted to run to the platform, but there were so many people that I couldn't get through. The nightmare of Stalin being killed haunted me and made me literally ill.

In our school there were only two Jewish boys. One, Iosif, was a rather unpleasant fellow. I didn't like him and we were never friends. As for the other one, nobody except me knew that he was a Jew, for he had a Ukrainian name. He lived next door to me and we used to walk to school together. I had seen his mother and father and was aware that they were Jews. We weren't friends, and our relations began and ended with the walk to school, but now I was tormented by the question: is it possible that his parents want to kill Stalin too?

One morning in the school playground things came to a head and the other boys started beating Iosif up. A big crowd gathered and everybody tried to kick or punch him. No explanation or incitements were needed – everybody understood that it was all right to beat

* In January 1953 nine prominent physicians, most of them Jewish, were arrested on orders from Stalin and accused of attempting to poison members of the Politburo, whose medical attendants they were. Two of them were beaten to death during interrogation and there was talk of banishing all Jews to Siberia, but the case was terminated on the death of Stalin (5 March 1953) and the doctors were rehabilitated.

him, that nobody would be punished for it. But for some reason the unhappy Iosif, instead of going home, staggered into the school and tried to show that he was a stout fellow, one of the boys, not in the least offended. The upshot was that he was beaten again during the next break and during the one after that; but he insisted, with a pathetic smile, on sticking to his friends, and the more they beat him, the more he seemed to invite them to continue.

After every break he would stagger into the classroom covered in blood, with swollen lips, still trying to talk as if nothing in the world were wrong. On each occasion he believed that it was all over now, that everything was finished and would be as before. But at the next break the same thing would happen all over again. All the teachers did was to say to him impassively: 'Go to the cloakroom and wash yourself.' And asked no questions.

I didn't join in. He was so revolting, with that pitiful, cringing smile on his broken lips, that I simply couldn't bear to go near him. I just waited miserably for it all to end. If only he had the sense to go away, or if they even killed him or something! I knew perfectly well that Iosif had nothing whatever to do with Stalin – was incapable of even thinking of murder. So why didn't I try to stop it? Worse still, the next morning I stopped walking to school with the boy next door, contriving to leave just a little bit late. Whether I felt shame or disgust, I do not know.

Stalin's death shook our life to its foundations. Lessons in school virtually came to a halt, the teachers wept openly, and everybody went around with swollen eyes.

One man shouted from the window of a hospital in a sobbing voice: 'Stalin's dead and I'm here!'

The rows and fights in the yard stopped too, and enormous unorganised crowds streamed through the streets to the Hall of Columns, where Stalin lay in state. There was something awe-inspiring about these immense, silent, gloomy masses of people. The authorities hesitated to try to curb them and simply blocked off some of the sidestreets with buses and lorries, while the waves of people rolled endlessly on. We boys managed to make our way via attics and rooftops to the roof of the Hotel National. The crowd below us surged forwards and backwards, like waves in the sea, and then suddenly, in one of the sidestreets, a bus shivered, toppled over and fell, like an elephant rolling on to its side. This vast procession continued for several days and thousands of people perished in the crush. For days, Gorky Street was littered with buttons, handbags, galoshes and paper. Someone had even stuffed a pair of galoshes into the mouths of the lions at the entrance to the Museum of the Revolution.

On the day of Stalin's funeral, factory sirens shrieked and wailed, and cars and locomotives hooted. Something terrible and irreparable had occurred. How would we live from now on? Our Father, to whom have you abandoned us? People said quite openly: 'Who is there to die for now? Malenkov? No, the people won't die for Malenkov!'

But the years passed, and we went on living just the same, or at any rate no worse, which was itself sacrilege. Life did not come to a halt. The grown-ups went to work and we went to school. Newspapers continued to appear, the radio to broadcast, and the yard went back to the old shouting and fighting. Stalin was mentioned less and less. And I was bewildered: hadn't God died, without whom nothing was supposed to take place?

Like threatening clouds, rumours began to spread about executions and tortures, about millions of Russians ill-treated in the labour camps. The doctors were released, Beria was executed as an enemy of the people, and another rumour spread like an obscure muttering: 'The biggest enemy of the people of them all was – Stalin!'

It was amazing how quickly people believed this, people who two years before had stampeded to his funeral and been ready to die for him. Now his misdeeds were announced at the Party Congress, and all the newspapers and radio stations, books and magazines, films and textbooks that had lauded his genius, began to condemn his 'mistakes' and 'distortions'.

All those people whose business it had been to praise Stalin for so many years now assured us they had known nothing about this Terror or, if they had, had been afraid to say so. I didn't believe the ones who said they had never known: how could you fail to notice the deaths of millions of people, the deaths of your neighbours and friends? Nor did I believe the ones who said that they had been afraid – their fear had brought them too many promotions. You might keep quiet out of fear, you might run away or go to ground, you might even humour the person you feared, but did fear oblige you to compose odes and dithyrambs, to become generals and members of the Central Committee? You don't get Stalin prizes and country houses if you're afraid. It was said that at the Party Congress, someone sent a note up to Khrushchev: 'Where were *you* at the time?' And that Khrushchev asked over the microphones: 'Who wrote this note? Please stand up!' Nobody, of course, got to his feet. 'All right,' said Khrushchev, 'I was where you are now.' Many people liked that answer, but I despised both Khrushchev and the author of the note. They both knew the truth, yet neither had the guts to say so openly. And neither of them was obliged to be in a public position where guts were needed; no one had forced them to be in that hall, so close to power.

How could it happen that people were still afraid to stand up? How could one man, or say ten men, seize power and keep all the rest in fear and ignorance? When did it all begin? Khrushchev seemed to think that he had explained everything, that he had given answers to all the questions. According to Khrushchev they had got to the bottom of it, released the innocent, spoken well of the dead, and life could go on. But for us, and especially for my generation, the questions were only just beginning. We had just had time to be taught that communism was the world's most progressive doctrine and Stalin the incarnation of its ideas when, hey presto, Stalin turned out to be a murderer and a tyrant, a terrible degenerate no better than Hitler! So what was the nature of the ideas that had produced a Stalin? What was the nature of a Party that, once having brought him to power, could no longer stop him? What difference did it make now whether they had been afraid or simply ignorant? After all, even now, when all had been revealed, they were still frightened to stand up and be counted. The first conclusion was self-evident: a system based on a single-party government will inevitably produce Stalins and then be unable to get rid of them, and it will always destroy all attempts to create an opposition or an alternative.

At that time a lot was said about inner-party democracy, but this struck us as unconvincing. Why should democracy be limited to the Party? Did that mean that the rest of us weren't human? We didn't elect the Party – they elected themselves. Did this mean that the same people who had produced and supported Stalin were again under-taking to establish absolute justice by introducing democracy among themselves? Were they planning to speak in the name of the people again, though the people had not elected them to do so? The same rogues who had lied about Stalin for thirty years, would carry on lying about party democracy. Who would believe it? If for the time being they had ceased killing millions of people today, where was the guarantee that this wouldn't happen again tomorrow? It was the same system, and the same people. No one had ever been punished or put on trial.

But who could they try? Everyone was guilty – those who did the actual killing, those who gave the orders, those who approved the results, and even those who kept silent. Everyone in this artificial

84

society had carried out the role assigned to him, for which he had been rewarded. Take my own parents, for example – modest, quiet, honourable people. But they were journalists, writing the very propaganda that had so vilely deceived me, that was created to justify the murders or hush them up. One long essay of my father's had been praised by Stalin, and on his personal instructions my father had been made a member of the Writers' Union – had become a writer! This had happened only recently, it seemed like yesterday. Everybody was delighted and congratulated him. The essay was broadcast over the radio and printed in *Pravda*, then published as a separate book. But what was there to be so pleased about? He had played his subordinate role and the chief executioner had rewarded him. What difference did it make to me how they justified their complicity, even if it was by the need to feed me?

And was I any better myself? It wasn't just that I ate their bread. I had been a Pioneer, I had participated in the work of this terrible machine whose end-product was either hangmen or corpses. Did it make it any easier that I hadn't realised what I was doing? Does a man feel better when he learns that by accident, without knowing it, he has been an accessory to murder? I recalled Iosif, whom I had not defended, and Ulyanov, whom I had tormented by invoking his namesake. I might have gone on like that, from rung to rung, from the Pioneers to the Komsomol and then into the Party; forty years later, perhaps, I would be waving to the masses from a platform or signing arrest warrants. And as I grew older, my children would say to me: 'Where were you, papa? Why were you silent? How could you allow all that to happen?' And my bread would stick in their throats.

Naturally I started reading voraciously, anything I could lay my hands on. And of course, one of the first to come to me in my darkness was Vladimir Ilyich Lenin. Ah, our beloved Ilyich, how many people has he lured into the darkness, how many supplied with a justification for their crimes! But to me he brought light.

Some years later, I had some friends I often used to visit – a couple and their little daughter; their grandmother lived with them, too. They were a quiet, lovable family who talked for most of the time about art and painting. One day I was surprised to find the entire family, including the ancient grandmother, engaged in a violent argument about Lenin. Each had their own understanding of what Lenin wanted, what he believed in and what principles he preached. They had no liking for Lenin, they were Christians, and I had never known them to take an interest in Lenin's views before. The thing that amazed me was that they were *quoting* Lenin, and each new quotation refuted the one before. I had never suspected such erudition in them. The following day I saw them again, and again they were arguing about Lenin. What the devil had got into them? And so it continued for a couple of weeks. The peaceful haven where I had been able to refresh my soul was destroyed. That's all it needs, I thought. This Lenin enters into people like Satan and sets them at loggerheads!

All of a sudden the whole thing was resolved. It turned out that because of the shortage of toilet paper, they had taken the complete works of Lenin into the lavatory. Naturally, each of them saw different pages of this opus, taken from different articles and sometimes from different periods, and of course they couldn't reach a consensus on what his beliefs were. And that is typical of Lenin and his dialectics. Just try it. Hand out his works to different people and ask their opinion afterwards: hardly two out of a hundred will agree. It is not surprising that there are dozens of Marxist-Lenninist parties in the world, and all of them genuine. Lenin had but one principle – to supply a theoretical basis for each concrete step that he took.

Still, I derived much benefit from reading Lenin. First of all it was a living history of the crimes of the Bolsheviks. The libraries wouldn't let Soviet citizens read the files of *Pravda* of twenty years ago, yet here was the entire revolution, the entire civil war, still living in Lenin's notes and comments! And knowing our later history, it was easy to see where it had begun.

From Lenin I went back to the Russian thinkers of the nineteenth century and stumbled across an amusing characteristic of theirs: all of them, sitting on their estates or in their city flats, loved to hold forth about the people, about the latent unplumbed forces of the people and about how the people would one day awaken from their slumbers and resolve everything, pronounce the ultimate truth, and create a genuine culture. It is understandable that they couldn't know what would happen at the outset of the following century – how the people would demonstrate its worth – and they made their judgment on the basis of their coachmen and yard-sweepers. That was the birth of the idea of a proletarian culture as somehow higher and superior.

To us who had grown up in the communal flats and backyards of this selfsame proletariat, living among them as equals, not masters, the term 'proletarian culture' sounded grotesque. For us it meant no mystical secret, but drunkenness, brawling, knife fights, squeezeboxes, obscenity and chewing sunflower seeds. No true proletarian would

have called this culture, because the distinguishing feature of the proletariat was a hatred of all culture, combined with a sort of inexplicable
envy. Culture was a witch they stoned. 'Intellectual' was an insult
hissed venomously by your neighbours.

With great curiosity I read further, devouring as many of the socialist
utopians as I could find. And I was astounded: all their utopias had truly
been realised by us! Realised, that is, as far as they could be by mere
mortals. We simply turned out to be the most conscientious and consistent exponents of these utopias. Please note that all these theories
presuppose a special type of people whom the ideal state will please,
people who are exclusively honest and objective, with the common
weal at heart – I wonder what happens to all the scoundrels in their
utopias?

Furthermore, it is considered self-evident that people who are born
and grow up in the new conditions will be quite different from before,
the sort of people, in short, who are needed for the new order. And this
is their fundamental error. They regard man as being born into this
world completely empty, like a vessel, and as malleable as wax, and
therefore they assert that there will be no more crime, dissatisfaction,
envy or hatred.

The amazing, naïve and inhuman faith of all socialists in the power of
re-education transformed our school years into a torture and covered
the country with concentration camps. In our country, everybody is
being 're-educated', from the cradle to the grave, and everybody is
obliged to re-educate everybody else. Conferences, meetings, discussions, political information sessions, surveillance, check-ups, collective
measures, Saturday working and socialist competition. For the in-
educable, heavy physical labour in concentration camps. How else
could you build socialism? All this was clear to me as a fifteen-year-old
lad. But ask any Western socialist what should be done with people
unsuited to socialism and he will reply: re-educate them.

In the Soviet Union they even made a serious attempt to turn apples
into pears, and for fifty years based biology on that belief. It is said that
for twenty years an eccentric Englishman cut the tails off rats in the
expectation that they would produce tail-less offspring, but nothing
came of it and he gave up. What can you expect of an Englishman?
No, that's no way to build socialism. He lacked sufficient passion, a
healthy faith in the radiant future. It was quite different in our country:
they cut off people's heads for decades, and at last saw the birth of a
new type of headless people.

This dream of absolute, universal equality is amazing, terrifying and inhuman. And the moment it captures people's minds, the result is mountains of corpses and rivers of blood, accompanied by attempts to straighten the bent and shorten the tall. I remember that one part of the psychiatric examination was a test for idiocy. The patient was given the following problem to solve. 'Imagine a train crash. It is well known that the part of the train to suffer the most damage in such crashes is the carriage at the rear. How can you prevent that damage from taking place?' The idiot's usual reply is expected to be: uncouple the last carriage. That strikes us as amusing, but just think – are the theory and practice of socialism much better?

Society, say the socialists, contains both the rich and the poor. The rich are getting richer and the poor poorer – what is to be done? Uncouple the last carriage, liquidate the rich, take away their wealth and distribute it among the poor. And they start to uncouple the carriages. And it turns out that there is always one carriage at the back, that there are always richer and poorer, because society is like a magnet: no matter which way you slice it, there are always two poles. But does this discourage a true socialist? The main thing is to realise his dream, therefore the richest section of society is liquidated first, and everyone rejoices because everyone gains from the share-out. But the spoils are soon spent, and people start to notice inequality again – again there are rich and poor, so they uncouple the next carriage, and then the next, without end, because absolute equality has still not been achieved. And before you know it, the peasant with two cows and a horse turns out to be in the last carriage and is pronounced a kulak and deported. Is it really surprising that the moment you get a striving for equality and fraternity the guillotine appears on the scene?

It is all so easy, so simple and so tempting – to confiscate and divide! To make everybody equal, and in one go, with one fell swoop, to resolve all problems. It is so alluring – to escape from poverty and crime, grief and suffering, once and for all. All you have to do is to want it, all you have to do is reform the people who are hindering universal happiness and there will be paradise on earth, absolute justice and goodwill to all men! It is difficult for man to resist this dream and this noble impulse, particularly for men who are impetuous and sincere. They are the first to start chopping heads off and, eventually, to have their own chopped off.

> Do not fear ashes, do not fear curses,
> Do not fear brimstone and fire,

88

But fear like the plague that man with the rage
To tell you: 'I know what's required!'
Who tells you: 'Fall in and follow me
If heaven on earth's your desire.'*

They are the first to put their head on the block or go to prison. Such a system is too convenient for scoundrels and demagogues, and they are the ones, in the final analysis, who will decide what is good and what evil.

You have to learn to respect the right of even the most insignificant and repulsive individual to live the way he chooses. You have to renounce once and for all the criminal belief that you can re-educate everyone in your own image. You have to understand that without the use of force it is realistic to create a theoretical equality of opportunity, but not equality of results. People attain absolute equality only in the graveyard, and if you want to turn your country into a gigantic grave-yard, go ahead, join the socialists. But man is so constituted that others' experiences and others' explanations don't convince him; he has to try things out for himself; and we Russians now watch events unfolding in Vietnam and Cambodia with increasing horror, listen sadly to all the chatter about Eurocommunism and socialism with a human face. Why is it that nobody speaks of fascism with a human face?

At around this time the Hungarian revolution occurred. After all the exposures, denunciations and posthumous rehabilitations, after all the assurances about the impossibility of repeating the past, we were now presented with corpses, tanks, brute force and lies all over again. Just one more convincing proof that nothing had changed at all. Boys just like us, fifteen or sixteen years old, were perishing on the streets of Budapest, rifles in hand, in defence of their freedom. Which was our side now, and which theirs? This was no longer a film or a game of war, where it was always our side against the Germans and we were always on our side.

On the one hand there was *our side* – the Russians, who were being cold-bloodedly sent in to kill. And on the other hand there was also *our side*, for I would have done exactly the same thing if I had been in the place of those young Hungarians. How we itched, in peaceful boring Moscow, maddened by our quiet humdrum life, for some

* From a ballad by Alexander Galich, a dramatist who turned to satirical writing after the death of Stalin and achieved enormous popularity in *samizdat*. He left the Soviet Union in 1974 and died in Paris in 1978.

89

action! It seemed to us that at any moment a dusty khaki truck would pull up outside our yard: 'Time to go,' they would say, and start handing brand-new machine-guns over the side. And we would swoop like a whirlwind through the attics and backyards, where we knew every rafter and every turn blindfolded, towards the centre, to the Kremlin's red stars. But the dusty trucks clattered past us over the cobbles, pedestrians walked uncaringly up and down, and women lazily exchanged insults. The kingdom of the dead. The days dragged by agonisingly, one after another, until it was all over and Hungary was strangled. It was clear that we couldn't wait any longer, we had to act. But how? I was ready for anything.

When some of the boys in school began to drop cautious hints about some new sort of organisation, I didn't even allow them to finish, I was so overjoyed. This is it, it's started, I thought. At last! Now for the machine-guns and we'll get going! And so I became a member of an illegal organisation. To my great sorrow there were no machine-guns in sight, and no one even talked of such things; on the contrary, our leaders from among the older boys said that the organisation had no political aims at all. But this was said meaningfully and with a knowing, conspiratorial look: it was clear that this was simply something that had to be said, just in case, in case someone talked out of place or gave way under interrogation, or in case we were being bugged. It was taken for granted that we were simply waiting for a signal to start, for the right moment, which one of our chiefs would recognise, and then. . . .

If someone started talking about communism or Hungary, he was stopped immediately: why talk about that? It has absolutely nothing to do with us. Do you think you have to convert *us*? The message was: a clever person should understand. We didn't even circulate forbidden literature, and we weren't recommended to try to get it. It was considered that we already understood the situation perfectly well and needed no further persuasion. From various hints dropped in passing, one was led to believe that there were very very many of us, virtually half the country was caught up in our network and only waiting for the signal. At one gathering in a forest about twenty-five miles from Moscow, I saw twenty people, and among the trees there were look-outs posted. At other meetings I noticed new boys I hadn't seen before, but according to our rules we weren't supposed to know one another, and it was even suggested that we should make a habit of using an alias.

In fact our entire activity consisted of conspiring and recruiting new members. First of all, it was explained, telephones and flats could be bugged, and on the telephone we should use only prearranged phrases that would sound innocent; in flats it was better not to talk at all. We also learned how to recognise a 'tail' and get away from him. A member you didn't know would take on the job of tailing you. You might have no warning, but you were supposed to be on the *qui vive* at all times. It was considered a great disgrace not to spot the tail, and afterwards you were told what you had done all day and where you had been. Similarly, you too might be given the job of tailing someone without being noticed. If you were discovered, you weren't supposed to show you knew, and you still had to prevent your target from getting away. But if you were the one being tailed, you had to try to find a way of giving your tail the slip and escaping. All these methods were carefully worked out and studied.

We were instructed how to behave during an interrogation: never admit anything – above all that you are a member of the organisation; don't recognise other members if they are shown to you; conceal your views and pretend to be a loyal Soviet citizen; feign surprise, perplexity, indignation, and use other psychological tricks during interrogation. Unfortunately, no one explained the legal side of interrogations to us. Generally speaking, the omniscience and omnipotence of the KGB were greatly exaggerated. It was held that there was bound to be torture, beatings and intimidation, and that the KGB would produce false written statements by other members, and so on. To a certain degree this was subsequently borne out as true, and my training stood me in good stead. But at the time no one paid us any attention.

The recruitment of new members was entrusted only to very few – you had to prove your abilities first. On the whole it was recommended to keep people under close and sustained observation at first, without getting too intimate with them. Talking politics was categorically forbidden. Future members of the organisation had to be selected not on the basis of their attitude or expressed beliefs, but according to quite different criteria. The person must be taciturn, reserved, bold and reliable. You had to establish that he had no particular vices or criminal connexions, and that he was not too trusting or stupid. Finally, when you had established that he was suitable, you had to introduce him to one of the leaders, and if he approved of your choice, someone else was nominated to recruit him. Your task was merely to make the introduction and then vanish.

There were many recruitment methods. The most common one was to recommend the organisation as one for cooperative mutual aid.

It was explained to me as follows: we are all in school at the moment and don't have any particular problems, but later we shall be living in more complicated circumstances and will have to overcome certain obstacles in order to make our way. It is very difficult to do this alone: you need reliable, confidential friends who, unexpectedly for outsiders, will give you their support, and you will correspondingly support them. If such an organisation grows big enough, we will prove very strong and will be able to accomplish practically *anything*. And that was about it. A completely innocent undertaking, and if a person didn't understand what we would be able to do, he was never told more, and he continued in the belief that he had been invited to join a mutual-aid organisation in order to further his career.

Such was the state of our minds and such the atmosphere then prevailing in the country, however, that the very mention of the word 'organisation', with the word 'secret' on top, would cause your interlocutor's eyes to light up joyfully, and it was immediately apparent that, like you, he had just been waiting for the truck with the machine-guns. Naturally, he at once sounded you out about the possibilities, and you gravely and meaningfully gave him to understand that intelligent people didn't discuss such nonsense, that the organisation didn't have any political aims. 'Aha!' he would nod enthusiastically, hastening to make it clear that he, too, was an intelligent man and realised that you couldn't talk about such things aloud. Afterwards, at the next assembly, you had to recommend him and present him to the others under an assumed name. If nobody objected, he became a member of the organisation and joined in the common work.

Only once did I come across someone who seemed to fit all the particulars but didn't understand the organisation's true aims. He was a radio enthusiast and was totally absorbed in his hobby. I don't think he had ever heard of Hungary and was totally indifferent to which country he lived in. He swallowed the idea of mutual aid entirely at face value and was constantly begging me to get him radio parts – he thought he had joined a secret club for radio amateurs. He used to regard our conspiratorial fussing with the indulgent air of a grown dog watching puppies at play.

Naturally I reported my failure, but such was the generally accepted atmosphere of ambiguity and understatement that it was impossible to explain what it was in him that was unsatisfactory. He was accepted and I felt discouraged. I could imagine his bewilderment if tomorrow they suddenly handed out machine-guns or we were all summoned to the Lubyanka. In fact, the game was conducted with such caution that if any of us had been arrested, we couldn't have said anything even if we had wanted to.

No matter where I went – to a Pioneer camp or simply to a country cottage on the outskirts of Moscow, or to another school – I was always told in advance which of our members were already there, how to get in touch with them and what to do. It was out of the question, of course, to turn down an assignment or refuse help to someone, just as it was to ask the purpose of the assignments you were given. Asking questions was in general frowned upon. Your knowledge was supposed to be sufficient only for carrying out the assignment, and then you were supposed to wipe what you had done completely from your memory. There was a whole system for checking whether people talked too much, and if even the leaders later asked you how the business had gone, the done thing was to remember nothing and express surprise at the question being asked at all. Needless to say, our parents never suspected what we were up to.

Whoever failed to carry out an assignment was disgraced, and no excuses were accepted. To arrive even five minutes late for a rendez-vous was an ineradicable blot. It was held that for a man of mettle there was no such thing as an unfulfillable task. Our stern warning to the headmaster to stop his punching had been sponsored by the organisation, and was regarded as aid to a beaten colleague. On another occasion, when I was on holiday at a cottage just outside Moscow, I was told that some things had been stolen from our boys while they were swimming in the river. They suspected some local youths who had been sunbathing all day in the vicinity. I knew these youths pretty well and was on friendly terms with them, so it wasn't difficult to persuade them to give the things back. But they were astounded that I knew about it.

Once as I was trying to give a training group the slip, I dashed into an entranceway. The group trailing me didn't see where I had gone, but if they started investigating the entrances they were sure to find me at once. This would be a great disgrace and I wondered feverishly what to do about it. As I dashed into the entranceway I had noticed a whole collection of cactuses in a window on the ground floor, and losing no time, I rang the doorbell of the ground-floor flat. An elderly woman opened the door and I told her that I was a collector of cactuses, was very keen on them and had happened to notice a number of unfamiliar species in her window. I must have looked pretty sincere, because she invited me in, treated me to some tea, presented me with a heap of cactuses and for a long time wouldn't let me go. With great difficulty

I finally extricated myself from the hospitality of the garrulous cactus breeder, and when I emerged triumphant into the street, there was nobody there.

My reputation gradually grew, especially as I was very successful at recruiting new members. Even earlier, I had had my own circle of friends who shared my views, and I now brought them all in with me. Furthermore, I put everything I had into it and was prepared to do anything to ensure our success.

Of course, we didn't devote much thought at this time to what our goal should be, and the curious thing was that we never thought of any possible adverse results or consequences. We didn't plan to create some sort of new order to replace the old. We neither attempted to calculate the strength of the enemy's forces, nor even to imagine what we might do in the event of success or, on the contrary, failure. We weren't interested in how realistic our scheme was. What we needed was an explosion, a moment of maximum tension, when it would at last be possible to exterminate all those vermin, when *our side* would suddenly rise up to their full height in every corner of Moscow and irresistibly storm all those prisons, Party committees, and ministries. On the one hand calculating and sharp to the point of cynicism, we were yet totally irrational and careless when it came to the most important thing.

How could these things be reconciled? The explanation was simple: each of us thirsted secretly – perhaps even unconsciously – for death. We had conceived a violent loathing for everyone older than us, who had been accessories to the monstrously vile deception. After those red-starred tanks, the pride and joy of our childhood, had crushed our peers on the streets of Budapest, a bloody fog blinded our eyes. The whole world had betrayed us, and we believed in nobody. We wanted to die shoulder-to-shoulder with comrades we trusted, with comrades we relied on more than ourselves in this sea of treachery. Our parents had turned out to be informers and provocateurs, our generals executioners – even our childhood games and fantasies were steeped in deceit. Only cynicism struck us as sincere, for noble words had become the small change of deception.

We smoked and swore like troopers, made filthy jokes in the presence of women, and drank vodka – ahead we could see only a void. We children of the socialist slums were prepared one fine morning to machine-gun the apathy and bite the dust. Which of us did not feel that there was no chance of winning? And what kind of a future did we face anyway? Liberty, equality, fraternity, happiness, democracy,

94

the people, were vile words from the vocabulary of vile leaders and red posters. We preferred to substitute oaths.

I don't regret those times and am not ashamed of our foolhardiness. All my life I have yearned for people who will stand shoulder-to-shoulder with me, no questions asked.

At last I was introduced to the leader of our 'branch'. Several times we met in the street and then I visited him at his home. We talked at length and in great detail, and I kept wanting to get down to brass tacks. What were we doing, after all? He was twenty-seven, a post-graduate who didn't in the least look like a leader of an underground organisation. It wasn't just that he was a lot older than me – that is to say, that he belonged to a leprous generation whom we detested – but his very appearance, his leisurely speech with its slight lisp, the piercing look he directed over the top of his spectacles, his ungainly figure, his balding forehead – in short, everything about him put me on guard and bewildered me. If I had been asked to try to recruit this fellow into our organisation, I would have turned him down.

'Society,' he said in his low toneless voice, 'is like an organism: it needs muscles and brute force, but it also needs nerves and a brain, eyes and ears.' He carefully hinted that he and I belonged to the brain, and I was supposed to be thrilled to be one of the chosen. He could be extremely persuasive and convincing, and never once strayed from the style of enigmatic ambiguity that dominated our organisation. He remembered exactly who all of us were, with every one of our strong points and weaknesses, but this was all somehow superficial and with-out feeling. I doubt that he realised he was the absolute master of a suicide squad. Our aspirations interested him only insofar as they helped him to exercise control. It seemed to me that he was interested in nothing but personal power, and I found it impossible to imagine him with a machine-gun in his hands, under a hail of bullets, or even under interrogation by the KGB.

I got on much better with his younger brother. He was only two years older than I, and much livelier and more comprehensible. I sensed in him the same impulse that moved the rest of us. He was deeply attached to his older brother and idealised him.

Eventually I came to an unexpected conclusion: there was nobody higher than these two: they were the leaders of the *entire* organisation, not just one branch of it. But this didn't discourage me in the least – from my point of view, even a few dozen people were a significant force. We just had to find ways of growing faster, of somehow attracting more people and infiltrating existing official organisations. We had to change our tactics.

The main thing to emerge, however, was that our inactivity now became pointless – no signal could possibly come and our expectations ceased. As it was, this inactivity was demoralising.

It turned out to be far easier to recruit people than to hold on to them. After the training in conspiracy and so on, the first rush of enthusiasm gradually gave way to boredom. Man cannot live in constant expectation. People began to drift away. For any activity would inevitably put the KGB on our trail.

We were faced with an insoluble contradiction: the organisation could become truly popular and effective only if it proclaimed its existence publicly and attracted allies and supporters, but that would also put an immediate end to its activities. The sentence for merely joining an anti-Soviet organisation was ten years in the labour camps.

But say we had announced our existence in some way, say we had discovered thousands wishing to join – how could we have established that they hadn't been planted by the KGB? How could we have continued to trust one another? More probably, we ourselves would have been taken for provocateurs.

The more we thought about it, the less we retained our faith in the possibility of illegal action. The situation was ridiculous – membership of an underground organisation guaranteed harmlessness to the regime. Plotting behind the scenes and, let us say, joining the Party for the sake of camouflage, a man could comfortably live out the whole of his life; he could work, go to Party meetings, and in every way appear to support the regime. He might even go and work for the KGB to improve his camouflage! But on the other hand, the slightest carelessness, and the whole secret organisation could be clapped in jail without having accomplished a thing. If a man wanted to act, he didn't need an organisation. On the contrary, it would only get in his way. Many years later, when I encountered various organisations in the camps, I understood that this was a key question we had been faced with, and I rejoiced that I had experienced these doubts while still a child.

Indeed, the 1950s and 1960s in Russia saw a mushrooming of clandestine organisations, unions, groups and even parties of different hues. It was forgivable for us youngsters to believe that we were doing great things, to conspire with our own shadows and bamboozle each other, making out that *our side* was everywhere and D-day would soon come.

But when you meet forty-year-old men in the camps, with a ten-year sentence for the same kind of activity, you can only shrug your shoulders. Even we boys had had the wit to grasp that you couldn't unite the entire country into such an organisation.

The logic of all beginners is more or less the same – they all start from square one, that is to say, the history of the Soviet Communist Party. We remember from the films and books we saw in our childhood that the Bolsheviks began by founding a party, then beavered away deep underground to distribute *Iskra* (The Spark) and *Pravda*, then gathered fellow spirits around them and in the end made a revolution. Responding to the wise proverb that says you should learn from your enemies, we fall victims yet again to the wiles of propaganda.

We forget that the Bolsheviks worked in conditions of relative freedom to establish tyranny, and not the other way round, that there was a high degree of freedom of the press and freedom of emigration, while the entire leadership sat in Zurich or Baden-Baden. We forget that there was a handful of professional revolutionaries, well supplied with money; that the entire Russian secret police force of that time was housed in a two-storey building too small even for a district police station today; that even in spite of this they were catching Bolsheviks almost every day. But nobody gave the Bolsheviks ten years' jail for propaganda – they were simply sent into internal exile, from which only the laziest failed to escape.

The basic propaganda literature, like *Das Kapital* and other 'classics', were freely and legally published in Russia and were even available in prison libraries. Their newssheets were published abroad, and since everything was so free and easy, were brought in across the virtually unpatrolled Russian border. And their circulations in any case didn't exceed two to three thousand. How often are we taken in by communist propaganda, forgetting that the Bolsheviks didn't accomplish any revolution at all, but developed their activities only after the February Revolution, in conditions of absolute freedom and backed by German money. The Provisional Government had no secret police at all.

How can grown-up people seriously believe that revolutions are the result of the activities of some underground organisations? In a nation where many political parties exist, private enterprise flourishes and there is no internal passport system, what sort of an achievement is it to have an underground? Especially when you don't even get hard labour for it? The question is, what's the point when you can do it legally?

The upshot of these propaganda delusions is that for twenty years people have struggled to emulate a mythical Bolshevik revolution – even now, not everyone has managed to clear his nostrils of its smell. It needs no more than three confederates gathered together for them to start searching for a name for their party. After that they write a constitution, a programme – and go straight to jail.

I have met political parties consisting of two, of five and of twelve members. The biggest of them all, the All-Russian Social–Christian Union for the Liberation of the People, added up to about 100. All they had time for was to write a silly programme and read Berdyayev (as if half the country wasn't reading Berdyayev anyway, without any parties!). The smallest party I ever came across consisted of one man, named Fyodorkov, and was called Direct Power to the People. Everybody in the prison, including the guards, simply called him DPP. He was a watchmaker from Khabarovsk, about fifty years old, short, stout and very quick in his movements, like a cuckoo-clock. At first he insisted on arguing with us, trying to prove the advantages of direct people's power, but then he reconciled himself to us and simmered down – if it's DPP so be it, and to hell with the lot of you. For a long time the KGB racked their brains over what to do with him – you could hardly try one man for starting a political party! Then they washed their hands of him and stuck him in a loony bin.

Thinking back on it all, I am proud that when I was only fifteen or sixteen years old, I and my friends started, not just the largest but also the best-concealed organisation that ever was, which lasted longer than all the others put together and was never once given away. Our secret was very simple: we recruited solely people of our own age – not only are there no KGB agents of that age, but at no age are people sincerer or purer. Our biggest secret of all, however, was that we never did anything: we didn't write programmes, we didn't swear oaths, we didn't keep lists, we didn't keep minutes of meetings, it was forbidden even to talk about politics or to have a name for the organisation. And if other illegal organisations had lasted as long as we did and had reached their natural limits, they too would have understood how impossible and unnecessary illegality was. They would have come to it, so to speak, experimentally.

We were luckier – we passed through this dangerous stage in our youth. And much later, in quite different times, we grasped another and more important truth: you cannot achieve democracy by going underground. The underground produces only tyranny, only Bolsheviks of a different colour. All I noticed at the time was that our leader, once he had our organisation's power in his hands, thought more of his own fortunes than the fortunes of the world. I didn't realise I had stumbled across an immutable law. I simply thought: 'What does he need it for?'

ALL this was a prelude, no more than a limbering-up. I still had not opened an account. You might say that I had only just clambered up the pine tree, and the notorious block of wood had not yet made its first swing. At this point, quite unexpectedly for myself, I gave it a shove, without in the least intending to.

I was in my last year at school, that is to say the tenth class, when some of us decided to start up a literary magazine, just for the fun of it. After so many years spent tediously studying the positive and negative heroes of classical Russian literature, we had been given very brief outlines of early twentieth-century literary movements. Naturally we were told that this wasn't literature at all, just literary juggling, which was harmful to the people and had been justly condemned by the Party. In passing our teachers gave us a handful of examples of this decadent prestidigitation, and these made a lively impact on the class. Everyone started writing parodies of them, weaving in incidents from school life. Before we knew it we had a magazine. Someone got hold of a type-writer, someone else offered his services as an illustrator, and all the rest were authors. Ten years of boredom exploded into a devastating parody of life at school and in the Soviet Union in general.

During the past few years various reforms had been introduced into the educational system. Learning was no more varied or interesting, but additional absurdities and stupidities were superimposed. For example, somewhere in the higher echelons it was decided that school was too divorced from life, that students were getting no training for work. As a result, special work lessons were introduced, followed by practical training on the job. One year we had to work in a factory, and the following summer we were sent out to work on a state farm near Moscow. This did indeed widen our horizons, though not in the manner planned by our wise Party.

Working in a bus factory in Moscow, my classmates and I saw for the first time what a Soviet enterprise is like – with all its deceptions, its hollow façade and its coercion. Nobody in the bus factory was in a hurry to work; the workers preferred to sit in the smoking room until the foreman appeared, when they all dashed to their places. 'Why should we hurry for the money they pay us?' said the workmen. 'Work's not a wolf, it won't run into the forest!' In the mornings they were almost all drunk or hung-over, and throughout the working day people would be regularly detailed to slip over the fence for some vodka. Only one man put in a full day's work. The rest hated him, and when pointing him out would rotate one finger meaningfully by the temple. They were always looking for chances to do him down, either by surreptitiously damaging his machine or by stealing his tools. 'Want to be a champion and raise the targets?' they said spitefully. It turned out that if one man exceeded the target, the target would be raised for all of them the following month, and they would have to work twice as hard for exactly the same money.

We quickly fell into the style of their work and learned their favourite ditty:

> Take the hammer, then the sickle,
> That do our Soviet land recall.
> Bang or reap, whichever you pick,
> It makes no odds, you'll get fuck all.

The turner to whom I was assigned for training, a young fellow barely older than myself, had a most original way of meeting the target. Once the foreman had told him the total, he only pretended to work. Then, when the foreman wasn't around, he would creep up to the big wooden shed where the finished parts were kept. There were two loose boards at the back. Nipping inside, he would quickly locate the boxes he needed in the dark and stuff his pockets with the necessary parts. Then he returned to the workshop by a roundabout route and spent most of the rest of the working day in the smoking room. I don't think my 'teacher' was the only one that was so crafty.

He and I were the youngest in the workshop, so it was natural that one of us would be sent for the vodka – the other stayed by the machine and pretended to be working. Towards the end of the day everyone cheered up, there would be a spring in their step, and for some unaccountable reason, they kept slipping out of the building. They would come back holding loosely wrapped packets or cartons, and then one or other of us young ones would have to skip over the fence again and wait for them to pass the packets carefully over to us. They would then leave by the proper exit and collect their booty. They stole practically anything that could be sold on the black market or used at home. One day they stole a whole bus engine, another day a roll of material for upholstering the seats. Paint, enamel, spare engine-parts were taken as a matter of course. At the same time the entire factory was festooned with colourful signs and slogans – 'We'll give! We'll catch up! We'll overtake!' – together with rising production graphs and pictures of scrubbed and smiling workers with their sleeves rolled up. On the placards factories such as ours were irresistibly storming the heights of communism.

Our temporary attachment to an agricultural establishment was no less enlightening. We were taken out to the State farm one evening and ensconced in a barrack hut. We spent the night on wooden bunks. At the crack of dawn we were awakened by a deafening burst of super-natural swearing. Tumbling out of the hut we discovered a couple of dozen peasant women shovelling a heap of rotten potatoes into a truck and cussing Khrushchev simply for the sake of it, to make the work go quicker.

'Nikita, screw you and up yours!' they yelled. 'He's having it off with Katy Furtseva, the fat hog, and having a damn good time of it as well, but we don't see our menfolk for weeks on end. Day and night we have to load these fucking spuds! Screw them! Fuck them! If only I could get my hands on that fucking Khrushchev!'

These potatoes were being taken out into the fields for planting. How on earth did anyone expect them to grow? But nobody cared about that. The peasants explained to us that they were paid for every ton of potatoes planted, so what was harvested didn't interest them. Soon it turned cold, the rain set in and we were sent out to weed beets by hand. This occupation struck us as absurd as planting those potatoes, which indeed it was. Naturally the whole of this State farm was also hung about with placards, banners, production graphs, and images of plump cows and buxom milkmaids.

The mud was impassable and vodka had to be fetched by tractor. We were amazed to discover that the State farm workers were unable to resign or leave the farm, since they weren't allowed to hold their own internal passports; and without a passport you were outside the law and could be arrested by the first town policeman to come across you. Nor could you get another job without a passport. Boys of our age were waiting for their call-up into the army as a salvation: when they finished their military service there was a chance they might find a city job instead of having to go home. The young girls thought of nothing but how to marry a towny and get away. Drunkenness, brawls and knife fights were everyday occurrences.

None of these experiences found their way into our magazine – we didn't consider them in any way relevant to literature. But indirectly and involuntarily, our new attitude to Soviet life showed through every line. There were ambiguous jokes, parodies and lampoons of the propaganda clichés that had made their way into Soviet literature. But none of us had the slightest intention of giving the magazine any political overtones – it was all just a joke.

When we had finished the magazine we invited the senior pupils to our empty room after lessons, and the literature teacher and the history teacher as well. To waves of laughter one of us read the magazine aloud. But when we looked behind us we were amazed to see that the two teachers were not laughing at all. Trembling, their faces pale and drawn, they assured us that the magazine was a failure, the jokes feeble and the whole thing politically wrong. We fell silent. Everyone felt embarrassed, and none of us really understood what was going on. We went home feeling as if someone had died.

By this time I was attending a different school. About two years previously, my father had obtained a new flat and we had moved to a new district, to Kropotkin Street. Our school had many children from the families of high Party officials and was considered to be one of the best; now, when some of the boys talked about the magazine at home, their parents grew alarmed and a row erupted. High-ranking committees visited the school almost daily, and we were called in for questioning and discussion; it was very odd to see our supposedly revered teachers casting awestruck glances at us, almost in horror. A hus hdescended on the school. It was whispered that our case was being dealt with by someone in the Central Committee. For the first time I appreciated how lucky it was that I had not joined the Komsomol. Komsomol members were dragged off to Komsomol meetings, where they were discussed, and obliged to recant, and given reprimands. I alone was allowed to go unpunished.

I don't know why, but the authorities had chosen to regard me as the ringleader, the scoundrel who had specially planned all this so as to cause unpleasantness to right-thinking people, and at a parents' meeting they did everything but scratch my father's and mother's eyes out. But then the wise Party functionaries came to a decision: let the collective itself, the boys, censure the culprits. This was a piece of typical Soviet hypocrisy, designed to create a simulacrum of public opinion and fake a unanimous vote of censure. But they had badly miscalculated, for boys who only a month earlier had been laughing heartily at the magazine could not bring themselves to make propaganda speeches, and while a few boys, who had been carefully instructed by their parents, made cautious speeches proposing that the magazine itself be censured as 'politically immature', they refused to censure the authors. However, even this moderate line failed to prevail. The basic mood of the school was feigned bewilderment, as if to say: what's so special about it, it's just another magazine, and very good too, we should publish another one. In the end the wrongdoers were invited to speak but we, too, refused to repent.

All of this was downright scandalous – and inadmissible from the Party's point of view. In the higher echelons, our magazine was pronounced an act of ideological sabotage, as a result of which the headmaster and I were summoned to discuss the matter with the Moscow City Committee of the Party.

I will never forget that journey to the City Committee with the headmaster, who was well over fifty, with a big bald head and a short fat body. At school we called him Roly-Poly. We sat side-by-side in the Metro train, like two naughty schoolboys who had been caught playing pranks (and were now awaiting their punishment). We felt so equal, and established such friendly relations, that he spent the whole journey sadly telling me about the village where he was born and brought up, about his children and domestic cares, and complaining of his health. I couldn't think of any way to console him. In fact, I began to feel my first pangs of regret for the blasted magazine. I told him that I would try to take all the blame on myself and get him off, but all he could do was shake his head sadly and complain about how ill he was.

At the City Committee headquarters some young men in dark suits, with placard-type regular features, ushered us into an office. Here I was made to wait, while the headmaster was led into the inner office beyond, where he stayed for about forty minutes; when I entered he was sitting at the table, all red and wiping sweat from his bald head.

About twenty men and women, most of them old, sat around an enormous T-shaped table, with worried frowns on their faces. They had sheaves of papers in front of them and were writing things down. At my appearance they swivelled round and fixed me with stern, gloomy regard. Strange to say, I experienced neither fear nor trepidation, nor even nervousness – I was overcome instead by a sudden surge of spiteful euphoria. This gaggle of important Party dowagers, this band of flabby, greying Party bigwigs, pompously gathered here to discuss a paltry school magazine – weren't these the very villains, the bloody executioners that a mere year ago we had been preparing to liquidate at the cost of our lives? It was they who held the country in fear and trembling, who had sent the tanks into Budapest, who were warping our souls!

I peered inquisitively at their expressionless faces. I was expecting to see cruelty, imperiousness, confidence and willpower, but saw only stupidity. Stupidity and cowardice. If only they might hear the stream of choice obscenities which any village woman directed at them daily. I think I must have grinned unpleasantly as I looked at them.

Suddenly they sprang to life and started fidgeting and talking all at once. They didn't like the way I was standing – why weren't my hands by my sides, and (of course) why didn't I wipe that smile off my face? And who had taught me to write this awful . . . this awful . . . this, this, this? Here the chief hog, sitting at the head of the table, raised one corner of our long-suffering magazine with two fingers.

'But why would anyone have to teach me?' I asked in surprise.

The menagerie stirred again. 'Where could you get such ideas from? You haven't lived long enough to see anything yet.'

Oh, so that's it! You sit with your backsides parked in your Party offices, reading nothing but Party directives, never go further than the lavatory, and I haven't seen anything, and mustn't think anything, and now you are undertaking to teach me. So that's it.

'Not at all,' I said, 'I've seen a great deal and I remember everything.'

My swelling rage was undammed, formed itself into words, and lashed their lacklustre faces. I didn't notice how it happened. I spoke about Stalin and his funeral, about how everyone had wept and then, hardly pausing to dry their eyes, had cursed and abused him; how I didn't believe them, either the ones who had been afraid or those who hadn't known. I spoke as if I were brandishing that long-awaited machine-gun and was simply explaining why they had to die. They tried to interrupt me, some were scribbling things down, but I forced them all to listen. I told them about the serfdom in the villages, about the drunkenness, the thieving, the endless lying – all of which sickened me to death, although I was still only seventeen.

When I had finished they were silent. Then, looking past me into

105

thin air, the chief hog spake: 'You have some very mistaken ideas, you are politically immature, you have been under a bad influence.'

Here the whole table came to life and fidgeted: 'Yes, yes, politically immature, yes, yes, a bad influence!'

'I have been discussing things here with my comrades and we have concluded that you need a spell of work, to temper you in the furnace of labour, to live a while in a proper workers' collective where you can straighten out your mind.'

'Yes, yes, to temper you,' rustled the table.

'It would be premature for you to study now. Instead of writing all this . . . this . . .,' again he lifted the corner of the magazine, 'you should have pulled yourself together and read the Five-Year Plan. You may go now.'

The block of wood had made its first swing and dealt Bruin a sharp knock in the ribs. The headmaster was sacked, my father was given a Party reprimand, the school was struck out of some inter-district competition, and I was recommended to spend the whole of my life being tempered in the furnace of work – i.e. fetching vodka, stealing spare parts and assimilating the wisdom of the workers: take the hammer, then the sickle . . . bang or reap . . . you'll get . . . fuck all.

When you read or hear stories about the concentration camps, about the mass terror and millions of liquidated lives, no matter how vividly it strikes your imagination or arouses your sincere indignation and disgust, it all stays somehow on an abstract plane. It doesn't change you personally in any way – your habits, the way you walk, or your handwriting – but, rather, disposes you to philosophical thoughts about how much evil there is in the world and how base man can be. It is quite a different thing, however, when the rotting block of the state lets you have it in the ribs. All they had done was forbid me to study and direct me to work in a factory, but I was beside myself with anger, and in a state of extreme nervous tension. Something had snapped inside me, and I was never again the same person.

Almost before I had left the City Committee headquarters I knew for sure that I would never go to a factory to be tempered in the furnace of labour – they would have to kill me first! This might sound surprising. Didn't I know what kind of a country I lived in and what to expect from that country? But the fact was, I was stunned. Where was my right to an education? What business was it of these dim-witted old men and women on the City Committee? Who were they to tell me what to do and what not to do, how to live my life and what work to take up? Till now I had been undecided what to do after school; but now, before even reaching home, I had decided irrevocably to go to university, even if I got a bloody nose for it. I wasn't a thing, but a human being, and nobody was going to push me around.

I still had to finish school, of course, but my school would never give me the reference I needed to enter university. So for the remaining six months of the school year I attended an evening institute for young workers. They assumed that I, too, was a worker somewhere, being tempered, and to confirm this they asked me to bring a certificate from my place of work. Certificate, certificate. In our paper state everything else is phantasmal – only a piece of paper can prove your existence. I forged the certificate myself: I asked a friend who worked to get a certificate for himself, blanked out his name, and wrote mine in instead – not for nothing had I got top marks in chemistry. Nobody bothered to check it: he's got the certificate, everything's okay.

After that I had to contrive a way of getting a reference for the university. Fortunately my class teacher, who knew my story, sympathised with me. Who knows, perhaps she or her family had also suffered at the hands of the regime, but in any case she didn't take much persuading. Relations between pupils and teachers at the evening institute were much simpler and more human than in school. The pupils were often older than the teachers, sometimes even family men, and there was none of that ideological education nonsense that you found in day schools. Anyway, she did it quite simply: she slipped my reference into a huge pile of other papers that she was giving the director to sign.

Now everything depended on me, and while the other school kids strolled around Moscow on vacation, I went out of town. Without telling a soul of my plans, not even my parents, I boned up on my subjects like a madman, day and night, so that by the time of the university entrance exams I knew all the books virtually by heart, from cover to cover. On the day before the closing date for applications, I sneaked back into Moscow. At the university I met a girl from my old school who was also taking the exams, so that right up to the last moment I expected to be discovered, and spent more time thinking about that than the work itself. Yet I could not forget that the competition was colossal – sixteen applicants for every remaining place – and added to the fear that someone would recognise and inform on me, my nervous tension was all but unbearable. I had to take five examinations; each time I quit Moscow afterwards so as not to run into anyone I knew, thus observing all the rules of conspiracy. Finally they put up a list of those accepted – I was among them. Now there was nothing anybody could do: I was formally a university student.

But this wasn't enough for me – it was now my turn to give the block of wood a shove. 'How can it be?' I thought. 'A pathetic school magazine with no politics in it and the whole menagerie gets in a stew, up to and including the Central Committee. That means they're afraid, this is what they fear the most. All right, that's what we need.' It was one thing to know theoretically that we had no freedom of the press or speech, but quite another to experience it in practice. Was there any guarantee that Stalinism wouldn't come back if they could sack people, issue reprimands and ban you from studying, all because of some paltry magazine? That is how it always begins. And would they say afterwards that nobody knew and they were all afraid?

It was a curious time, the late 1950s – and the further it recedes into history the harder it becomes to arrive at a correct appreciation of it. Now they call it 'the Khrushchev thaw'. But what happened in fact? What did Khrushchev actually do? Having condemned Stalin and shown a glimpse of the State kitchen, the cannibals' kitchen, to the public gaze, he took fright and sounded the retreat. It was fortunate that there had been time to release the prisoners – though even that, as I discovered subsequently, was due not so much to Khrushchev as to Snegov.

A close friend of Khrushchev in the old days before the purges, Snegov himself had done time in a concentration camp; when Khrushchev came to power he let him out.* Snegov had been a committed communist and remained one, despite the camps, despite the terror he had lived through. This doesn't surprise me. People of the older generation who remembered the days before Stalin did not equate the idea of communism with Stalin as we did. It seemed to them that if it hadn't been for Stalin distorting Lenin's beautiful concepts, everything would have been fine. It was hard for them to realise that Stalin, with all his brutality, was an organic consequence of Leninist ideas and of the very idea of socialism itself. And so it was hard for them, although they condemned Stalin's obvious crimes, to doubt the correctness of the underlying ideas, ideas for the sake of which they had lived and them-

* A. V. Snegov, an 'Old Bolshevik', was jailed and tortured during Stalin's great purge of the 1930s and spent seventeen years in labour camps before being rehabilitated in 1956. He was mentioned by name in Khrushchev's 'secret speech' to the 20th Party Congress denouncing the crimes of Stalin.

selves participated in the liquidation of class enemies. Their rejection couldn't go that deep. Some law of psychological self-preservation forced them to believe that only Stalin was guilty, not they. A man cannot, near the end of his life, acknowledge that the whole of it, and everything in which he believed, was a mistake, or even worse, a crime.

Even those of us who had experienced the denunciation of Stalin when fourteen or fifteen years old, had found it hard to accept, and were left with a trauma for the rest of our lives; people twice our age, however, could no longer wake from their dream and commit psychological suicide. During the late 1950s, therefore, the reigning idea remained a slightly liberal variant of communism: Lenin continued to be an authority, Yugoslav socialism was a model of the correct embodiment of correct ideas, and none of the innovations went further than Tito.

But Snegov, despite his communist faith, had assimilated convict psychology and convict ethics in the labour camps. When Khrushchev appointed him as his deputy in the rehabilitation commission, Snegov realised how unstable the situation was, and during the two years he was in the post, hastened to release as many prisoners as possible. By the time he was removed only 40,000 or so were left in the camps. It was during this time that the softest camp regime in the history of the Soviet Union was established, and old cons still hark back to those times as to a legendary era, a real golden age. There are legends of commercially run canteens where you could pay for your food, just like outside; of a time when the didn't force people to work, but practically everybody volunteered, since they were paid. Now the whole thing seems incredible.

Early in the 1960s all this came to an end. The golden age had lasted for only three or four years. For Khrushchev it had been nothing but a political game, part of the struggle against his enemies in the Central Committee, who were more closely associated with Stalin's repressions than he. Now nobody knew what tomorrow's decisions would bring, how to interpret the criticism of the personality cult or where this concept began and ended. A handful of books critical of the cult slipped into print, but even here it was halfhearted: you could criticise life during Stalin's time, but no later (and not fundamentals!). The district party secretary could now be shown as a negative personality, but the regional secretary was invariably positive and by the end of the novel had established Khrushchevian justice.

The power of the KGB, although trimmed, remained enormous, and political arrests did not cease but were merely reduced in scale. Was this thanks to Khrushchev and his 'thaw'? I think not. Mass political terror had ended right after the death of Stalin and was never renewed. This had nothing to do with Stalin or Khrushchev: mass terror was simply no longer possible – the ruling clique's instinct for self-preservation had done the trick. The implacable logic of terror is such that, as it increases, it becomes uncontrollable and is usually turned against the terrorists themselves. No one was guaranteed safe from the bullet: having shot all their political opponents and class enemies during the 1920s and 30s, the communists were no longer able to halt the terror; it became a weapon in the intra-party struggle and a weapon of total repression, without which the Party could no longer live or rule. Suddenly it turned out that two-thirds of the delegates to the Seventeenth Congress of the Party were enemies and had to be shot, and by the end of the 1940s practically the entire membership of the Politburo had been replaced.

Later I met a man whose story excellently illustrated the mechanics of this accelerating process. It happened in 1947. A colonel in the tank corps, he was arrested on a false denunciation and accused of high treason. There was no evidence of his guilt and none was sought. All that his interrogators wanted from him was new names and new victims. They demanded that he name the people who had recruited him for foreign intelligence, and they tortured him cruelly. He was prepared to sign any idiocy against himself, but not to incriminate his totally innocent friends. At last, feeling that he could no longer hold out against the torture, and fearing to write a false denunciation of someone while in a delirium, he did something that took even himself by surprise.

The interrogation and torture was being carried out by three KGB investigators – one chief investigator and two assistants. One day when they were demanding that he name the enemies who had recruited him, he suddenly pointed his finger at the chief investigator and said: 'You! It was you, you bastard, who recruited me! Don't you remember? On manoeuvres outside Minsk, in 1933, in the birch grove!' 'He's raving, he's gone mad, take him away!' said the chief investigator. 'No, no, why do that?' said the other two with sudden interest. 'It's very interesting, let him go on.' He never saw that chief investigator again – he was probably shot. One of the assistants took his place, the case was quickly brought to an end and my acquaintance was dispatched to a camp with a 'quarter' (twenty-five years).

It is easy to understand that once the madness of the mass terror had come to a halt with the death of Stalin, there were no enthusiasts for starting it up again. And now, when so many years had elapsed, when there had been a turnover in both the punitive personnel and the governing elite from natural causes, it was simply out of the question to return to those times: the system had become bureaucratised, had put on fat, and it was now impossible to bring back the atmosphere of universal spy mania and suspicion.

Like the end of that geological process whereby a continent is formed, beginning with earthquakes and eruptions of lava, the system was gradually hardening, petrifying and arriving at a state where further changes were no longer possible, because no one wanted them. The people wanted nothing more to do with revolutions or struggle: they knew instinctively that a revolution would bring them nothing but endless disaster, bloodshed, starvation and a new tyranny. Nor did their rulers want more terror or upheavals, which they knew would end by destroying them as well. The 1960s saw not so much a thaw as a cooling down, an ossification.

Nevertheless there *was* a thaw and a melting at the end of the 1950s and beginning of the 1960s, only it took place not because of Khrushchev and not at the top, but in the hearts and minds of ordinary people. Having survived the nightmare, people needed a respite in which to make sense of what had occurred. It was this process that partly captured and motivated Khrushchev, not the reverse. After the climax of 1956, Khrushchev's whole effort was directed towards opposing the process, opposing the thaw.

Khrushchev's destiny was tragic and instructive. Of course, after the shock we all got from the unmasking of Stalin, no communist leader would ever again be loved by the people or would ever earn from them anything but jokes and jibes. But equally, no one, it seems, would ever provoke such unanimous and bitter hatred as Khrushchev. Everything about him was irritating: his inability to express himself intelligently, so typical of most communist leaders both before and after him; his fat grinning mug (with failing harvests and food shortages on every side, he went right on grinning – a fine time to enjoy himself); his trips abroad; his feverish passion for superficial reforms. But all his initiatives provoked only ill-will and mockery. It is not difficult to understand. Before he came along there was the same starvation, the same lack of freedom, the same fear and hopelessness, but faith in the bewhiskered god somehow obscured all the rest. Khrushchev removed that faith, and although the obvious truth of what he said was not called into question, the bitter sorrow and resentment provoked by the death of the god were unleashed on him.

Even worse, by depriving people of their illusions, he made them look back and see the whole of their former life as it really was. All of a sudden people started blaming him for what had been revealed. The unviability of the whole system and the incompetence of the leadership became evident. But worse still was the fact that he essentially changed nothing at all: he didn't root out Stalinism, he didn't put the economy right, and he didn't give the people their freedom. Instead he attempted to sell people the same old illusions that had just been so graphically exposed. His naïve promises of communism by 1980 provoked only mirth. I think that he was the last communist ruler who truly believed in the possibility of building communism and endeavoured to bring it about. But nobody needed his communism any more, nobody, besides him, believed it was possible any longer. The deception was so obvious to everybody that even the moles saw through it.

Finally he was nothing but a poor parody of Stalin. Having failed to break the old system, he became its victim, and gradually, in place of the personality cult of the adored Stalin, people were given a personality cult of the hated Khrushchev. Therefore, when he was ultimately removed, he had no supporters at all.

It is amazing: the man ruled for ten years and didn't win for himself a single supporter. Only a few people in Moscow, who saw in Khrushchev a guarantee against the return of Stalinism, regretted his departure. Some ventured the theory that he was the personification of that centuries-old dream of the Russian people – to have an Ivan-the-Fool on the Russian throne. But the more knowledgeable said that a better comparison was with Rasputin.

Interestingly enough, the process of inner thawing that began during his rule evidently affected Khrushchev personally as well. People who saw him after his removal from power said that he had changed enormously, that he was upset by the lack of gratitude towards him and, once out of power, quickly assimilated the point of view of society as a whole. Once in 1970 we all gathered at Pyotr Yakir's* place to sign a routine petition in support of Alexander Solzhenitsyn in connexion with his being awarded the Nobel Prize. As usual, Yakir never

* Pyotr Yakir, son of the brilliant Red Army commander, Iona Yakir, served seventeen years' hard labour from the age of fourteen after his father's execution in 1937. Yakir got drawn into the dissident movement after the Sinyavsky–Daniel trial of 1966, and in 1969 wrote a celebrated open letter denouncing the rise of 'neo-Stalinism'. In January 1972 he addressed an appeal to the UN in support of Bukovsky and in June that

left the telephone and called around Moscow to collect the signatures of friends. Somebody jokingly suggested that he should ring Khrushchev – after all, it was on his orders that Solzhenitsyn had first been published. No sooner said than done. Nina Petrovna Khrushchev answered the telephone and passed it to Nikita.

'Have you heard the news?' asked Yakir. 'They've given Solzhenitsyn the Nobel Prize!' 'Of course, of course,' said Nikita cheerfully, 'I've heard. I get all the news from the BBC.' 'And what's your opinion about it? After all, you were the first to let him be published.' 'Yes, I remember.' Then, after a pause: 'Well, they don't give Nobel Prizes for nothing.'

Of course, we didn't go so far as to ask him to sign our petition, but I think that if he had lived another ten years as an ordinary citizen, he would have joined the protesters. He was moving in that direction, and his memoirs, of course, did not get out by accident.

One way or another, the atmosphere of those years was one of springtime, hope and expectation. There was the World Youth Festival in Moscow in 1957, then the American exhibition in 1958 – the first swallows from the West in our entire Soviet history. All this talk about 'putrefying capitalism' became ridiculous. The importance of these events was comparable to the exposure of Stalin. Then there was the unexpected rapprochement with Yugoslavia and the beginning of the quarrel with China; there were foreign tourists, and a small quantity of rare but nonetheless attainable goods imported from the West. Moscow was transformed before our very eyes. In place of the crime-ridden slum city of my childhood, with its gang of youths in high boots, raincoats and pleated caps, there rose a city whose inhabitants thronged the bookshops, crowded into halls where poets gave public readings and packed the Sovremennik Theatre. The music drifting through the windows on summer evenings was no longer Utyosov's ersatz pop, but jazz and rock-and-roll, bought secretly on the black market. It was recorded from radio on to old x-ray film, and these 'records' were then sold in millions by enterprising individuals. If you held them up to the light you could see people's rib cages on them. And that provided their name: 'Rock on the Ribs'. Young men started

---

year was himself arrested. In August 1973 he was tried, together with Victor Krasin, on charges of anti-Soviet agitation, made a public confession of guilt and was sentenced to three years in normal-regime labour camps. After one year, however, he was pardoned. His autobiography has been published as *A Childhood in Prison* (Macmillan, 1972).

fitting themselves out with narrow trousers in the Western style – so narrow that it took a heroic struggle to get into them at all. And although the Komsomol vigilantes used to catch them at first, beating them up and slitting their pants with scissors, nonetheless the fashion caught on and soon the entire Komsomolarchy was going round in them too.

A beggar operating on the Sadovy Ring, on trolleybus route в, used to board the bus, take off his cap, and declaim in a loud voice to no one in particular: 'Greetings to you, comrade Tito, you've become our brother dear! According to our bold Nikita, you're not to blame, so never fear. Help an old soldier fighting for a decrease in world tension!' He was generously treated by everyone.

Throughout Moscow, office typewriters worked overtime, clicking out – for the personal pleasure of the typists or for their friends – the poetry of Gumilyov, Mandelshtam, Akhmatova and Pasternak. It felt as if everyone was gingerly straightening numbed limbs after ages of sitting still, of people trying to twiddle their fingers and toes and shift position as their bodies pricked with pins and needles. It seemed there was nothing to keep them sitting still any longer, but they had lost the habit of moving and had forgotten how to stand on their own two legs.

The rebirth of culture in the Soviet Union after half a century of plague recapitulated all the stages in the development of world culture: folklore, epics, tales passed from mouth to mouth and from generation to generation, songs by troubadours and minstrels, poems, and finally prose – novels, dissertations, philisophical treatises, topical articles, open letters and appeals, journalism.

One day someone ought to erect a monument to the political joke. This astonishing form of creation is especially popular in the socialist countries, where people are deprived of information and a free press, and public opinion, banned and suppressed, finds expression in this form. Packed to the hilt with information, a Soviet joke is worth volumes of philosophical essays. The simplification of the joke exposes the absurdity of all propaganda tricks. The joke has survived the hardest times, stood its ground, multiplied into families of jokes, and in it you can study the entire history of the Soviet regime. It is as important to publish a complete collection of jokes as it is to write a true history of socialism.

In jokes you can find the thing that has left no trace in the printed sources – the people's opinion of events. For every question there is an answer. For instance, what did the people think of the exposure of Stalin's personality cult? When Stalin's body was removed from the

Mausoleum and buried under the Kremlin wall, a wreath appeared on his grave with the following inscription: 'To the posthumously repressed from the posthumously rehabilitated.'

Or: one day Lenin's body disappeared from the Mausoleum. They started a search for it and frisked the Mausoleum. Inside they found a note: 'Gone to Zurich to start all over again.'

Or: how will this era go down in the encyclopaedias? 'Hitler, a petty tyrant of Stalin's time. Khrushchev, a literary critic of Mao Tse-tung's time.'

And, of course, there are the jokes about the KGB. In Egypt they discovered a mummy. The world's leading egyptologists gathered there, but couldn't establish which pharaoh it was. Then three Soviet egyptologists turned up in plain clothes. 'Leave us alone with him,' they said. Their request was granted. A day passed. Then another and another. No news. On the fourth day they emerged triumphant: 'He's Rameses the Twenty-fifth.' The others were dumbfounded. 'How did you find out?' 'He confessed of his own accord, the bastard.'

A Jew goes to his rabbi and asks: 'Rabbi, you are a very wise man. Tell me, is there going to be a war or not?' 'There will be no war,' replies the rabbi. 'But there will be such a struggle for peace that no stone will be left standing.'

And what do Soviet people say about 'rotting capitalism'? 'It may be rotting, but what a lovely smell!' and they inhale voluptuously.

And there are hundreds of thousands of such jokes, every one a poem.

I would erect a monument to the typewriter, too. It brought forth a new form of publishing, *samizdat*, or 'self-publishing': write myself, edit myself, censor myself, publish myself, distribute myself, go to jail for it myself. *Samizdat* began in the 1950s with the poems of banned, forgotten and suppressed poets: everything that couldn't be published officially because of censorship ended up in *samizdat*. Now *samizdat* counts two Nobel Prize-winners among its authors.

While we're on the subject of monuments, we also need a monument to a man with a guitar. Where else would scratchy, amateurish recordings of songs sung to the guitar be secretly distributed in millions of copies at the risk of instant arrest? I remember when I first heard a voice, accompanied by a guitar, softly singing about the backyards of Moscow, about my beloved Arbat – and even about the war – in a way in which no one had ever sung before. There wasn't a single false note of official patriotism in those songs, but so much sincerity, so much of our yearning and pain, that the authorities could not tolerate it. The idiotic and spiteful persecution of Bulat Okudzhava in the late 1950s was virtually the first campaign against a poet that took place before our very eyes.

A little later he was joined by Alexander Galich, whose songs are still secretly copied by prisoners in the labour camps. The first question put to every new arrival in the compound is: 'What new Galich songs have you got?'

As time went by, more and more of these unseen figures with guitars sprang into being. They weren't given any halls for their performances and every song might earn them a prison sentence. Therefore only the few and the lucky could boast that they had actually seen them. Their predecessors in the dawn of history had it easier: no one jailed the minstrels or dragged Homer off to a lunatic asylum, accusing him of blindness and bias. For us Galich was nothing less than a Homer. Every song of his was an odyssey, a journey through the labyrinths of the soul of Soviet man.

At that time, our *samizdat* culture was only just coming into existence. No one was thinking of awarding it Nobel Prizes. I myself, having accidentally blundered across it in the darkness, saw in it the only possibility of living, the only alternative.

In the summer of 1958 a statue of Mayakovsky was unveiled. At the official opening ceremony, a number of official Soviet poets read their poems, and when the ceremony was over, volunteers from the crowd started reading theirs as well. Such an unexpected and unplanned turn of events pleased everybody, and it was agreed that the poets would meet here regularly. At first, the authorities saw no particular danger in this, and one Moscow paper even published an article about the gatherings, giving the time when they took place and inviting all poetry-lovers to come along. Young people, mainly students, assembled almost every evening to read the poems of forgotten or repressed writers, and also their own work, and sometimes there were discussions of art and literature. A kind of open-air club came into being. But the authorities could not tolerate the danger of these spontaneous performances for long, and eventually stopped the gatherings.

I hadn't gone to Mayakovsky Square at the time and knew of them only by hearsay. But now, after the whole business of the magazine, I regretted that I hadn't. I could have found kindred spirits, and together it would have been easier for us to defend ourselves and our right to originality. That humiliating sense of being unfree, that sense of outrage I had experienced when outsiders attempted to dispose of my life, had cut me to the quick and I was eager to fight back as energetically as I could. In September 1960, therefore, after entering the university, a friend who lived near the Square and another in drama school and I agreed to start up the readings once more. Soon they were taking place regularly again and attracting an enormous number of people. We swiftly got to know the 'veterans' from the earlier readings and were overjoyed to discover that they were feverishly active on other projects too. Apart from disseminating the works of poets who had long been banned, they were also collecting and distributing their own poetry in *samizdat*. Their friend Alexander Ginzburg had just been arrested for bringing out three numbers of a poetry magazine called *Syntax*,* but they were planning to bring out some new verse collections – *Phoenix*, *Boomerang*, *Cocktail* – and others with similarly whimsical titles. They also made a point of attending official Soviet lectures and discussions, where they would speak up, ask questions and start genuine arguments on real issues. Since the original readings they had got to know an enormously large circle of widely differing people: scholars, writers, artists. My own circle of acquaintances grew with startling speed. As for the readings themselves, they attracted all that was best and most original in Russia. This was exactly what I had been looking for all this time.

About a hundred years ago, young people of our age devoured socialist pamphlets and discussed socialist utopias; whoever hadn't read Fourier or Proudhon was considered an ignoramus. The password with us was to know the poetry of Gumilyov, Pasternak and Mandelshtam; and whereas the tsarist detectives had had to study socialist treatises in order to infiltrate the youth of that time, our KGB agents were willy-nilly obliged to become devotees of poetry. Freedom of creation and the problems of art and literature had become central to society, when the

---

* *Syntax*, edited by Alexander Ginzburg in 1959–60, was the first *samizdat* literary magazine. *Boomerang* (1960) was edited by Vladimir Osipov and *Phoenix* (1961) by Yuri Galanskov. The editor of *Cocktail* is not known.

Ginzburg was sentenced to two years in normal-regime labour camps for editing *Syntax*. In 1964 charges of possessing 'anti-Soviet literature' were preferred against him and then dropped. In 1966 he compiled and smuggled to the West the celebrated *White Book*, published in the West as *On Trial* (Collins, 1967), on the trial of Sinyavsky and Daniel, for which, in 1968, he was sentenced to five years' imprisonment in strict-regime camps on a charge of 'anti-Soviet agitation and propaganda'. Some time after his release he became the chief representative in the Soviet Union of the Russian Relief Fund for Political Prisoners (financed largely by Alexander Solzhenitsyn), and a member of the Helsinki Monitoring Group in Moscow. In February 1977 he was arrested on unspecified charges. In July he was convicted of 'anti-Soviet agitation and propaganda' and sentenced to eight years' imprisonment in special regime labour camps.

biggest revolutionaries turned out to be the nonconformist artists and 'formalist' poets. This wasn't because we wanted it so. It was because the authorities denied all freedom of creation and insisted on ramming socialist realism down everybody's throats. The resulting situation was paradoxical: in the West many of the avant-garde were communists, while in our communist country the avant-garde were regarded as outlaws.

Our crowd was immensely heterogeneous. Some were interested only in pure art, and they fought ferociously for its right to be pure. Throughout the ages such purists have been regarded as totally apolitical, yet these views now put them in the very forefront of the political battle in Russia. There were those like myself for whom the right of art to be independent was merely one point of opposition to the regime, and we were here precisely because art happened to be at the centre of political passions. There were those like the author of some lines that I can still remember from that time:

> No, not for us can it be to spray bullets
> At the green-columned marching throng!
> For that we are too much poets
> And our enemy is too strong.
>
> No, not in us will the Vendée reawaken
> At the decisive reverberant hour!
> Ideas must remain our token,
> The cudgel can never be ours.
>
> No, not for us can it be to spray bullets!
> But to mark the significant dates
> The epoch created poets,
> And they the soldiers create.

Among the people circulating in Mayakovsky Square at that time were a lot of neo-Marxists and neo-communists of various kinds, but they no longer counted. That tendency was dying out and receding into the past. It had appeared in the 1950s as a natural reaction to Stalin's tyranny: taking the classics of Marxism–Leninism as their starting point and making their appeal to them, people endeavoured to force the authorities to observe their own wonderful principles. But the authorities had long since ceased to take note of the prophets displayed on the Party façade and were guided by considerations of their own self-interest. Meanwhile, the more people tried to elucidate these unshakable Marxist principles, the more convinced they became that they didn't exist, whereas what did exist led inexorably to Stalin.

Later, others camouflaged themselves with Marxism for demagogic purposes, believing it was both more convenient and safer to criticise the regime from that point of view – to belabour the regime, so to speak, with the collected works of its own beloved Lenin. But since most people even remotely able to think for themselves went much further in their political development, these voices began to sound out of tune. The popularity of Lenin and the rest had fallen so low that this kind of criticism began to sound more like a compliment than an indictment.

It strikes me that many people in the West overlooked this point and too often thought of the movement for human rights in the USSR as one more variety of neo-Marxism. This is because the few people in the movement who managed to retain a sincere faith in socialism with a human face were united with everyone else in their protest actions and their practical activities. But all of us were fighting for the human face, and most of us had had more than enough of socialism.

We were fighting for the concrete freedom to create, and it was no accident that many of us – people like Galanskov, Khaustov, Osipov and Edward Kuznetsov – later merged with the movement for human rights. We all got to know one another in Mayakovsky Square.

The poetry readings right there on the square, in the centre of Moscow, created an extraordinary atmosphere. They were usually held in the evenings and on Saturdays and Sundays, and hundreds of people turned up. Many of the readers were excellent professional actors and others were first-class original poets: Shchukin, Kovshin, Mikhail Kaplan, Viktor Kalugin, Alexandrovsky, Shucht, and so on.

One of the works most often read in the Square was Yuri Galanskov's *Manifesto of Man.*★ It was read both by the author and by some of the actors. To this day I cannot say whether it is a good poem or not, and I'm in no position to judge – it is too intimately bound up with my whole recollection of those times. We perceived the *Manifesto of Man* as a symphony of rebellion, as a summons to resistance.

> I'll go out on the square
> and into the city's ear
> I'll hammer a cry of despair. . . .

★ *Manifesto of Man* appeared in the *samizdat* journal *Phoenix 1966*, which Galanskov also edited. In 1968 Galanskov was tried together with Ginzburg, Alexei Dobrovolsky and Vera Lashkova – in 'the trial of the four' – and sentenced to seven years in strict-regime labour camps. He died in the camps in November 1972 of peritonitis following an operation for stomach ulcers.

used to ring out over Mayakovsky Square like words just discovered that very moment. Yuri's poem expressed exactly what we felt and what we lived by:

> This is me,
> calling to truth and revolt,
> willing no more to serve,
> I break your black tethers
> woven of lies.

Like him we felt that out of this despair and this rebellion, a free and independent personality could be reborn and grow.

> I don't want your bread
> kneaded with tears.
> And I'm falling and soaring,
> half-delirious,
> half-asleep . . .
> And I feel
> man
> blooming in me.

And indeed, this really was a manifesto of man, and not some narrowly political manifesto.

Just imagine. This was being recited in the heart of Moscow, in the open air, in that same Moscow where seven to eight years previously you would have had ten years stuck on you for those selfsame words, even if you whispered them, before you could say Jack Robinson.

Deprived of their former freedom of action and maddened still further as a result, the authorities were not intending to tolerate such liberties: almost from the beginning they organised provocations, detained the readers, noted their names and informed their faculties, since the majority were students. The faculties then took their own measures, which consisted basically of expulsion. Formally speaking, the punitive measures taken against us were determined by the city committee of the Komsomol and the Komsomol's operational staff, but in fact it was the KGB. From time to time some of the lads were searched and had collections of poetry and other *samizdat* material confiscated. KGB plainclothesmen would provoke fights in the Square, or attempt to disperse us, or keep us away from the statue at the appointed time by cordoning it off. But none of that could stop us, and in any case the crowd was always on our side.

Simultaneously the Party press started a slander campaign against us. Their favourite argument was that we were all parasites, good-for-nothings who didn't work. (The latter accusation was sometimes formally true in that, on the orders of the KGB, some of us had been chased out of the university and were also prevented from getting jobs.) But the vilification was good publicity for us, and more and more people found themselves drawn to the readings in Mayakovsky Square.

In April 1961, Yuri Gagarin's space flight had just taken place, and the day had been proclaimed a holiday. Crowds of tipsy people filled the Moscow streets to overflowing. It happened that we had arranged a reading for that day to mark the anniversary of Mayakovsky's suicide. At the appointed hour the square was absolutely packed. Many strollers joined us simply because they saw a crowd and wanted to know what was going on. We ourselves were uncertain as to whether we should postpone the reading or not, but in the event, it was decided to go ahead. The atmosphere was tense in the extreme and plainclothesmen were ready to pounce at any moment. At last, when Shchukin started reading, they let out a howl and made a dash through the crowd in the direction of the statue.

We usually formed a ring round the readers in order to foil any provocations, though we could always rely on the audience to take our side. And we had done that this time as well. But the plainclothesmen were itching for trouble and the crowd was full of bystanders, some of them drunk. A gigantic fist-fight broke out. Many people had no idea who was fighting whom and joined in just for the fun of it. In the twinkling of an eye the entire square was in an uproar: people were either fighting already or elbowing their way through the crowd to join in. The police were generally unpopular anyhow and on this occasion their appearance provoked a great deal of anger; at one point I feared that the crowd would overturn the police car and kick it to pieces. But somehow or other the police succeeded in bundling Shchukin and Osipov into a car and extricated it from the crowd. Shchukin got fifteen days 'for reading anti-Soviet verses' and Osipov ten days 'for disturbing the peace and using obscene language'. (This last was especially silly since Osipov* was known to dislike obscene language.)

This episode alone indicates what an extraordinary time it was. The

* Vladimir Osipov was sentenced to seven years in labour camps later in 1961 for anti-Soviet agitation and propaganda. In 1971, after his release, he founded the *samizdat* journal, *Assembly*, and in 1974 another journal, *Soil*. In November 1974 he was sentenced to eight years in strict-regime labour camps for 'anti-Soviet agitation and propaganda'.

uncertainty and instability of the leadership and Khrushchev's fear of making a bad impression in the West stayed the avenging hand of the security organs. Also, the absolute openness and legality of our activities nonplussed the KGB – they kept trying to discover the illegal organisation 'standing behind us'. They didn't make any arrests, however, evidently fearing to 'frighten off' the mythical organisers.

I knew all these details very well at the time, thanks to my old contacts from the conspiratorial organisation, many of whom now worked for the Komsomol city committee and even the Komsomol executive, which was officially responsible for breaking up the poetry readings and which worked in close cooperation with the KGB. Generally speaking, we had a lot of sympathisers among the Komsomol officials at that time, and I would get fairly accurate information about impending moves against us and was able to warn the others.

We were constantly being raided, and were sometimes detained for several hours. Often, when they detained one of us, the plainclothesmen would turn us in to a police station and give fictitious evidence of bad behaviour. Sometimes the police punished us, but more often they simply let us go – their interdepartmental hatred for these self-appointed police officers from the KGB never abated.

That spring of 1961 I tried to get my friends among the Komsomol officials to help me establish an official club under the aegis of one of the Komsomol district committees. They willingly gave us the club but at the same time tried to introduce certain limitations and control. Our club's first venture – an exhibition of nonconformist artists – was banned, and the club closed before it could open properly.

I was also summoned twice to the KGB for questioning. Up till then I had attracted no particular attention since I never took part in the readings myself and my function was purely organisational. Besides arranging the actual readings, I worked at securing the safe departure of the readers from the square. While the reading was going on, of course, the crowd was their protection, but as the evening drew to a close you had to lead the readers, one at a time, through the crowd and see them home or to a safe place, unnoticed by the plainclothesmen. Sometimes they had to be given a change of clothes or at least a different hat, or hustled into a car, or some ruse had to be thought up to distract the plainclothesmen. On each occasion it called for a great deal of resourcefulness. The crowd continued to stand around until there was no one left to read, at which point it dispersed. Then came the hardest bit of all – we too had to disappear. Sometimes the KGB's pursuit of us turned into a straightforward chase; we would scarcely have been able to get away if I hadn't grown up in those parts and known every connecting yard in the neighbourhood.

Although I had been detained several times in the past, only now, after my venture with the club, and particularly after our refusal to go on with it, did the KGB take an interest in me. And it *was* somewhat suspicious that without ever having been a member of it, I had such extensive contacts with the Komsomol leadership and could spend days and nights in the offices of the district committee (where we had been hoping to start the club) attending practically all the meetings. There was also something odd about the whole business of the club: the initiative had been approved by the city and district committees of the Komsomol, we had brought in a mass of paintings of 'undesirable tendencies', and although the exhibition was promptly banned as an ideological diversion, we had nonetheless succeeded in showing them unofficially for a couple of days. Elsewhere we had been planning to set up a printing shop for the publication of poetry, but wind of that reached the KGB. As a result, I was twice hauled in for questioning.

No case had been started against me and therefore I would have been within my legal rights not to talk to them at all. Unfortunately, all my training for this eventuality had been psychological, not juridical, and I hadn't the faintest idea of my legal rights. Instead of simply refusing to talk I wriggled and squirmed, made myself out to be a Soviet patriot and even wrote out a statement, congratulating myself on having pulled the wool over their eyes. Without naming or incriminating anybody else, I created a completely false impression of myself. Evidently they decided that I was a yielding, pliable sort of fellow – the worst thing that can happen when dealing with the KGB. Only much later did I realise how much harm I had done myself.

Meanwhile, events accelerated. In the autumn of 1961 I was kicked out of Moscow University. As a matter of fact, soon after I had gone there and the moment it had been discovered that I was supposed not to be there, the authorities had started looking for ways to expel me. Formally my position was entirely in order and there was nothing for them to seize on. There were no written instructions saying that I was to be excluded. But, as always, the Party acted illegally and under-handedly, resorting to backstairs methods. When the first group of exams came along in the winter of 1960–61, I discovered I was not to be allowed to take them. What was the matter, I asked in surprise? All my tests had been taken and passed at the proper time. 'We don't know,' they replied in the registrar's office. 'There must be some misunderstanding. Come back tomorrow.' But time was running short. I was in danger of missing the closing date for completing the session in time, and if that happened they would have every right to kick me out.

Luckily I still had my student record card with me and hadn't handed it in at the registrar's office. Taking advantage of this blunder, I went straight to my tutors and asked them to let me take the examinations without an admission ticket. I explained that there had been some sort of mix-up in the registrar's office, that they had omitted to give me a ticket. Both my tutors in chemistry and mathematics – two of my favourite subjects – liked me well enough, and seeing I had my record card with me and had completed all my tests, they agreed to let me take the exams without a ticket, provided that I brought them the ticket later. And that is what I did. When the registrar's office later started to tell me that I had failed to finish the first session, I had the enormous pleasure of brandishing my exam record card under their noses. There was absolutely nothing they could do, and so I got through my first semester.

Towards the end of the second semester the authorities refined their methods, calculated their moves better, and prevented me from even taking the tests. Sensing that this time I wouldn't be able to beat them, I gave in and resigned from the university voluntarily, giving poor health as my reason. This gave me the formal right to reapply the following year.

But the following autumn, when I reapplied, they refused me. The Komsomol had opposed my reinstatement, they told me. 'I don't know what's the matter,' said the registrar, 'you'd better go and find out. The official reason for rejecting you is that you don't conform to the ethos of a Soviet student.'

I caught the secretary of the Komsomol for the entire university in the midst of preparing for some sort of tourist expedition – a routine group exercise. She flew into a rage at my effrontery: 'You've got a nerve coming here and asking questions! Haven't you already been told that you're forbidden to study at the university? Don't you read the newspapers? There's no room for people like you here!'

It was true that a campaign had been started to smash the Maya-kovsky Square readings and our names had often appeared in the newspapers, where we were virtually called enemies of the people. The conversation was obviously pointless: when I said something about the right to an education, she merely snorted. After that I was invariably referred to in Soviet newspapers as 'the student who failed to graduate' and who had been 'expelled from the university for failing his exams' – and still am.

To tell the truth, I wasn't very sorry about what had happened. It was clear that the authorities weren't going to let me study. And life at the university was anyway so dull and featureless that it filled me with disgust. The teaching system was little different from school. Attendance at lectures was compulsory. Many of the subjects we studied were Party disciplines, completely useless to my growing interest in biophysics. There were also military studies, and that damned physical training, which I couldn't stand. It was like living in a barracks – there were specially appointed prefects to see that you went to the lectures, and if you failed to turn up, they reported you. The students had no rights whatsoever, especially if they came from out of town on scholarships. For these scholarships and for hostel accommodation, complete obedience was demanded. Many students informed on their comrades so as not to lose their position. They had absolutely no means of defending themselves – and still don't to this day. You could be expelled from the university for the least little thing and with no explanation – just go and try to complain afterwards to the Minister of Education.

To hell with them all, I decided. Anyway, I have no time for it now, I've got better things to do!

Indeed, I really did have better things to do. My informants told me that the readings were due to be completely crushed. Orders had at last come from above to round us up at all costs. News of our doings had begun to filter out to the foreign press, and by October 1961, when the Twenty-second Congress of the Party was due to be held, everything had to be quiet.

In August they had arrested Ilya Bakstein. He was a very sick person, having spent most of his childhood in hospitals with tuberculosis of the spine. He had never performed in the square or read poems, and the fact that they chose to arrest the most helpless and least fit of us all, showed the KGB's intention to try to use him to build a case against us.

Now, as if let off the leash, the KGB stopped at nothing. Just before we were due to meet again they brought snowploughs on to the Square and let them loose on the crowd. The ploughs circled round and round the statue, keeping everyone at bay. We were summoned and threatened with reprisals.

Late one night, after one of our readings, I was on my way home when a car suddenly drew up beside me. A group of young men bundled me inside and drove off with me. We had often been picked up before this and detained for several hours and questioned, so I wasn't surprised at first. After quite a long time, half an hour or more, we drove into a courtyard where there was a sort of office in a basement. It was curious that nobody was in the basement at all, apart from the people who had brought me here. I was led into a big windowless room with no furniture.

We had barely got inside when the man on my right suddenly punched me in the face. Almost simultaneously another tried to punch me in the solar plexus and knock me down, but I was already on my guard and turned away. I swiftly leapt into the corner, pressed my back to the wall and attempted to guard my face and my solar plexus with my arms.

They beat me for hours. One of them grabbed my hair and pulled my head downwards, trying to smash his knee into my face at the same time. Another took this opportunity to punch me in the back as hard as he could, aiming for my kidneys. All I thought of was how to keep myself from going down on the floor, for then they would have crippled me with their boots. I hardly knew where I was, my head was spinning, and I had difficulty breathing. They stopped for a moment, and one of them leaned over me and stroked my cheek with a voluptuous smile. Then they started beating me again.

It was four in the morning when they pushed me out into the street. 'Don't ever go to the Square again, the next time we'll kill you,' was all they said.

The last days of the readings were upon us. Bystanders had somehow been sifted out and disappeared, and the groups were dwindling, but this led to an even greater intimacy among the remaining few. It grew harder and harder to organise the readings, and even more complicated than before to get the readers away safely and unnoticed, one at a time. Many of them no longer lived at home, but had gone into hiding with friends. Still, every performance left us with an inexpressible sense of freedom and rejoicing. There was something mystical in this reading of poetry to the nocturnal city, the isolated windows in which lights still burned, and the late-night trolleybuses. Even now, many years later, I feel a special, intimate attachment to the friends who held out to the bitter end in Mayakovsky Square.

On the morning of 6 October 1961, three days before the Twenty-second Congress was due to open, we were all arrested. I suddenly woke up in bed with the feeling that someone was staring at me. It was true. Captain Nikiforov of the KGB, the one who had interviewed me in the spring, was sitting at the bottom of my bed. How he had entered the flat I do not know. A car was waiting by the front door to take us to the Lubyanka, the chief investigation prison and headquarters of the KGB.

Offices, corridors, staircases, and people everywhere, bustling back and forth with papers, folders, briefcases. In one office I was cross-examined, in another threatened, and in another I found, not KGB officers at all but kindly father-figures and dear friends. I was tempted with jokes and treated to tea. Then there was more shouting and fists banging on desks: 'Quit being so obstinate, we know everything!' No beatings. No torture. That, I suppose, was still to come. I was led from one office to another, and everywhere there were crowds of people.

The main things were patience and endurance. What did they know? What did they want?

'Here is a pen and a sheet of paper. Write down all you know.' Oh yeah, smart aleck. You won't get all I know on to one sheet of paper.

Two things gradually emerged from all the wheedling, shouting and threats. They were interested, first in what I knew about a planned attempt on Khrushchev's life and, second, in a document I had composed and discussed with some of the other fellows.

Now it was true that not long before this, rumours had circulated to the effect that one of our fellows was planning to assassinate Khrushchev. This would have been a monstrous stupidity, and we were appalled. After lengthy inquiries and investigation we succeeded in establishing that one little group had had a theoretical discussion one evening on the subject of political terror as an instrument of struggle; terror was condemned as both senseless and harmful. The question worrying everybody was: what to do if a new Stalin appeared? Would it be justified to murder him? The majority concluded that the murder of Stalin would not have led to any changes. The Party would have simply promoted a new one, since there were plenty of candidates. It had long been clear that in our system the fortuitous death of the Führer would not entail political changes. Rather the reverse – when the time was ripe for such changes, the Führer would suffer either an enigmatic death or an open execution. The murder of Khrushchev could bring us nothing but a fresh wave of intensified repressions. Despite our hostility to him, even we could see that.

The KGB decided to use this discussion as a pretext for arresting even those of us who weren't present that evening, and went to great lengths to spread more rumours about the intended assassination. Apparently this made it easier for them to get Party sanction for the arrests and for all the other decisive measures they were taking to liquidate the readings on Mayakovsky Square.

The other point was also incidental and had no criminal content. My Komsomol friends had not understood why we didn't want to hold the readings under the aegis of the Komsomol, why we didn't join them and didn't trust their 'inner-party democracy'. To explain this, and at their request, I had written out a couple of pages of argument: my principal objection was to the Komsomol's utter dependence on the Party, their red tape, their dictatorial method of leadership, and the rest of the usual Party paraphernalia. If the Komsomol were autonomous and independent, permitted its members to discuss political questions openly, and became a proper social force, then, I argued, we would be able to work with it. My friends in the district committee typed up these arguments on the committee typewriter and arranged to hold a discussion of them. I for my part presented them to my Mayakovsky Square friends at one of our meetings in Yuri Galanskov's home. None of us regarded any of this as illegal, and when Edward Kuznetsov asked me for a copy in order to read it more carefully at home, I willingly gave him one.*

Now it turned out that the document had been found during a search of Eddy's home, and he testified that he had received it from me. Naturally I confirmed his statement without the slightest hesitation. How were Eddy, Galanskov and I, not to speak of the others present, to know that the KGB would dignify this unfortunate document with the solemn title of 'Theses on the Dissolution of the Komsomol' and pronounce it anti-Soviet? As if we hadn't discussed dozens of such statements during the preceding months!

The stubbornness of the KGB's questioning about the circumstances of our meetings and conversations put me on guard, and I refused to give any more testimony so as not to name any more names. I didn't even tell them who had typed the 'Theses'. I gave evasive answers about the obvious facts of my acquaintanceship with many of the Square regulars blaming my poor memory as an excuse. It turned out that I had been quite well prepared after all.

They kept us at the Lubyanka all day. In the evening they returned

* Kuznetsov was sentenced in 1962 to seven years in the labour camps for 'anti-Soviet agitation and propaganda'. In 1970 he was one of the chief participants in the celebrated attempted hijacking in Leningrad, for which he was first sentenced to death and then to fifteen years in special regime labour camps. His *Prison Diaries* (Vallentine, Mitchell, 1975) is one of the best books to emerge from the dissident movement.

with us to search our homes. Naturally these same 'Theses' were lying in my desk drawer. It had never even occurred to me to hide them. They found nothing else of consequence in my room. They confiscated some poems and my own short stories. The search ended late, at about midnight, but I wasn't arrested, and I was allowed to remain at home.

My parents were terrified, and the occurrence did little to improve my already complicated relations with my father. I can't say that we were in open conflict – there was just mutual dislike between us. In his own way he was a very honest man and was devoted to his subject – the fate of the countryside. He had been born and brought up in a village in Tambov Province and had spent all his life writing about rural matters. He actually believed in collective farms and thought the liquidation of the kulaks was justified (perhaps because he had taken part in it himself during his youth). Lenin was his highest authority, and he attributed all the subsequent impoverishment and ruin of his beloved collective farms to Stalin's influence. But that was not the issue so much as personal factors. He was a generally difficult, despotic sort of person. He disliked me, I think, because I had turned out to be not at all the sort of person he would have wished. It is strange how cruelly fate revenged itself on him for this dislike. Right up until his death fourteen years later, even after he had left my mother and me, he continued to incur regular reprimands and penalties from the Party for having brought me up 'incorrectly'. Eventually he was almost not published any more, and they started deleting about half of every article that did get through. He was endlessly summoned hither and thither for discussions, and every time I landed in jail, or Soviet propaganda took it into its head to abuse me in print, he was punished in some way.

On this occasion, however, he unexpectedly displayed dignity and contempt for the KGB. At the very height of their search of the room which I shared with my mother, he suddenly came in and said to the plainclothesmen in a deeply angry and suspicious tone: 'I suppose you'll be rummaging in my room next, will you?'

'No, no, not at all,' fussed the plainclothesmen, and soon made themselves scarce. He slammed the door after them and locked himself in his room again. He was capable of sitting there for a whole week without speaking to anyone, and emerging only rarely to go and eat in the kitchen.

From then on we found ourselves being regularly interrogated by the KGB. All of us who were questioned as witnesses – Galanskov, Khaustov and about twenty other people – used to meet after the interrogations to discuss the situation and exchange advice on how to answer. In effect, none of us added anything to our evidence of the first day, despite the investigators' cunning.

It was now that I learned for the first time about a witness's legal rights. Alexander Sergeyevich Yesenin-Volpin,* recently released from the Leningrad Special Mental Hospital, read us a whole lecture on the subject. He had come to the Square one day, listened for a bit, and looked around. At our first meeting he hadn't impressed me much – he was an eccentric sort of fellow wearing a tattered fur cap, and he spent the whole evening holding forth about the need to respect the law. But his words had been of practical help, and now none of us allowed himself to be confused or was tricked into blabbing.

Meanwhile we decided, nevertheless, to spoil the opening day of their Party Congress. On 9 October the Square went into action for the last time – we held readings throughout Moscow, not only by Maya-kovsky's statue, but also by Pushkin's and several others, and also in front of the Lenin Library. This last was the most important – the others were a diversionary manoeuvre. That evening, more than a little tight from drinking in the corridors, the Congress delegates began to emerge from the Kremlin gates. Seeing the crowd by the Library, they came over to it, listened to the poems and applauded, and when an attempt was made to disperse us, they even intervened on our behalf. One of the delegates, well under the weather, drew several of us aside and warmly thanked us, assuring us that we were doing great things and very necessary work. Of course, we immediately complained to these delegates about the way the KGB was harassing us and dispersing our meetings, beating us up and doing other illegal things. Some of them promised to make representations so that we wouldn't be touched any more. But I don't think they did, since after that the readings were officially banned and anyone who dared continue would have found himself behind bars.

Again the Party press heaped mountains of slanders on us. Of me it

* Yesenin-Volpin, a mathematician and son of the famous 1920s poet, Sergei Yesenin, had spent varying periods in mental hospitals since 1949. In 1959 he had sent to the West a philosophical treatise and collection of poems, published as *A Leaf of Spring* (Thames & Hudson, 1961), and in 1965 founded the 'Constitution Day demonstrations' that later became an annual event. He became a prolific contributor to *samizdat* on legal problems and in February 1968 was forcibly committed to the Kashchenko Mental Hospital for protesting against the 'trial of the four' (Ginzburg, Galanskov, Dobrovolsky and Lashkova). He was released again in May. He then became the chief legal adviser to the Moscow Human Rights Committee (led by Andrei Sakharov) until his emigration in 1972. He now works at the Massachusetts Institute of Technology.

was inevitably said that I was 'a failed student' and had been 'led astray by the good life my father gave me'. The reporter had noticed that my father was a member of the Writers' Union and made the rest up out of his head. How could he know our true relations? But this had unexpected consequences: my father began to feel uneasy about his hostility to me and, not without embarrassment, bought me a suit – the first, I think, I had ever had in my life.

The fate of our arrested comrades was decided four months later in the harshest possible way. Ilya Bakstein, with the curved spine, got five years in the labour camps, and Kuznetsov and Osipov seven years each. Nothing more was said, of course, about that fantastic assassination plan. They were convicted of 'anti-Soviet agitation and propaganda', in other words for the readings and discussions in Mayakovsky Square, and for the poetry. The Moscow court also attempted to accuse them of creating an anti-Soviet organisation, but that charge, too, was later dropped, since the investigators were unable to invent a plausible organisation. My 'Theses' were used to incriminate Eddy and figured in one of the charges against him: 'the possession and dissemination of anti-Soviet literature'.

The trial was closed to the public, of course. They didn't even want to let anyone in to hear the sentences. But our great legal wizard Alik Volpin, a copy of the criminal code in his hand, proved to the guards that the pronouncement of a court sentence must always be open to the public.

Alik was the first person we had ever come across to speak seriously about Soviet laws. We used to make fun of him. 'You really are cracked, Alik,' we would laugh. 'Just think what you're saying. What laws can there be in a country like ours? Who pays any attention to them?' 'That's the whole problem – that no one pays any attention to them,' replied Alik, not in the least disturbed by our mockery. And when they let some of the lads in to listen to the sentence, he exulted. 'Look, you see. We've only ourselves to blame if we don't demand that our laws be observed.' But the rest of us shrugged our shoulders.

Little did we realise that this absurd incident, with the comical Alik Volpin brandishing his criminal code like a magic wand to melt the doors of the court, was the beginning of our civil rights movement and the movement for human rights in the USSR.

The literary period in the slow awakening of Soviet society was coming to an end. Poets and readers were being sent away in deadly earnest to absolutely real labour camps. Not soldiers and not conspirators, but poets:

No, not for us can it be to spray bullets!
But to mark the significant dates
The epoch created poets,
And they the soldiers create.

It was an epoch that couldn't stomach poets – they had to become
soldiers.

I didn't go to the court, although I was listed as one of the witnesses
to be called. I was shamed by one absurdity: Eddy, who had merely
borrowed my ill-starred 'Theses' to read, was in the dock, while I, who
had written them and given them to Eddy, was only called as a
witness. In such circumstances I was ashamed to remain at liberty, let
alone appear in court. But the lads told me afterwards that after
pronouncing sentence the court announced a separate finding, according to which proceedings should be instituted against me as well.

We all continued to meet frequently, but we no longer went to the
Square. Every one of us was expecting reprisals and these meetings were
no longer as jolly as before. Several of us had been put away in lunatic
asylums and all we could do was wait our turn. I found this waiting
intolerable. Wandering about Moscow in the evening, I strove to think
what to do next. Arrest was inevitable, so I had nothing to lose.

The thing that tormented me most of all was my impotence. There
was absolutely nothing I could do to get back at the scum for the
violence and insults they were visiting upon us. If only I could think of
something, even spit in their faces! The very thought of how they had
beaten me kept me awake at nights. Then there was the university,
Mayakovsky Square, hump-backed Ilya in jail. Brazen lies flooded in
from all sides just as before, as if nothing had happened. All this drove
me to distraction.

Unable to think of anything better to do, I organised an exhibition
of paintings by two nonconformist artists in a private flat. The exhibition attracted many visitors. For a short while it was just like old times,
a kind of demonstration against the Party control of art. The KGB,
however, was not caught napping: three of them came to the exhibition, gazed for a long time at the pictures and silently went away. Then
they summoned the tenant of the flat, threatened to kick him out of his
job, deprive him of his flat and virtually throw him in jail. The
exhibition continued for over ten days. At that point I was daily awaiting arrest. The KGB brazenly trailed me everywhere, scarcely bothering
to hide.

I felt an upsurge of even more bitter anger: why should I wait submissively to be arrested and allow them the pleasure of devouring me like a rabbit, slowly and quietly, savouring the taste? Swiftly shaking them off when they least expected it, I skipped out of Moscow. They were left standing waiting for me outside an entranceway while I was already on the train. The wheels clacked as it carried me past stunted copses and impoverished villages, and early the following morning, at some junction, I awoke joyfully to the sound of locomotives calling to one another and the coupling of carriages. Then, its bronze wheels clattering heavily over the rails, our locomotive moved on and hooted from somewhere up ahead of me, as if yawning. The carriage jerked, swayed and creaked, and we were off again – onward, onward, to Siberia. Stifling Moscow, where every window stared suspiciously at your back, fell far behind in the past. Let the secret police look for me now on one sixth of the earth's surface!

Through some friends in Novosibirsk I got myself taken on a geological expedition, and within a week we were bumping through the trackless wilds of the taiga towards the east. Tomsk, Krasnoyarsk, Irkutsk, Baikal, Chita – 6,000 miles by ex-army truck. Every evening by the camp fire – tea out of a smoke-blackened pot, songs and yarns. New impressions, new faces, and no one standing over you. There is no boss in the taiga, other than lumbering Bruin. Only occasionally, when passing through hamlets, did we catch sight of the poverty and hopelessness of Soviet life. But then we were back in the taiga again, with its impassable tracks and mosquitoes like clouds of dust, so that you could hardly draw breath.

Suddenly, between Irkutsk and Lake Baikal, we came across fifty miles of beautifully asphalted roadway, with all the little villages along it looking incredibly neat and tidy, and as gaily painted as Easter eggs. At the far end of the road, beside the lake, there were two luxurious modern bungalows with avenues of trees and a golf course. What wonder was this? And what for? The explanation was very simple. It turned out that Eisenhower and Nikita had been supposed to come here in 1960. Things hadn't worked out, however, and here these bungalows still stood as a monument to Soviet–American friendship: a piece of America in the midst of the trackless Soviet wilderness.

Beyond Baikal we stumbled across another wonder – a marble road. This also had a simple explanation: hard by, it seemed, there were marble deposits, but with no means of transporting the marble it had seemed a shame to waste it, so they had paved the road with marble chips to reduce skidding. In another place the paving again attracted the attention of my geologist friends. They climbed out of the truck and began tapping with their hammers: surprise! It was zinc ore. About a mile further along the road it changed to lead ore. It turned out that in the vicinity there were two smelting plants adjoining each other: one for lead, the other zinc. But they were administered by different authorities and situated in different districts, therefore one dumped the zinc ore that it couldn't use, and the other its lead ore.

Further on we came to the taiga and bogs again, where not even tractors could penetrate because it was too marshy. The villages were few and far between, and very primitive. Log cabins with plank roofs. Wind and rain had endowed everything with a grey, abandoned look. And the Siberians, descendants of transported convicts, were a gloomy people who glowered at you distrustfully and answered your questions laconically and unwillingly.

We stayed one night with a peasant in one of the villages. Inside the hut there wasn't room to swing a cat, yet there were six children sleeping on shelves, with one pair of boots between them for going outside in the winter. 'How do you manage?' we asked. 'Somehow.' We exchanged glances and left him half our tinned food – we would make up for it by hunting and fishing.

I heard that two years before us some cartographers in a helicopter had discovered a village that no one knew about. Some Old Believers who had broken with the official church had been living there since the turn of the century, and had cut themselves off from the outside world. Lucky people! They knew nothing of the revolution, the world war, collective farms. It was a rich, densely populated village of a sort you rarely see nowadays. There was plenty of news to tell them. And of course, they were immediately herded into a collective farm and an end was put to their prosperous, carefree life.

The further east I went, the more I realised that while it was easy to escape the KGB, there was no escaping Soviet life. Everywhere it was the same, only greyer than in Moscow.

It was just getting dark when we reached the Chinese border. What a strange sensation, to be on the border. Here, on this side, the steppe and the knolls were ours. Over there, across the Argun river, they were Chinese. The border ran down the middle of the river and there were no visible signs of it – neither posts nor barbed wire. And the border was virtually unpatrolled. Nothing but small military outposts, about four miles apart, manned by drunken officers and soldiers. And not even these were visible on the Chinese side. At one post we were warned not to light big fires, not to swim across the river, and not to fire in that direction. I felt vaguely disturbed by all this – I had never been so far away from home before. Everything seemed strange, the alien stars, the oversized flowers on the steppe, the somehow disconcerting silhouettes of the mountains on the Chinese side. The border was there and yet it wasn't. All I needed was to swim a hundred yards across the Argun and I would find myself in a different world, with different customs. Nobody would be pursuing me any more, nobody would be trying to catch me and drag me off to jail. Or would they? Were they really so very different from us?

It was already late and the others were asleep. My fire was blazing, despite the warning, and specks of red light were dancing on the Chinese shore – inside China. I was alone on the outer edge of our country, my only company the midges and moths, which kept flying inquisitively out of the darkness and into the flames, only to fall and burst with a soft plop, like rain falling. And the river splashed quietly and indifferently against both our shores.

So there was no border after all!

Early next morning at dawn, as we were having breakfast, a Chinaman rode past on the other bank, driving a small herd of horses before him. Drawing level with us, he removed his cap and said in Russian: 'Good day to you.' 'Good day to you.' we replied across the river. Then he turned to bellow at his horses: 'Get a move on, you fuckers!' and drove out of sight.

In the autumn of 1962, with heavy heart, I returned to Moscow. I knew that they would arrest me, but what could I do? I couldn't stay in hiding for the rest of my life. As it was I'd spent nearly six months wandering about Siberia. There was nowhere to escape to, there was no place for me anywhere in this enormous country. And then there was the thought that maybe this suited them very well? What difference did it make whether I was in jail or hiding away in Siberia? Either way I wasn't bothering them, so long as I was out of their sight.

I began wandering round Moscow by night again, walking down its crooked backstreets and gossiping with the old detached houses of the Arbat. In the autumn, when the trees turned yellow and the wind blew the wrinkled leaves along the streets, and the smell of acrid smoke came wafting from the gardens and the boulevards where the leaves were raked into piles and burnt; in winter, when hoarfrost etched every cornice and every railing; and in spring, when the cornices dripped icicles and every sound rang out loud and clear, as in a cathedral – in every season these old houses were my only friends. Each of them had its own unique personality and history. It was as if they still bore the imprint of another, vanished life, and I knew literally all there was to know about their former owners. A chipped pediment here or the shape of a window there, the carved doors, the stucco ornaments, the worn steps and the garden railings, each had a tale to tell about the family dramas of now vanished occupants – stories that could have been regarded as tragedies only in the placid calm of the last century. I indulgently heard them out, smiling at the naïvity of their adventures:

'Lucky people. . . .'

No matter how much you anticipate arrest, it always comes un-expectedly and at an awkward time. It was seven months after my return to Moscow before they arrested me, that is when I had already stopped expecting it. I had been introduced to the wife of an American correspondent by a friend of mine, and visiting her one day I spied a copy of Djilas's *The New Class* on her bookshelf. I had known of the book for some time, but had never had an opportunity to read it. Catching my greedy look, the correspondent's wife gestured to me to say nothing, since the flat was bugged. She took the book down and handed it to me. Talking aloud on a completely different subject, she gave me to understand that the book had to be returned the next day.

It seemed stupid to read it at breakneck speed, skipping pages in order to return it in time. I therefore decided to make a quick photographic copy so as to be able to read it later at my leisure, without hurrying. I photographed the whole book, returned it silently to its owner and set about developing the films. I spent the night making prints and fell asleep only the next morning. That evening the KGB struck. It was Captain Nikoforov again, with four others. Naturally I had no time to hide anything – the work was unfinished and I still had several pages to print. They didn't look for anything else – it seemed they knew what they had come for. As is usual on such occasions, they assured my mother they would let me go immediately, that they were just taking me for a chat with their boss. I had long been used to the idea of being arrested and the only thing that worried me was how my mother would take it. So I too did the best I could to convince her that I would return at once, and was in such haste to leave, putting on such a casual air, that I only succeeded in frightening her all the more. They took me straight to a solitary cell in the Lubyanka.

As far as I can remember, cell number 102 was small and right under the roof, so that on the window side the ceiling sloped down to head height. There was only room for a cot, a bedside table and a latrine bucket. The door was so narrow that it couldn't even accommodate a food flap – they had to open the door to feed me. The exercise yards were on the roof, on the seventh floor – you were taken there in a lift: tiny squares, like deep wells, the walls covered in sheet iron, with barbed wire strung along the top. The minute window in the cell was at chest height and the top part opened just a fraction. It was impossible to see anything out of it. All I could hear was the guard being changed below in the courtyard: 'Objectives to be kept under observation are the windows of the isolation prison and door number two. Guard handed over. Guard accepted.'

On the first night, strangely enough, I slept soundly. It was a little odd to be sleeping without a sheet and directly under a blanket, which was all prickly. It was also uncomfortable sleeping with the light on, and like all novices on their first night in jail, I knocked on the door and naïvely asked them to put out the light.

'Not allowed,' they replied through the door.

On the fourth or fifth day I was taken to see General Svetlichny, the then head of the Moscow security service. A luxurious mansion, the former residence of Count Rostopchin, mayor of Moscow during the war with Napoleon, had been linked to the KGB headquarters by a special enclosed passageway. High stuccoed ceilings, parquet floors, carpets everywhere, tall carved wooden doors leading from room to room, and people hurrying in and out. After four days in my cell I was dazzled by this magnificence. I felt that at any moment I would round a turn in the corridor and bump into ladies in crinolines and gentlemen in powdered wigs gravely chatting together.

The general, a little man with a big head, like an evil dwarf, was sitting behind a high desk. Two other men – the head of the investigation department, Colonel Ivanov, and my investigator, Captain Mikhailov – were sitting to one side, and all three of them were wearing civilian clothes. The questioning didn't last long, and since I sullenly refused to answer their questions, the general came straight to the point. Brandishing my arrest warrant in one hand, he said emphatically: 'If you don't tell me who gave you the book and who helped you, I'll sign this and you'll go to jail. If you tell me, you can go home this minute.'

It would be interesting to know how many people, leaving this gilded office, have gone on to become diplomats, writers or academicians, making speeches at international forums, lecturing their children on morality and referring to their sense of duty. Reliable, respected people. Ladies in crinolines and gentlemen in powdered wigs.

No one but this evil dwarf knows the secret of their success. All they needed to do was append their signature, or even just make a little cross or leave their thumbprint, in the best traditions of the Middle Ages. Nothing terrible. And he would lock the document away in his fireproof safe.

Only much later did I discover that they knew perfectly well who had given me the book. They weren't at all interested in having my testimony, they just wanted to turn me into a nark, which was why they had arrested me. The reason for this was to be sought in my first encounter with the KGB in the spring of 1961, when I had behaved as I had been instructed, giving evasive answers and pretending to be a Soviet patriot – thinking, in my naïvety, that I had outwitted them. It was then, it would seem, that they had marked my dossier accordingly, which was why they hadn't jailed me together with the others last autumn and even now weren't reckoning on holding me.

But one glance at me this time was perhaps enough for them to realise their mistake. I exuded so much hatred, was so obviously thirsting to tear them limb from limb, that their question became a mere formality. I don't remember exactly what I said to the general – something very insulting about the KGB's activities during Stalin's time. And for the lack of any more effective instruments of destruction, I expressed myself in such choice Russian language that he merely shook his head and signed the warrant.

I remember I was very dissatisfied with myself when I got back to my cell. Such a unique opportunity, a real live general of the KGB! How much there was to say to him – he would have remembered it for the rest of his life. Two or three days later I re-lived this scene all over again and got so carried away that when the investigator called me in for interrogation, I let him have it full blast. Yet I was still dissatisfied when I got back to my cell.

After about a month I was transferred to Lefortovo. Apart from the old case based on the Mayakovsky Square readings, I was now also accused of 'processing and preparing anti-Soviet literature with the intention of distributing it' – i.e. having two incomplete photocopies of Djilas' book. The charge of intending to distribute it was based on the fact that I had tried to make two copies, not just one.

I refused pointblank to talk, and during the whole of my time there I signed only one statement – concerning my attitude to the communist regime and the KGB. In it I wrote that I would never allow them to decide which books I should read and which I shouldn't. And beyond that, despite my interrogators' cajoling and shouting and desk-pounding, I refused to sign anything at all. They showed me some fictitious statements purporting to contain other people's testimony against me, promised to let me rot in jail or to send me to the back of beyond, but I remained silent. It's true they didn't beat me, but I don't think even that would have helped. I was too angry.

'Don't worry,' I thought. 'Just let me hold out till the trial. Then I'll give you an earful. You'll wish you'd never got involved.'

After a while they virtually ceased summoning me for interrogation. 'Don't you see,' said the investigator sadly, just before the end, 'I hate it when a case doesn't come out well. I hate it the way an artist hates it when his picture doesn't come out as planned.'

*It seemed to me that I had spent my whole life in Lefortovo. I would fall asleep and only dream that I was free and at home. And then I would wake up to those same Lefortovo walls again. All new initiatives and hopes, all thaws and freezes, ended in the Lefortovo cells, or else began in them. Almost every three years, like the swing of a pendulum, I would find myself there again: in 1963, 1967, 1971, 1973, and now 1976. It was the old struggle between the bear and the block of wood.*

*It was here that they brought me the first time, still warm and palpitating and full of impressions. It was here that I totted up the pluses and minuses, agonised at night over the fact that I had achieved nothing again, recalled my childhood and slept off the effects of my feverish life 'at liberty'. Here I witnessed the ultimate in human degradation and the pinnacle of human honour. Here I had first started to build my castle and had laid its foundations. Here I was brought from Vladimir in 1973, my body emaciated and my head swimming, when they hoped to force me at last to repent and recant.*

*The prison governor, Colonel Petrenko, would come and visit me in the evenings, when he was tipsy, like an old friend.*

*'All right, tell us,' he would say, 'you've seen all the prisons and camps now, so you can compare. Tell us – how do I feed you, eh?' And when he heard me sing the praises of the Lefortovo kitchens his face would be wreathed in a broad smile.*

*'You know,' he would say, 'I'd like to take you by the arm and lead you round all the cells in Lefortovo, so you could repeat your words to everyone. The point is, I've got prosecutors in here now for taking bribes. Yesterday they were eating shashlik à la Karsky and turning their noses up even at that, and now they don't want to eat their gruel, and they keep complaining! Of*

course, Lefortovo prison's not what it used to be, times have changed. Take this man here,' he poked his finger at the chest of the sullen block guard standing to attention by his side, 'now this man remembers what they used to do here in the old days. But it's not like that any more!'

In Stalin's time Lefortovo had been a torture prison. 'What? You want Lefortovo?' the investigator would threaten the stubborn prisoner, and the latter's heart would burst – anything you like, only not Lefortovo! It was in the basements here that they had liquidated Yezhov,* and torture had ended for a time. Only for a time.

Here they always required just one thing of you – repentance. For this reason the very walls of Lefortovo must have been steeped in remorse. Prisoners groaned and tossed and turned, unable to sleep: prison reminded them of everything they had ever done in their lives to be ashamed of.

I always felt remorse in Lefortovo, not because of what I had been arrested for, as the investigators wanted, nor in the way they wished. But I invariably dwelt on all the things I had to reproach myself with.

The first time, in 1963, I kept thinking for some reason of the hare we had killed on that Siberian expedition. It had happened one night, our car was travelling downhill. It had just stopped raining, the road had grown soft, and the surface was a pudding of clay. Suddenly a hare leapt out from one side, ran about ten yards in the glare of the headlights and sat down in the road. It was all hunched up and covered its head with its paws, as if cowering in fright.

'Aha, run him over! Get that hare!' we all cried. 'We can have him for supper.' And a second later came a knock on the underside of the car. Reaching the bottom of the slope, we went back for the hare; soon he was stewing in the pot.

The others laughed at me, but I couldn't eat it. I don't know why, but suddenly I realised that my life was about to change. Everything had come easy to me before, but it wouldn't any longer.

It seemed to me that this hare was the main reason I was sitting here in Lefortovo; I thought of him most of all. I hadn't killed him, and in any case the slope was steep and slippery after the rain and it would have been impossible to brake in time. But I had wanted his death, wanted it for a split second, and that was enough. Later I often killed birds or even hares while out hunting, but I never thought of them afterwards.

The very appearance of Lefortovo prison – with its shape in the form of a letter к, its wire netting stretched between the catwalks, so that the block officer sitting at his table in the middle of the wall could keep all the guards and all the corridors in view, the mysterious tongue-clicking with which the guards

* Nikolai Yezhov was chief of the NKVD from 1936–8 and directed Stalin's 'great purge' of those years. In 1938 he was accused of 'excesses', replaced by Beria and killed.

signalled their approach to one another when leading a prisoner – all this had astonished me that first time.

The prison regime in those days had been quite different from what it became later. Prisoners under investigation weren't allowed to have either pencil and paper or newspapers. There were no calendars in the cells either, and you had to use a method peculiar to Lefortovo if you didn't want to lose track of the days. Hanging on the wall of every cell was a copy of 'Regulations for the Investigation Prisons of the KGB'. 'Regulations', PRAVILA, was printed in capital letters at the top, just beneath the string on which the card hung. This word became your calendar. If you hung a scrap of paper on the string in such a way that it covered one of the seven letters, and then moved it along each day, you could count off the days of the week: P was Monday, R Tuesday, A Wednesday, and so on. But the worst part was that they wouldn't let you sleep during the day. You would be woken at six a.m. and had to spend the rest of the day sitting on your stool. If you started to doze off the guard would rap on the door: 'No sleeping! Sleeping isn't allowed!'

After that the regime had been gradually relaxed. In 1965 they allowed you to have Pravda, and by 1967 you could lie on your cot during the day and there were calendars in every cell. The cons were also free to buy pencils and exercise-books from the prison shop. And after 1970 you were in clover: you got a ten-pound parcel from home every month. By then it was sheer pleasure doing time in an investigation prison – they even gave you a shave twice a week.

The barber who used to work at Lefortovo was a sergeant-major called Yashka – nobody ever called him anything else, although he was over fifty. Skinny, inevitably sloshed or hung over, and with a huge store of jokes, Yashka would fly into the cell with his inevitable suitcase, swiftly set out his instruments, cracking jokes all the while, and just as speedily start shaving you. It was no joke, shaving a whole prison in one day, you had to look sharp. Conversations with him usually centred around one of two topics: drink (as an expert he was able to give us the latest communiqués from this front) and Stalin. In his youth Yashka had been a member of Stalin's bodyguard and had even received a personal testimonial from him, so he always spoke of him with veneration and invariably called him Uncle. In later years, when prisoners were allowed to handle razors, Yashka no longer shaved us, but simply distributed them and collected them again. This meant that he spent less time in each cell, but he never missed an opportunity for a brief chat.

Despite his sociability, Yashka had always been very careful and never said a loose word. And if there was an informer in the cell, he was always extremely cold. In fact, you could infallibly judge who your cell-mate was by watching Yashka's behaviour. Was he still here, I wondered, or had he perhaps retired? I would love to see how he behaved in the presence of my cell-mates now.

141

# 4

THIS first time in Lefortovo, in 1963, they put me with an informer, of course. His name was Alexander Sinis and he was a brash young man of about twenty-five who had been given eight years for currency offences. They had even written a satirical article about him in the newspaper, which he used to show to everyone as proof of his credentials. He approached me from every possible angle, trying to persuade me to split: it makes no difference, he would say, they know everything anyway, but if you split you won't have to do so much time. I had already heard a thing or two about stool-pigeons from Volpin and the others, so I shot him a line. Every time he came back from being questioned, where they evidently slated him for his poor work, he would dream up some new ruse for getting me to take him into my confidence. At last he said that he was being moved to the Krasnaya Presnya transit prison, where he would be allowed a visit from his wife. He went on at great length about how lax they were at Presnya, what the regulations were and how easy it would be to pass on any request to his wife. Seeing that this didn't interest me either, he openly suggested that I write a note to my friends outside. I gave him some non-existent address and he dashed out with it.

His tricks now strike me as primitive, almost childish, but at the time I was in two minds. Maybe it was just the fellow's nosy character – maybe he was as concerned for other people as he was for himself? And if I held back, it was rather for fear the cell was bugged. Besides, I had been trained since childhood never to say certain things to anybody. Otherwise, who knows, I might have shared my worries with this personable cell-mate.

Stoolies must have existed for as long as there have been prisons.

They have been described in literature hundreds of times and everybody knows about them. But it is one thing to know about them in the abstract, and quite another to believe that this fellow you share your bread with, crack jokes with and talk to, is only pretending to be your friend. It's difficult to live side-by-side with someone for months on end, knowing he is your enemy and concealing your thoughts and emotions from him. After all, there are only two of you, and there's nobody else to talk to. One way or another, they always put investigation prisoners in Lefortovo into a cell with stoolies, and very often it proves effective.

Despite a widely held opinion, stoolies aren't regular KGB employees, but are ordinary prisoners. Having been given a long stretch, usually for currency or other economic offences, they are destined for the labour camp. But at this point the godfather summons them and starts explaining the advantages of working as a stool-pigeon, promising to get them a pardon or a provisional discharge when half their sentence is done, together with an assortment of other favours and privileges. Few of them ever refuse – the advantages are too obvious. They sign a formal certificate of collaboration, and for written communications and reports are assigned a code name.

This agent is then put into a cell with a prisoner under investigation, having first been equipped with a story – a version of his own case that he can tell to his cell-mate. More often than not his story is fashioned to resemble the case of the prisoner being investigated, at least in its general outlines, so as to prepare the ground for sympathy and trust to develop between them. However, according to the regulations for employing such agents, it is forbidden to equip them with a political story.

The stoolie's task isn't necessarily limited to the ferreting out of secrets. He must try to incline his cell-mate to repentance and convince him to make a clean breast of everything to the investigators of his own accord. In addition, he must keep track of his cell-mate's moods, especially when he returns from interrogation, must detect which of the investigators' tricks has had the greatest effect, find out what his cell-mate most fears, what his weaknesses are, and so on. You might think all this is very primitive and crude, but it works. In fact it hardly ever fails with an inexperienced victim.

Beginning in 1961, the KGB had started bringing lots of cases for embezzlement, large-scale bribery, currency operations, and so on. Such cases had led to investigations of factory and State farm directors, government officials and cooperative managers, that is to say a section of the population that had a completely conformist Soviet psychology and was completely unprepared for it. Every single one of them had valuables stashed away somewhere – gold or government bonds. So the KGB's most important task was to locate these treasures. The stoolie would start whispering to his victim: 'Give it up! Why are you hanging on to all that gold? You can't take it with you when they shoot you. Do you think it's *you* they need, with all your deals? Gold is what they need, and precious stones. If you give it up voluntarily they'll let you go, or at the very least give you a shorter sentence.'

More or less the same message came from the investigator. So why not believe them? 'It's true the regime robs us right and left, all it wants to do is squeeze as much as it can out of us.' And it would begin to look to them as if they could bargain with the Soviet regime.

I remember how in 1967 they brought into my cell an elderly man, past sixty, a director of a textile factory. For days on end he would sit motionless on his cot, staring at the same spot, then suddenly leap up, strike his head with his fists and run around the cell, wailing: 'Idiot! What an idiot I am! What have I done!' Gradually I got his story out of him. It turned out that he had just spent nine months in a KGB prison, and for nine months had kept his mouth shut. Practically speaking, there were hardly any charges against him at all, except for trivial things worth two or three years. And his investigation was almost over. But his stoolie whispered that if he gave up his buried treasure, they'd reduce his sentence. And the old fool took his advice and handed in gold and diamonds to the tune of three-and-a-half million roubles. The first thing they did was stick a new charge on him for the illegal possession of valuables, and after that he had to explain where he had got them from. As a result, he not only got fifteen years himself, but sent down nine other men as well.

The story was very typical. The famous Roifman, who was at the centre of the first of the 'textile' trials, also kept his mouth shut, so that not even the stoolies could talk him round. Then he was called in to see Semichastny, the head of the entire KGB, and Malyarov, the Deputy Public Prosecutor, who gave him their sincere Party word that he wouldn't be shot if he gave up his riches. Roifman believed them, handed in his valuables – and was shot.

There were many ridiculous aspects to this form of bargaining. Underground millionaires are reluctant to part with their accumulated riches, but they don't want to lose their lives either, so they start giving up their gold bit by bit, swearing each time that this instalment is the last. But the investigators and the stoolies are perfectly well aware that there is more to come, and they keep up the pressure. 'Listen,' they tell him, 'the October holidays will soon be here, the anniversary of the Revolution. Give us a bit more for the anniversary and they'll probably lop a couple more years off.' So he hands in his gold in instalments – some for 7 November, some for 1 May, then for Constitution Day and maybe even for 8 March (Women's Day). The investigator gets his bonuses, the stoolies early release, and the millionaire – a bullet.

These millionaires are for the most part an unpleasant mercenary bunch, ready to sell their accomplices down the river at the drop of a hat, and it was with them, apart from the stoolies, that I usually ended up sharing a cell (politicals under investigation are not allowed to share a cell, in case they teach one another how to behave). There are, however, some engaging fellows among them. In 1963 I shared a cell for a while with Iosif Lvovich Klempert, the former director of a dye factory. His case was a serious one, running to millions. There had even been a satirical article about him in the newspaper: 'The Arbat Millionaire'. He knew he would be shot, but he wasn't in the least downhearted. 'I've lived my life to the full,' he used to say cheerfully, 'far better than any of them ever could!' One thing bothered him, though. He missed his brandy, especially in the evenings.

The way he had been caught was most instructive. While he was stealing, fixing deals and illicit operations, and filling his pockets, nobody touched him and he got away scotfree. But one day he took it into his head to build a block of flats for his workers – up till then they had lived in barrack huts. It was all because of his pride – why should *my* workers have to live so badly? Officially the state would allow him no money for workers' housing. He pushed and prodded and explored, but it was no use.

'What's the matter with me, I'm not poor, am I?' he thought at last. 'The money's only buried, I can't do anything with it.' And he built a whole block of flats at his own expense – threw up a damned great block good enough even for government workers. 'There you are, enjoy yourselves and remember Iosif Klempert!'

Before the workers could move in, there were inspections and inquiries: where did the money come from, out of which fund? And they nabbed him. Later, during the investigation, his other operations came to light. He put up a firm front, dug in his heels to the last and handed no money over. But after he was sentenced and his appeal for clemency was rejected, he too broke down. He began handing his money over bit by bit, buying himself a month or two of extra life each time. When the money ran out, he recalled all sorts of undiscovered episodes and testified against other people, again buying himself an extra month or two each time. Overall he bought himself two additional years of life, but in the end they shot him just the same. It was not surprising, therefore, that in this bargaining between the KGB and people who had robbed the state, the arguments of the stoolies were hard to resist.

In time I got so used to the stoolies that I began exploiting them for my own ends. If you think about it, they depend more on you than on the KGB. After two or three days I could usually tell if my cell-mate was a stoolie, and if he was, I would give him an ultimatum: either he worked for me or I would denounce him, and he would have as much chance of an early release as of seeing his own ears. Not one single one resisted. Some even owned up of their own accord and themselves proposed that we pull the wool over the KGB's eyes. It was from them that I learned about the KGB's recruiting and work methods, and I usually insisted on them giving me their code name and enlistment date at once. This was to make sure they didn't try to wriggle out of it later.

The result of this operation was that in effect I changed places with the investigators. I knew everything about them, while they learned nothing about me. After all, it was easy to determine which direction the investigation was headed in, and what they knew, from the nature of the questions the stoolie asked. And by misinforming them through him, it was possible to lead them into such a blind alley that they would end up tearing their hair out.

The stoolies I have had through the years – some insolent, some timid, some intelligent, some stupid, some so cunning that you'd never have guessed. On the other hand, I shared a cell in 1967 with a certain Prisovsky, who was so stupid that he couldn't even tell his story properly and got all mixed up. After that he turned bashful and shut up completely, asking no questions and never starting a conversation. I even began to doubt my instinct – maybe he wasn't a stoolie after all, but just shy. It was around then that Semichastny was sacked and Andropov became chairman of the KGB. We read about it in the newspaper and I said to this fellow: 'Well, fancy that, how interesting. I used to know his daughter.'

About a week later my investigator said: 'You used to know Tania Andropov, I hear?' He couldn't contain himself. He was just a petty functionary and here was the boss's own daughter. Maybe there would be changes: a new broom sweeps clean. But I didn't know her at all, I had only heard that Andropov had a daughter.

There was another one in 1971 – I even felt sorry for him. He was completely the wrong man for the job. He wasn't stupid, just inexperienced. This was his first time inside, and all prison life was totally new to him. He slipped up the very first day and fell for the most elementary ruse.

According to his story, he was still under investigation, and he said that he had been in for only two months. But it was obvious that he didn't know the prison at all. All I did was ask him if he had had his fingerprints taken yet. He said yes. They are usually taken during the first week after your arrest. 'And where do they do it now?' I asked. 'Is it still in the same block as the bathhouse?'

'A–ha,' he nodded.

But they had never been taken there, and if he had been an investigation prisoner, he wouldn't have forgotten that fact.

And so I pounced on him. He admitted that he had been in Butyrka prison up till now and had been given seven years for economic offences but was frightened of going to the labour camp. His health was already pretty bad and he was afraid he wouldn't survive. He had lost one leg in the war. He had been head of a construction department. His name was Ivan Ivanovich Trofimov. He blushed and began making excuses, saying that he had never intended to say anything bad about me. For a long time afterwards I played on his guilt: 'How do such things happen, Ivan Ivanovich? You fought at the front, lost a leg – it was much more frightening there, I suppose. I never expected an old soldier like you to agree to become a traitor and inform on his cellmates.'

He would be almost in tears: 'You see,' he said, 'I never thought I'd be capable of it. It's my damned health, I won't survive the camps. I have children. It was only for their sake I agreed. My eldest boy went to the university this year. They threatened to throw him out unless I agreed.'

And it was obvious that he really was ashamed. He did everything I told him – diligently, like a schoolboy. It was not fear that drove him, but conscience, and when we were due to be separated and put into different cells, he beseeched me: 'Rescue me! I'm frightened to refuse – they'll expel my boy and finish me off. You know better than me how to get them to send me to the camps – I can't hold out here!'

Usually I did not reveal to the authorities that I had unmasked their agents – it was not to my advantage to arouse suspicions, and I preferred them to think that I was a simple-hearted, trusting sort of

147

fellow. But I took pity on the old man: I wrote a statement to Andropov and a confidential complaint to the Prosecutor. He was taken off at once, and a week later I established beyond all doubt that he had left Lefortovo. God grant that he survived the camps.

Soon after him I came across the most cunning informer of all the ones I have encountered. He was a man of about forty, powerfully built, energetic, a former officer and paratrooper. He had been kicked out of the army after a brawl and then worked as a volunteer in Kolyma, mining gold. And it was because of this gold that he had been nabbed. He travelled to Moscow on holiday and sold it until he was caught. He was investigated at Butyrka and got five years. It should have been more, but he managed to persuade them that the gold hadn't been stolen from the State mine, but was native gold that he claimed to have stumbled across. He told me that he was already in the camp when they suddenly transported him back to Moscow again – it seemed that new incidents had come to light and he was now threatened with fifteen years, or perhaps even the death penalty. He was a canny customer and I couldn't catch him out at all; none of my favourite tricks worked. But Yashka the barber invariably clammed up when he saw him.

Out of old habit I used to say to him: 'Well, how are you, Yashka? A bit hung over this morning?'

But he simply compressed his lips and looked away: 'To some people I'm Yashka and to others I'm Yakov Mitrich, sir.'

The worst possible sign.

This cunning informer's name was Gritsai. He came from the Ukraine, from the town of Galich. And from the very beginning he made it plain that *he* didn't trust *me*. Naturally, if that was the case, I was supposed to be off my guard – by his reckoning, at least.

When Gritsai arrived, my investigation was virtually over, but the KGB was hoping that after the trial I would grow more talkative and careless. This often happens to people: they think there's nothing more to lose, everything is over. And the KGB was also interested in what I was preparing to do *at* the trial. I didn't let on, of course, that I had guessed what Gritsai was. On the contrary, I pretended to open my heart to him, made him my best friend, and in that way managed to accomplish quite a bit through him.

He was extremely anxious to know why I was so sure that everything that took place in the courtroom would become known abroad. Who would do it? My family? 'What a hope!' I laughed. 'What family? They're so stupid they don't have a clue what's going on.

They'll sit through the trial from start to finish and God help me if they know at the end of it how many years I got. Women – what use are they? But just you see. The KGB's overreached itself and invited two foreign correspondents to the trial as witnesses.'

It worked like a charm: my mother and sister were allowed into the courtroom and the two correspondents were kept out, although they had been called by the KGB itself. There were several more tricks of that sort that I managed to pull off through him.

Just before he left the cell, not long before my own departure for Vladimir, Gritsai announced that his case had been closed – they hadn't been able to pin the new incidents on him and were having to ship him back to the camp again. True enough, a couple of days later he was taken away, but when they took him out they led him not towards the exit but into the prison interior, to another cell. His bosses had made a slip, but they had evidently concluded that it didn't matter any more – I was going away anyway.

A year later, when I was brought back to Lefortovo in connexion with Yakir's case, I accidentally heard the continuation of Gritsai's story.

A huge trial of diamond thieves was underway, involving over forty defendants, and the prison was chock-a-block with them – there was one in just about every cell. At the courthouse they were able to meet during the intervals and exchange a few words. This meant that virtually the entire prison was linked through them. Naturally I used them to find out which of our boys was in which cell, and all of a sudden I stumbled across Gritsai. He was still there, still telling the same story. It turned out that almost all the diamond thieves knew him too – they had almost all shared a cell with him and were filled with admiration.

'What an operator!' they said. 'Getting off charges like that. It would have been curtains for him for sure! Scared the wits out of all the witnesses and then scrammed. Now they've closed the case and he's off to the camp to finish his fiver.'

When I explained that he was a stoolie, they didn't want to believe me at first – he had made an amazing impression on them. But there was no way of reconciling his story with the fact that he had been in Lefortovo as long ago as 1971, and they were reluctantly obliged to agree with me.

The diamond case was by far the biggest at that time and it's no wonder that Gritsai was set on to them. An entire Moscow diamond factory ended up in jail: out of fifty people working there, forty-eight were arrested for stealing diamonds. And they caught masses of buyers as well. It turned out that the KGB had been aware of the stealing for five years or so, but had left everyone alone, hoping to find out who the stones went to, who bought them and where they were hidden. And periodically it raked these hoards in. Maybe the KGB would have gone on shearing these diamond sheep to this very day – it was clean work, but one day Kosygin visited the factory, was photographed with the champion workers and foremen and handed out some sort of awards. At once the KGB pounced – it needed to prove its usefulness, to show you couldn't go anywhere without it. Political calculations, as usual, outweighed economic ones, the gigantic 'diamond case' came into existence and the factory was closed.

The tasks and methods of the KGB have changed little since Stalin's times, but whereas then they needed a plethora of enemies and plotters to scare the people with, they now need the machinations of swindlers and racketeers. The only difference is that there really are racketeers everywhere and there's no need to invent them. The spirit of enterprise is indestructible in man.

You should have seen the fantastic cases that passed through Lefortovo in the 1960s. I used to write their appeal requests for them and they used to give me their sentences to read – some added up to a weighty volume and were neatly bound, like a book. Dozens of pages would be taken up with interminable lists of all the valuables that had been confiscated from them – an infinity of rings, bracelets, diadems, tsarist gold coins, ingots, valuable china, pictures, icons and heaps of gold and diamonds. Whole enterprises would be beavering away – helped by Party committees and socialist competitions – while the profits were siphoned off into the private pockets of deputy ministers and management chiefs. And the opposite also occurred. Entire industrial complexes existed on paper, appeared in the plans and were allocated funds by the State – even the Section for Preventing the Embezzlement of Socialist Property was on their payroll – whereas in actual fact their sites were occupied by virgin Russian forest or an expanse of steppe. Poor old Chichikov with his dead souls was nowhere in it!

Khrushchev wasn't very far from the truth when he said in one of his speeches: 'If people in our country would cease stealing for even a single day, communism could have been built long ago.' But the thing he failed to understand was that, without this stealing, the Soviet economic system wouldn't work at all. Without these rigged figures and manipulations, hardly a single target would be met, and without this private, hence illegal, initiative, nothing at all would be produced in our country. All these collective and State farms that have become showplaces, with turnovers in the millions, wouldn't have survived for one minute if they hadn't been managed by clever swindlers. From the point of view of humanity at large, these millionaires have committed no crimes. Only Soviet justice considers financially rational conduct of the economy to be criminal.

I remember once sharing a cell with a character whose only crime was that of behaving as a normal commercial entrepreneur, doing no harm to anyone. He went to the coalmine and offered to remove their slagheaps for them for a moderate fee. The director was pleased – he had already had several reprimands for those slagheaps – and they were in the way. Then this chap went to some collective farms and offered their chairmen some cheap slag for building their cowbarns. The chairmen were also happy. He next went with the collective-farm trucks and some peasants and removed the slag from the mine. Everyone gained from it, all parties were in raptures and a mass of financial problems was solved at a stroke – and my enterprising comrade got six years in jail for it.

Preoccupied as we were with the problem of intellectual freedom, we didn't notice that the regime was in effect trying to destroy Russia's emergent underground capitalism. This economic 'opposition' had representation at the top among the so-called economists and 'managers'. They had no special theories, and all their proposals could be reduced to one simple thought: if the economy was to grow, you had to pay people real money for their labour, and not tie down the economic initiative of the managerial personnel. Even from the point of view of Marxism, economics should come first, not ideology.

By the early 1960s it was obvious that the economy was disintegrating, and people thought seriously about the possibility of a new NEP. They could see that at the very least it was essential to introduce wide economic reforms and greater incentives. A number of interesting new industrial experiments were carried out, and these were written up ecstatically in the newspapers. The early euphoria passed, however, for the experiments illustrated all too clearly the superiority of the capitalist method over socialist methods of running the economy. It was clear that if they were extended countrywide, although they would lead to rapid economic growth, they would also restore all those 'ulcers' of capitalism that Soviet propaganda so loved to frighten us with: unemployment, inflation and 'production anarchy'. That is to say, it would be a market economy, and the State would no longer be able to maintain its control over economic life. More importantly, it would render the Party's control of the economy both superfluous and impossible.

Naturally this led to a submerged but desperate struggle between the 'economists' and the 'ideologists'. The ideologists' chief ploy was to paint a picture of the universal pillage and plunder that was in store for us, with the economy out of control. Losing control of economic life, the Party would lose control of the country's life as a whole. The economists' plans, in fact, excluded the leading role of the Party, but they couldn't say this openly. This muffled war was fought out between the Party and State bureaucracies beneath the banner of the economic reforms, whose necessity was acknowledged by all. Even Brezhnev, in his confidential letter to the Central Committee in December 1969, admitted the desperate position of Soviet industry.

It was this struggle that necessitated the economic trials – the new equivalent of the terror of the 1930s. We know that in the short period between November 1962 and July 1963 over eighty economic trials took place in dozens of cities of the Soviet Union, resulting in 163 death sentences. It is amazing that the West, with all its Sovietological institutes, completely misread the meaning of these trials. And it is laughable to recall the protest made by Bertrand Russell, who saw nothing but anti-semitism in the sentences. It would make as much sense to see only anti-semitism in the persecution of the Trotskyist opposition.

Judicial repression alone, of course, would not have been enough to secure victory for the ideologists – the decisive stroke came from the West. As an alternative to broad internal reforms, the ideologists proposed a plan of 'peaceful advance', or détente. They gambled on receiving extensive economic aid and a trade boost from the West. Why introduce dangerous reforms if you can get what you want in a package from abroad? Wheat could be sown in Kazakhstan and harvested in Canada.

Symbolic of all this was the fate of Ivan Nikiforovich Khudenko, a senior financial adviser working for the Council of Ministers of the USSR, with the rank of deputy minister, who in 1960 volunteered to carry out an economic experiment in the State farms of Kazakhstan. Khudenko's proposals were extremely simple – a system of complete self-financing and financial autonomy with, above all, a realistic scheme of material incentives. Payments were made for achieved results, and not for the effort expended. The experiment was fantastically successful: the employment of men and machines was reduced by a factor of ten to twelve, the cost price of grain by four; the productivity of each worker was increased sevenfold and his salary fourfold. Khudenko had demonstrated that the introduction of his system into Russia's agriculture would enable production to be quadrupled while the number of people employed in agriculture could be reduced from thirty million to five.

Enthusiastic newspaper articles and films appeared about Khudenko's experiment, but nobody seemed in a hurry to apply his system, and in 1970 his State farm, Akchi, was closed down at the height of the season: the farmworkers were neither paid any wages nor recompensed for the money they had invested in advance. Khudenko and his workmen turned to the law and carried their struggle into the courts, where the case's ups and downs reflected the struggle going on in the Soviet leadership. Court decisions were several times annulled in favour of new ones. Certain organs of the press continued to write about the valuable nature of the experiment, but in August 1973, Khudenko and his deputy were convicted of 'sequestering State property' and sentenced to six and four years respectively. Some of Russia's chief financial experts continued to protest against the sentences even after the trial had ended, but on 12 November 1973, Khudenko died in a prison hospital.

This was far from the only instance of judicial suppression of the new economic tendencies. The mid-1960s had seen a phenomenal rise throughout the country of what were known as 'Torch' clubs – voluntary associations of technicians and engineers who carried out commissions for technical projects, the introduction of new technology, and the rationalisation of existing systems. Engineers and research workers who could not carry out these projects on salary for their institutes and offices during the day, were able to do so splendidly and with record speed in their free time, on their own initiative, unhampered by Party and union committees and in return for a decent fee, and in doing so provided the state with a profit of many millions of roubles. But during the 1970s, when détente was in full swing and Russia was importing Western technology and capital, every one of these clubs was closed down and their leaders clapped in jail.

These trials in the 1970s would not have gone so smoothly had there not been a psychological preparation in the form of the earlier trials of the underground millionaires. The State had shown it would take the economic management of the country in hand, intimidate people with reprisals, and expose the ugly, predatory essence of this burgeoning capitalism. It also sounded convincing to the broad masses: 'If everybody stopped stealing even for a single day, we could long since have built communism!' Aha, there's the enemy – stop that thief!

But they succeeded in crushing the opposition and by the mid-1970s the propaganda trials of the embezzlers had come to an end, as if everyone in Russia had stopped stealing. The trials were no longer needed. They even allowed a polemic to appear in the *Literary Gazette* on the problems of economics and law. Academicians, Heroes of Socialist Labour, factory directors and leading economists wrote that the economic laws and regulations were so chaotic and contradictory that in practice, every single one of them was committing a crime every day. And since it no longer had any political significance, even Brezhnev had his say, too, promising to improve the chaos of economic laws and regulations.

What didn't end, though, was the eternal war between the citizenry and the authorities. The moment people devised a means of augmenting their niggardly incomes, the State pronounced this means outside the law. If a man buys a car, you might be forgiven for thinking that it's nobody's business but his own. But no, round come the police – where did he get the money from? But it doesn't even need to be a car. Go to a restaurant too often and you also get yourself noticed. The swine know that the ordinary Soviet citizen doesn't earn enough to buy a car or eat out in restaurants.

Every summer the walls are repainted at Lefortovo prison. In 1963 they were dark green, in 1967 olive green, in 1971 grey-green, and now you can't make out what colour they are. And if you were to remove the time strata layer by layer, like paint, you would uncover the great edifice of socialism, and expose the petrified remains of all the creatures it was considered necessary to eliminate in each period. When I first saw Lefortovo in 1963, I was astonished to find only two storeys out of four occupied, and the other two empty. No more than about eighty cells were in use. Each contained two or three prisoners, so there couldn't have been more than about two hundred there in all, and a half of these were stool pigeons. Did the KGB really need to arrest so few to maintain the Soviet Union in a state of fear? Then I realised that that probably *was* all that was needed. Imagine that Hitler had stayed in power not for thirteen, but for dozens and dozens of years. Would he then have needed the gas ovens? Who would he have needed to burn? Lefortovo alone would have been sufficient for him, provided he used his head.

But then, of course, I couldn't know all the details of how this machine worked. My prison career was only just beginning, and in any case I didn't stay for long – soon I was sent for psychiatric examination at the Serbsky Institute. My case wasn't acquiring any shape, my artists weren't able to compose a clear picture, not even with the help of their stoolie. Hence the asylum.

It is ridiculous to think now of how pleased I was then when I learned that I had been pronounced unfit to stand trial. I had already heard a great deal from Alik Volpin and others about the Leningrad Special Mental Hospital on the Arsenal Embankment, and by all accounts it was a better place than a concentration camp. You weren't driven out to work, you were fed somewhat better than in the camps, nobody tried to treat you, there were no punishment cells, you could sleep during the day, you had a visit once a month, and you could even get books from home. Alik told us that during his time the patients were almost all politicals and completely normal. He had introduced me to many of his fellow-inmates in 1961, and they all said the same.

In Stalin's time it was regarded as a virtual salvation to be sent to a mental hospital instead of the camps, and some psychiatrists saved people's lives that way. It was true that you were always required to recant, to admit your guilt and to agree with the diagnosis. And eventually you had to admit that thanks to your stay in hospital your condition had improved. Without such an admission the doctors would have had no way of signing you out or the court of releasing you – there was nothing to show that the patient was no longer dangerous. But in Stalin's time this didn't bother people much: the authorities could squeeze much worse out of you by interrogation.

To resist openly was considered highly dangerous – they might classify you as chronically insane and dispatch you to Sychovka, a colony for chronic madmen, from which no one ever emerged. Apart from Sychovka, there were only three prison mental hospitals in the country: in Leningrad, Kazan and Rybinsk. This last was for people who went mad in the camps.

Shortly before my arrest in 1963, Khrushchev declared somewhere that the USSR no longer had any political prisoners and that no one was dissatisfied with the system – the few who still expressed dissatisfaction were simply mentally ill. Not many people took his words seriously at the time – this wasn't the only rubbish he was continually spouting. But this was not the premier's little joke, it was a directive, and it signified a major turn in punitive policy. Khrushchev seriously intended to build communism, and that meant: the church must disappear completely; there must be a return to ideological unanimity; material abundance must come about of itself, with no particular expenditure; criminality must disappear; and the State must gradually wither away. But the problem of criminality was a major snag. Not only was it not diminishing, it was on the increase. As for unanimity, there was not much to be said about that: recent risings in Alexandrov, Murom and Novocherkassk spoke for themselves. The intelligentsia, too, was getting out of hand. So what could Khrushchev do? Having denounced Stalin's crimes, he was in no position to return to the methods of the terror, to have show trials and mass arrests. At the same time, he had a pathological fear of that thaw which, by an irony of history, still bears his name. Party discipline was disintegrating and some sort of neo-Marxists had made their appearance.

Khrushchev figured that it was impossible for people in a socialist society to have an anti-socialist consciousness. Consciousness is determined by existence, and criminality was a logical impossibility in a society overflowing with maize. Just try putting on a show trial, however, and you'd never hear the end of it. Anyway, how could you organise such things without using torture? Khrushchev had no intention, and no means, of bringing back Stalinism in full measure. Everybody knew where it would end. The conclusion that suggested itself was a model of simplicity: wherever manifestations of dissidence couldn't be explained away as a legacy of the past or as a provocation by world imperialism, they were simply the product of mental illness, which, as is well known, is something that a communist existence alone cannot cure.

Soon they were explaining to law students that theirs was a dying profession, and the law faculties began to limit enrolment; the State would no longer need their services and their work would be taken over partly by citizens' courts and partly by psychiatrists. Here and there they even closed some prisons – a legacy from the dark ages of the tsars – while special psychiatric hospitals began to spring up like mushrooms. On churches the Central Committee passed a special decree – they were all to be demolished within ten years. The intelligentsia was brought into line by a plenary session on ideology. The KGB was told to abandon Stalin's thesis on the intensification of the class struggle and was given a new ideological directive on the intensification of psychiatric illnesses as progress was made towards the building of communism.

The KGB had its own difficulties. At all times, and of course especially at the very height of Stalin's illegalities, the arrested had been made to confess their guilt, repent, lay down their ideological weapons, and condemn their mistakes. At that time it had been relatively easy to accomplish – with beatings, all-night interrogations and torture. But now the security men found themselves in the period of post-Stalinist humanism and they were no longer allowed to beat and torture the people they were investigating. And if the KGB investigators weren't able to frighten, cajole or in some way blackmail the prisoner, it would appear that they weren't up to their job, couldn't persuade the prisoner to lay down his ideological weapons. Two or three such failures were enough to get you thrown out of the KGB for incompetence. The numerical demand also changed: whereas at one time the idea was to grab as many counter-revolutionaries, spies, saboteurs and other enemies of the people as possible, now every such case was regarded by the higher echelons as an instance of failure to re-educate the masses. It would be quite a different matter, however, if the prisoner were a madman – in that case no one would be to blame.

If everything had gone according to the Party's overall plan, crime would have disappeared completely, and in place of the mass terror, spy-mania and other mistakes of the personality cult, we would all have been looking apprehensively at one another to see who was a loony and who wasn't. Tens of millions of temporarily sick citizens, including certain members of the Politburo, after a brief course of treatment, would have rejoined the healthy ranks of the builders of socialism. And who knows, we might perhaps have seen the time when two-thirds of some Twenty-seventh Party Congress had to be treated for mental illness.

For the time being, everyone was satisfied – the KGB, the Party bosses, Khrushchev, the psychiatrists and the dissidents. A few dozen individuals – almost everyone arrested around that time on political charges – turned out to be lunatics, and they were all delighted: we won't be sent to the camps! True, there were a few exceptions. A man called Kovalsky, himself a clinical psychiatrist from Murmansk who had been arrested for anti-Soviet propaganda – like most of us – wasn't in the least pleased. 'Fools,' he said, 'what are you feeling so relieved about? You haven't the slightest idea what a psychiatric hospital is like.'

Perhaps to demonstrate the truth of his observation, or else simply to amuse himself, he tried to prove to us that we really were crazy: first, because we had come into conflict with society, whereas a normal person adapts to society; and secondly, because we had risked our freedom for the sake of stupid ideas, neglecting the interests of our families and careers. 'This,' he explained, 'is called an obsession with self, the first sign of a paranoidal development of the personality.'

'But what about you? You're a lunatic yourself,' we replied.

'Yes, of course I am,' he agreed cheerfully, 'only I'm already aware of it and therefore half-cured, while you aren't and therefore still have to be treated.'

I saw my principal doctor just a couple of times, no more, and she said more or less the same thing. And so did the specialists on the panel of doctors that was called to examine me and pronounce on my case. They asked me all the same questions: why was I in conflict with society and with its accepted norms, why did my beliefs seem of overwhelming importance to me – more important than my liberty, my studies or my mother's peace of mind? For instance, I persisted in going to Mayakovsky Square. Yet I knew it was forbidden, I had been warned. Why did I continue going there? Why didn't I keep to the university?

In fact, it was by no means easy to answer their questions. If I said that society was to blame for my conflict with it, it emerged that everyone around me was wrong, and I alone in the right. Clearly I would sound like a madman. And what could I say about my beliefs? One of the boys quoted Lenin, who had also been in conflict with society and had been exiled to Siberia for his beliefs. But all you got as a result of that kind of tactic was a note in your case history: 'Suffering from delusions of grandeur, compares self with Lenin.' No matter which way you turned, normal, sincere answers merely supplied further evidence of your sickness. And if you dared mention persecution by the KGB, a persecution complex was unavoidable. Even when they ended by asking me whether I considered myself to be ill, my negative answer proved nothing: what madman regards himself as mad?

We also helped the doctors without realising it. After so many months of prison-cell life, it was pure joy to meet so many fellow-spirits all at once, from all over the country, and to exchange names, anecdotes and jokes. Everyone in our political isolation ward in section 4 of the Serbsky Institute talked about his case, his friends and his plans, and at first we did not realise that the old women attendants were taking it all in and relaying it to the doctors. For example, I told the boys all about a book on palmistry that I had read just before my arrest, and later I learned that this had been incorporated into my case as yet another symptom of illness. Another man, Sergei Klimov, went on hunger strike for reasons best-known to himself. For several days they refused to isolate him and he was obliged to lie in the same cell where we all had our meals. Finally we lost our tempers and announced a similar hunger strike by the whole lot of us, demanding that he be isolated and saved from the torment of watching us eat. This hunger strike, too, turned up as a symptom in our dossiers.

But we weren't in the least afraid of being called lunatics – on the contrary, we were delighted: let these idiots think we're loonies if they like, or rather, let these loonies think we're idiots. We recalled all the stories about madmen by Chekhov, Gogol, Akutagawa, and of course *The Good Soldier Schweik*. We laughed our heads off at our doctors and ourselves.

It is interesting to note that at this time a number of people charged with economic crimes were also examined by the panel of psychiatric experts, but none of them was pronounced mad.

In early autumn our entire company of political loonies was transferred back to Lefortovo, and it was then that we got our first unpleasant shock: they had no intention of actually allowing us in court – we had all been tried *in absentia*. My hopes of meeting my judges face-to-face collapsed. I had not been intending to justify myself – my aim had been to accuse. And I had been planning to do it in such a way that this trial would have cost them dear. Now it turned out that they had got away scotfree with punishing me again.

I learned all this only from my mother, who was allowed to visit me in September 1963. It was a very brief visit, lasting only an hour – and this in the presence of a guard who kept interrupting us. We were brought to a room with a wide table running down the middle; I sat on one side, my mother on the other. Passing things or even touching was strictly forbidden. Mother was intimidated by these circumstances and could barely bring herself to speak at all. I made an effort to comfort her as best I could. But I was literally writhing with impotent rage. According to law, my trial should have been a proper one, with the witnesses questioned and the evidence examined, but the procedure in fact had occupied less than an hour, she told me. The charges were read out, followed by the conclusions of the panel of experts, and a resolution was passed obliging me to undergo compulsory medical treatment for an indefinite period.

Thus I was officially recognised as sick, not responsible for my actions. Still, no one seemed in any hurry to send me to a hospital – all of us remained incarcerated in Lefortovo, where they told us they had no orders to send us for treatment yet, and anyway there were no beds free. Only in December did they send us away – some to Leningrad, some to Kazan. It is a very painful moment in prison – parting from people who have become your friends. Who knows if you will ever see them again?

They brought us to Leningrad early one evening and shepherded us straight to the bathhouse at the Special Mental Hospital. There the first thing the orderlies did was to crop not only our heads, but also our armpits and crotches – all with the same clippers. Sergei Klimov made as if to resist when they went for his magnificent new moustache. 'Change the clippers at least!' What a hope. The moustache came off. They twisted his arms behind his back and thumped him in the ribs: behave yourself!

We could see the situation was bad. The orderlies were criminal convicts who had been sent here to do time as hospital attendants instead of going to the camps. They were like savage dogs, and here they had people to brutalise with impunity.

We were given the usual convicts' garb to put on, our things were taken away from us, and we were led to our cells in groups of three. The drill here was to place all new arrivals in block 1 to begin with, the observation section. Once upon a time, until 1948, this had been an ordinary prison. The buildings were old, and the damp, cold cells were ordinary ones, like in Lefortovo, with a peephole and food flap and bars over the windows. Only there was no toilet, not even a latrine bucket: mental patients weren't allowed to have heavy objects around. To relieve yourself you had to hammer on the door and ask the guard to take you to the communal toilet at the end of the corridor. But he never had any time, and never felt like it.

'What's all that knocking for?' he would bellow from afar.

'I need the toilet!'

'You can wait!' What does he mean, wait? You start hammering again. 'I'll teach you to keep knocking like that! I'll break every bone in your body!'

'But I have to go to the toilet, officer. I can't wait any longer!'

'Piss on the floor!'

And so on all day. If you pushed him too far, he would set the orderlies on you and you would wish you'd never asked.

The next morning, one of my cell-mates started yelling slogans the moment he opened his eyes: 'Enough of this Bolshevik slavery! Liberty and an amnesty for the people! We need to organise a free, independent and autonomous Ukrainian State! Give the people their national costume!' He went on yelling like this all day long, without pause, until lights out. I learned that he had done seventeen years in

Vladimir prison for Ukrainian 'bourgeois nationalism' and had gone mad there. Here he was ruthlessly beaten – the guards were sick of listening to his slogans. Every day they would unlock the door, and half a dozen orderlies would pounce on him like wild dogs. The first day I made an effort to go to his assistance, but was punched so hard that I was sent flying under the bed and was barely able to crawl out again. There was no way in which I could help him. Yet I could not stand by in silence and watch him being beaten black and blue.

Our other cell-mate took no interest in anything and merely sat there with a blissful smile on his face. He was in for murdering his children and had a mania for swallowing things. Immediately after murdering his children he had cut off his ears and eaten them. In the hospital he had already swallowed a set of chessmen, and they dared not give him even a spoon.

For a time I thought I would never leave the cell alive. Every time the orderlies burst in to beat my Ukrainian cell-mate, I insisted, like a fool, on trying to stop them, and naturally got a helping as well. According to regulations, the nurses were supposed to write up an observation record for each patient. With this man, in order to explain the bruises, scratches and other marks, they wrote that he had 'become violent' and himself attacked the orderlies. Seeing this note in the record, the doctor would then prescribe injections of sulphazine or aminazine for the patient. And when my cell-mate attempted to resist the injections, he was beaten up again. Of course, neither the beatings nor the injections could change him in any way, so he kept on yelling his slogans, growing gradually quieter and quieter, day by day, as if fading away. As for me, the danger was that my interventions would take me into that vicious circle too, from which I would never be able to escape.

The true masters in the psychiatric hospital are the junior service personnel: the orderlies, the nurses and the guards, who together form a sort of clan. If you don't come to terms with them, they will kill you or torture you. The first two months in the hospital are the most important. You establish a reputation which is hard to change. The nurses are too lazy to observe the patients properly, they write approximately the same thing each day, copying their earlier notes. Yet the doctors never meddle in this area and rely entirely on what the nurses tell them.

I don't know how I would have ended up if they hadn't transferred me to another cell. Apparently even the orderlies were fed up with me interfering. But there was another reason as well. I suddenly received a letter from my mother, in which she wrote that she would be coming to visit me in just a few days. Handing me the letter, the nurse unexpectedly smiled a kindly smile: who was my mother, where did she work, who was my father, she asked, and so on. Now the usual procedure in hospital is for letters to be read by the doctors and then passed on unsealed, but it was clear from her questions that she too had read the letter. I immediately realised what the position was: I had long known that to people not living in Moscow, every Muscovite is virtually a member of the government, for it seems to outsiders that we are all living there cheek by jowl and can do anything we want. (When I was in Siberia, I needed only to tell the locals I was from Moscow for them to look at me with a mixture of apprehension and inexplicable admiration, as if I was Gogol's inspector-general.)

Two more murderers shared my new cell with me. One, a fat man of about fifty, had killed his mother and suffered from laughing fits. He began with a grin, followed by a series of short giggles which would gradually gather momentum until he could no longer stop himself. His face turned purple, his eyes bulged from their sockets, he gasped for breath, choked, and the whole of his bulky body shook with irrepressible laughter. Between attacks, he would lie silently on his cot, never speaking to anybody and never replying to questions. He fixed me with his spiteful, watering eyes, and then, as if having spied something unbearably funny in me, he would launch into peals of hysterical laughter again, gradually working himself up into a near fit. The other man, whose name was Kostya, had killed his wife and had attempted to stab himself as well. There was a broad red scar on the left side of his chest. This Kostya tormented me with stories about how his wife had deceived him and how he had discovered and hounded her – it was impossible to tell what was true and what was fantasy. If anything, the stories were worse than the slogans and the laughter.

Around the cell there was a constant clamour of shouting on all sides. The prison was so poorly constructed that you could hear when somebody was being beaten up, even on the other floors. In a cell opposite ours a young fellow would keep yelling intermittently: 'Soviet spacemen will be the first to land on the moon! Soviet spacemen will be the first to land on the moon!' His cell-mates were evidently teasing him, because his yells grew louder and louder, until finally the orderlies burst in and beat him up. It turned out to be true that every time he shouted his tiresome prophecy, his cell-mates would answer *sotto voce*: 'American!...', which provoked him to absolute frenzy, but the nurses just kept noting that he was 'violent', and he was mercilessly pumped full of aminazine. Towards the end of my stay in that section, I met him during one of our exercise periods. He was sullenly skulking along the fence and there was so much disillusionment, and so much disdain for mankind in his expression, that I couldn't resist asking him: 'Well, whose spacemen are going to be first on the moon?'

'The Americans,' he muttered with great reluctance, looking away from me.

Once a day we were allowed out for exercise – everyone from all of block 1. A dreadful crowd of madmen in tattered clothing, in ragged caps and reefer jackets, and wearing the boots that were issued just before we exercised, spilled out into the special yard enclosed by a high fence. Most of the prisoners were murderers; no more than ten per cent were politicals.

My Lefortovo friends were dejected; not a trace remained of that joyfulness with which we had greeted the news that we were lunatics. In fact, the Leningrad Special Hospital was just an ordinary prison with detention cells, bars on the windows, barbed wire, a high wall, armed guards, and where the 'patients' had restricted rights to correspondence and food parcels. (Theoretically the guards weren't supposed to shoot at a mental patient trying to escape. But how were they to tell a patient from one of the crooks working as orderlies? Naturally, the safest thing was to shoot, and that had already happened on some occasions.) Added to all the usual prison worries were the worries specific to psychiatric detention – indefinite confinement, compulsory treatment, beatings and the total lack of any rights. There was also no one to complain to, for every complaint got lodged in your case history as yet one more proof of your insanity. None of us were sure if he would ever leave there alive. Some of our fellows were already in trouble – they had had injections and others were getting pills. It was no simple matter to prove that you were sane, or at least on the road to recovery. What doctor wanted to overturn his colleagues' diagnosis or take responsibility for discharging you? It was far easier to go along with things. It was well-known that although, formally speaking, our de- tention was supposed to be indefinite, in practice murderers were usually held for five or six years and our sort for two or three – that is, if you submitted completely, were involved in no conflicts and had no bad reports on your observation record.

A central commission of psychiatrists came about twice a year from Moscow and was shown all the patients. But it could discharge patients only if this were recommended by the hospital, and in certain instances the recommendation was ignored. To get a discharge the doctors bluntly demanded that you acknowledge your sickness and condemn your previous behaviour. This they called 'criticism', a critical attitude to the symptoms of your illness, which served as proof of your recovery.

Among the patients, there was one, Nikolai Nikolayevich Samsonov, a geophysicist and winner of a Stalin Prize, who categorically refused to undertake this 'criticism' and had now been in for eight years. He had been put away in 1956 for sending a letter to the Central Committee demanding a more consistent exposure of Stalin's crimes. They tried everything they could – injections, beatings, putting him in a cell with violent patients – and had irrevocably undermined his health.

On the whole there were three main 'remedies for violence' – that is to say, punishments. The first was the injection of aminazine, which made the patient fall into a permanent doze or stupor and cease to be aware of his surroundings. The second was sulphazine or sulphur. This remedy inflicted excruciating pain on the patient and induced a high fever for two or three days. The third remedy, the 'roll-up', was considered the worst of all. For some sorts of offence a prisoner would be tightly wrapped from feet to armpits in a wet sheet or strips of canvas. As the material dried out, it shrank, inflicting terrible pain on the prisoner and scorching his body all over. Usually the prisoner would quickly lose consciousness, and it was the nurses' job to keep a watch on him. Once he was unconscious, they would loosen the roll-up slightly to give him a chance to breathe and come round, and then tighten it again. This would be repeated several times.

In view of the open tyranny and terror that reigned unchecked in the hospital, our total lack of rights, and the unbridled sway of the orderlies, we were skirting the edge of an abyss. Two of the boys sharing a cell started wrestling out of sheer boredom. One of them turned awkwardly, cutting his temple on the radiator, and asked one of the nurses for some iodine. She at once wrote into their observation records that they had grown violent, and they were both given sulphur injections. You had to be on your guard every minute of the day, and somehow stay on good terms with the attendants and nurses.

On the top floor of block 1 were the padded cells where the violently insane were prevented from banging their brains out against the wall. Patients there were stripped naked and kept in solitary confinement, and it was said that they were also beaten without quarter. One inmate had been killed there quite recently – they had broken his back. Another died in the roll-up – they didn't loosen it in time. No culprits were ever brought to account, of course, and the dead men were simply 'booked out'.

Block 2 was supposed to be for medical treatment, but in fact the treatment was the same everywhere. True, there were also special wards in block 2 for the administration of insulin shock treatment. And section 7 was the stamping ground of the ferocious medical assistant, Victor Valeryanich. He was an out-and-out sadist and was badly upset if no one was wrapped in a roll-up during his shift. One of our crowd, Anatoly Belyayev, sentenced for telling jokes about Khrushchev, somehow got engrossed in his reading one night and didn't notice the call for lights out. For this, Valeryanich put him into a roll-up – and, naturally, noted in his record that he had been violent.

On the whole, however, Valeryanich was an exception. The prevailing atmosphere was one of apathy, indifference and cynicism. Just as a surgeon is not disturbed by the sight of blood or a mortuary attendant by corpses, so the nurses, orderlies and doctors were inured to cruelty. It went without saying that the patient was not human, that he couldn't and shouldn't have any desires or human feelings; and a few of the doctors frankly called the hospital 'our little Auschwitz'.

The threat of punishment hung over each of us constantly. At the slightest provocation the orderlies and guards would yell sadistically: 'What? Do you want the roll-up? A dose of sulphur?' And if aminazine injections were once prescribed for you, they continued automatically, and the time to stop was forgotten. They injected on such a mass scale that after a while the needle would no longer go into your buttocks. One day I was taken to the physiotherapy room to get some heat treatment for my tonsils – the damp Leningrad climate had worsened my chronic tonsillitis and I was running a temperature. There I was confronted by a fantastic spectacle: lying face-down on trestle beds was a row of men with their naked backsides exposed to special heat lamps. They had been injected so often with aminazine that the needles no longer penetrated their muscles, and it was necessary to soften them up to get them to absorb the infiltrates so that the 'treatment' could be started again.

When a sane man finds himself in such a place his first thought is to set himself off from the mental patients, to stand apart and convince himself and others that he at least is different. A small group of sane men were to be found in every section, making up a sort of 'club' of normal people in the midst of this sea of madness. Their attitude to their insane fellow-inmates was usually every bit as hostile as that of Valeryanich, and they were often even crueller to them than the orderlies, as if to underline their superiority and sanity. Savage jokes and mockery at the expense of the madmen became almost a necessity. In a large ten-man cell in block 2 there was a young fellow of about nineteen called Sapronovich. He was obsessed with the idea that he had to destroy the entire Western world, especially America. He was constantly pressing imaginary buttons to launch rockets with atom bombs. 'We've got to blow up America! Destroy them! Kill Kennedy!' he used to shout, pressing his buttons. For some reason he particularly hated Kennedy.

'Sapronovich!' the sane inmates used to say. 'Come over here! Look, here's a real button, press that!' And they showed him the button by the door used for summoning the orderlies and guards. Gradually they got him so accustomed to the button that he used to stand there pressing it for days and days on end. The orderlies quickly tired of answering these false signals and would often beat him up, give him injections or put him into the roll-up, but nothing helped.

That autumn Kennedy was assassinated. Sapronovich's persecutors couldn't miss such a magnificent opportunity to make fun of him. They brought him the newspaper with the news. 'Hey, Sapronovich, you've done it now. You thought it was just a joke, didn't you, pressing all those buttons? Now look – they haven't found the murderer yet, they're hunting for him, but you won't be able to hide here very long, you know. They'll find you. Everybody knows about those buttons you were pressing.'

Sapronovich was terrified and stunned. For a whole week he lay on his bed with his head buried under the blanket. He didn't even get up to eat – he was afraid to look out. But the end result of all this was quite unexpected: he began to recover and stopped pressing his buttons.

Occasionally it happened the other way round, and someone inside the small circle of the 'normal' suddenly broke down and began raving, talking to himself and behaving strangely. Whether it was the end of some temporary improvement or whether he had really gone out of his mind, the effect on the rest of us was traumatic. Just a few days ago you had been able to talk to him, sharing your hopes for release and laughing together at the 'loonies', but now he himself was indistinguishable from them. It erased more of the borderline between us and them, between the normal and the abnormal, and this was the worst betrayal of all. That was why, after a while, you grew preternaturally suspicious and spent much of your time covertly examining your neighbours to see whether their behaviour was entirely normal, or whether they were displaying just a superficial propriety or a temporary improvement. Were they not perhaps concealing their madness?

It sometimes happened that you could find no one in your entire cell to have a game of dominoes with or speak frankly to. And then you were no longer sure who was mad and who wasn't: me or them? Even the orderlies began to seem like angels. Who knew where the borderline lay? Who would tip me off when *that* had begun? I would wake to these grey Leningrad mornings, wander aimlessly round the cell, listen for hours to the hoarse voice of some maniac moaning in the cell opposite; I would go out once a day into the exercise yard among this crowd of tattered madmen and wander up and down the fence. What would change? The colours, sounds, smells? Would the fence grow whiter or the sky darker? Perhaps it had already begun? Perhaps that was me hoarsely groaning, and the sound only seemed to be coming from the cell opposite? Me sitting on the bed, rocking back and forth, clutching my head in my hands and groaning. We always see our own actions as so logical and justified. But how could I find out, whom could I ask?

In an attempt to shut myself off from everything going on around me I concentrated on my English books. All day long, from reveille to lights out, I picked my way through the word jungles of Dickens or Fenimore Cooper, trying not to look around me, trying not to listen, and living the imaginary life of the books' heroes. After about a month of this I was horrified to discover that I had begun to think in English. I even found Russian difficult to speak, and when my mother came on a visit, I caught myself translating from English to Russian before I answered her. Here it was, it was beginning! My blood ran cold. I think our greatest fear was that by the time our release came, if ever it did, we would be past caring and would no longer be aware of the difference between freedom and captivity.

One young fellow in our cell was a former Intourist interpreter by the name of Karaulov. Externally he was entirely proper and the uninitiated would have taken him for normal. But he had one eccentricity: he was frightened that someone would eat him. Whether this was because he thought his flesh was particularly tasty or whether for some other reason, I don't know, but it only needed someone to stare at him for him to cringe and try to move nearer the door. Naturally, they used to make fun of him whenever they could. In the evening someone would say in a loud voice, addressing his friends so that everyone could hear:

'Boys, has anyone got any salt?'

'Yes, I've got a bit. What do you want it for?' replied his friends, playing up to him. Karaulov would literally freeze with horror and only his eyes would dart from side to side, looking for a means of escape.

'Got a knife?' continued his tormentors unsparingly.

At this point Karaulov could stand it no longer and with a wild animal-like scream would leap to the door and ring for the orderlies to come. He stayed in there for about three years and in the end seemed to be more or less cured, so they discharged him. Many years later I accidentally bumped into him in Gorky Street in Moscow. Outwardly he seemed completely normal and I grew curious to know if he remembered his former phobia. After several minutes' conversation I suddenly said: 'Well, Karaulov, are you still afraid that somebody will eat you?' His eyes immediately rolled anxiously from side to side. 'What,' I said, 'even here, in the middle of Moscow?' 'Who the devil knows?' he muttered and dashed into the crowd.

I have met desperate men ready to risk their lives for a trifle, but never one who was prepared to risk his sanity. Any man would, I think, prefer death. It was well understood that we all had one way out in reserve, and there had to be no chance of us finding a piece of metal or glass in the exercise yard. We weren't even allowed to have matches. Our towels had to be hung over the back of our cots at night so that they could be seen through the peephole. You weren't allowed to cover your head in bed, and you had to sleep with your arms outside the blankets. And the duty orderlies looked regularly into your cell. But there was one *method* they didn't know of, a *method* we used to tell one another about in a whisper. This was one right that we wanted to keep for ourselves.

To try and escape was hopeless – we were too closely watched. Orderlies, guards, nurses and doctors – all of them watched us and one another. I did all I could to dissuade one particular fellow, but it was impossible to stop him: the following day they were due to start treating him. The result was a matter of indifference to him, there was no other way out. And then I told him about the *method*, in case he was caught.

They say he miscalculated when he jumped from the wall: he had counted on landing on a passing truck, but he missed. We heard three shots being fired, one after the other, but the guards either missed or fired into the air, then they raced round the cells, counting everyone.

He was brought back and locked in a cell in block 1. They beat him endlessly, then put him in a 'roll-up', then kept him for a month on sulphur injections. It was two months before I accidentally ran into him again, on my way to meet a visitor, and I had difficulty recognising him: a skinny, sallow old man with feverishly gleaming, sunken eyes.

He didn't recognise me and I passed by. I doubt whether he remembered the subject of our conversation.

A man gets used to everything and gradually grows a sort of thick, insensitive skin. You have to learn not to see anything around you and not to think about home or expect release, to adapt yourself to this life in such a way that it passes over you without, as it were, touching you. Everything taking place around you becomes unreal, like a play, and is at once forgotten. Gradually I managed to develop this detachment. There was only one thing I couldn't get used to. In the evenings you could hear the tyres of the Leningrad trolley-buses swishing by on the other side of the wall, and for me this sound was like being tortured with electric shocks – everything around me stood out with excruciating clarity and solidity. No, not every kind of life is better than death.

I had no need to resort to the *method*. I was very lucky: I wasn't given a single pill or injection the whole year I was in the Leningrad Hospital. Soon I was transferred to section 10, the best, where they even unlocked the cells during the day and you could walk along the corridors. It was the only section where the orderlies' reign of terror didn't exist. Lieutenant-Colonel Leonid Alexeyevich Kalinin, who ran it, an old man of nearly eighty, didn't believe in the existence of unprovoked aggression by patients. 'I've been a working psychiatrist for fifty years now,' he would say to orderlies when they tried to convince him that a patient had been 'violent' and attacked them, 'but I don't remember a single case of the patient attacking first. You must have done something to provoke him.'

I, too, had never seen a patient attack someone without reason, but the reason was not always easy to guess. One day I only just succeeded in getting away from one husky fellow who jumped on me as I passed his bed. The reason was that he regarded an area of floor around his bed as his territory, and he was prepared to slaughter anyone who stepped inside it. It was extremely important to find out your neighbours' quirks as quickly as possible, so that you could live in safety, and the main thing was never to fear them. They could smell fear and hostility like animals.

Kalinin was a legendary figure. He absolutely refused to recognise the Moscow school of psychiatry and immediately transformed the Moscow schizophrenics that were sent to him into psychopaths, alcoholics or malarials. 'Tell me, have you ever been bitten by mosquitoes?' he would ask insinuatingly in his soft, old man's voice, and some sixty-year-old gaffer, scratching his head, would be obliged to admit that, yes, it had sometimes happened. This admission was enough to diagnose the patient as suffering from the pathological after-effects of malaria.

'Do you drink vodka?' he would ask tenderly of some husky murderer.

'I do on occasion.'

'A lot?' Kalinin himself never drank or smoked, and therefore considered alcohol and tobacco to be the root of all evil in this world.

'Sometimes. I used to have a drop during the holidays and on pay-day,' the assassin would squirm.

'Did you drink again when you were hung over?' asked Kalinin sympathetically.

'Occasionally. . . .'

Who doesn't drink nowadays? Who doesn't resort to the hair of the dog? It seemed ridiculous and implausible to deny it, and so they were diagnosed as alcoholics.

Having been warned of his hobby-horses, I boldly looked him in the eye at our first meeting and announced that I had never seen any mosquitoes in my life – there weren't any in the capital of our fatherland. I had long ago given up alcohol and didn't even care for a beer.

'Perhaps you used to go out of town sometimes?' said Kalinin, nothing daunted. 'With your friends? On a tourist trip? You know, sometimes you don't even notice the mosquitoes.'

He could feel me slipping out of reach. But I was implacable and even denied myself the tourist trip. If only he had known about the clouds of mosquitoes that had besieged us in Siberia! He kept me under observation for about a month but I, too, had become skilled in these matters: I was on the friendliest possible terms with the nurses and orderlies, played chess with the medical assistant in the evenings, exchanged compliments with the sister, and treated all the guards to cigarettes. The notes in my observation record evidently read more like a recommendation for Party membership than a mental patient's behaviour record, because a month later he called me in again.

'It seems to me that you are here by mistake. I can't find anything wrong with you.'

I assured him I had always held this point of view myself, but for some reason had not been believed, and would be only too pleased if he would now clear up the misunderstanding. We parted on extremely good terms. But my joy was premature: it turned out that failing to find anything wrong with me, the old donkey had taken it into his head to declare me a malingerer. He actually put in a request to the administration to have my diagnosis annulled and to return me for investigation by those same individuals who had failed to come up with a case in the first place. He calculated that they would be delighted by his discovery!

Now I was in danger of getting permanently stuck midway between Leningrad and Moscow. The struggle between the Moscow and Leningrad schools of psychiatry was then at its height. Leningrad refused pointblank to accept either the authority of Professor Andrei Snezhnevsky or his theory of 'sluggish schizophrenia'. I don't think Snezhnevsky created his theory especially to satisfy the KGB, but it was unnervingly apt for the needs of Khrushchevian communism. According to the theory, this socially dangerous disability developed very slowly, without showing any outward signs or in any way impairing the patient's intellect; and the only people who could diagnose it were Snezhnevsky and his pupils. Naturally the KGB strove to ensure that as many of Snezhnevsky's pupils as possible sat on the psychiatric panels called to adjudicate the political cases, and later, in the early 1970s, Snezhnevsky succeeded in practically subordinating the whole of Soviet psychiatry to himself. In 1965, however, he was regarded in Leningrad as a charlatan, and the moment his 'schizophrenics' arrived there, they made an instant recovery.

A pawn in the medical dispute between the two schools of thought, I was destined to remain a prisoner until it was resolved. Traditionally, the only way to resolve a dispute over a diagnosis was to hold a scholarly debate between all the interested parties, but no one ever knew how long this process would take. The only good thing about it was that in the meantime I wasn't given any treatment.

Section 10 had more politicals in it than any other – about thirty-five or forty men out of fifty-five. The majority consisted of 'fugitives', people who had tried to skip over the Soviet border: by water – in rubber dinghies; under water – with aqualungs; by air – in home-made helicopters, gliders and rockets; on foot; in ships' holds; and beneath railway wagons.

And every one of them was, of course, demented, for what normal person would want to flee at a time when, after all the mistakes, the contours of true communism were at last beginning to grow visible? A few of them had crossed the border successfully and been handed back – one by the Finns, another by the Poles, a third by the Romanians.

Another numerous group consisted of men who had tried to enter a foreign embassy. Simple Soviet people have this naïve belief that you can somehow be smuggled abroad direct from one of the embassies – all you have to do is to get yourself inside one. Their cases were more complicated: there was no law against entering an embassy, so what could they be charged with?

A man called Pintan had fled Latvia at the time when Soviet troops invaded, and throughout all the intervening years he had lived in Australia, where he had worked as a docker and raised a family. Finally, he heard rumours down-under about the Khrushchev 'thaw' and was drawn back home to see how his countrymen were faring. He arrived with all his family and was willingly admitted. But when he had had a look at the thaw and decided to return to Australia, complications arose. He had never taken the trouble to apply for Australian citizenship and had lived with his old Latvian passport – in Australia nobody cared what passport you held. In our country, however, they cared a lot – the Soviet Union doesn't recognise an independent Latvia. And they explained to citizen Pintan that for all these years he had been a citizen of the USSR without realising it. Pintan found it absolutely impossible to assimilate this artless concept, so he kicked up a fuss, attempted to break through into his beloved Australian Embassy, and was now being treated with aminazine for his delusions.

Another fellow had actually succeeded in entering the American Embassy. To do this he had made himself up as a black. They explained to him, as was the custom, that there was no underground passage leading directly from the American Embassy to the far side of the globe, and that to depart from the country legally you needed permission from the Soviet authorities. He was obliged to leave the embassy, but at this point it started to rain, and our black man suddenly began to turn streaky under the noses of a couple of policemen. This natural phenomenon attracted the lively interest of some plainclothesmen who just happened to be strolling outside the embassy entrance. Soviet judicial psychiatry justly concluded that only a madman would voluntarily wish to change from being white to being black, and then apply to go to America, where, as is well known, they lynch even their own blacks. Now these racial whims of his were being eradicated by injections and he was well on the road to recovery.

There was a French communist, Romanian by extraction, Nikolai Georgievich Prisakaru, who had been oppressed by the fetters of capitalism. He had felt suffocated in his native Marseilles – France had nothing left of that equality and fraternity heralded by the fall of the Bastille. And he had only one dream left in his life, one hope: the Soviet Union. That was why he had come.

At the shoe factory in Moldavia, where he was given the kind of skilled work he could do, he was astonished by the pay: it wasn't enough to buy a pair of the very shoes he was producing. Here was an obvious isolated shortcoming that needed to be put right in accordance with the only true doctrine. Calling the workers together, he attempted to explain to them the current tasks of the proletariat and suggested they go on strike.

'I am convinced that *our* Party's central committee will support us! It's in the interests of the workers,' he said, trying to convince the surly workers. They must have thought that he was talking about the French Communist Party – I can think of no other explanation for their agreement to strike.

Within a few days the plainclothes representatives of the avant-garde of the proletariat were already taking him to have his head examined – not even French communists are insured against mental sickness. In the Leningrad Special Hospital he behaved modestly, sorrowfully swallowing his aminazine and patiently enduring the universal jokes at his expense. At the beginning he attempted to explain to us in his broken Russian that communism in the Soviet Union was still not the proper communism, like they had in France, and ascribed his failure to the machinations of the Vatican. But his vocabulary was pathetically limited – he knew only three words properly in Russian: 'gruel' (which he pronounced with a French accent), 'my' and 'love'. And when the food servers scraped the bottom of the urn and shouted: 'Who wants some gruel? There's half a bowl left!' – he would leap up from his place and, bowl in hand, beat everyone to the counter: 'Gruel, my, love!'

Apart from the 'fugitives' and the people who had tried to enter embassies, there were about a dozen men in section 10 who were there for 'anti-Soviet propaganda' – jokes, literature, leaflets – and several for 'espionage', i.e. contacts with foreigners. Also Mikhail Alexandrovich Naritsa, the first writer to send his manuscripts abroad clandestinely. This particular mental ailment was to become endemic throughout the Soviet Union, but at that time it was still a novelty and we regarded Naritsa with something akin to envy – at least he was in for something worthwhile.

In the mornings we used to go to workshops, and although work wasn't compulsory, a desire to work was generally regarded as a symptom of recovery. Also, the workshops constituted our only link with the other blocks, where a number of politicals were also confined. Most people worked in the tailor's shop, but about five of us worked in the bookbinding shop. I didn't need to prove that I was recovering – I was in any case considered sane – but I did the bookbinding because the psychiatry textbooks were brought there for repair and I could read them on the sly.

Everyone mainly lived in anticipation of the central commission, which came from Moscow about once every eight months. All our hopes rested on it. Jokes about lunatic asylums usually begin with the arrival of a commission. But our commission truly was a joke. It was in session for no more than two to three days, and in that time was supposed to examine 1,000 patients, each of whom got one-and-a-half to two minutes at the most. Each one was asked two stereotyped questions: what is your attitude to your illness and case (i.e. are you expressing 'criticism')? And what are you planning to do after your release?

The overwhelming majority of the political inmates readily expressed criticism – it seemed senseless to resist. They reasoned approximately as follows: it would be better for me to get out, do a bit of good work, and land up inside again, than to spend the rest of my life senselessly sitting in this loony bin. Who am I defending my principles against? The psychiatrists? All I'll get for my pains are sulphazine injections. Moreover, after a few years particularly stubborn patients were dispatched to the dreaded Sychovka as chronic lunatics unamenable to treatment. In those years nobody left Sychovka alive.

This false repentance, this false confession of sickness struck everyone as so reasonable and justified that nobody even bothered to be ashamed of it or conceal it from his cell-mates, but on returning from the commission readily related his experience in every detail, even acting out the scene and mimicking the different parts. One escapee even wrote a verse to the chairman of the commission, Professor Tarubarov, and gave it to him:

> Tarubarov, my dear man,
> Send me home as quick as you can.
> Not one embassy have I seen,
> Across the border I've never been.
> Tarubarov, my dear man,
> Send me home as quick as you can!

But the psychiatrists were far from satisfied with a formal repentance – they wanted to be sure. Therefore, about five months before the commission arrived, they set traps for the people who were due to be discharged. Nurses, guards and doctors would start picking on them, insulting them and trying to make them lose their tempers, and if the patient couldn't endure it or reacted in some way – in short, if he behaved like any normal person – the staff would immediately take out his case history and note that 'his condition had changed', and there could be no question of his discharge by the next commission.

These traps not only were set for the politicals, but were normal practice. Any doctor proposing to discharge a patient had personal responsibility for this recommendation, and naturally the doctor wanted to be sure that in provocative conditions, his charge wouldn't repeat his former behaviour. Let us say that if the orderly gave you a clip on the ear or took away your food and you responded by 'becoming violent', where was the guarantee that you wouldn't be picked up again outside? Out there, in everyday life, you would have to put up with far worse. And if you hadn't achieved the necessary degree of humility, hadn't learned to control your reactions, then it was better to keep you here a bit longer. You weren't yet fit for life among normal Soviet people.

You had to be constantly on your guard, not allowing yourself to relax even for a second, controlling every gesture. And you couldn't believe a single word that was said by the nurses and doctors.

Patients were not supposed to know the commission's conclusions. Those about to be discharged were usually given to understand as much in a tête-à-tête with the doctor. But this secrecy was also exploited in an attempt to provoke the patient. After seeing the commission, he would be confidentially informed that he was more or less discharged already and would be released in two to three months' time, after the court had sat. (The court was a complete formality, since it hardly ever rejected the decisions of the commission.) It was now that a man displayed all the true feelings he had concealed before the commission – and it was now that they watched him even more closely than before, deliberately annoying and provoking him. He, for his part, thought he already had one foot outside; his case had gone to the court and the doctors could no longer stop him. There were instances when a man was actually led out to the gatehouse for what looked like his final release. He would say goodbye to all his friends, pick up his bags and walk off convinced that he was on his way to freedom. But on his way out, those last fifty yards, the nurses would still be trying to provoke him and get him to drop his guard, and it was known for a man to be turned back at the very gate. Truly, these provocations alone could send a man out of his mind.

I myself had no need to repent or fear a trap. Having denounced me

175

as a malingerer, Kalinin demanded that my case be referred back to the KGB investigators. The resulting situation was farcical. Evidently the KGB panicked: the members of the commission insisted that I was sick, while Kalinin virtually accused them of aiding and abetting a criminal to evade justice. The more naturally I conducted myself, the more proof I provided to the commission of my 'sickness'; to express criticism and repentance, on the other hand, would have only strengthened Kalinin's position. He lost, and I was discharged with the diagnosis: 'suffering from psychopathy of a paranoidal type in the stage of compensation'.

What a whimsical thing life is! If I had owned up to the mosquitoes I would have languished in there for the next three years while Kalinin queried my diagnosis and made a malarial case out of me. But the decisive role, of course, was played by the KGB. (There was one other fellow in our section not suffering from mosquito bites, a straight-forward murderer by the name of Lavrov. Grandpa Kalinin announced that he was a malingerer, and for Lavrov this meant the firing squad. The things he got up to! He tried to gnaw through his veins, attacked the orderlies and even ate his own excrement – all to no avail. Kalinin would say in his low, soft voice: 'Listen, Lavrov, you've been eating your excrement, but you're wasting your time. I shall still pronounce you sane.' And he really did consign the fellow to the firing squad.) I can imagine Kalinin's bewilderment and indignation when they pre-vented him from 'denouncing' me. Evidently he seriously regarded his colleagues' behaviour as a plot against the authorities, and was still living in those times when lunatic asylums were used to save political prisoners from the firing squad and the extermination camps, and when it was the duty of a patriot to denounce them. I was later told by some psychiatrists that in the 1930s Kalinin had been a well-known informer but now had failed to grasp the new trends and didn't understand the tasks of psychiatry in a period when communism was being constructed on all fronts. And not long afterwards he was pensioned off.

On 26 February 1965, I was discharged into the care of my mother as a convalescent paranoiac. I had nothing to fear from provocations, and I walked to the gatehouse with a carefree and cheerful heart. I said goodbye to the boys and slipped away – ahead was freedom. No orderlies, no injections, no bars – live and enjoy yourself. As I was taking my leave, one of the boys said:

'The moment you get outside the gates you'll forget about us, you won't even write any letters. That's the way it always is. Everyone who leaves here promises the earth, and then doesn't even send a postcard!'

'Well, what now?' said another. 'Work, study, marriage – and that's that. When you meet us on the street you won't even recognise us.'

Well, perhaps some people can manage all that – perhaps. But now, ten years later, I can still remember our *method*, and still remember the swish of the trolleybus tyres fading away into the Leningrad night.

# 5

Is it possible to feel nostalgia for the madhouse or homesickness for jail?

Only yesterday, stifled by that atmosphere of madness that impregnated everything, like pitch, the deck of a ship, all you could dream of was: Lord, let me get out of here! You didn't need very much, did you? Why were you eternally discontented, eternally looking for something better, and poisoning those simple, priceless moments of happiness that were always accessible to you if you really wanted them? What use to a man were riches, luxurious palaces and the constant pursuit of pleasure, when a simple bread roll, bought for five copecks at the railway station and gnawed unhurriedly as you ambled down the street, were more precious to you than anything in the world?

Drunk on the hurly-burly of the streets, on the mass of human faces and colourful apparel, you would board a tram and rumble along the boulevard. There would be no need to peer suspiciously at others and become tense each time they asked you a question. Each new crossroads, each street, would be as full of people as words of meaning. And you would be able to get off at any stop and mingle with the crowd, stunned by the colours and the sounds. Or jump off while the tram was still moving.

The main thing was to want nothing, desire nothing and strive for nothing; then the warm evening twilight, the lights in the windows and the scraping of thousands of feet would come to you like unexpected gifts. And the scent of the fields, the intoxicating resinous aroma of pine-needles the gurgling of water. . . . You would tramp the dusty lanes from deserted village to deserted village, sleep the night in haystacks, and when you were woken by the morning chill, you would stride across the fields wrapped in morning mist. All you needed was not to think of the morrow, not to wait for it, and then every ray of sunlight would be a miracle, every morning a discovery.

But the moment you cross the threshold of your jail, this idyllic dream goes to hell. The first person you see, the filthy wooden fence across the street, smothered in tattered posters, the peeling tram, the hurrying crowds of people and the dead grey blocks of flats – all seem no more than a stage set, with no relation to you at all. The movement, faces, colours and sounds fill you with unbearable pain, and as the tram climbs screechingly up the hill, you stare at the rubbish-strewn floor beneath your feet and wait. Whenever someone comes too close to you, you curl up inside: hurry up and go by. This noisy world won't tolerate the uninvolved – it pushes you, pulls you, orders you about, makes demands on you, threatens you and tells you to be careful.

What do you want of me? Leave me in peace, let me alone. Don't touch me. I want to squat right here, alone, and stare into space, seeing nothing. I need to crawl into some burrow where it's damp and dark, because I have to slough off my old skin and grow another. The old one hurts me too much. Quiet, don't shout. Your loud voices produce only a guffawing echo inside me, a hollow echo, as in an empty building, and no words can provoke my thoughts to respond.

But this world is so virtuous, has so much cruel desire to save you. It's full of the kind faces of your family and friends, their obliging bustle, their advice and officiousness. They drag you from place to place by the scruff of your neck, like a bitch its pups, and all you can do is smile stupidly – after all, you should be grateful. What can you say to them, what answers can you give so as not to look a complete idiot? They've all grown so clever and are expecting you to make profound observations, but you have absolutely nothing to say, you're empty. You and they are living in different dimensions, in different rhythms. I was so comfortable with my simple, youthful idiots. Why did they push me out? Now I understood my former cell-mate. He had shot his wife, his mother-in-law, his father-in-law and a neighbour. Looking round, he then caught sight of the cat and shot that too. So it wouldn't look at him so quizzically.

To hell with your bread rolls! On my first day I drank myself into the middle of next week. Thrusting my head out of the carriage window to meet the oncoming wind, the smell of smoke and the electricity poles flashing by in the dusk, I gazed ahead at the crimson glow of Moscow approaching in the distance. I didn't know what I would do or how, but one thing I knew for sure: there would be no more quarter given on either side – by them to me, or me to them. From now on it was no holds barred in this war between us.

Slowly, as after an operation when the anaesthetic wears off and your sense of feeling returns, bringing a wave of dull, unendurable pain with it, and the pain mingles in your consciousness with the smell of bandages, iodine, carbolic and the white walls of your hospital ward, life came back to me. Who was it said: I think, therefore I am? On the contrary: I feel pain, therefore I live.

Again I wandered through the back lanes of Moscow communing with the Arbat mansions, but no longer was I surrounded by the benevolent phantoms of the last century with their naïve fantasies – this time I had my own phantoms. I wandered into our old yard, where the houses still stood with their blue-painted inscriptions: TBD. Just as before, aged crones sat sunning themselves, children swarmed in the dust, the washing was hung out to dry. The grey building of my old school stood at the top of the rise, just as before, but it no longer evoked bitter memories – all the ghosts on my conscience had remained behind in Lefortovo.

I walked again along the river embankment with my grandmother, through Red Square and into the Alexandrovsky Gardens.

> Who the emperor-bell durst raise,
> And swing the emperor-cannon?
> What gallant doffs not his cap
> At the holy gates of the Kremlin?

Nobody tipped his cap, and crowds of people were pouring past, jostling and pushing, like ants – like ants at the bottom of a mug. Where were they going? And why?

Pushing my way into the hurly-burly, I ran and jostled with them, trying to catch their rhythm and sense, like a splinter of wood carried along by a torrent. Where were we going? And why? I kept thinking that every person I passed would turn out to be a comrade, a phantasmal former inmate from *there*, and after exchanging a swift, wordless, understanding glance with him, I would hurry on towards the mouth of this torrent, to its destination.

Oh, this world! So serious and so preoccupied. So much mysterious significance in it. I shall never be able to understand it, and it will never come any closer to me. I detest its aimless efficiency. I carry my anguish through it, but the tall, modern glass and concrete buildings laugh complacently down at me:

'*Soviet spacemen will be the first to land on the moon.*'

I run like a frenzied ant at right-angles to the well-trodden paths of the other ants. I want to break out of this city, into the forest, but the heavy grey station building calls after me:

'*Piss on the floor!*'

And even this kindly old Moscow house, all cracked with age and covered in wrinkles and looking at me through its window-spectacles, asks in an insinuating voice when I approach it trustingly:

'*Have you ever been bitten by mosquitoes?*'

Once I had wanted to study biology. I was curious to learn about the spring that pushes the tender stalk upwards out of the seed, unfolds the leaves to the light and paints the butterflies. And now, looking at the green boulevards, I recalled a young fellow I had seen only in the exercise yard – he lived in a different section. I never asked him anything about himself, didn't want to know whether he was normal or not, and didn't even know his name. We simply walked in silence along the wall. He had piercing dark-blue eyes – not pale-blue, but dark-blue. One day, with an enigmatic smile, he beckoned me over to the corner, where some grass had thrust itself under the wall, and showed me a flower – his flower, which he had concealed from everyone. It was a misshapen flower, with two calyxes growing out of one head.

I bought a roll for five kopecks and chewed it slowly, but there was no taste or joy in it.

When I grew tired, I would wander round to see one or other of my old friends – most of all, Yuri Titov. We had known each other since the Mayakovsky Square readings and he was one of the two artists for whom I had arranged the exhibition shortly before my arrest. I watched him for hours as he painted his pictures. Whether it was his room, packed to overflowing with books and icons, familiar to me down to the last little detail, or his measured manner of speaking, his unhurried movements, the smell of paint and the semi-darkness, I do not know, but only here did I get the feeling that time had stopped, that there was no need to run after it; and then the paintings – enormous canvases depicting a smoke-blackened, burning God and a deserted earth consumed by fire – had a soothing effect on me. Most of the time we were silent. But at nights we would get drunk, watch God writhing in his flames and the dead black expanse of the earth. There was no more mercy in the world.

All we could hear outside our windows was the swishing tyres of departing trolleybuses.

As if to spite me, Moscow smelt of nappies, and the entire male population seemed to be pushing prams up and down the boulevards. My friends had all married, acquired children and vanished. Occasionally I would bump into somebody trotting home from work, his eyes fixed on the pavement.

'Sorry, old chap, no time. It's the wife, children, work.'

The former man had disappeared. All that remained was a man-unit, who could not quite walk upright on his own two limbs without additional support from a pram.

Mainly owing to Yuri Galanskov's efforts, a few of the boys from the Square were still making verse anthologies. But even this activity no longer had much life in it – the time for that had passed. There was something new in the air, new ghosts were haunting Moscow. There was more and more talk of Stalin being rehabilitated. Soon after Khrushchev's removal there were rumours of some sort of lists – was it 2,000 or 5,000 individuals who were due to be repressed in the first instance? Shelepin was singled out as the candidate for a new Stalin.

What use was verse at such a time!

Battalions of prams with babies in them moved through the city like columns of tanks. The parents hoped that they themselves didn't figure among those 5,000. And the limousines flew to the Kremlin like black lightning to check the lists.

Why are Leningraders such plotters? Where do they get their underground psychology from? Moscow is like one big hotel, you can always find whoever you want there, and people are always glad to introduce you without being asked. The Moscow flats are crowded with people; there's such a racket going on that you can't even hear your own voice. In Moscow kitchens they sit up all night, arguing and arguing. In Moscow you can turn up with a crowd at a friend's house in the middle of the night and no one will be surprised. If you've got a bottle with you they'll be overjoyed. And by morning the argument will inevitably come round to the ancient theme – when did it all begin? In 1914? In 1905? Or was it the Decembrists who screwed the whole thing up? Some go back still further and heap the blame on Peter the Great: he was the villain of the piece. Raped poor old elemental Russia, who gave birth to a bastard that has plagued us ever since.

At least one of his crimes is self-evident – he built St Petersburg, a city of plotters. He built it with malice aforethought, probably when he was hung over, which is why the city is permanently enveloped in fog, which poisons everyone with a passion for plotting. The Petersburgers lurk in their homes, storing up their secret thoughts, and see every acquaintanceship as a clandestine link.

Arriving in Leningrad from the Moscow station one early spring morning, I wandered down its dazzling, deserted avenues and admired the sumptuous architecture. Every building is an aristocrat, looking condescendingly down its nose at you. But all you need to do is penetrate behind the façades, into the maze of damp, gloomy, well-like courtyards, and it hits you at once – *this* is its home, *this* is the source of that Leningrad underground psychology. You can talk to Leningraders only one at a time, in a whisper, and they never introduce you to anyone else: 'Oh dear no, I live alone – I don't have any friends.'

'Gaffer', one of my former cell-mates in the psychiatric hospital, seemed created to arouse the immediate suspicions of the Soviet man-in-the-street – he looked too much like a foreign spy in a Soviet film. Short, fat and bald, peering watchfully out through thick-lensed glasses, he was the very image of an agent of world imperialism. Even schoolchildren used to stop in the street and stare after him – should we call a policeman? Making my way to his home by way of Leningrad's backyards and backstairs, I invariably intercepted wary looks from his neighbours: 'Another visitor for our spy.'

Gaffer lived with two aged aunts, and although he was already pushing fifty, he couldn't escape their continual ministrations. 'Boris darling, you've eaten nothing to speak of since morning,' one of them would say. 'Put a warm sweater on, it's cold today,' the other would chime in.

'Come on, Auntie, that's enough now. After all, this is ridiculous,' Gaffer would reply in his nasal voice. 'I beg you to stop it, that's enough.'

Despite all this he was an arch-conspirator, had already done three spells in the mental hospital and was so inured to leading a double life that by now he virtually plotted with himself. Each time he was released he was restored to membership of the Party and got himself a job in the ideological sector – writing articles for the Party press or working as an instructor. In short, he 'wormed his way into a position of trust' and 'camouflaged himself'. One day in Moscow he went with me to visit a typical rowdy Moscow flat and was overcome with indescribable horror. 'This is a trap,' he hissed in my ear, 'we've all been had. We must leave at once.' And I could never get him to come back to Moscow again.

From Party sources Gaffer already knew all the details about the lists and the proposed rehabilitation of Stalin, and naturally he wasn't sitting back and doing nothing. He had a regular plot going. Friends were hard to find in the Leningrad fogs, but conspirators were ten a penny. Looking twenty years younger, he scurried about Leningrad, busy with his conspiratorial meetings, secret rendezvous and negotiations.

In just the same way they must have slipped into the Petersburg fog in March 1881, holding their neat packages. An hour later in front of the Summer Garden, just where the tsar's carriage turned to go down the Moika, there was the sound as of an iron fist smiting the roadway, a flash of flame, a column of fire rising into the air, and the snorting of wounded Cossack horses. And it didn't matter that enraged janitors beat up all the students they could find afterwards, and that the new tsar took immediate measures to have the troublemakers captured, for from that moment on, the edifice of our history began to totter. Tell me now, when did it all begin – in 1905, in 1914 or in 1917? Blinded by this bomb, generation after generation manufactured more and more bombs and again disappeared into the Petersburg fog.

It always seems so tempting, so simple and so justified – surely it's fair to pay the villains back in their own coin? To answer the Red Terror with the White Terror, the White with the Red? Look, they are torturing us, they are beasts, not human beings! Why can't we torture them? Watch, they are openly robbing us – what are we waiting for? Their impunity only encourages them, unties their hands. And if the state is exercising coercion anyway, why not use coercion in the name of justice, and in the name of their salvation too?

Well, for them, perhaps, carrying their neat little packages to the Summer Garden, this seemed irrefutable. But I was born in a year when the whole of mankind, whether it wished to be or not, was at loggerheads over the colour of its concentration camps – brown or red. One thing was clear to me: man's liberation couldn't come from outside. It had to come from within, and until the majority of us had freed ourselves of the psychology of the underground, of the rage for justice, our descendants were doomed to go on arguing in their kitchens: when did it all begin? Like ants at the bottom of a mug.

Sergei Petrovich Pisarev was the diametrical opposite of Gaffer. As a fourteen-year-old boy at the height of the First World War, he had run away from home to fight for his tsar and native land. He was already at the front when they caught him, and to stop him running away again, they sent him back on a prison transport together with a shipment of convicts. On the way back, in Rostov jail, he met some arrested Bolsheviks and after that became a communist to the marrow of his bones. The jails he had been in! During the Civil War it was in Denikin's counter-intelligence headquarters under sentence of death, in 1937 it was Lefortovo, in 1953 the Leningrad Special Mental Hospital, and nothing could shake his communist faith. But in spite of that, he was at constant odds with his proletarian government.

In 1935, when a friend of his was arrested, he tried to secure his release by writing protests and even collecting signatures. Naturally, by 1937 he himself turned out to be 'an enemy of the people'. He was cruelly tortured and his back was broken on the rack in Lefortovo, but he signed nothing. With his back broken he was flung like a dog into Butyrka prison and left there to peg out. He lay there a whole year, unable to move a muscle. His cell-mates fed him and carried him to the latrines. For a whole year he wrote petitions in tiny, tiny hand-writing on scraps of toilet paper. Not for himself, but for his illegally arrested comrade. His cell-mates only laughed: 'Who are you writing to? Your petitions get no further than the guards. Save the paper – we don't have enough as it is.'

A year later he was suddenly called out of the cell. What for? Nobody knew. With great difficulty the guards lugged him to the Deputy Public Prosecutor. This official opened a folder and said: 'You wrote?' And at this point Pisarev saw all his scraps of paper neatly pinned together and numbered. 'Your comrade,' said the Prosecutor, 'was indeed an honest communist, innocently arrested by a band of enemy saboteurs who had wormed their way into the security organs. Now they have been exposed and will receive their just punishment. Unfortunately, your comrade did not live to see this day – he died under interrogation.'

It turned out that much had changed during the past year. Yezhov, the head of the NKVD, had been shot, together with his cronies, who had turned out to be 'enemies'. Beria had been appointed as the new chief of the NKVD and the tortures had been bought to a halt. There was a kind of 'Beria thaw' at the time, which few people remember now.

Having been released in this miraculous way, Pisarev limped off to the Central Committee and assured them that everyone sharing his Butyrka cell with him had been equally innocent, and had incriminated themselves only under torture. He got many of them off.

In 1953, at the height of the campaign against the Jewish doctors alleged to be plotting against Stalin, Pisarev sent Stalin a memorandum in which he asserted that the whole 'doctor–wreckers' case was a falsification and the Interior Ministry 'mendacious from top to bottom'. He was immediately consigned to the Leningrad mental hospital. But even there he carried on writing his endless petitions and smuggling them out surreptitiously during visits. After Stalin's death Pisarev won for himself not only complete rehabilitation, but also the annulment of his diagnosis. Further, exploiting his contacts with the Central Committee, he managed to get a special commission appointed to investigate the Serbsky Institute and the Leningrad and Kazan mental hospitals; it established that large numbers of sane, innocent people had been incarcerated there for political motives. Many of them were released immediately.

Naturally Pisarev was rehabilitated in the Party each time he was released – not for camouflage, as in Gaffer's case, but because he remained a sincere believer in communist doctrine. He considered himself a follower of Lenin. Such was his detestation of Stalin that he could never bring himself to utter his name, referring to him invariably as Djugashvili. Stalin, in his view, had staged a coup d'état in the thirties and exterminated the true Leninists. 'The Party has been completely regenerated,' he used to say. 'In these conditions we are obliged to join the Party in order to provide it with healthy new blood. Take yourself – you are an honest man. Your place is in the Party, to struggle against the degenerates from inside.'

Such logic was incomprehensible to me. I didn't believe in communism, whether of the Leninist or Stalinist varieties. How could I join the Party?

Pisarev lived in a tiny little room, crammed with Marxist classics and old files of *Pravda*. After one rehabilitation he had been awarded a ludicrously small pension, but even that he spent entirely on books. He lived on condensed milk. Knowing his situation, friends used to leave tins of it around for him surreptitiously, pushing them unobserved into some corner or other. Sometimes, at some particularly critical point in his ceaseless battle against the 'degenerates', he was obliged to go into hiding, and then he would live with one of his friends.

Pisarev also knew about the lists and the proposed rehabilitation of 'Djugashvili', and of course was fighting on this front too, dispatching endless petitions to all levels of the Party.

I listened to him with interest, but was unable to adopt the same position. Not only was the inner-party struggle for the purity of Leninism unacceptable to me, but I wasn't prepared to appeal to the authorities in any way, since that would have amounted to a *de facto* recognition of them on my part. Even taking a simple job in a State enterprise would have meant giving *de facto* support to a regime founded on coercion.

More and more often I found myself visiting Alik Yesenin-Volpin. After getting to know one another in September 1961, before the rout of the Mayakovsky Square readings, and later during the interrogations connected with them, we used to see one another fairly often, and for a while we worked in the same research institute. He was running a seminar there on semantics, and I used to go and listen to him. Then, when I was in jail, he visited my mother. This was a general rule of his – to visit prisoners' families, even if he didn't know them. And naturally the first thing he did was to explain the laws to everyone.

I was astounded by the serious way in which he discoursed on rights in this country of legalised coercion. Didn't the KGB say to us quite openly: 'Give us the man and we'll find a charge for him'? No more than ten years ago it had been revealed that these same laws could coexist with the murder of almost twenty million innocent people. The very author of our constitution, Bukharin, barely survived to finish it before he was shot. What sense was there in expounding our laws? It was like expounding humanitarianism to a cannibal. Alik himself had been twice committed to prison mental hospitals for reading his own verse – and this not even in the Square, but at home, to a circle of friends. Wasn't this enough to convince him? In short, he struck me as being in the same mould as those dyed-in-the-wool Marxists whom not even prison could enlighten.

Alik's permanently dishevelled aspect, total impracticality, inability to adapt to his surroundings and absolute indifference to his appearance completed the picture, making him an exemplar of the eccentric professor. And he really was a first-rate scholar – of mathematics and logic. What was so striking and endearing about him was his absolutely childlike naïvety and defencelessness, quite unexpected in a forty-year-old man. It was this quality, I think, that was prized by most of his friends, almost all of whom had gone through Stalin's camps. As for his theories on legality, his friends regarded them indulgently as a forgivable eccentricity, shaking their heads with a smile when he launched into one of his expositions.

Whether it was his constant preoccupation with logic that set its seal on him, or that he had chosen this subject precisely because of formal logic's affinity with his mode of thinking, I do not know, but all his arguments were strictly constructed according to logical theorems.

Every proposition, from his point of view, had to be either true or false. He completely denied the relativity of these concepts and got very angry over the common inexactitudes of everyday speech, regarding them as virtually the root of all human misfortunes: we introduce lies, ambiguity and vagueness into our lives, and then we juffer the consequences. But given that in real life the truth of any sudgement is always conditional, all of Alik's arguments became encrusted with digressions, reservations, parentheses, exceptions and qualifications, and he invariably ended up with the problem of whether and how much a word corresponds to what it denominates, terminating in such a semantic jungle that nobody had the slightest idea any longer of what was being said. Only Alik, turning his shining light-blue eyes on his interlocutors, still thought that everything was utterly simple.

It is easy to imagine what happened when Alik came into direct conflict with the Soviet punitive apparatus. I remember that some years later he was summoned for questioning by the KGB in connexion with some case or other. His wife, knowing from experience how the whole thing might end, kindly warned the investigator not to proceed with his scheme, but her advice was spurned. Two hours later Alik was drawing assorted circles, squares and diagrams on a statement-blank in an effort to explain to the investigator just one of his simplest thoughts. Four hours later, after completing a short course in the theory of numbers, they had at last reached the problem of the denominator; the dazed, sweating investigator rang Alik's wife and begged her to come and fetch her husband. Naturally she refused, quite rightly considering that it was the investigator's own fault for not listening to her in the first place. 'That's your problem,' she said.

Luckily, on this occasion Alik had been called as a witness, not as the defendant; otherwise the investigation would have ended in a psychiatric examination. Psychiatrists were not mathematicians or logicians either; 'truth' and 'falsehood' were not the objects of psychiatric study. Therefore all investigations of Alik ended in an identical manner, with his consignment to a psychiatric hospital of a special type for particularly dangerous patients. What other result was possible? Imagine, for a moment, that the KGB has taken it into its head to arrest a computer. On the other hand, the computer simply won't understand the ambiguous language of the investigator's questions or of Soviet law. Its logical circuits will give out answers of the 'true–false' variety, and if an attempt is made to get an extended answer, it will simply cough out a long perforated ribbon with an infinity of units and zeros on it. What would you have them do with it? I guarantee that the case would end, as with Alik, in the mental hospital.

I used to argue fiercely with Alik, sometimes into the small hours. And not only because at the age of nineteen one tends to argue with everybody, but also because his entire line of reasoning and all his premises were unacceptable to me, and nothing he said seemed to have any application to real life. But returning home early in the morning, still burning with indignation, I would suddenly discover, to my horror, that I had completely accepted one or other of his arguments.

His central concept was the *position of a citizen*, which offered a laughably simple way out of all my dilemmas.

These dilemmas began at the point where I was required to be a 'Soviet man'. This concept is so diffuse and demagogic that you never know exactly what obligations it carries with it. 'Soviet' means someone enthusiastically building communism, wholeheartedly endorsing the policies of the Party and government, and angrily condemning world imperialism. And supporting whatever else our propaganda will dream up tomorrow. The official ideology created a mythic image of Soviet man, and each new invention it made became a directive for everybody.

This concept of 'Soviet man' was really the starting point for all the illegality in the country. Every ruler that came along filled it, as he did the concept of 'socialism', with anything he wanted to put into it. And if you tried to argue with it afterwards at Party meetings, there were no criteria. The supreme judge in this question was the Central Committee. And any interpretation differing from theirs was in itself a crime. 'You are a Soviet man,' says the KGB detective, 'and therefore obliged to help us.' And what can you say in reply? If you're not Soviet, what are you? Anti-Soviet? That alone is worth seven years in the labour camp and five in exile. And Soviet man is obliged to collaborate with our glorious security organs – that's clear as daylight. What was I kicked out of the university for? For not conforming to 'the ethos of a Soviet student'.

Alik Volpin argued, however, that there was no law obliging us to be 'Soviet people'. A *citizen* of the USSR, on the other hand, was quite a different matter. We were all citizens of the USSR by virtue of having been born on its territory. But there was no *law* obliging all the citizens of the USSR to believe in communism or to help build it, or to collaborate with the security organs or conform to some mythical ethos. The citizens of the USSR were obliged to observe the written laws, not ideological directives.

Then followed the concept of Soviet power. Are you against Soviet power, or for it? I could think what I liked, but if I officially announced that I was against it, that would be 'anti-Soviet propaganda'. Again seven plus five. What was I to do – lie about it? Or consciously break the law? But this was not necessary. According to the constitution of the USSR, the political foundation of Soviet power was the power of the Soviet of Workers' Deputies – a sham body that had less authority than the average policeman. There was no mention of any party whatsoever in this section of the constitution.

'Do I object to the power of some parliament that calls itself the Soviet of Workers' Deputies?' reasoned Volpin. 'No, I don't. Especially since it is nowhere mentioned that it has to have only one party. True, they might have found a more felicitous name for it.'

This line of reasoning was extremely important, since in practice the authorities simply proclaimed as anti-Soviet everything they didn't like. According to strictly juridical criteria, none of us was committing a crime so long as we didn't directly assail the power of the Soviet of Workers' Deputies. And who was going to do that?

In creating our laws mainly for propaganda purposes, our ideologists had overreached themselves. Actually, there was nothing to stop them from not bothering with a constitution and simply writing: 'In the USSR everything is forbidden except what is expressly permitted by decisions of the Central Committee of the Communist Party of the Soviet Union.' But this would have led to unwanted complications, and would have made it harder to spread the Soviet form of socialism among the gullible abroad. Therefore they wrote a constitution with a plethora of rights and freedoms which they simply couldn't afford to grant, rightly supposing that nobody would be reckless enough to insist on them being observed. Volpin's idea, therefore, came down to this. We reject this regime not because it calls itself socialist – there is no law defining socialism and therefore citizens are not obliged to know what it is – but because it is based on coercion and lawlessness, tries to impose its ideology on people by force and obliges everyone to lie and be hypocrites. We wish to live in a State ruled by law, where the law is unshakable and the rights of all citizens protected, where it would be possible not to lie without risking the loss of our freedom. So let us live in such a State. We, the people, are the State. Whatever we are will mould the character of the State. A close examination of the laws we have been given fully supports such an interpretation. Let us, therefore, like good citizens of our country, observe the laws as we understand them, that is as they are written. We are obliged to submit to nothing but the law. So let us defend our laws from being encroached upon by the authorities. *We* are on the side of the law. *They* are against it. Of course, there is a great deal in Soviet law that is absolutely unacceptable. But not even the citizens of free countries are completely satisfied with their laws. When citizens don't like a law, they seek by legal means to have it reformed.

'But *they* can't get by without using coercion,' we objected to Alik. 'If they were to introduce a strict observance of the law, they would simply cease to be a communist State.'

'Actually, I agree with you,' Alik would say in a conspiratorial whisper, and everyone would burst out laughing.

'You're crazy, Alik,' we used to say. 'Anyway, who's going to listen to you with your theories about the law? They'll go on jailing you, just as they did before. What difference will it make?'

'Well, if somebody breaks the law and encroaches upon my legal rights, as a citizen I'm bound to protest. I am obliged to fight back with all legal means. And above all, with publicity.'

And again everybody laughed. 'Now he wants publicity! Where are you going to get it from? Is *Pravda* going to help you?'

But having had our laugh, we were obliged to agree that if you answered lawlessness with lawlessness, there was precious little chance of ensuring observance of the law. There was simply no other way. In exactly the same way, answering violence with violence would only multiply violence, and answering lies with lies would never bring us closer to the truth. Once again our dishevelled computer was in the right.

Alik's idea was both inspired and insane. The suggestion was that citizens who were fed up with terror and coercion should simply refuse to acknowledge them. The point about dealing with the communists is that to acknowledge the reality of the life they have created and to assent to their notions means *ipso facto* to become bandits, informers, hangmen or silent accomplices. Power rests on nothing other than people's consent to submit, and each person who refuses to submit to tyranny reduces it by one 250-millionth, whereas each who compromises only increases it. Surely our Soviet life was actually nothing more than an imaginary schizophrenic world populated with invented Soviet men building a mythical communism. Weren't we all living double and even triple lives? The inspiration of this idea consisted in eliminating the split in our personalities by shattering the internal excuses with which we justified our complicity in all the crimes. It presupposed a small core of freedom in each individual, his 'subjective sense of right', as Volpin put it. In other words, a consciousness of his personal responsibility. Which meant, in effect, inner freedom.

Let us suppose that this point of view were adopted by large numbers of people. Where would the Central Committee be then with its ideological directives? What would the KGB do with its army of informers? A citizen has nothing to hide, and no need to justify himself – he merely observes the laws. And the more openly he does so, the better.

'But what will you do, Alik, if they change the laws tomorrow so that they can't be interpreted in your way any more?' I asked.

'Then I shall probably cease to be a citizen of this country.'

This was totally beyond the comprehension of mere mortals. What did he mean – was he going to flee across the border? Alik launched into a long disquisition on a citizen's right to leave his country and, of course, to return to it again, supporting his argument with quotations from something called the Declaration of Human Rights. We merely shrugged: 'He's raving again!' I wonder how many of us who shrugged then are now in Vienna, Rome, Tel Aviv or New York? But only Volpin leaned out of the train that took him to Vienna and made a speech on the need to struggle for the right of re-entry.

While these legalistic and semantic arguments were going on in Moscow kitchens, events knocked on the door. Soon after my release from the special hospital, I had made the acquaintance of Valery Yakovlevich Tarsis. This was only a few months since Khrushchev had been removed from power and replaced by the triumvirate of Brezhnev, Kosygin and Podgorny. Tarsis, meanwhile, surrounded by foreign correspondents, was giving a press conference in his Moscow flat.

'Mr Tarsis,' they asked him, 'what is your opinion of the changes in the Soviet leadership?'

'The great Russian writer of fables, Krylov, once wrote: "And you, my friends, no matter how you sit, to be musicians never will be fit." '

What was this – a hallucination? Only a couple of months ago I had seen a man doing eight years for merely writing a critical letter to the Central Committee, and another was still inside for whispering jokes about Khrushchev into a friend's ear. A third was accused of espionage for being acquainted with foreigners. And if I really hadn't taken leave of my senses and wasn't seeing things, Tarsis, all those present and all their relatives and neighbours were destined to find themselves in the Lubyanka by evening. I doubted if they would even be allowed to leave the flat.

Tarsis was organising these press conferences almost every day and nobody seemed to be bothered. Miracles never cease! Who was this untouchable Tarsis?

'The whole thing is a gigantic provocation by the KGB,' explained our underground thinkers. 'They're trying to tempt us into the open and flush us out of our cover. Tarsis is just a decoy, a trap.' And they dug still deeper into their burrows.

No, no, don't think you can impress a weathered Soviet subject by this seven-day wonder of a Tarsis! Thank God we've survived the NEP, the Trotskyist conspiracy, the Bukharinite opposition, the 'rootless cosmopolitans', and the 'doctor-wreckers'. We've learnt a thing or two along the way, we weren't born yesterday, you know. Tarsis won't get us to bite, try some other fool. The main thing under socialism is to survive. Self-preservation! If some provocateur starts cussing the regime out loud, the first thing to do is answer him back, loud and clear, so that everyone hears you. And then run to the KGB as fast as your heels can carry you, so that nobody beats you to it.

It is possible that Tarsis himself would have argued approximately the same way twenty years before. He had gone to university, joined the Party, fought at the front and become a Soviet writer. But the years went by, he was almost sixty, and still there was no glimmer of light. During Khrushchev's thaw Tarsis revealed his views somewhat more openly than other more cautious and respectable people, and by 1960 they had completely stopped publishing him. It was then that he started sending his manuscripts secretly abroad.

This method of publication, which later became traditional, had begun with Boris Pasternak, and began to seem particularly alluring after he had won the Nobel Prize. But every underground writer, whether he kept mum or added his voice to the nationwide chorus of righteous condemnation, grimaced over Pasternak's response with annoyance: 'The old man muffed it! No guts – he's refused. Just let 'em try giving the prize to me, I wouldn't let it go. . . . Not even if they shot me. Company in distress makes the trouble less.'

When the cautious publishers in England released Tarsis's first book there under a pseudonym, he immediately exposed the pseudonym and demanded that he be published under his own name.* And it was this that saved him. Naritsa, whose manuscript was published in Germany under the pseudonym of Narymov, revealed himself too late, and he

* The title of the book was *The Bluebottle* and the pseudonym was 'Ivan Valery'.

got three years in a mental hospital. But with Tarsis it was different: Khrushchev was somewhere abroad at the time, and one of his entourage showed him the book, in which Khrushchev himself was depicted. Naturally he flew into a rage and gave orders for Tarsis to be incarcerated in a lunatic asylum. It had to be done quickly – there was no time for arrest, charge, examination and dispatch to a special mental hospital, because the scandal was escalating all the time – so he was pushed into an ordinary city mental home, the Kashchenko Hospital. But the scandal was growing, and although it was not very big by today's standards, they had to let him out after three months. An enraged Snezhnevsky himself flew back from some international symposium where people had ventured to ask after Tarsis, and personally released him, making all sorts of excuses as he did so.

Then they summoned Tarsis to the KGB to see Semichastny's deputy, General Perepelitsyn.

'Mr Tarsis,' purred the general tenderly, 'we understand what an important writer you are, a major talent. You could be of so much benefit to our people. Why don't you describe the good sides of our life? There are so many good things here, we have so many achievements to our credit.'

Tarsis was unmoved.

The general changed his tactics. 'You know, Mr Tarsis,' he said in that same tender tone, 'you are just an ordinary mortal. A motor car might accidentally run you over. Nobody is insured,' and he shook his head in commiseration.

'What of it?' replied Tarsis. 'A crown of thorns will suit me very well. Remember, no one will believe you even if I am run over by accident or a brick falls on my head. Abroad they will still think that the bloodstained secret police killed Tarsis. Therefore, not only will you not kill me, but you'll even look after me and move heaven and earth to see that I don't die.'

In 1964, not long before the fall of Khrushchev, a new book by Tarsis was published in England, *Ward 7*, in which he described his adventures in the Kashchenko Hospital. The book had an enormous success and quickly became a bestseller. After that Tarsis lived exactly as if no Soviet regime existed around him at all, gave interviews and press conferences, sent new manuscripts abroad, and even bought himself a new car – to the chagrin of all the other writers in the housing project where he continued to live. People – especially foreign correspondents and tourists – flocked to his flat to look at the eighth wonder of the world. And everyone waited with bated breath for this Tarsis to be arrested, knocked down by a car or otherwise crucified.

It was some kind of crazy dream! What use was it to patrol the borders, have customs searches, maintain censorship, keep watch on foreigners and support an army of KGB agents when you had this man sitting in the middle of Moscow and saying whatever he liked out loud, giving interviews and publishing his books in England? And in the evening you could hear everything he said via the BBC! Where was the Iron Curtain? For the first time in history there had appeared in the Soviet Union a man they couldn't jail.

If older and more experienced people tended to give Tarsis a wide berth, the younger ones never left his side. And it was around this time, in early 1965, that a new wave of young poets appeared and attempted to resurrect the readings in Mayakovsky Square. They christened themselves with the strange name of SMOG, which was said to stand for the Russian words for 'boldness, thought, image and depth', or, alternatively, 'the youngest society of geniuses'. I don't know about genius, but they certainly showed plenty of courage. They held several meetings in the square, began circulating their verse in *samizdat*, organised debates, appeared in public wherever they could, and, through Tarsis, practically all of them succeeded in getting published abroad. The number of Russians now publishing abroad with impunity thus rose to several dozen, which was extremely important. Official Soviet literature naturally refused to recognise them, didn't publish them and banned their appearances, but still the authorities couldn't bring themselves to jail such a large number all at once. The poets had wide circles of acquaintances and, taken together with the circle that had formed at the time of the first public readings, constituted a significant force. We were already seriously thinking of organising on the spur of the moment a Russian section of the PEN club and applying to join International PEN, when there occurred an event that was to have extraordinary repercussions – the arrest in September 1965 of the two writers, Andrei Sinyavsky and Yuli Daniel, for publishing their books in the West.

It was difficult to say at the time what had impelled the authorities to take this step. Did they wish in this way to scare off others thinking of publishing abroad and thus sever this burgeoning tradition at the root? Did they think that it was time to whip the increasingly unruly intelligentsia into line and take revenge for their failure with Tarsis? Or did they simply get carried away in their hunt for the unknown mystery men and find themselves unable to halt the momentum? At all events, it looked at the time as if this was the start of that plan to bring back Stalinism, and Sinyavsky and Daniel were simply the first of the proposed 5,000.

I think also that the circumstance that they published abroad under pseudonyms and not under their own names was significant in the whole affair. First of all such behaviour amounted to a virtual proof of guilt according to the KGB's logic: if a writer plotted and practised concealment, he must have known that he was committing a crime. From the point of view of propaganda the case also seemed a winner – it had the flavour of a detective novel. Look at these secret enemies stealthily turning into writers, concealing themselves and sabotaging us on the sly. They write one thing here and something quite different over there! It's all the same to them what they write, as long as they get paid for it. Yes, you could build quite a story round those pseudonyms. Furthermore, this evasive and indecisive position allowed the KGB to suppose a shortage of courage or even a definite absence of principle in the two writers, and they may have hoped that both would repent of their sins and help the KGB to stage a major, open show trial.

The KGB also calculated, of course, that this complication of the pseudonyms would somewhat delay and weaken the public reaction abroad, or at any rate preclude any protests before the trial. In short, as in Naritsa's case, the pseudonyms did Sinyavsky and Daniel an extremely bad turn. They were undermined by their underground psychology.

At first the KGB's calculations seemed justified, for the West's first reactions to the arrests were belated and muted. Only after a month or so did the foreign press start writing vaguely about the arrests of – was it two or three writers? – mixing up their real names and their pseudonyms, and the whole thing seemed highly doubtful. The authorities, of course, introduced additional confusion, reassuring 'progressive public opinion' abroad, denying the fact of the arrests, permitting so-called 'controversial' poets to make occasional trips abroad, publishing a few 'controversial' articles on literature, and so on. The general impression was given that 'the new leadership is occupying a tolerant position' with regard to the creative intelligentsia.

Fairly soon, however, Western literary circles grasped the fact that these arrests were aimed at the entire 'liberal intelligentsia', as they liked to call it, and were designed to serve as a sort of touchstone for the new Soviet chieftains. A certain edge was given to the whole affair by the award of the Nobel Prize for Literature that year to the Soviet

Party functionary, Sholokhov. This opened up the possibility, which struck everyone as highly ingenious, of addressing a number of appeals to him on humanitarian grounds. He for his part, carrying out his Party duties, naturally talked a lot of nonsense at the award ceremony. The world community of authors now moved into action, there was a torrent of protests, letters, appeals and telegrams, and even the openly communist press was obliged to respond to them. In short, the affair escalated into a scandal of such proportions that if the ponderous juggernaut of the Soviet state had been able to stop, it would have done so. But the system of repression was so unaccustomed to adjusting actions, so incapable of acknowledging its mistakes, and was possessed of such brazen insolence and dumb arrogance that only the threat of a complete break with the civilised world could have forced it to its senses at that moment.

Once having blundered into it, they put up a bold front to cover the stupidity of the Sinyavsky and Daniel arrests, and totally ignored world public opinion.

In later years we were often astounded by the idiotic stubbornness of our authorities and their reluctance to look at the obvious facts, all of which did them catastrophic harm. This self-destructive obstinacy may strike us as incomprehensible, but that is because we forget that a regime of terror cannot behave otherwise. Where it differs from a democratic regime is precisely in not being responsive to public opinion. In such a State, the individual cannot have any rights – the least inalienable right possessed by a single individual instantly deprives the regime of a morsel of power. Every individual is obliged from childhood to absorb the axiomatic fact that never in any circumstances or by any means will he be able to influence the regime one jot. No decisions can be made other than on initiatives from above. The regime is immovable, infallible and intransigent, and the entire world is left with no choice but to accommodate itself to this fact: you may humbly beg its indulgence, but never demand your due. It doesn't require conscious citizens demanding legality, it requires slaves. In just the same way, it doesn't require partners, it requires satellites. Like a paranoiac obsessed by a fantastic idea, it cannot and will not recognise reality – it tries to realise its delirium and to enforce its criteria on everybody else. We will never be rid of this terror, never acquire freedom and security, until we refuse categorically to recognise this paranoid version of reality and oppose to it our own reality and our own values.

Thousands of books have been written in the West and hundreds of different doctrines created by the most prominent politicians to find a compromise with this kind of regime. They are all evading the only correct solution – moral opposition. The pampered Western democracies have forgotten their past and their essence, namely that democracy is not a comfortable house, a handsome motor car or an unemployment benefit, but above all the ability and the desire to stand up for one's rights. Neither atom bombs, nor bloody dictatorships, nor theories of 'containment' or 'convergence' will save the democracies. We who were born and have grown up in an atmosphere of terror know of only one remedy – the position of a citizen.

There is a qualitative distinction between the behaviour of an individual and that of the human crowd in an extreme situation. A people, nation, class, party or simply a crowd cannot go beyond a certain limit in a crisis: the instinct of self-preservation proves too strong. They can sacrifice a part in the hope of saving the rest, they can break up into smaller groups and seek salvation that way. But this is their downfall.

To be alone is an enormous responsibility. With his back to the wall, a man understands: 'I am the people, I am the nation, I am the party, I am the class, and there is nothing else at all.' He cannot sacrifice a part of himself, cannot split himself up or divide into parts and still live. There is nowhere for him to retreat to, and the instinct of self-preservation drives him to extremes – he prefers physical death to spiritual death.

And an astonishing thing happens. In fighting to preserve his integrity he is simultaneously fighting for his people, his class or his party. It is such individuals who win the right for their communities to live – even, perhaps, if they are not thinking of it at the time.

'Why should I do it?' asks each man in the crowd. 'I can do nothing alone.'

And they are all lost.

'If I don't do it, who will?' asks the man with his back to the wall.

And everyone is saved.

That is how a man begins building his castle.

And so it came about that in November 1965 a number of people started distributing typewritten leaflets among their friends containing a 'Citizens' Appeal'. The text, calling for a mass meeting to demand a public trial for Daniel and Sinyavsky, had been composed, of course, by Alik Volpin. It ended: 'You are invited to a public meeting on 5 December at six p.m. in the public garden in Pushkin Square, beside the poet's statue.

'Please invite two more citizens by showing them the text of this appeal.'

Of course, there were plenty who opposed the venture. As usual, they said it was a KGB provocation designed to 'flush them out', and so on. A majority, however, was in favour of the idea, and even a pessimist like Yuri Titov said:

'Aha, at last these intellectuals have come up with something sensible.'

The appeal circulated through the well-tried *samizdat* channels that only yesterday had been circulating the poetry of Mandelshtam and Pasternak and literary anthologies. These 'channels of trust' were our greatest achievement of the previous ten years, and thanks to them, practically the whole of Moscow knew by December of the impending meeting scheduled for Constitution Day. Remembering our experiences in Mayakovsky Square, I was sure that chanting slogans was a hopeless and dangerous undertaking. Placards with slogans on them were better from every point of view, and so I arranged for several of the boys to prepare them.

At first our enthusiasm knew no bounds and the main subject of conversation in Moscow was this demonstration. But the closer it got to Constitution Day, the more pessimistic and even fearful people became – nobody knew how the enterprise would end. The regime was capable of anything. It might herd the whole lot of us into lunatic asylums or worse. Nevertheless, whatever one thought, we were on the eve of the first free demonstration in the country since 1927.

On 2 December, I had just succeeded in handing the last packet of appeals to a SMOG member in the Moskva cinema on Mayakovsky Square, and was on my way out, when I was surrounded at the street exit by a crowd of KGB agents. For some reason they seemed to think that I was armed and were shaking in their shoes. They crowded tightly round me from all sides so that I didn't have time even to lift a hand, and hustled me into a waiting Volga. There was one on either side of me, and one, the group leader, sitting beside the driver. 'Hands on the back of the seat in front of you. Don't move and don't look round.'

'Can I smoke?'

'No.'

They took me to the nearest police station and searched me. I had kept one copy of the appeal for myself in order to make further copies, but they found nothing else. I was taken into the duty room. 'Sit there.'

It was suspicious that they hadn't taken me straight to the Lubyanka or Lefortovo. What were they waiting for? Further orders? I struck up a conversation with the policemen. 'KGB picked you up? Done nothing at all, I bet?' they asked sympathetically. 'Fine bloody detectives they are.'

The policemen's hatred of the KGB was nothing new and had often been our salvation in the past. I exploited it now, too. I fished my little notebook out of my pocket, which had some addresses in it, and destroyed it. My policemen didn't turn a hair. Who knew whose addresses were in that book – perhaps their own sons'?

'Where are they taking me?'

The policemen shook their heads – they clearly didn't know.

About twenty minutes later I was called into the office. A woman in an overcoat was sitting behind the desk. Before her she had a sheaf of papers and my copy of the appeal. 'Hello. Sit down. How are you feeling?'

Ah, that was it, a psychiatrist. I could tell at once by the smile: only psychiatrists smile with such knowing condescension. And her look was that of a woman inspecting a small insect: 'Oho, where do you think you're going, silly boy!' All of a sudden, as if having downed a glass of vodka, I was plunged back into Leningrad hospital with its crowd of ragged idiots. I could even smell the hospital.

Whatever I said now and whatever gesture I made would be noted down in my medical record. And that was irremediable. It is useless to argue with psychiatrists. They never listen to *what* you are saying, only to *how* you are saying it. You daren't get hot under the collar, otherwise there will be a note: 'Over-excited, morbidly sensitive to subjects that have emotional significance for him.' And aminazine is guaranteed. If you are too downcast and sullen, a depression is noted. And you can't be too cheerful either – 'inadequate reactions'. Indifference is terribly bad: 'emotional apathy, inertia' – a symptom of schizophrenia.

Don't look guarded, suspicious or secretive. Don't argue too confidently or insistently ('over-estimates his own personality'). Above all don't hesitate, but answer quickly and as naturally as you can. No efforts that you are able to make later will erase what she writes down now. She is the first to see me, and her word will go. Priority in psychiatry goes to the first person to examine a patient. Ten minutes later, there may already be an improvement. God and Stanislavsky help me!

I responded in an equally friendly and cheerful tone of voice, as if speaking to my own mother:

'Hello. Thank you, I'm feeling fine.'

A few routine questions: name, address, date of birth – she was checking my sense of orientation. How mediocre and predictable they all are. Next she would ask me what today's date was. What *was* it? Yes, 2 December, three days till the demonstration. No, she didn't ask. Hmm, it seemed that I had won the first round. They would still put me away, of course. But the main thing was not to give the old bitch anything to write about.

'We are hospitalising you on the instructions of the Chief Psychiatrist of the City of Moscow.'

'What for?' I said with absolutely natural surprise, as if I had never been in a mental hospital in my life. 'I'm not disturbing anybody. I haven't attacked or bitten anyone.'

But that didn't fool her at all.

'And what's this?' she said, pointing to my blasted leaflet, and again there was a superior glint in her eye, as if to say, I know these lunatics and their antics. He runs around town with a pocketful of leaflets and then pretends to be surprised when he's caught. And it was useless to protest. Even dangerous. The psychiatrist is always right.

'But I've only just found it. Didn't even have time to read it,' I said, neutrally, more for the sake of appearance than anything else and in order not to remain silent. None of this was important any more. The main thing was for her not to write too much. It seemed that I had won the last round as well. In the hospital it would begin all over again. I would have to talk and talk on the subject of that leaflet.

Only on the way to the hospital, when drawing a deep breath after this conversation, did I think to myself despondently: 'Damn, that wasn't much of an excursion. Nine months in all. And now is the time to act – everything is just beginning.'

One thing was good: the orderlies were a cheerful pair and we spent the whole ride swapping jokes about Lenin. And in this way I was delivered to the loony bin – City Psychiatric Hospital No. 13, in Lublino.

'Jump out, subversive. We're there.'

A normal city hospital is paradise compared with a special hospital, and although they dumped me in the section for violent patients, where the bolts were thicker and the regime harsher, I had settled down comfortably within a couple of days. My greatest recommendation was that I had been brought there on the orders of the KGB – nobody after that had the slightest doubt about my normality. The doctors, medical assistants and orderlies were all young fellows of my age or a bit older, and we found a common language at once – in some instances, even common acquaintances.

After the first chat with my doctor, Dr Arkus, I was sure not only that he would not attempt to 'treat me', but that he considered me completely normal and would do everything in his power to get me discharged. But that was no simple matter. As always in the Soviet Union, they find it easy to put people away, but letting them out is a real problem. It needed the agreement of the chief doctor, or of a whole commission. And that wasn't all: they could only *inform* the Moscow Chief Psychiatrist of their opinion; he took the final decision, since I had been committed on his instructions as a 'socially dangerous patient'. Nobody knew what the intention of the authorities was – they merely suspected that the plan was to return me to Leningrad as an 'uncured' patient who had been 'prematurely discharged'.

By the next day my friends had sniffed out my whereabouts, and a whole crowd of them came to see me. Naturally, all conversation centred on the forthcoming demonstration and its possible consequences. The general mood was uncertain. The incident with me had increased fears that they would incarcerate the lot of us. Enthusiasm had drastically ebbed – what if no one decided to come to the demonstration? I was very much afraid that these fears would prevail, so when Yuri Titov asked me straight out whether they should go ahead and hold it or not, I replied that if they didn't, it would rebound on me, it would look as if everything had collapsed without me, that I was the chief instigator. In actual fact, it wouldn't have affected me at all, but I wanted to tie them down with some sort of moral obligation. This, of course, was dishonest of me and in doing it I was pushing them to do something partly against their will. To a certain extent, however, this was a decisive moment.

All through 5 December I was on tenterhooks. I even thought of trying to escape from the hospital. Time dragged on endlessly. It was only the following day that the boys came and told me the details of what had happened.

By six o'clock in Pushkin Square a mass of inquisitive onlookers stood in a solid wall round the square and even across the street. Near the statue strolled a number of groups and individuals, looking for all the world like accidental passers-by, but consisting of participants in the demonstration, KGB plainclothesmen and foreign journalists. Somebody had even turned up with a pair of skis over his shoulder so as to have a plausible excuse if anything went wrong: he had just returned from a skiing trip out of town and had stopped in the square by chance to see what the crowd was all about. Alik Volpin had been brought to the square by a friend of his, a legless invalid, in his invalid carriage – anything else would have been stopped. As I expected, no one took the risk of shouting slogans, and there was a moment when they had no idea *what* to do. Seeing that nothing terrible was happening, the crowd gradually grew bold and inched closer to the statue, while a solid group formed in the centre consisting of about 200 people. The situation was saved by my friend, the artist Yuri Titov. After our conversation in the hospital, he had gone home and, without saying a word to anyone, had prepared some paper placards saying: 'Respect the constitution', 'We demand an open trial for Daniel and Sinyavsky', 'Free Bukovsky and the others arrested for preparing a demonstration' (the day before the demonstration Vishnevskaya and Gubanov had been picked up*). He had brought these posters to the square under his overcoat and now, in the thick of the crowd, he pulled them out, unrolled them and started to hand them round to the others. For a brief moment the placards unfurled over the heads of the crowd, but the KGB men instantly snatched them away, tore them up and crumpled them, while their holders were bundled into cars and driven off – about twenty people all told. In the ensuing confusion, Galanskov clambered on to the statue's plinth and shouted: 'Citizens of free Russia, come closer to me!'

Some plainclothes citizens of free Russia instantly rushed at him, knocked him to the ground and dragged him to a car.

At the police station where everyone was taken, KGB detectives were in charge, interrogating them and examining the placards. 'What are you trying to say with this slogan, "Respect the constitution"? Who is it aimed against?'

'Against whoever doesn't respect it.'

'And who is that?'

'Well, for example, people who break up peaceful demonstrations.'

From Alik Volpin they confiscated a placard demanding an open trial for Sinyavsky and Daniel. However, the detective who had snatched the placard away on the square had torn it so neatly in two that now, when the remaining halves were put together again, it read: 'We demand a trial for Daniel and Sinyavsky.' Evidently the word

* Yulia Vishnevskaya, a poet, was briefly committed to a mental hospital for taking part in this demonstration against the Sinyavsky–Daniel trial and emigrated in 1971. Leonid Gubanov, a member of SMOG, wrote poetry for *samizdat* and was also committed briefly to a mental hospital.

'open' had so enraged the detective that it was still clenched in his mortal grip.

All of those picked up were held for a couple of hours and then released.

Later I found out that not even the dispersal of the demonstration had gone according to the authorities' plans. Initially they had been intending to use not the KGB but vigilante detachments of Komsomol members. But they had run into some unexpected opposition, and at a special meeting where the KGB and Party authorities gave them their instructions, the Komsomol members had suddenly rebelled. The overwhelming majority were students, and they objected to being used as a crude police force without their opinion being asked. 'Let us read what these writers have written and then we'll decide what to do,' they declared. So the KGB had somewhat hastily changed its plans; and subsequently a number of the rebels, including my school friend Ivachkin, were kicked out of the Komsomol.

It was generally felt that the moment for the demonstration had been exceptionally well-chosen. Our fellow-citizens had stirred after all. And although the demonstrators continued to be persecuted by extra-judicial measures – being expelled from the university and sacked from their jobs – public opinion had come down on the side of Sinyavsky and Daniel.

At last Soviet propaganda capitulated to the double pressure from within and without, and at the beginning of January, *Izvestia* printed a long article on the subject – the first publication anywhere in the Soviet Union to mention the case. Naturally the article tried to make capital out of the pseudonyms, and Sinyavsky and Daniel were portrayed as hypocrites who allegedly praised the Soviet Union in the Soviet press whilst underhandedly slandering it abroad. The article was called 'The Turncoats'. But even here, Soviet propaganda was unable to sustain the right note – as usual, it lacked the necessary subtlety. The article's strident, vulgar tone, its arbitrary quotations taken out of context, and above all its brazen anticipation of the court's verdict, with its accusations of anti-Soviet propaganda and of virtual treason – all this provoked an avalanche of protests from both inside and outside the country.

The authorities were obliged to make haste and inspire workers' letters supporting the article. The one scenario kept in reserve for every eventuality was wheeled into action: indignant letters from agronomists, milkmaids, steelworkers and deer-breeders. All that remained was to organise meetings in factories and collective farms to complete the picture of nationwide condemnation. Even the *Literary Gazette* could not resist exploding into furious comment. In short, a perfectly normal Soviet propaganda orgy got under way, the underlying principle of which was to scream as stridently as you could so that nobody else could be heard. As in the nursery rhyme:

> Whoever loudest barks bow-wow
> Is always in the right, you know.

Naturally it led to the opposite results. By the time the trial of Sinyavsky and Daniel opened in February 1966, the scandal had reached global proportions. But then, in order to blur the picture somewhat, the authorities suddenly allowed Tarsis to go abroad. As if to say: it's only the 'turncoats' we put on trial – the ones who do it openly are even free to go abroad. At the same time, of course, they adroitly rid themselves of Tarsis, not knowing what else to do with him. You have to hand it to them: two such events as the departure of Tarsis and the trial of Sinyavsky and Daniel were bound to blur and contradict one another, spoiling the clear picture in the public mind of the situation in the USSR.

'Mr Tarsis, why were you allowed to come to England, while Sinyavsky and Daniel have been put on trial?'

What could he say to them? Grandad Krylov had never expressed an opinion on this particular subject. What emerged was that either Sinyavsky and Daniel were criminals or Tarsis was simply mad. How were Western people to understand that everything in our state is subordinated to the needs of propaganda and misinformation? Krylov's time was gone forever.

But this could not save them either.

On 10 February 1966, the Sinyavsky–Daniel trial began – the first show trial of the post-Stalin era, the prototype of a whole series of trials which were to follow. It was held behind closed doors, of course, although it was called an open trial. Only specially selected spectators with special passes were allowed into the court to listen. There were no passes for foreign correspondents. The Soviet press, on the other hand, whipped itself into a frenzy. Almost every day there was a newspaper article headlined: 'From the Courtroom'. You want publicity? Here you are then, get a basinful of our Soviet publicity. You want legality? Here's our Soviet legality.

But floods of protests, petitions and open letters were pouring in. They came from people who remembered Stalin's old labour camps –

Vorkuta, Norilsk, Karaganda, Kolyma and Djezkazghan – and also from people who were anxious not to acquire memories of those places. It was risky to 'know nothing' and becoming dangerous to 'be afraid'.

Tens of thousands of cigarette-paper-thin sheets began to circulate from hand to hand, bearing a typewritten text that was barely legible – the 'last words' of Sinyavsky and Daniel. For the first time at a political show trial, these made clear, the defendants had refused to recant or acknowledge their guilt, or beg for mercy. And this was *our publicity, our victory.*

Meanwhile, my own affairs were becoming more and more tangled. The doctors of City Mental Hospital No. 13 refused to accept that I was ill and sent their findings to the Chief Psychiatrist of the city of Moscow, Yanushevsky. They weren't in a position to release me, but in their findings they broadly hinted that inasmuch as no medical indicators were observable, they would be hard put to it to hold me in the hospital any longer. Since it was not a place of detention, it was, alas, ill-equipped for such a purpose, and they were unable to guarantee my complete isolation. In other words, I might run away, and they would have few grounds for preventing me.

In fact, it would have been as easy as pie for me to run away. The staff treated me with such sympathy and understanding that they would have held the doors open for me, if only I had given the word. And would have called a taxi to take me home. But the authorities would immediately have interpreted escape as proof of my 'social dangerousness'. The Leningrad Special Hospital would have been guaranteed. So what? I could run away to Siberia again, couldn't I? But I decided to stay and fight it out to the end. At all events, these positive findings by a hospital where I had been under observation for a whole month gave me a chance to prove my fitness.

The most sensible thing for the authorities would have been simply to release me, but their idiotic obstinacy and faith in their own omnipotence tripped them up yet again. For it was emerging that nobody had been punished for our defiant demonstration. And so, faithful to their tradition of beating one to frighten the rest, the authorities resolved not to let me out. They would let my soul rot in a series of lunatic asylums.

In mid-January I was hastily transferred to another hospital – Hospital No. 5 in the village of Troitskoye, about forty miles from Moscow. They were hoping that the doctors in the new hospital would turn out to be more cooperative, and also by this time news of my case had filtered through to the Western press, and they were afraid lest Western correspondents started paying me calls. My new hospital, the celebrated Stolbovaya, was situated outside the zone in which foreigners were permitted to travel.

This hospital, which had been built at the beginning of the century, was intended for the compulsory treatment of people found guilty of petty crimes: stealing, prostitution, speculation, vagrancy and similar 'untypical' acts of the Soviet citizenry. It held a minimum of 12 to 15,000 patients. The majority of them really were chronically sick, and many had spent virtually their whole lives in there, especially the ones without relatives or whose relatives refused to have them at home. Yegor, for instance, blind and with an improbably large head, like an embryo, had been here since birth, and was now pushing forty.

'Well, how are things, Yegor?' the others used to ask him cheerfully.

'Things are fine, my head's still mine,' he would answer in his rasping voice, like a robot.

There were paralytics with their tongues hanging out, living out their days here; slow-moving idiots, like seals; skinny schizophrenics; epileptics falling into fits at hourly intervals; and, of course, in every section a small fellowship of sane, absolutely normal people, consisting mainly of Moscow pickpockets, burglars, robbers.

My fellow-passenger in the loony van turned out to be an elderly, dyed-in-the-wool Moscow thief by the name of Sanya Kashirov. For a moment he looked at me searchingly and then said in a low voice: 'Got any dough?'

'Some,' I said, equally quietly.

'Give it here, they'll take it off you when they frisk you. It'll do for today, tomorrow we'll drum up some more,' he said in a businesslike tone of voice, pushing my ten-rouble note into a matchbox. 'I'm a good cobbler. They all know me there. We shan't go short of money.'

It was true. The moment we arrived and were taken to see the doctor in the reception office, she clasped her hands and exclaimed: 'Ah, Sanya! You're back again! Listen, I've got some heels that need mending. They're new shoes, I've only just bought them. Will you be staying long? Where do you want to go – 4B again?'

Only afterwards did she turn her attention to me, but Sanya headed off all questions and simply said: 'This one will come with me to 4B.'

Without even glancing into my file or reading the dread instructions of the KGB and the recommendations of the Chief Psychiatrist, the doctor assigned me to section 4B. No inspection, no questioning, no search. That's what it means to make friends with a good cobbler. 'Okay, Sanya, I'll call in this evening when I come off duty. I'll bring the shoes with me. All right?' she called after us as we left.

It was the same in the section. We had barely arrived when the nurses clustered around Sanya as if he were a long-awaited guest, and vied with one another to tell him about their felt boots, their shoes, their soles and their high heels. A good cobbler is in general a rarity nowadays, and out here, forty miles from Moscow, was unheard of. People could scarcely travel to Moscow every time their children needed their boots stitched or their shoes soled. Sanya was in great demand.

The section was absolutely chock-a-block with about 200 men. People were sleeping on the floor, on benches and on the dining tables. You had to wait months for a bed, in a living, moving queue. As a punishment for some misdemeanour the doctor could confiscate your bed – your greatest blessing – and move you to the floor. To get a bed, people used to bribe the orderlies. But two beds were immediately made available for Sanya and me, side-by-side and with a small table between them – two loonies were turfed out to sleep on the dining-room floor. Even the sister in charge was generosity itself, issuing us new flannelette pyjamas, warm brown dressing-gowns, and slippers. In short, we were treated royally, like foreign tourists at the Hotel National.

The community of the sane numbered about eight in our section and consisted exclusively of professional crooks who had often been here before. While the scholarly world was engaged in debating, writing treatises and conducting research into sluggish schizophrenia, the Moscow thieves had swiftly discerned its advantages. Instead of sweating it out for five years in the labour camps, felling timber and rotting in punishment cells, how much better it was to be squatting in a mental ward for six to eight months. Earlier convictions were disregarded, you didn't lose your residence permit, and there was no need to work. It was a piece of cake. They had all done some time in the labour camps and were in no hurry to go back. A clever man needed only one appearance before the Kashchenko Hospital commission to secure himself a reliable diagnosis till the end of his days. Some of them had been here a dozen times already – the equivalent in the camps would have cost them fifty years. When they were let out, they went stealing again, then they were readmitted, and invariably returned to their favourite section 4B as if coming home.

Thus the atmosphere in the section was that of a den of thieves.

There was no need to ask the orderlies to bring vodka, they themselves volunteered to run and fetch it. A glass went to the orderly and the rest to you. So long as there was money. On the first evening, Sanya and I put my ten roubles into circulation. I was so unused to vodka that after a couple of glasses I was completely pickled, but the orderlies gently put me to bed so that the duty doctor wouldn't notice me when doing his rounds, and then ran to the shop for a further supply. And so it went on every day. In the mornings we got over our hangovers, at lunchtime we drank, and in the evening we got sloshed.

One day we drank ourselves under the table. Nobody had any money left, not even the orderlies, and nobody would lend us anything anymore. What were we to do? At this point one pickpocket said to the orderlies: 'Let me out for an hour. I'll just take the bus to the station and back, and then we'll have some dough.'

No sooner said than done. He was dressed up in normal clothes and an orderly went with him just in case – to cover up if he was caught: don't worry, it's just a lunatic I'm taking to the hospital. It worked, and an hour or so later they came back with twenty-five roubles. And off we went.

My companion, Sanya the cobbler, once complained to me that he never seemed able to give up drinking. Being a cobbler, it was difficult for him not to drink. Wherever you got a job outside, they all drank like fish. How can you resist it? He had thought of laying off in here – what a hope! And it was when drunk that he had been caught picking somebody's pocket, an episode of which he was thoroughly ashamed: his real speciality was burglary.

It would have cost nothing at all to run away from here – or rather, it cost exactly thirty roubles. If you paid this to the orderly he would bow you out of the door and even take you to the bus-stop. One day even a legless man got away on his crutches.

Of course, the doctors couldn't possibly not have known what was going on. From time to time the duty doctor would come across someone drunk and then, as a form of punishment, have him transferred to the section for 'violent patients', to Dr Pozdnyakov, who was renowned for his sadism. Pozdnyakov had two favourite devices, 'three on five' and the 'riding breeches'. 'Three on five' was three injections of 5 cc of sulphazine, two in the buttocks and one under the shoulder-blade. After this, the feverish victim felt as if he was being crucified and was unable to move hand or foot for the pain. The 'riding breeches' was a procedure for pumping the thighs full of saline solution, so that they swelled up until they looked exactly like riding breeches.

The pain was hellish and it was impossible to walk. But not even the threat of savage punishments like these could restrain my underworld friends from getting smashed, though on the whole they were rarely caught. None of the orderlies or nurses had an interest in that happening, and they always hid the patients when they were drunk.

For the rest, the doctors pretended they knew nothing. They were all part of the same vicious circle. The service personnel robbed the hospital of everything they could carry away, especially food. The supplies were plundered so mercilessly that it would have been impossible for the patients to live off the hospital food, and most of us ate what we got from home – luckily there were no restrictions on food parcels – and the available food was simply given to the ones with no families outside. The whole village of Troitskoye lived off the hospital too, and regarded it as a source of supplementary income.

During the day the sane patients gathered in the dining room, while the loonies were chased into the corridor. There was a television set, and we also played cards and drank there. Practically no attention at all was paid to the loonies, except when some comical madman wandered in and some fun was to be had from teasing him. I immediately made inquiries, of course, about the possibility of obtaining a radio. This turned out to be extremely easy to arrange. In one of the other sections they had a combined television set and radio, and the orderlies swiftly agreed to swap it for our television set.

Every morning when we sat down to breakfast, I tuned in to the BBC, and while the loonies gulped down their gruel, the epileptics writhed in convulsions and the schizophrenics sat motionless over their bowls, staring unseeing into space, we listened to the news from London: letters and protests over the Sinyavsky–Daniel case, a transcript of the trial itself, Tarsis' interviews and statements in London. My underworld friends simply shook their heads – the things that go on! But they began listening with particular interest after my name also came up a few times. From then on I no longer needed to worry about switching it on in time – the orderlies did it for me and we all stopped talking.

So there you have a symbolic picture of our glorious fatherland! An enormous madhouse where everything is looted down to the last rotten spud, where the whole shebang is run by a handful of the 'sane', where even they are drunken crooks who prefer to disguise themselves as schizophrenics, and where they sit and listen to what London has to tell them about life in their homeland.

'How are things, Yegor?'

'Things are fine, my head's still mine.'

My doctor at Stolbovaya, Bologov, was neither a brave man nor a man of principle. After the city hospital's findings about my sanity, it was easier for him to confirm those findings than refute them. For three weeks or so he kept an eye on me, and on a couple of occasions summoned me for a chat. He knew, of course, that I was drinking with the orderlies and mixing with the thieves, and this for him was the best possible proof of my fitness – neither group would have had anything to do with me at the least sign of abnormality. In effect, he had had no doubts about my health from the very beginning. The example of Hospital No. 13 had shown that there was no danger in reaching such findings, and it wouldn't ruin his career. So he wrote that he didn't regard me as sick. At this point the authorities had another opportunity to release me without fuss, and again they let it pass. Instead, in the middle of February, I was unexpectedly transferred to the Serbsky Institute in Moscow.

There wasn't much the Serbsky Institute could do: two hospitals, one after the other, had declared me sane. Furthermore, thanks to Tarsis, my case had been attracting a lot of publicity abroad, and the Serbsky Institute preferred to 'abstain'. But there was one legal peculiarity they were able to exploit. Formally I had never been arrested, charged or even held on suspicion, and no case had been instituted against me. Therefore, from the legal point of view, the Institute of Forensic Psychiatry was not empowered to examine me. There could be no question of discussing the issue of 'fitness to plead', since I had never been charged with anything. Therefore, without officially refusing to examine me, the Serbsky Institute simply requested the KGB to forward the incriminating evidence, so that they could study it and come to a decision on the question of my fitness. Twist and turn as they might, the KGB could find nothing to send – they hadn't anticipated such a turn of events.

What the argument came down to, in fact, was the old question of the diagnosis. In 1963 they had given me two diagnoses: psychopathy and possible schizophrenia. The Leningrad Special Hospital had rejected the diagnosis of schizophrenia and discharged me as a psychopath. Now, two more hospitals had also denied that I was suffering from schizophrenia. And the Serbsky Institute was tending to take a similar view, which absolved it from the necessity of contradicting the old diagnosis (no one now disputed my psychopathy because no one was interested in it). But if the KGB could overturn the decision of the

Leningrad hospital and get the diagnosis of 'schizophrenia' to stick again, it would invalidate my discharge from the Leningrad hospital. This would then give them grounds for sending me back to the Special Hospital on the basis of my old case, without the need to institute a new one, as a patient who had been wrongly treated and therefore not properly cured.

At this point my mother became seriously alarmed and, overcoming her timidity, began writing complaints to all and sundry. From all departments of the Prosecutor's Office she got replies serenely informing her that everything was legal and there were no grounds for complaint. Actually, that is what the Prosecutor's Office exists for in the Soviet Union – to send such replies. And I think that this was the point at which my mother experienced a sharp awakening – the sort that the working man experiences when he first comes into conflict with his own regime. Until this point – in no way differing here from the many others who had lived through decades of Soviet terror – she had cultivated in herself a safe submissiveness. And a habit of not even admitting to herself her true attitude to the world about her. From the office to home, and from home to the office. The main thing was not to look around you, not to have a perplexed expression on your face, otherwise you might find yourself suddenly being summoned somewhere and asked what you were staring at. You get sucked into this kind of life so gradually that you can no longer make out which of the thoughts in your head are reserved for public consumption and which for private. And if you force yourself for long enough to be pleased with everything you see, you will gradually grow accustomed to regarding your surroundings as normal, and propaganda slogans repeated for the millionth time will become assimilated by your consciousness.

Man can get used to anything, accustom himself to any loss and accommodate any absurdity. But there is in man a kind of spring, a limit to his capacity for elasticity, beyond which something inside him snaps. He then ceases to believe in what is going on.

One friend of mine, whose husband had been harassed for many years for no reason at all, received a notice asking her to report to the police station.

'Don't take your passport with you,' said her friends.

'Why not?'

'Because they'll take it away and cancel your residence permit. And you'll be left without a roof over your head,' they explained.

'What?' she said in astonishment. 'But where's the justice of it?'

Something similar happened to my mother. Where was the justice of it? I wasn't supposed to be arrested, I wasn't supposed to be charged, they couldn't find anything wrong with me, I wasn't supposed to be getting any treatment, and yet they had been holding me in detention for half a year and insisting that there were no grounds for complaint. Driven gradually frantic by these brazen answers, she worked her way up to the most senior departments, insisted on being received by the bosses and bawled them out.

My old friend General Svetlichny, head of the Moscow section of the KGB, was also raging mad. It so happened that he was one of the people my mother managed to see. In Count Rostopchin's sumptuous mansion, with its high moulded ceilings, carpets and gilded doors, where I had once had a vision of elegant ladies in crinolines and gentlemen in powdered wigs, there occurred a conversation between two people thirsting for justice.

'That's enough, he'll never come out again!' roared the evil dwarf with the over-sized head, tramping wrathfully over the Count's parquet floor. 'I'll see him rot in those lunatic asylums first! Enough!'

And this was the only honest answer my mother ever got the whole time. After that it was the endless letters again: 'Everything is legal. There are no grounds for complaint.'

Meanwhile I remained in the Serbsky Institute, waiting to see how the whole peculiar business would end. Professor Lunts himself, the omnipotent Lunts, who had incarcerated thousands of sane men in lunatic asylums on orders from the KGB, was at a loss, and asked me curiously: 'Well, what's to become of you now?'

This was the first time he had been unable to oblige his masters, and he was intrigued by the ensuing situation.

Daniil Romanovich Lunts, Chief of the No. 4 (Political) Department of the Serbsky Institute, loved to chat with his well-read patients about philosophy and literature, especially if the conversation occurred in the presence of colleagues. He liked to parade his erudition, quoting from memory the works of authors of whom modern Soviet man has never even heard, or of whom at best he can read in the *Dictionary of Philosophy*: 'Bourgeois idealist, reactionary thinker of such and such a century. In his works expressed the interests of the exploiter class.' To his younger colleagues such erudition bordered on the fantastic and gave him an irreproachable authority.

But for him it was not difficult. Born into a highly intellectual, professorial family, he had been raised on such books. His youth had coincided with that crazy time when any half-educated proletarian, having more or less mastered the *Communist Manifesto*, could become a 'red professor', and in this context Lunts' knowledge became useless, and he deeply resented the 'cooks' children' who had come to govern the country and who, he thought, were obsessed with 'overvalued' ideas. However, he realised only too well how dangerous it was to contradict a paranoiac, especially one that is in power. Therefore, following the best traditions of the Russian school of psychiatry, he had skilfully entered into this madness himself and soon looked so orthodox that even his own parents feared to speak frankly in his presence.

The farther things went and the more drastic the times became, the more hotheads disappeared in the whirlpool of events, and in no time yesterday's 'red professors' were being shipped out to Siberia to fell timber and build roads. Lunts, however, continued to grow and grow, and it seems that he had already come to regard himself as invulnerable, when suddenly, overnight, he found himself on the edge of an abyss. The year was 1953 and it suddenly turned out that he was nothing less than a Jew, a progeny of that leprous tribe of 'enemies' and 'wreckers' whom the supreme leader had decreed should be transplanted to the land of eternal ice. He never forgot those several months of mortal fear when, dismissed from his job, defamed and accursed, he trembled in his flat, waiting for the inevitable nocturnal knock on the door.

The danger passed, he recovered his responsibilities and honours, and it even became possible once more to show off his wide philosophical knowledge without risk: but he never again escaped a certain servile haste in his movements and a sweating twitch in his hands whenever he was summoned *there*. Because of the type of work he did he was often summoned – without ceremony, like one of their own, underlining the trust and respect they had for him – and this afforded him a secret pleasure, evoking an irresistible desire to shine, to guess what was wanted before the words were out, or without any words at all, and to do it, to do it so that it was absolutely watertight.

He was prized for his tact and cultivation. How often did the general line of the Party twist and turn? Yesterday the Leninists were jailing Stalinists, tomorrow it would be the other way round, and every time you could expect commissions and investigations. But with Lunts you could sleep easy. He never botched a job – not like the others. For them it was simple – they simply handpicked their 'own' commission, which would rubberstamp any diagnosis they liked, without effort. Before you could say Jack Robinson, yesterday's political commissar would be diagnosed as a congenital idiot, and a Party stalwart with an irreproachable record as a third-degree alcoholic. Lunts could suit a diagnosis to a man's particular character so aptly, dig up such out-of-the-way facts, and psychologically prepare his patient so skilfully that you could show him to an international commission afterwards.

He didn't, of course, recognise the theories of Snezhnevsky, for whom everyone was a schizophrenic, at the very least of the 'sluggish' variety (that is, whose schizophrenia only *he* could spot). Lunts quite rightly saw these theories as a threat to his own position as a 'master case-maker'. Who would need all his subtleties if everyone were a schizophrenic and all you had to do was show him to Snezhnevsky?

Naturally I didn't know all these details then, but during my many evenings discussing Bergson, Nietzsche or Freud in his office, beneath the lithograph of the great French humanist Philippe Pinel, who had freed the mentally sick of their chains, I found myself wondering why he was spending so much time on me. After all, he had told me that he hadn't been appointed to observe me this time, since I wasn't a criminal case. Was it out of boredom?

With his thick, convex glasses and disproportionately wide mouth, he looked like an enormous frog, especially when, at the end of our philosophical conversations, he thoughtfully croaked: 'I wonder what's going to become of you?' As if we had spent the entire evening speaking of nothing else. He was probably thinking to himself: How do they think they can wriggle out of this one without me? Maybe I'll still be called?

Finally, in the spring of 1966, on the orders of the Central Committee, a 'neutral' commission of four professors was established to resolve my tangled case. The KGB simply took the easiest way out and secured the inclusion in it of two supporters of Snezhnevsky – Morozov and Rotstein. Although he wasn't a member of the commission, Lunts was present and gave his opinion. I was summoned for no more than five minutes and, of course, tried not to supply them with any more 'symptoms'. But they weren't interested in me at all – the basic argument between them was over theoretical questions that were only indirectly connected with me.

The vote was of course split fifty–fifty: two professors found that I was suffering from 'sluggish schizophrenia' and two professors didn't. Again the future was completely dark. Lunts looked quizzically at me again – what was to become of me now? And so I stayed at the Serbsky Institute till the summer.

I really don't know how it would all have ended — perhaps I would still be in the Serbsky Institute today. More likely, however, they would have sent another commission consisting entirely of Snezhnevsky's disciples, and by now, whatever remained of me would be kicking around somewhere in the Leningrad Special Hospital, or even further away from the public gaze in one of the other special hospitals that have since been opened in the provinces.

But the case had inspired too much publicity by now. On the instructions of Amnesty International, an English lawyer, Mr Ellman, came to Moscow and contacted the director of the Serbsky Institute, Dr Georgi V. Morozov, with a request to visit him. He also asked for a meeting with me. I don't know what Mr Ellman made of his conversation with Morozov, though I can easily imagine the latter's line of reasoning.

For some reason Morozov expressed not the slightest surprise at the fact that a foreigner was demanding that he give an account of himself, and he didn't even seem to regard this as 'interference in our internal affairs'.

'Bukovsky?' he repeated, with a frown. 'I don't remember. I'll have to look and see if we've got a patient by that name.' And he started riffling through some papers on his desk. 'Oh yes, here he is. He was found to be suffering from schizophrenia, but the treatment has helped a lot and we shall soon be discharging him.'

In this way the eight-month scientific argument over my psychiatric condition was brought to an abrupt end. No certificates, no explanations, no apologies. I beg your pardon, who detained you? You simply imagined it all.

And for another three months after my release my mother continued to receive belated replies from the various departments of the Public Prosecutor's Office: 'No grounds have been found for your complaint. The investigation is being carried out according to normal judicial practice. Your son has been detained in accordance with the law.' Truly we were born to make Kafka live.

# 6

In 1966 the West for the first time began to take an interest in the real state of affairs in the Soviet Union. Only one tiny corner of the curtain had been lifted, but even that partial revelation had provoked a storm of indignation. What would happen if the rest were revealed?

From our point of view, for the first time we had witnessed the power of publicity and been convinced by it, and seen the fear and confusion of the authorities. Insolence and obstinacy still ruled the roost, but the authorities had suffered a colossal setback. For how much longer could they continue to cling to their self-destructive arrogance? For the first time in our closed society, the germ of public opinion had created a crack of light. Our eyes were witnessing the birth of a movement in defence of civil rights. It was necessary to make haste and not let it die out, to keep the indignation from subsiding.

But the authorities had also not abandoned their plans to resurrect their version of Stalinism. In an apparent effort to compensate for their setback, and above all to scare off any newly emboldened citizens, they swiftly prepared a new offensive. Our December demo had caught them unawares – the Criminal Code didn't provide any penalties for that sort of activity. There was, of course, the article covering mass disturbances, which was used to cover uprisings, but that would have been excessive even for our sort of justice. To correct their oversight, therefore, the authorities passed a Special Decree of the Presidium of the Supreme Soviet of the USSR, dated 16 September 1966, introducing article 190:3.

Wholly in keeping with Soviet hypocrisy, the article didn't even mention the word 'demonstration' but contained a reference to 'the organisation of, or active participation in, group activities involving a flagrant breach of public order, or explicit refusal to submit to the lawful demands of representatives of authority, or the interruption of transport or of the work of State or social institutions or enterprises.' Presto! Just try to prove that free demonstrations are banned in the Soviet Union! It's all lies! Slander! All that is banned are group activities involving a flagrant breach of public order. But at the same time, any Soviet citizen accustomed to the swivels of the pole of the law knew perfectly well what this article was aimed at. Not only did it make demonstrations a crime, but also strikes ('interrupting the work of State or social institutions or enterprises'). For all or any of this, three years' imprisonment was prescribed.

The same decree simultaneously introduced article 190:1, prescribing three years in the labour camps for 'the systematic dissemination by word of mouth of deliberately false fabrications bringing the Soviet State and social system into disrepute, and equally the preparation or dissemination of such fabrications in written, printed or any other form'. Formally speaking, the only difference between this new article and the old article 70 lay in the matter of *intent*. Article 70 required intent to subvert or weaken the Soviet regime, whereas 190:1 didn't, so that the sphere of possible repression was widened. Outwardly everything looked perfectly decent: it wasn't freedom of speech or of the press that was banned, but slander. But here too, the Soviet citizen, accustomed to arbitrary rule and hypocrisy, quite justifiably saw it as a reaction against the growth of *samizdat* and the loosening of tongues. Slander was a word that could be applied to everything the authorities didn't like.

The laws of the Soviet Union do not recognise the category of political crime ('we have no political prisoners!'), and crimes like treason, agitation, ideological sabotage and so on, are assigned to the category of 'specially dangerous state crimes'. However, people convicted under these articles had been held separately from ordinary criminals in special concentration camps. But now it was proposed to keep anyone convicted under the new articles in the normal criminal camps, and even the investigation of these cases was supposed to be conducted by the Public Prosecutor's Office and not the KGB. All this further underlined the fact that these articles had nothing 'political' about them.

This typical display of hypocrisy considerably hampered the campaign of protest against the new articles. We found ourselves in a vicious circle. Although they obviously encroached upon constitutional liberties, the articles didn't formally contradict the constitution, so that it was difficult to call them anti-constitutional. Such an assertion would itself be considered slander. One could only demonstrate that the very intention of the authorities in bringing in these articles was anti-constitutional after their application had become clear in practice. And even then the authorities would be able to say that one couldn't generalise from individual cases.

However, the articles aroused such universal unease that a group of writers, academicians and Old Bolsheviks appealed to the Supreme Soviet not to accept this amendment to the Criminal Code. Among the signatories to this letter were such prominent people as the composer Shostakovich, the writers Kaverin and Voinovich, the academicians Astaurov, Engelhardt, Tamm and Leontovich, and the film director Romm. The signature of A. D. Sakharov also appeared for the first time on this letter. The letter was cautious in its phraseology and merely pointed out that these new articles were 'contrary to Leninist principles of socialist democracy', 'opened the way to the subjective and arbitrary interpretation of any statement', and could 'form a potential obstacle to the exercise of liberties guaranteed by the constitution'. No reply was received by any of the signatories, and at the end of December 1966 the Decree was confirmed by the Supreme Soviet.

On 5 December 1966, the anniversary of our first demonstration, another 'public meeting' was held in Pushkin Square. Several dozen people gathered there at six in the evening, removed their caps and simply stood there for five minutes. It was decided to do this every year to honour the memory of the victims of coercion. The authorities reacted nervously and attempted to disperse the assembled crowd, but no one was arrested.

It is difficult now to remember everything we did at that time. There were no leaders and no led, there was no allocation of roles, and no one was actively pushed or persuaded. But despite the complete absence of organisational forms, the activities of the protesting community were astonishingly well-coordinated. From outside it was difficult to see how this came about. The KGB, as of old, spent its time looking for leaders and plots, secret hiding-places and addresses, but every time they arrested a supposed 'leader', they were astonished to discover that not only had this not weakened the movement, but in many instances it had even strengthened it.

As when those brain specialists thought for so long that the brain contained special command centres and a hierarchical structure of control, yet each time they succeeded in isolating one of those 'centres' they observed to their astonishment that a completely different 'centre' suddenly took over its functions, so that essentially nothing had changed From outside it seemed as though the brain cells were occupied with superfluous and even pointless work, duplicating one another and carrying out the same functions. It would have been much more rational for there to be specialisation, subordination, commands and absolute compliance. It would have made for much greater order. But no, such a principle is unacceptable to a living organism. Similarly each of us, like a nerve cell, participated in this amazing conductorless orchestra, spurred on only by a consciousness of our own dignity and a sense of personal responsibility for what was happening around us.

We weren't playing politics, we didn't compose programmes for 'the liberation of the people', we didn't found unions of 'the plough and the sword'. Our sole weapon was publicity. Not propaganda, but *publicity*, so that no one could say afterwards: 'I didn't know.' The rest depended on each individual's conscience. Neither did we expect victory – there wasn't the slightest hope of achieving it. But each of us craved the right to say to our descendants: 'I did all that I could. I was a citizen. I fought for the observance of the law and never went against my conscience.' It wasn't a political struggle, but a struggle between the *living* and the *dead*, the *natural* and the *artificial*.

Nobody 'instructed' Alexander Ginzburg to collect documents on the trial of Sinyavsky and Daniel (the so-called *White Book*), or Yuri Galanskov to produce the literary anthology *Phoenix-66*; nobody obliged Vera Lashkova to type all this out, or Victor Khaustov and myself to organise a demonstration when they were arrested.*

Arrests followed one another in quickening succession. The first one to go was Radzievsky. Then, on 17 January, Lashkova and Galanskov, and on the 19th, Dobrovolsky and a few days later, Ginzburg.† The aim was to frighten us off, to make each of us feel that he would be next. To make us retire into our corners, behind locked bolted doors, go down on our knees and whisper: 'Lord, let it not be me!'

* Khaustov, a worker, was tried separately from Bukovsky in February 1967 and sentenced to three years in normal-regime labour camps for helping to organise the demonstration.

† Paul Radzievsky, a worker, was arrested for assisting Galanskov to duplicate some documents for use in *Phoenix-66*, but was later released without being tried. Vera Lashkova had typed out parts of *Phoenix-66* and the *White Book* and in January 1968, at the 'trial of the four', was sentenced to one year in the labour camps. Alexei Dobrovolsky was sentenced at the same trial to two years in strict-regime labour camps for helping Ginzburg and the others.

Perhaps it was this that filled us with an irresistible urge to step forward and shout: 'Here I am! Take me, I'm next. Nobody is afraid of you!' It is sickening to be at liberty when your friends are in jail. When well-known writers were arrested the whole world would be up in arms. But you couldn't expect that now. Who would be disturbed by the arrest of a typist or a junior worker?

There were only two days in which to organise the demo, which meant there was no time to distribute leaflets, as on the previous occasion. Victor Khaustov and I simply went round all our friends – about thirty people in all. We prepared our slogans with care and put them on cloth banners, even nailed them to poles. On 22 January, a couple of dozen of the boys gathered in my flat. Two more groups were to leave from other places. Nobody spoke much – everything was done in silence. Everybody understood that we wouldn't be coming out of it as lightly as last time. Some of us would go to jail. Khaustov and I took full responsibility as the organisers, but who could tell – maybe they would grab the lot of us? It was a new article and nobody had yet been convicted under it.

Probably the only one to speak was Alik Volpin. This time he opposed the demonstration, particularly the slogans. For now we were demanding not an open trial, but simply the release of the fellows who had been arrested. And there was one other slogan: 'We demand a review of the anti-constitutional decree and Article 70 of the Criminal Code.' Alik, of course, protested against the word 'anti-constitutional' – formally speaking, the text of the articles introduced by the new decree didn't contradict the constitution.

'Never mind,' I said, 'let's find out what lies behind this new decree. We'll conduct a legal experiment. If it isn't anti-constitutional, they won't arrest us.'

Again we read through the text of article 190:3, and planned accordingly: don't commit a breach of public order, don't resist representatives of authority, hand over the banners at once if they demand them and go quietly. There was no question of us interrupting transport or the work of any offices – from that point of view, Pushkin Square was an ideal place. We decided not to shout anything, the slogans would suffice. Volpin attempted to write something out for us, some sort of instructions on what to do if arrested, but nobody wanted them.

'Never mind, it's clear enough, anyway,' said Andrei.

'Don't bother, old chap,' said Yulia Vishnevskaya.

Actually, I needed those instructions for the trial. Everyone present should testify that we had had no *intention* of violating article 190:3, and then there would have to be a whole legal argument over the question of intent.

Shortly before six p.m. we made our way to the square from three different directions. It was ten minutes by trolleybus from where I lived. We travelled in silence. Each of us was filled with gloomy determination, like a kamikaze pilot about to ram the target with his plane. Not far behind us came our KGB shadows – they had been on our heels all day.

The weather was killing – about thirty below zero – and this made the street lamps, Pushkin's statue and the lights in the windows stand out all the more clearly and sharply, like a stage set. There were few people in the streets.

We were carrying the banners beneath our overcoats, three of them, and what we feared most was that there would be no time to unfurl them. But nobody interfered with us. Everything was empty around us, as though frozen to death. The entire crowd of about forty people instantly moved towards us, facing us in a semicircle.

'Higher, we can't see,' said someone quietly.

And we stretched our arms up, holding aloft the three white ribbons of cloth with dark blue letters on them, which stood out clearly in the frosty air.

A tall figure, wrapped tightly from head to foot, approached the crowd and stood at one end.

'Aha, a nark,' said Yulia gloatingly.

'No, it's not, it's Boris Yefimov.'

And for a second I was overcome with a sudden fear: what if nothing happens? The whole calculation was that they would confiscate the banners and arrest us. Surely we wouldn't have to take them home with us again? I hadn't banked on going home at all.

Suddenly five men came dashing out of the darkness on our right and hurled themselves upon us, shouting. No uniforms and no armbands. Mugs red with cold.

'Disgusting things to display!'

'I'll knock your eye out, you swine!'

Representatives of authority with their lawful demands.

They ripped off our banners, but Khaustov was still holding on to his and a 'representative of authority' was trying in vain to detach the banner from the pole. Khaustov and I had made that banner ourselves, nailing it on thoroughly and professionally. He had a job as an up-holsterer and had supplied some special sort of nails.

At last three of them knocked him over and started to twist his arms behind his back.

'Victor, don't resist!' I called out. 'Take it easy, don't resist!'

He quietened down and was quickly dragged from the square.

Everybody began talking and moving, and only then did I catch sight of one other young fellow standing with one of the banners under his arm and holding on to Boris and Yulia. The two of them stood there quietly, ready to go wherever they were told, but the fellow remained alone and was obviously undecided what to do. Quite young – younger than me. He was embarrassed and confused, and I could see that he felt terribly ill at ease. He was waiting for us to push him out of our circle and then he would leave with a clear conscience. But the opposite happened. He was taken for one of us and someone in the crowd called out:

'Hide the banner under your overcoat, they'll be back again in a minute.'

'Go away, go away, while nobody's looking.'

For a second he hesitated, then abandoned the two of them and strode away swiftly, without looking back.

It was all over. We felt cold and uncomfortable.

'Let's go,' I said. 'We've done what we came for. Let's go somewhere and get warm.'

About ten of us, including me, moved slowly off to the trolleybus stop. The crowd split up into little groups, all animatedly discussing what had happened.

'What happened, what was it?' asked some chance passer-by.

Some time later, after I had gone, the plainclothesmen came back and grabbed Vadim Delaunay and Yevgeny Kushev. Kushev had taken it into his head to shout: 'Down with dictatorship! Free Dobrovolsky!' Delaunay was released, but Kushev was taken to Lefortovo. Ilya Gabai was detained by two policemen on orders from the KGB, but he too was released after his name had been noted down.*

These details were subsequently repeated a thousand times by witnesses, investigators, prosecutors, judges and lawyers, were intentionally twisted or accidentally distorted, until, at last, after being filtered

---

* Delaunay was an amateur poet. He made a confession of guilt at his subsequent trial with Kushev and Bukovsky, and was conditionally sentenced to one year in normal-regime labour camps. Kushev also pleaded guilty and got one year conditionally. Ilya Gabai, a teacher and editor, was supposed to be tried together with Khaustov, but his case was adjourned and after four months he was released without charges. Later, in 1973, he committed suicide after persistent interrogations by the KGB.

through the judicial process, they settled into the wooden phrases of the sentences.

Evidently the authorities themselves were at a loss what to do with us. Vadim was arrested only three days later, Gabai and myself after four days. Again the days dragged by in Lefortovo, with its interrogations and informers. Reveille, breakfast, exercise, lunch, supper, lights out, reveille, breakfast, exercise, lunch, supper, lights out.

'Get ready for the bathhouse.'

'What, bath day again? Another week gone.'

The investigation of a political crime in the Soviet Union is a very special procedure that cannot be accommodated in any criminal code. It was no accident that the KGB's best investigator was professionally incapable of conducting a normal criminal investigation, and would have been unable to solve even a paltry case of pocket picking. In criminal practice a case is started after a crime has been committed. A murder, let us say, takes place, and that is the basis for instituting a case, 'the case of the murder of citizen so-and-so'. The investigation examines the circumstances of the murder, its links and connexions with certain people, considers which of them might be the murderer and investigates their relations with the victim. Finally, if they are lucky, they find the murderer and start collecting evidence of his implication in the crime, taking fingerprints, blood samples, and so on. If the evidence is insufficient, he is left alone and they look for another possible murderer. If they don't find one, the murder case remains unsolved. But everything is precise: the witnesses are only witnesses, the murder suspect is suspected only of murder, the investigator is simply an investigator, and the defence counsel simply counsel.

In a political investigation, however, the case is instituted against *the man*, because in the opinion of the KGB and the Party bosses *his time has come*. They have accumulated an assortment of denunciations revealing his utterances, intentions, contacts and influence on others, or showing him as being in somebody's way or, on the contrary, refusing to cooperate, or knowing too much and talking about it or, on the contrary, not wanting to know at all. In short, he's ripe for it. More often than not, a whole circle of people is considered ripe for putting away – they need to be brought into line; a few jailed and a few baited and hooked. Then the KGB inspects them and chooses the man who looks the most vulnerable and most likely to crack, the most likely to compromise; or, on the contrary, they choose someone whose arrest will have the greatest shock effect on all the others. Or even someone who has been the least active of them all, in order to make the rest feel responsible: 'You see, you're all right, yet he (she) is in jail'; or: 'You involved him in your affairs and now he's got to pay for what the rest of you did.' Or else they knock off everyone *around* someone who is very active, hoping to arouse suspicions that he is still free because he's collaborating with the KGB.

There are exceptional cases, of course, when the arrest is forced by unexpected circumstances, as with our demonstration, but even then the investigation is conducted according to the usual rules as summed up in the well-known phrase: 'Give us the man and we'll find the charges.' If a man is arrested on a criminal charge, he is not accused of murder in general, or robbery in general, or of being a swindler in general, but of the murder of someone, the robbery of someone, or of concrete examples of swindling. But in political cases the charge is formulated in terms of the article that is being invoked, and the facts are selected in the course of the investigation: whatever can be used to confirm any testimony, any confessions or materials found in a search, will later be incorporated into the formal indictment. They also tend to arrest you, or search you before an arrest, on the most unlikely pretexts: conspiracy to assassinate the General Secretary of the Communist Party of the USSR, or refusal to pay alimony to your abandoned family; attempted escape abroad, or conspiracy to rob a bank. They simply take the most colourful of the denunciations they have received of the chosen victim and present them to the Party bureau (without whom not one arrest can be made): 'You see what sort of a man he is and what he's come to! It's high time to put him away. He's spreading propaganda, taking bribes and has beaten his wife. We'll take him in first for the fight with his wife, then we can see what else there is that seems useful.'

And a case is started against citizen N. A whole team of investigators is assigned, and day by day, hour by hour, they minutely examine citizen N's whole life – it cannot be that this citizen has never done anything of 'that sort', we don't have such spotless people in our country. All right, so he didn't want to murder the General Secretary, but he criticised him when drunk, praised America, greased somebody's palm or sold something that 'fell off a lorry'. As in Kafka, the guilt reveals itself. Investigating the case of our demonstration, they arrested five people, and although there were no more than fifty in the square, they searched a hundred, raking in, of course, large quantities of *samizdat*. This gave them both the means to scare people and the hope of picking up something else.

But what interests the team of investigators above all is citizen N's private life: who did he sleep with, where, when and how often? Who of us hasn't sinned? And if such a sin comes to light, they can make various uses of it. In the first place, citizen N has a wife and he is not at all keen for her to find out. Secondly, the citizen he sinned with has a husband who will be a willing ally of the prosecution and will recall, invent or corroborate as many incriminating items as he can about citizen N. Thirdly, what won't this lady sign to prevent her husband from finding out about it? And so on. There is no end to the number of possible combinations – all you need is the time to put it down in writing. And finally you get a beautifully distinct picture of citizen N's immoral character, his true nature, so to speak, and this will come in very handy for the trial and the newspapers.

The task of a political investigation is thus not to disentangle the crime, but above all to collect compromising material. Its duty is to elucidate why it is that citizen N, who to all intents and purposes is wholly Soviet, grew up in a Soviet family and was educated in Soviet schools, has turned out to be so terribly un-Soviet. This has to be established and communicated to the higher echelons in the Party hierarchy, so that conclusions can be drawn and measures taken.

According to Party dogma, a man is incapable of arriving at certain thoughts on his own, just like that. There has to be someone's 'influence', either that of bourgeois propaganda (discover how it got through!) or of some anti-Soviet individual (uncover him and bring him in for observation!). In the last resort, the investigation is obliged to confirm that not enough educational work has been done with citizen N. This is very bad, and means that one of his Party colleagues at work or in the faculty will be reprimanded. But they prefer not to take the matter that far and therefore urge him: 'Come on now, think. Who was it that influenced you? Who?'

Of course, before the investigation is completed citizen N, under the weight of all the incriminating evidence, is supposed to repent, to acknowledge his mistakes or, at the very least, to regret what he has done. Otherwise the investigators themselves will catch it in the neck: a political investigation is in the first instance the re-education of a sinner, and the investigator is both an educator and a political instructor.

The investigator's main weapon is the average Soviet man's ignorance of the law. From the day of his arrest until the conclusion of the investigation, citizen N is held in complete isolation from the outside world and is not allowed to see a lawyer. No copy of the

Criminal Code is made available to him, and even if it were, what use would it be? So he must try to decide on his own what to say and what not to say, what rights he has and what he hasn't.

A man arrested for the first time is usually convinced that he is going to be tortured, or at the very least beaten. The investigator is in no hurry to disabuse him of this belief. On the contrary. 'All right,' he mutters menacingly, 'if you won't own up of your own accord, so much the worse for you.' What it is that will be 'worse' is never explained.

As a rule a man decides that the best course of action is to confirm everything that the investigator already knows. What difference does it make? He knows it anyway. So long as you don't give him any new facts or implicate new people. And this seems a particularly good move, because every time you refuse to answer they fling back at you: 'You're not sincere.' This way you can confirm your 'sincerity' with certain facts without, it seems, yourself being broken. This is the commonest mistake. To give evidence confirming what the investigation already 'knows' is to give them hard currency at the official rate in exchange for Soviet roubles. Whatever they 'know', from agents or telephone tapping or simply pure supposition, cannot be included in the investigation record for submission to the court. By confirming what is doubtfully 'known', a man turns it into a juridical fact, into hard evidence.

Even when they read you the testimony of somebody who has 'repented', you should never confirm it. One man's testimony, particularly if he is the accused, is one thing; he may still change it or, in the last resort, deny it in court. But the testimony of two people is a much more serious matter, and it will make it much harder for the man who has 'repented' to deny his former penitence in court. Even the most insignificant facts, details and minutiae, which seemingly have nothing whatsoever to do with the case, should on no account be confirmed (or related) – they will later be shown to someone over your signature and this other person will be told: 'You see, he confessed everything. He even told us such tiny details as these.'

Furthermore, the investigator taking down your statement is bound to twist everything you say. Instead of 'meeting', he will write 'criminal gathering', instead of 'views' – 'anti-Soviet views', instead of 'gave to read' – 'distributed'. And it's a bit awkward to refuse to sign it afterwards – look at all the work the man has done writing it down.

It is amazing how difficult Soviet man finds it to say 'no', 'I don't wish to reply', 'I won't tell you'. He prefers to speak vaguely: 'sort of', 'as if', 'perhaps'. The investigator, of course, writes down 'yes', and adds a whole sentence of his own, making it into an extended 'yes'.

Then there's the informer in your cell, and the investigator's hints about the hard time your wife and children are going to have.

And when, at last, they close your case and you are allowed to meet your lawyer, it is too late. The injustice people do themselves out of ignorance! Themselves and others.

The investigator's second weapon is the witnesses. Everything said above applies to them too, but for the witness it is even harder. A witness in a political case is not just a witness, but a suspect. Today's witness, tomorrow's prisoner, and the basic characteristic of a witness is the desire not to become a defendant. In some cases it is even difficult to make out why one person becomes a witness and another the accused. They are both equally 'guilty'; it's just that it suits the investigation that way.

A witness is immediately informed that it is a criminal offence to refuse to testify, and another to supply false testimony.

'Did or didn't citizen N say to you that there was no democracy in our country?'

Who doesn't say it! It doesn't sound very convincing to deny it. And if you do they'll nail you for false testimony. 'You know, I don't remember. Sort of. . . .'

'Good enough,' says the investigator soothingly, 'we know he did. Now that Thursday at your place, for example, when you were sitting round the table. You also told a joke about Lenin's widow, Nadezhda Konstantinovna Krupskaya. Right?'

'Maybe,' says the witness uncertainly. 'I don't remember.'

He particularly doesn't remember telling a joke himself. And the investigator enters into the record: 'Yes, that Thursday citizen N made anti-Soviet remarks in my home, asserting that there was no democracy in the Soviet Union.' The vilest slander on the most democratic system in the entire world. A dead cert for article 70. What lawyer can help you now?

Anyway, it is only in criminal cases that the lawyer is there to help you. In political cases the lawyer is, as a rule, there to help the KGB, having been appointed – or, as official jargon has it, 'admitted' – by them. And if the joint efforts of the investigators, informers and witnesses, combined with his ignorance of the law, haven't succeeded in bringing citizen N to repentance, then it is the lawyer's turn to take a hand. Not only will he point to the Criminal Code, but he will cite cases from his own practice to show that sincere repentance is a mitigating circumstance: 'Repent, even if it's only a formality, and you'll get a shorter sentence. Five years instead of seven. Otherwise it'll be impossible to defend you.'

This is the reason the KGB never has any 'unsolved cases'. If they had to admit that they had pointlessly arrested citizen N and pointlessly held him in Lefortovo prison, there would be the most almighty scandal. Somebody would have to be demoted, somebody put out to pasture, and somebody transferred to the far side of Siberia as senior investigator of particularly important cases – to root out anti-Sovietism among the polar bears.

Never in our history has a court acquitted anyone arraigned on political charges. The most that can happen is that they hand out a suspended sentence – if, that is, the repentance is particularly handsome. After all, the first concern of our Soviet judges must be to educate the masses. And what sort of an education is it if even a fool can see that citizen N is being tried, even by our standards, for next to nothing at all? With not even a doubtful episode over money or 'moral decay' to help things along? How can an enemy of the proletarian regime be morally pure? And when they haven't found any evidence of the influence of bourgeois propaganda.

And if they let him go, it is well before the cases reaches the court, and not after having 'acquitted', or better still having 'pardoned' him (he's still not convicted and not even brought to court, but pardoned!), or in the last resort, 'for lack of proof of guilt'. No, it's run and enjoy yourself, dear fellow, while we dig up some more dirt on you, you won't get very far. That's what they did with Ilya Gabai in our case – let him go in order to arrest him properly two years later, with none of your nonsense about lack of proof.

My position during the investigation was clear and simple: 'I am a citizen of this country and have acted within the framework of its Constitution. Yes, I was the organiser and an active participant in the demonstration. That is my constitutional right and I made use of it. I invited my friends to take part in the demonstration, made the banners, took them to the square and held one of the banners myself. I refuse to say exactly whom I invited, who helped me to make the banners and who came to the square, since these things have nothing to do with the charges against me. I can answer only for my own actions. Before going to the square I instructed my friends how to behave. I read them the text of article 190:3 aloud and warned everyone present not to commit a breach of public order, to submit to the demands of the authorities, not to resist and not to interrupt transport or the work of any institutions. None of us violated any of these requirements during the demonstration. It was those who interrupted us and tore our banners who flagrantly violated public order. I demand that they be traced and criminal proceedings instituted against them.' And like a model citizen I wrote hundreds of complaints demanding that the disturbers of the peace be speedily brought to book.

On the tenth day I was charged under article 190:3. The charge said that 'learning of the arrest of his friends Lashkova, Dobrovolsky, Galanskov, etc., with the aim of securing their release and in violation of the procedure established by law for addressing the competent organs on questions of this nature, he embarked on a course of unlawfully expressing his demands and his disagreement with article 70 and articles 190:1 and 190:3 of the Criminal Code of the Russian Federal Republic, was one of the organisers of activities that constituted a flagrant breach of public order in Pushkin Square, Moscow, on 22 January 1967, and took an active part in those activities.'

'Do you understand the charges?' asked the investigator.

'No.'

At this point we changed roles, and now it was he who had to give the explanations. But how could he explain? The Soviet regime is not accustomed to giving explanations, it can only make demands.

'I don't understand where you got this "aim of securing their release" from. What is the "procedure established by law for addressing the competent organs"? How could I violate it if I didn't even try to use it? Why was the method of expressing my demands unlawful – after all, it was wholly constitutional – and above all, what did my "flagrant breach of public order" consist of?'

I was visited by prosecutors, section chiefs and some plainclothesmen, who endeavoured to explain it all to me, waving their arms about and puckering their foreheads, but without moving the matter forward one inch. How do you explain that it is all right to demand the liberation of Greek political prisoners, but not of Soviet prisoners? And where, in what law, is it written that the 1 May demonstration in Red Square is not a breach of public order, while ours in Pushkin Square was? And not one of them could get past the article in the constitution which states in black and white that citizens of the USSR are guaranteed the freedom of street processions and demonstrations.

I crushed them with laws, pinned them down with articles and stunned them with paragraphs: admit it, honestly and truthfully, tell the whole truth that there is no freedom of demonstrations in the USSR, that you categorically forbid everything you don't like. Now it was they who began to slip into vagueness: 'maybe', 'sort of', 'as it were'.

'Yes, but you are a Soviet man.'

'I am a citizen of the USSR.'

'What opinions do you hold?'

'What does that have to do with my case? I hope you're not holding me in jail for my opinions?'

'Do you admit your guilt?'

'How can I answer that when I don't understand the charges? Tell me.'

Under the law they were obliged to explain them to me.

'You can't?' A whole sheaf of complaints went flying off on the instant: they don't want to explain the charges to a poor prisoner in jail. I've been here six months and I still don't know what for! And from on high the answer was handed down: 'Explain to the accused.' The machine had been short-circuited. That is what sometimes happens to computers: lights flash on and off, something clicks, the machine whirrs and no decision comes out. The position of a citizen was proving to be invulnerable.

To begin with, of course, they wouldn't give me any copies of the Criminal Codes. I received a visit from the prison governor, Colonel Petrenko, with his shaggy grey eyebrows sticking out from under a Caucasian fur cap. 'It's not allowed.'

All right. I wrote another sheaf of complaints and threatened a hunger strike. No more than two days went by before Colonel Petrenko put himself to the trouble of coming to see me again, saying almost tearfully: 'We haven't got any codes, we've turned the whole library upside down. All I've got is my own copy with a dedication from Semichastny. What do you want me to do – give you that?'

I took not only his presentation copy, autographed by the then chairman of the KGB, but also a copy of the Criminal Procedure Code, complete with commentaries, and a whole pile of assorted legal literature. The only thing they couldn't find was a copy of the constitution. But I was adamant and on the fourth day, puffing and blowing, the deputy governor, Lieutenant-Colonel Stepanov, came running in with one.

'Here you are, I've brought you the constitution,' he said in his comical provincial accent. 'But it's for the Russian republic, I couldn't find one for the USSR. Still, they're both the same. Bought it myself. Cost three copecks. Never mind, we'll settle up later.'

Petrenko and I became the best of friends. He would come to my cell, make an effort to knit his shaggy brows into a stern frown beneath his fur cap, gaze thoughtfully at my empty shelves and ask: 'Why haven't you got any food?'

'I've eaten it all. It's all gone.'

'When is your next parcel due?'

'Not for a while yet. In a month.'

'Write an application. I'll allow you an extra one.' And then he would leave.

He himself was a former investigator and now, reading my endless complaints, he could see clearly that the investigation had run up a blind alley. There was nothing to charge me with.

Meanwhile I was devouring the criminal codes as if they were detective novels, memorising them like multiplication tables, and was discovering to my amazement how many rights I really had. And I started to make the fullest use of those rights.

Now I openly made fun of my investigators, deluged them with complaints and forced them to write out my statements ten times in a row.

It was summer, the heat was killing, and my investigators sweated away, dreaming of shady woods. 'Vladimir Konstantinovich! Surely that's enough? How many more times can it be copied?'

Round about the middle of summer they came up against a total deadend and started a new investigation under article 70. But this time they began with caution and stealth, not telling me the new charges. What a hope! The law's the law. Tell me the charges and then ask your questions. Another stream of complaints from me: Illegal investigation! Criminals! Put them on trial!

Two of the boys, Kushev and Delaunay (Khaustov by now had been tried separately from us and given three years), had repented and were writing tearful epistles to their investigators. For them it was all terrible – prison, bars, guards. Six months without their families and the future a complete blank. But for me the whole thing was a picnic and never again did I have as much fun as I did then. The case kept spawning more and more disasters for the KGB. Suddenly it emerged from the evidence of two of the policemen that they had detained Gabai on the direct orders of Colonel Abramov of the KGB, who had been in charge of dispersing the demonstration in the square.

Finally the case ground to a complete halt and there was nothing more to talk about. My investigator started calling me in just for the sake of it, for a chat. With all the squabbling going on, neither of us had noticed how friendly we had become, and now he found it boring if he let a day go by without arguing with me about something or other. He himself lived in the provinces, in Yaroslavl, and like all provincials was ashamed of how badly informed he was. 'Well, tell me about one of your books. What about that book by Djilas that you were charged with in 1963? What sort of a whatsit was it?'

'Do you mean to say they don't let you read them? Don't they trust you either?'

'Not likely. All you get to read in my job is what you turn up in the searches. And back in Yaroslavl there's nothing to find. Total darkness.'

He listened with rapt attention, like people listening to a lecture in a planetarium: 'Is there life on Mars?' I told him everything I could remember from the books I had read in *samizdat* – let him take it all back to his Yaroslavl and tell his friends there. They were human beings, after all, and dying to hear something new.

In some ways he quite appealed to me – tall, with a broad forehead and a frank, open face. He didn't care for our case or the role he had been assigned to play in it. Our farewell was even touching. In the war he had been an artillery man and now he told me how the boys in his battalion had occupied some rise and continued firing to the last man. They had all perished, but without surrendering. 'Then the Germans,' he said, 'buried them with full honours. A general came and personally attended the funeral, taking off his hat and ordering a salute to be fired. That was correct, you should always respect a worthy opponent. I too feel that – ' here he broke off, made a motion as if to offer me his hand, but couldn't quite bring himself to: what if I didn't take it?

I later learned that he left the KGB soon after that. I don't know if it was true, but in my opinion he wasn't a bad fellow at all.

The investigation was brought to an end by the Deputy Public Prosecutor, Malyarov. Taking pity on the secret policemen, he refused to prolong the term of investigation, and wrote across the corner of my complaints: 'Close the investigation and bring the case to trial.' The Great Holiday was approaching, the Fiftieth Anniversary of the Soviet regime, and this shameful trial was hardly the best present from the ardent men in blue to their beloved Central Committee.

But now, at the eleventh hour before the trial, they made a last desperate attempt to avert a scandal. Through the defence lawyers representing my co-defendants came a proposal that I petition the authorities to be sent for a psychiatric examination. 'The chief thing is to wait till the holidays are over,' they assured me. 'Then there will be an amnesty and you will be freed. You'll get the best of both worlds.'

That didn't suit me at all. The fact was that I had the KGB by the throat, and it would have been unpardonable stupidity on my part to let them slide out of it now and not bring me to trial. Anyway, what a crazy idea – that I myself should apply to be examined! That was simply putting my head in a noose. And amnesties were never extended to loonies anyway.

'All right, if you won't spare yourself, what about Kushev and Delaunay? Why should you spoil their lives for them? They won't get long to do, of course, but still, it's a conviction on their records.'

But I categorically refused and they went away disillusioned. My own lawyer, Dina Isakovna Kaminskaya, took no part in this haggling. She merely said: 'Decide for yourself,' and listened in silence to our conversation. It was this, I think, that suddenly made me realise that a miracle had happened: I had an honest lawyer.

The usual position in political cases is that the relatives, or the defendant himself, can choose only a lawyer who has an 'access permit to inspect secret records'. Given that these 'access permits' are issued by the KGB, naturally it goes only to people they can trust. Before the trial these 'defence counsel' work the defendant over, persuade him to repent and give the necessary testimony, and even try to worm some information out of him in which the KGB is interested. At the trial they begin by announcing that as honest Soviet citizens they condemn the views of their client, are horrified by the depths to which he has fallen, and can venture nothing other than to beg the honourable court most humbly for leniency, taking into account his youth (or, on the contrary, advanced age), his inexperience, lack of previous convictions, poor health, difficult childhood, his young children, sincere repentance, readiness to redeem his guilt and the harm he has caused society, by engaging in honest labour. There have even been curious cases when the lawyer got so carried away by his role as an indignant Soviet citizen that the judge had to stop him and ask, 'Comrade counsel, are you for the defence or the prosecution?'

Naturally this was the sort of lawyer I was expecting, and I had resolved to dispense with a defence counsel altogether, which fortunately is allowed under the law. I had therefore greeted Kaminskaya, who had been chosen by my mother, with reserve. What did my mother know of such things? Nor did it help when she referred to her friendship with Kallistratova: sitting in my Lefortovo cell, I hadn't heard a thing about Victor Khaustov's trial or about the courageous and brilliant way in which Kallistratova had defended him. Only later, after the other lawyers suggested that I ask for a medical examination, did the ice of my distrust begin to melt. Soon the whole world rang with the names of our valorous lawyers – Kallistratova, Kaminskaya, Zolotukhin, Zalessky, Aria, Monakhov and others. For the first time, defence counsel began to seek acquittals at Soviet political trials, professionally demonstrating the absence of guilt. This had the effect of an exploding bomb. Maybe the defence could not influence the court's decision, whose outcome had in any case been decided in advance by high Party circles, but that wasn't where we looked for victory.

By the time our trial came around in the summer of 1967, it was clear even to the naked eye how completely the case against us had collapsed. After five months of fruitless investigation, Gabai had been released. True, they still kept trying to pin a criminal charge on him, but nothing came of that. Radzievsky, one of the arrested boys for whose benefit we had organised the demonstration, was released: thus we were to be tried for 'illegally' demanding the release of the arrested men, one of whom had already been released by of all people – the KGB. The others had still not been brought to trial, and who could say that they wouldn't be released as well? Our case had dragged on for seven months and the investigation was terminated by order of the Public Prosecutor. They still hadn't succeeded in charging us under article 70.

None of the witnesses questioned, including the detectives and police, had seen us in any way committing a breach of public order. The thugs who broke up the demo admitted that they had been hired by the KGB. The demonstrators testified unanimously that I had previously instructed them not to disturb public order, and to submit to the demands of the authorities. Furthermore, in the square itself, I had called on Khaustov not to resist, and this was noted in everybody's testimony. All that remained now was to complete the rout of the KGB during the trial itself. Therefore I prepared to take an active part in it and not give them a moment's rest, and I planned to denounce them to maximum effect in my final statement to the court.

It was probable that they would refuse to let anyone into the courtroom, as had happened with the trial of Sinyavsky and Daniel. But their final words had somehow become public knowledge anyway, and I was hoping that my friends, too, would find a way of noting down my speech. Even if they didn't, I was determined to behave as if I was addressing the whole country. Simply for the moral satisfaction of it.

Apart from denouncing the KGB and demonstrating the monstrous illegality of this trial, I also intended to expound the aims of our demo and point out the anti-constitutional character of the political articles in the Criminal Code, all in strict accordance with the citizen's position

235

I had adopted. I would announce this position publicly for the very first time, and taking advantage of the general interest in the trial and the tension of the proceedings, attract maximum attention to it. In short, I prepared a speech of about an hour and a half, which was a mistake. Whoever would remember such a long oration?

Knowing how the trial of Sinyavsky and Daniel had been conducted, I foresaw that the judge and the prosecuting counsel would try to prevent me from speaking, would interrupt the witnesses and do all they could to take the proceedings into their own hands. I therefore made a detailed study of the Procedural Code and thought out all the legal moves that would enable me to conduct the trial the way I wanted it. I particularly expected clashes with the judge, and therefore had worked out a whole programme of action. From my experience of meeting investigators and prosecutors, I knew how badly informed Soviet jurists were about procedural law, and therefore I was sure that a reference to some obscure and forgotten article would stump the judge completely. And it was hardly possible for him to thumb through his code in the middle of the trial and demonstrate his incompetence.

In the code, for instance, I read that I had the right to make remarks on the judge's conduct of the trial and to insist that my remarks be included in the court record. I doubted whether this article had ever been used since the code was adopted, and of course the judge wouldn't remember it. I couldn't use that device indefinitely – it would cease to be effective after a while – and so I decided that I would resort to it five or six times and suddenly halfway through the trial, enter a plea for the judge to be removed: I would generalise my remarks and announce that the judge's conduct of the trial demonstrated prejudice. The procedure for removing a judge promised a lot of fun. According to the law, a judge cannot participate in the hearing of such a plea – he is the object of the pleader's distrust. The two people's assessors, without the judge, are obliged to retire to the deliberating room alone and find a correct formula for their reply, since reasons have to be given for their decision. The assessors are usually completely illiterate in legal matters, submissive and without initiative – I relished in advance the nonsense they would write in their decision, once left to their own devices and without the judge to dictate to them. Meanwhile, the judge was obliged to quit his position as chairman and go and sit in the body of the court. All in all it would be a pretty humiliating procedure.

There were three of us being tried together: Delaunay, Kushev and I. Khaustov had been tried long before, since the authorities found it more convenient that way: he could in some sense be charged with 'resisting the representatives of authority'. He got three years.

On the morning of 30 August 1967, we were brought from Lefortovo to the Moscow City Court, in Kalanchovka Street, and locked in special cells in the basement. Just before ten, our escort guards led us into the courtroom and the dock.

I had been looking forward to this as to a celebration: for once in my life I was getting a chance to speak my mind loudly and clearly. But I was terribly nervous and feared that I would be unable to conduct the trial as I wanted, that I would lose my nerve and jumble my words. Yet the moment I set foot in that courtroom, with its inexpressibly stale, government smell, dingy walls, official chairs and grubby ceilings, all my tension drained away. No solemnity, no festivity, no tragedy – only official conventionality, bureaucratic boredom and public apathy. I was amused to see that on the raised judges' rostrum, directly beneath the massive coat of arms of the Soviet Union, some joker had scratched in large letters that one-syllable word that decorates all walls, all public conveniences and all school desks in Russia: prick. This indeed was the sign of the zodiac under which our whole trial was to pass.

The judge, a woman of about forty-five, rather affable, not in the least hostile or overweening, directed the proceedings with the expert automatism of a priest celebrating mass. For her it was just another working day. The assessors dozed, propping their heads on their hands, the escort guards yawned, and the body of the court was filled with plainclothes security men playing the role of 'the public'.

Thousands of shaven-headed men had shuffled in a long grey file through this courtroom before the gaze of these judges, assessors and guards, had received their melancholy sentences – five, ten, fifteen years, or the firing squad – and disappeared. It was fine for the poets of old to write odes about captives in picturesque rags rattling their chains, about gloomy dungeons and bloodthirsty executioners. Nowadays they no longer sent you to the block, where you had a chance of turning to the people, bowing from the waist in all directions and exclaiming: 'Good people! On this holy cross I swear that I am innocent!' Then putting your head on the block: 'Here, do your worst, heathen!' Now it was more like dispatching goods from a warehouse: 'Sign here and here and here. Stand over by that wall, Okay. Next.' The man yawns and looks at his watch – how long till dinner time?

None of your odes and ballads – just that one-syllable word. The best possible poem.

Looking at that miserable courtroom, not only did I not feel like making any speeches, but I didn't even want to open my mouth. Wasn't it going too much against the grain to pretend that I could take this farce at face value?

'Citizen judges, Citizen prosecutor, Citizen witnesses. . . .'

The sentence was all prepared in their pockets, all it needed was to be signed. Monotonous questions, monotonous answers – everything was known beforehand, had been prepared in advance. 'I don't understand the charges. I plead innocent.' Mortal boredom.

I was saved by the prosecuting counsel. He had a face of rare obnoxiousness, and when he began, with a nauseous smirk, to explain that it was only fair to expect someone after seven months in jail to trim his opinions, I was overcome with silent rage. What a slimy cheapskate, this paper-chewer. Measures everybody by himself. One day in jail and I bet you'd sell your own mother! All right, I'll make you sweat for that soon.

Everything went by the book. The judge tried to interrupt me a few times, but I was prepared and shot her down with one of the articles I had ready. This did indeed damp her ardour, and for the rest of the three-day trial she hardly interrupted me at all, except occasionally for the sake of appearances, so as not to be reprimanded afterwards. And there was no need to ask for her removal.

When it was time for the cross-examination of witnesses – those same 'representatives of authority' who had torn our banners down – we and our lawyers laid into them till the feathers flew. (They didn't dare to call the police as witnesses – the testimony they had given during the investigation had been highly unwelcome to the KGB.) These 'auxiliary policemen', despite the careful instructions given them by the KGB, came out of it looking pretty sick. They all confessed that they had had no identifying armbands, none of them could describe any 'breaches of public order', and a few of them let slip that they had been warned in advance that a demonstration was due to take place, and had been sent to disperse it. The whole thing looked ridiculous.

The following day our friends who had taken part in the demo were cross-examined. They all gave splendid answers, and my pals in the dock were visibly cheered: it's always easier when you see some familiar faces. The most surprising thing was that the witnesses weren't bustled out of the court when they had finished giving evidence but were allowed to stay, and naturally they did everything they could to memorise the proceedings.

On the third day there was the summing-up. The counsel for the prosecution had been backed into such a corner that he was obliged to argue that the very holding of a demonstration was a breach of public order. At this point the defence counsel piled into him: what about the constitution?!

Tying himself hopelessly into knots, the prosecuting counsel finally said: It is forbidden to demand the release of persons arrested by the KGB. That undermines the authority of the security organs. It is forbidden to demand a review of the law. It is permitted to express disagreement with the actions of the authorities only 'according to the established procedures'. Any other method is automatically a breach of public order.

My two co-defendants had grown so cheerful now that in their final words, although expressing regret for what had occurred, they refused to acknowledge their guilt. I myself spoke at great length – at too great a length for such a trial. But I said everything I had wanted to. I shook my three copeck constitution under the prosecuting counsel's nose, launched thunderbolt after thunderbolt, and just before the end, said that the first thing I would do after my release would be to stage another demonstration.

I must have spoken too strongly, because glancing around the courtroom from time to time, the frightened faces of my friends and the ashen face of my mother seemed to tell me that they were witnessing a catastrophe. Only Alik Volpin nodded his head approvingly, as if nothing in the world was wrong.

As was to be expected, the sentences corresponded word for word with the indictment, as if this absurd three-day trial had never taken place. I got the scheduled three years, and the other two were each given a year's suspended sentence. On parting, we embraced. I knew they faced a harder time than I did: freedom can be much worse than prison, and after the 'repentance' they had displayed in court, they were destined to repent again and again. God grant that they would find the strength to master themselves and remain human.

On my way from the courtroom to the prison van, which stood in a closed inner courtyard, one of my friends opened a window above and threw out a whole armful of cornflowers, which cascaded on to my head and on to my guards as well. I took these cornflowers back to my cell.

'What's this?' said Petrenko with a frown. 'Flowers? Well, now....' but turned away and said no more, though flowers in prison are 'not allowed'.

Two months later an amnesty was proclaimed to mark the fiftieth anniversary of the Soviet regime, but in its decree the Presidium of the Supreme Soviet said that the amnesty did not extend to those convicted of 'organising or taking an active part in group activities that constitute a flagrant breach of public order'. Three whole extra lines in the decree, yet in the entire Soviet Union there were only two people in jail on that charge: Khaustov and me.

There was one other strange consequence of these events: my old friend General Svetlichny, the head of the Moscow KGB, the evil dwarf with the outsize head, suddenly went into retirement.

I was in the labour camp in January 1968 when the trial of Galanskov, Ginzburg, Lashkova and Dobrovolsky was held. This was yet one more attempt by the authorities to intimidate the intelligentsia and force it to see things their way. But whereas official propaganda had seen fit to pass over our trial in silence – except for one short paragraph in the *Evening Moscow* newspaper – the 'trial of the four' was accompanied by a deafening howl from the Soviet press. The authorities again tried to make out that they had been put on trial not for their opinions, but for 'plotting', having 'secret links with centres of subversion' and 'slander'. But that was just for export. For the Russian people the trial was an open threat – just see what will happen to you!

Once more, as in the Sinyavsky–Daniel trial, we saw the collision of two points of view, two concepts, two ways of life: one furtive, underground and schizophrenic, the other open, appealing to the law and actively standing up for civil rights. This trial demonstrated with extraordinary clarity the link between underground psychology and official tyranny: you could not have one without the other.

The trial was in some ways reminiscent of the theatre of the absurd. They were talking about the same articles of the Criminal Code, using the same terms and expressions, yet different people had totally different concepts of what lay behind them.

The charges, the court and official propaganda insisted on their own *ideological prescriptions*, whereas the defendants, their defence lawyers and the witnesses invoked their *legal rights*.

What do we regard as most fundamental – ideology or the law? That was the question posed by our trials, and on the answer to it depended, not the fate of the accused but the entire future life of our country.

The fate of the accused had been decided in advance – the ideological State could not afford to have a civil-rights point of view imposed upon it. And Yuri Galanskov, ashen-faced from the pain of his stomach ulcers throughout the five-day trial, fighting back his agony and resisting the taunts of the court and the prosecuting counsel, was destined to die in the camps before the expiry of his seven-year term.

But we ourselves were responsible for deciding our future, and after Larisa Bogoraz and Pavel Litvinov appealed to world public opinion, letters of protest flowed in a never-ending torrent: the Novosibirsk letter, the letter of the Ukrainians, the witnesses' letter, the letter of the 79, the 13, the 224, the 121, the 25, the 8, the 46, and the 139. Whole families wrote, individuals wrote. A sailor from Odessa, the chairman of a collective farm in Latvia, a priest from Pskov, an engineer from Moscow. Writers, scientists, workers and students from every corner of the country.

They were kicked out of their jobs and the university, stripped of their titles, pilloried in the press and at meetings. One or two of them recanted, but the rest only became more determined and obstinate, and their numbers grew and grew. Look at the signatures under those first letters and you will see the names of people who, either that year or a few years later, were to become the accused themselves. New arrests, new trials – and new protests. Repressions became a normal feature of life, and the trials that repeated those first trials of ours across the country became a ritual: the crowd at the court entrance prevented from attending the 'open' trial (as Ilya Gabai once said, 'standing outside the closed doors of an open trial'), the knot of foreign correspondents (in Moscow), shrill articles in the press, the lawyers' speeches, the defendants' final words and the invariably swingeing sentences. And again protests, protests, protests. It turned out that there was so much happening every day – persecutions, reprisals, arrests – that a bimonthly information journal had to be published in *samizdat*: *The Chronicle of Current Events*. And *samizdat* in general was no longer a purely literary affair: there were open letters, articles, pamphlets, dissertations, research monographs. And, of course, trial transcripts. The more furiously the regime raged, the broader and stronger grew the movement – just try and make out who was the bear now and who the block, and how it would all end.

How galling it was to have to rot in a camp at the most exciting time! The only thing that reassured me was that among all the other *samizdat* documents circulating inside the country was a transcript of our trial, compiled by Pavel Litvinov. At least the three years would be worth something; what we said had not passed into oblivion.

# 7

'HEY, brother, how about a game? That's a nice-looking sweater you've got on.'

Having kicked around a few transit prisons and transports in my time, I already knew something of the underworld, its habits and customs. It was madness to play cards with crooks – the cards were marked and they knew every trick in the book. There are experts who can pick any card you care to name, even with their eyes closed. They live for cards. All day long they turn them over in their hands, shuffle them, finger them so as not to lose their touch, and once they choose a victim they strip him naked. But to refuse is to show weakness, to get off on the wrong foot, and I was going to have to live with them for three years.

'Okay,' I said, 'but make it preference. There's enough of us, we can write down the pool – should keep us going all night.'

This took him aback. Preference wasn't a crook's game. But what sort of a crook refuses a game of cards?

'Okay, brother, but tell me what sort of a game it is and how you play.'

I explained it to him and his cronies. Preference is a complicated game, almost like chess, and it takes a long time to learn and grasp it. They sat down unwillingly, but what could they do? They tried to fiddle along the way, of course, but I never turned a hair. Fiddle away my friends – if you don't know the game you won't win. Especially at preference. Within an hour or so I had cleaned them out.

'All right,' I said, 'you can take your things back. They're no good to me. And now I'll teach you to play properly.'

We got so carried away that we were at it all night – and became the best of friends.

The crooks display extraordinary respect for political prisoners nowadays, and if you are honest and firm with them and don't break their underworld code of ethics, they will always help you out of a tight corner. But the questions they pester you with! Somehow it's taken for granted that if you're a political, you must be 'educated' and know everything. And suddenly you find yourself acting as a walking encyclopaedia for the whole camp. You have to resolve endless arguments about how many generalissimos there have ever been (for some reason they had it fixed firmly in their minds that there had only been three generalissimos – Suvorov, Stalin and Franco), how many miles it is from Tula to Tambov, or which is further south – Kiev or New York? Your word is law. Naturally they all came to me to write their complaints – I was the only political in the entire camp.

I was always amazed by how quickly they recognised what people were like, divined their weaknesses and were able to predict what they would become in the camp. On the one hand there was this fantastic instinct and cunning, on the other an astounding naïvety, trustfulness and cruelty, as in children.

The world of the 'hoodlums' or 'thieves' is extraordinarily interesting as a model of purely popular lawmaking. Of course, there are virtually no more 'thieves under the law' in existence these days, but their 'ideology' is still terribly vital, has penetrated almost all strata of the population, is particularly popular with our youth now, and evidently will never die. Even the guards live by the same concepts. The 'hoods' ideology' represents a distillation of youthful impulses to boldness and resourcefulness, combined with notions of a genuinely independent life. It is natural that exceptional, heroic natures, especially when young, should find themselves drawn to it.

I think that the sources of this ideology are to be found in the Russian folk epics and in the legends about heroes, knights and justice-loving outlaws. I can see little difference between the ideology of some prince with his retinue, laying his surrounding region waste and exacting tribute from the vanquished, and today's gangleader with his gang. And they don't regard their exploits as in any way shameful either. On the contrary, the thieves' basic ideal bears a close similarity to the concept of justice held by some legendary knights, and consists in the belief that they are superior people, while all the rest of the population, the 'peasants', are their tributaries. They never steal, they merely exact their 'due' – which is literally the word they use. In relations between themselves they are outstandingly honest, and theft among themselves – like theft in general in the camp – is regarded as the worst possible crime.

However, I don't know much of the history of this subject. I know only that in the 1930s and 40s, and even into the 50s, the 'thieves' movement' in the country was extraordinarily strong. Their first and most fundamental idea was non-recognition of the State and complete independence of it. A genuine 'thief under the law' was under no circumstances supposed to work, not even under duress. He had no home: outside prison he lived in various thieves' dens with his underworld girl friends. Not only were they obliged to live by stealing, but each thief had to keep to his own narrow 'speciality' and was unable to change it. The tribute they collected in this way was not supposed to be divided equally between them – it was handed over to the gangleader to share out as he thought fit, 'according to justice'. It is interesting that gangleaders were never elected. They were recognised on the strength of their thieving authority (just like the Politburo). The thieves' world had a complex hierarchy and that, too, was established not by elections, but by the 'recognition' of degrees of authority. And it was this hierarchy that determined how the money would be distributed and what was each man's 'due'.

There also existed a mass of unwritten laws, and only the most authoritative thieves were permitted to interpret them and act as judges in disputes. Thieves' courts, or 'regulators', were also an ancient and original example of popular lawmaking. I had many opportunities to observe them in the camps. Since I enjoyed a certain amount of trust, I was even able to be present at them, though not, of course, as a participant. They were based on a sort of processing of claims litigation, if I may put it that way. A thief's trial couldn't be called by the whole community, there could only be a personal claim by an injured party, or an accusation made in the presence of the most authoritative colleague – or perhaps of a whole assembly. Grievances were almost never resolved by conciliation – one of the parties was adjudged guilty, and the winning party had then to be personally recompensed by the loser (compensation might be exacted in any form, from murder or rape to a simple beating or the acceptance of material payment). And only if the losing party refused to submit to the court's decision did the judge step in and exercise his power to enforce it. Until that had been done, no one could interfere.

Thieves' law protected only those who observed it. Anyone who seriously violated it found himself outside the law (this was also decided by a 'regulator') and after that, any thief might deal with him as he pleased, without having to fear the consequences. A man who had been in any way connected with the authorities (wearing an armband, for instance, or squealing on a colleague) could never ever have the right to attend a thieves' gathering. He couldn't even be quoted as a witness. There was also an oath – the 'swearing-in'. A thief's word was his bond. Once said – done. There were also assemblies to decide questions of importance to everyone. In short, a whole system of laws.

According to tradition, a thief or an outlaw was always a dashing knight-errant, a handsome young cavalier, agile and elusive, harsh but just, and enjoying universal esteem. There exists a mass of stories and songs in which the thief appears as a romantic hero. Thieves traditionally lived in 'families' and regarded one another as 'brothers'.

In accordance with their aristocratic position, they had to be masters in the prisons and camps. Prison for a thief was a home from home. He had to live in the lap of luxury there, with his own servants, a homosexual as his paramour, and with all the non-thieves voluntarily paying him tribute. A thief didn't have the right to steal in prison or take things by force – others had to bring things themselves. He could win at cards and even cheat or 'pull tricks'. But at the same time he was obliged to assist a fellow-thief in trouble and show generosity and magnanimity. As for the people he beat at cards and cheated (hoods on the fringes of the underworld), they were obliged to go and grab or steal what they needed. A thief was obliged to stick up for the 'peasants' who paid him tribute, protect them from the depredations of other thieves and maintain justice among them. Traditionally he could not allow himself to be released from jail but was obliged to escape. He had no right to work, of course, but was formally assigned to a brigade that worked sufficiently to cover his norm as well as their own.

In this form the 'thieves' movement' existed until the mid-1950s. It had for a long time been expanding and consolidating itself, because the authorities saw it as a support and exploited it, setting the thieves at the throats of the politicals, who shared the camps with them in those days. But in the early 1950s, the level of professional crime rose so steeply that the authorities decided to put an end to it. They launched a new slogan: 'The criminal world must exterminate itself.'

The authorities succeeded in provoking hostilities by creating a new breed of thief – the 'bitches' or 'Polish thieves', as they preferred to call themselves. The difference was not very great. The bitches were those thieves whom the authorities succeeded in forcing to work,

employing the most savage measures and frequently obliging them to choose between life and death. After this they were given 'command' of certain camps, that is to say, were made brigade-leaders, foremen, and so on, and now it was they who forcibly drove the other prisoners out to work. It was then that the celebrated 'underworld war' broke out, when thieves and bitches could no longer exist side-by-side in the cells and camps – one or the other had to be killed. The camp administration, of course, forced the thieves into bitches' camps and bitches into the arms of the thieves, and a veritable slaughter took place. In short, there are practically no thieves 'under the law' in existence nowadays, except, perhaps, for a few dozen living out their lives in various jails (I managed to meet a few in Vladimir).

But their ideology has not died out, and with certain adjustments has continued to flourish to this day (because of the harsher conditions outside and the stiffer regime in the camps, they are allowed to work, live at home, not escape, and so on). A certain modified version of their code of honour – if you like, a kind of slum psychology – continues to exist. Furthermore, their basic principles and criteria have become so widespread that it is possible to regard this ideology as far more popular than the communist one. In essence, it differs little from the real ideology of the Party leadership, and both worlds bear a startling resemblance to one another.

The main hotbeds of the thieves' ideology are the reform colonies for juvenile delinquents. The regime there, judging by accounts I have heard, is exceptionally savage – everything is based on beatings, inciting the youths against one another, the artificial elevation of some over others and a system of collective responsibility: one boy's offence brings down punishment on them all, thus embittering relations between them. Naturally the strongest and most determined come out on top, and everyone gets used to living according to the laws of brute force, while the heroic halo of oral legends about the brotherhood of thieves endows this life with legitimacy and sense. When released, they carry this mythology all over the country, recruiting new admirers. And having been brought up in this spirit, they do not find it easy to escape it. The world they have created in the camps is exceptionally cruel and caste-ridden, steeped in privilege and abounding in harsh rules, an ignorance of which can cost a novice extremely dear.

So here I was in the camp, in the settlement of Bor. Three hundred miles south of Moscow. About twenty-five miles from Voronezh. In the living compound were nine barrack huts – six for sleeping, one canteen, a school and a bathhouse. A terrific crush. Every hut partitioned into four sections, each containing sixty to eighty men. Two, and in some cases three, vertical tiers of bunks. No room to turn over in the morning. About 2,000 men in the camp altogether. Both the living and the work compounds enclosed by multiple barbed-wire fences, a raked strip, and watch-towers with armed guards in them.

The compound was decorated with production appeals, productivity charts, and special 'educational' stands and signs. One side of our barrack hut was covered with an enormous wooden board. At first you couldn't make out what had been painted on it by one of the camp trusties, but peering closer you guessed that it represented a weeping woman sorrowfully resting her head on her hand. Underneath was an inscription in capital letters: '*Do your best to earn an early release, my son!*' After that came a picture of a whole family – little children with their mother: '*Your family is waiting for you.*'

All the fences and free walls were covered with the sayings of great men: '*Man – what a proud word! Gorky*'; '*Everything in a man must be beautiful – his face, his clothing, his soul, his thoughts. Chekhov.*'

On the wall of the canteen was painted: '*He who doesn't work, doesn't eat.*' And it was true. Those who refused to work were dumped in the box where they got bread and water every other day.

On the gates leading to the outside world they had written: '*Back to liberty with a clear conscience.*' This was the godfather setting his nets. What he wanted is for men to own up voluntarily to unsolved crimes. Admit it yourself and you'll do less time. Naturally, no one was fool enough to own up, but the more crafty ones did a deal with the godfather. For an extra food parcel from home they owned up to some trivial offence for which they couldn't be made to do extra time. Photographs of these crafty dodgers were also pinned up by the gates, beneath the legend: '*They confessed their crimes.*' Food packages for them, and recognition for the godfather.

Deals of this sort are completely acceptable to the authorities. They begin during the investigation period: the investigators try to persuade prisoners to confess to some unsolved crimes so that they can write them off: 'Here, admit to a couple more robberies. What difference does it make? It'll just mean six instead of four.' In exchange they promise you some sort of indulgence or simply bring you vodka. If you don't agree off your own bat, they try to wring a confession out of you by force. A police investigation is a ferocious affair. They are instructed to have a 100-per-cent solution rate, so how else are they going to do it?

Every barrack hut also had a stand with photographs on it: 'Productivity champions', but instead of the usual smiling maidens in headscarves looking out at you, you found shaven-headed criminal mugs. *'Do remember, tell your friends, honest work homeward sends,'* was written in foot-high letters. And there was an enormous red board in the centre of the compound: *'We the convicted, like the entire Soviet people, swear...'* to fulfil, overfulfil, catch up, overhaul. And every barrack hut had its wall newspaper in a glass case, laboriously complied by prisoners on the road to reform':

'The convicts Ivanov and Petrov are working well and have met their production norms. They have started on the road to reform and are members of the internal-order section. The convicts Sidorov and Fyodorov, on the other hand, have been avoiding work, have failed to meet their norms and violated the terms of their custody. For this they have been committed to ten days in the punishment isolator.' Followed by a cartoon showing Sidorov and Fyodorov behind bars.

However, the 'reformed' never did any real work. The administration put them into the sort of jobs where they could earn their percentages with no effort. That's the way work is organised in the camps: in one job you are guaranteed 150 per cent of the norm for doing nothing at all, while in another you can slog away all day and be lucky if you get 70 per cent.

The first thing that struck me when I arrived in the camp was the vast number of people wearing red ribbons, stripes, triangles and diamonds on their sleeves. They comprised at least a half of the prisoners, if not more. (When I was sent to a political camp in 1973, no one wore armbands. Even the *polizei* – that is, people convicted of collaborating with the Germans during the war – who now collaborated with admin as members of the camp's collective council, preferred to play it down, and didn't wear their armbands.)

This was the sio, Section of Internal Order, for which there was a derisive alternative based on its Russian initials: 'the bitch begs for mercy'. 'Firmly on the road to reform', 'taking an active part in collective life' – these were the phrases admin would use when pleading for these prisoners' early release, after they had done a half or two-thirds of their sentences (depending on the charges). In fact, it meant collaborating with the bosses, establishing rules to suit their convenience, informing on fellow-inmates – all dressed up to look like a voluntary prisoners' organisation, a species of 'self-government'. There could be no question of any real self-government. There was simply a second tier of assistants working to secure an early release. And of course, they could do anything they liked. One of them could punch you in the mouth and that was all right. But if you punched him back – article 77:1: 'terrorising a prisoner who has started on the road to reform' (eight to fifteen years or the firing squad). Naturally it was the ones who had 'started on the road to reform' who, with the blessing of the administration, terrorised the rest of the camp population.

This terror can reach a point when it is no longer endurable. Then you get a camp rebellion and a revolt breaks out. A few of the 're-formed' are killed, others are crippled, battered with stakes or cut up with knives. To save themselves they clamber on to the fence, under the protection of the machine-guns, or run to the guardhouse to seek refuge with their masters. Sometimes the rebels set fire to the barrack huts. For a short time the camp remains under seige, with doubled guards in the watch-towers; then military reserves are summoned and enter the compound to suppress the revolt. An investigation is instituted, the 'ringleaders' and chief culprits are identified and are given a show trial, usually in the camp itself, and sentenced to be shot (or fifteen years is added to their sentences). For a time the camp is quiet – the prisoners 'on the road to reform' keep their horns in: scenes from the recent rebellion are still too fresh in their memories. But the years go by, the personnel changes, the past is forgotten, and the whole thing begins all over again. These rebellions were a common occurrence in the 1960s.

The camps' basic objective is economic gain, so that admin's first concern is to see that the plan is fulfilled. Both their personal careers and their bonuses and perks depend on this. Soviet law and the reigning ideology agree that forced labour is the 'basic method of re-education'. Everything in camp depends on the work and everything is subordinated to its interests.

Beyond the fence was the work compound, with its furniture factory.

There is nothing drearier than a camp muster on a dark winter's morning. Aroused by the hoarse wheeze of the factory klaxon, with the scraps of some misty dream still floating around your head, you run first to the stinking canteen, which is billowing clouds of steam like a bathhouse, hastily gulp down some slops with fishbones swimming in them, and then dash off at full speed for the main gate, buttoning your reefer jacket as you go. There, huddled up in the cold, you wait for the overseer in his sheepskin coat and felt boots to count the grey mass of stooping cons into fives. It was at the very end of 1967, in numbingly cold weather, that I arrived in the camp, and halfway through winter again when I was released in 1970. And all three winters, as if to spite me, were exceptionally hard.

'Fourth brigade. First five, second, third. . . .'

Hands thrust into the sleeves of their reefer jackets, cap earflaps pulled down and tied beneath the chin, the solid grey mass moves unsteadily and disjointedly forward, shifting from one foot to another, trying to hoard its warmth.

Ahead, through the gates, loom the indistinct silhouettes of the box-like workshops and the boiler-house chimney in the work zone, and from somewhere comes the sickening screech of an electric saw: some ox is already at his bench. Only one thought pierces your foggy brain. Which is the best workshop to sneak into, and where's the best place to hide so that the brigade-leader doesn't find you till lunchtime?

But the brigade-leader has already found you under the central-heating pipes and the two of you, hoarsely cursing, hating one another and the common enemy, trail off to your workshop. With frozen fingers you unscrew some nuts, tool up your blasted lathe, but nothing seems to go right and you keep on dropping things. An hour passes, another. The monotonous drone of the motor, rhythmic, identical movements – gradually your fingers acquire their usual dexterity, and the heap of finished parts grows bigger and bigger.

'Hey, you'll wear yourself out!' yells the man on the next bench through the workshop din. 'Let's go for a smoke!'

'Wait a minute, I'll be through soon. Not many to go.'

Suddenly, with a wave of disgust, you become aware of the pleasure you have been getting from your dexterity, from doing a job well and the desire to finish it properly. This must be the way a woman feels when she has been raped: she screams and struggles and scratches, then quietens down, then is suddenly revolted and ashamed to feel the physical pleasure it has given her.

Will any con ever forget or forgive that frozen feeling of 'I can't go on', that intolerable loathing of lathes, workshops, norms, brigade-leaders and oneself? For the rest of your life you will detest the very word 'work'.

A furniture factory is not the hardest sort of work, except for the loaders, the people who work in the kilns, and the men in the timber store. It isn't the hardness of it, but the humiliation.

I have seen men break their arms or legs to get off a few days' work. It is difficult to do this for yourself, and in our camp there was a specialist at breaking bones – a tall thin fellow who worked in the timber store. He would place the arm or leg across two thick pieces of wood and give it a quick blow in the middle with a felt boot stuffed with a log. He could do simple or compound fractures to order.

Others chopped off their fingers with an axe, swallowed nails, inflicted burns on their hands. If you took some powdered sugar and inhaled it for a time, you could give yourself genuine tuberculosis. And there were countless methods of raising your temperature. The surest way was to inject fish fat into your veins (needles could always be had from the addicts).

All these things were called 'hornswoggles' and were, of course, strictly punished. The medical unit, as a rule, would refuse to treat known hornswogglers, and admin would throw them into the box There, like dogs, they had to lick their own wounds without medical treatment. They used to slit their veins or swallow spoons simply to get the doctor to come.

It wasn't always easy to recognise a hornswoggler, and the medical unit preferred to regard anyone who fell ill as a malingerer. Occasionally you couldn't even get them to take your temperature or give you a pill.

'Go on, go on! Get back to work!' they said to everybody, out of habit, without distinction. Only those 'on the road to reform' were in a better position. There were instances when cons died for lack of treatment.

There was a constant sea of mud everywhere, and scab was endemic. The medical unit didn't like this at all – after all, it was highly infectious. And to begin with they tried to quarantine the scab-sufferers in hospital. But it quickly proved unworkable, the disease spread too far. Those who couldn't catch it injected resin glue from the factory under the skin in their groin or between their fingers and you couldn't tell the difference!

But it wasn't easy to get into the medical unit anyway. It was situated in the work zone, where the factory was. So you had to go to work to get anywhere near it. Well, once you had gone to work you couldn't be so bad, could you, you wouldn't die. So you could work. In short, everything was designed for the fulfilment of the plan. But then, what else were prisoners for?

A criminal camp offers you a complete cross-section of society, the entire country in miniature, and in camp life you can find a microcosm of the Soviet people's attitude to the law and their social position.

The majority of people in Soviet criminal camps are not degenerates or professional crooks. According to our most accurate estimates, the number of prisoners in the Soviet Union is never less than two-and-a-half million – that is, one per cent of the population, every hundredth person. And usually it's more. If you take into account the fact that the average term of imprisonment is five years, and recidivists account for not more than twenty to twenty-five per cent of the prisoners, it emerges that almost a third of the Soviet population has passed through the camps.

Such a high percentage of criminality is artificially maintained by the State, above all for economic motives. Prisoners are a cheap (almost unpaid) work force that can easily be moved, at the authorities' discretion, from one branch of the economy to another, sent out to do the heaviest and most unprofitable types of work and into undeveloped territories with a harsh climate, to which you can persuade a free work force to go only by paying extremely high wages. It was no accident that in Voronezh region when I was there, they had only ten camps (one administrative unit). In the Perm region, further north and closer to the Urals, where I went in 1973–4, there were about fifty camps (five administrative units). There were about the same number in the Kirov, Tyumen and Sverdlovsk regions and in the Komi Autonomous Republic.*

This was how all the great construction projects of the USSR had been built: dams, canals, roads, polar cities. By forced labour, almost entirely hand labour.

The average prisoner's earnings are 60–80 roubles a month, compared with 140 roubles for free workers on similar jobs. Half of this is deducted by the State, and a quarter goes to pay for food, clothing and maintenance. Thus a prisoner's real wage is 15–20 roubles a month. Out of this he can spend from three to seven roubles a month in the camp canteen, depending on what his sentence was. His incentives to work are all negative, that is they consist basically of assorted punishments for evasion of work or failure to fulfil the norm. Furthermore, the workers are removed from the sphere of normal consumption, which given the Soviet Union's permanent shortage of goods, is very convenient for demand-management. Meanwhile, goods that are not in demand by the population (mainly low-grade food products) are unloaded on to the prisoners, who have no choice in the matter. Prisoners also don't need housing – they build their own barrack huts.

* Perm is in the northern Urals. Kirov and Sverdlovsk are just west of the Urals, in European Russia, while Tyumen is east of the Urals, in western Siberia. The Komi Republic is further north than any of these, in the extreme north-east corner of European Russia.

In short, if a general amnesty were suddenly called tomorrow, it would precipitate an economic disaster. That is why, since Stalin's time, there have in effect been no amnesties. There have been a few decrees under which almost no one was freed, since all prisoners convicted of the most frequent charges were excluded. In Khrushchev's time, instead of amnesties they developed the concept of early release (and later of suspended sentences) with compulsory assignment 'to national economic construction sites', or, as it was called, 'to the chemistry'. This category of prisoners is altogether unquantifiable. It usually includes short-timers (up to three years) who are directed to the very heaviest and lowest-paid types of work. If a 'chemist' commits some sort of misdemeanour, he is dispatched to a camp to serve his full time (time served 'at the chemistry' doesn't count). It is an extremely convenient form of release.

It is difficult to say whether the State Planning Agency, Gosplan, gives direct instructions to the Ministry of the Interior as to how many offenders should be arrested each month to maintain the national economy at the requisite level. Given the Soviet Union's centralised planning system, this is perfectly feasible. I think, however, that the matter is handled slightly differently. From somewhere up above, from the very highest reaches of the Party, an instruction is handed down: step up the struggle against, let us say, hooliganism. It's not that there are more hooligans about than usual, but rather that at a given stage in the building of communism, their existence suddenly becomes particularly inadmissible. And a nationwide campaign is inaugurated to promote the struggle against hooliganism. The Presidium of the Supreme Soviet publishes a special decree, social institutions are mobilised to assist the overstretched police force, judges are issued with guidelines, and slogans appear all over the place: '*No mercy for hooligans*', '*Make the place too hot for hooligans.*' Every province, every region must arrest more hooligans than it did before the 'struggle' was 'stepped up'. How, otherwise, could you report back that you'd done your job?

But up at the top, at the point where all these reports converge, they are outraged to discover that as a result of the campaign, the number of hooligans in the country has steeply risen. My word, this hooligan's a pigheaded brute! Won't give in! And there comes another decree – on yet another stepping-up of the struggle against hooliganism. More instructions to the police, directives to the local authorities and clarifications to the judges, and the concept of hooliganism begins to stretch like a rubber band. A man loses his temper and swears at someone – hooliganism. A husband has a row with his wife – hooliganism. Two schoolboys have a fight – hooliganism. And monstrous sentences, up to five years! How else can you prove your zeal and demonstrate that the struggle is truly being stepped up? The statistics for hooliganism start to climb dizzily, the prisons are overflowing, the judges are exhausted, and battalions of provocative young hooligans are being shipped out to work on the Bratsk Hydroelectric Station or the Baikal–Amur Railway. God defend you from falling foul of one of these regular campaigns – you are bound to be dispatched to a far-away construction project for the glory of communism, because one campaign has a fatal way of leading to another.

On the principle of the feedback circuit, this campaign might continue to grow to infinity – after all, it can't be stopped so long as the number of hooligans continues to grow. And you never ever get a directive to 'relax the struggle'. Instead they simply choose some other offence to have a campaign about, and the word goes out from high Party circles: 'Step up the struggle against embezzlers of socialist property!' And everybody heaves a sigh of relief: at last the hooligans can be left in peace. Their numbers decline steeply, and up at the top somebody registers a victory over hooliganism. The number of prisoners falls slightly until the new campaign gains momentum, and then rises sharply again.

This is approximately how the purges and campaigns against enemies of the people worked in Stalin's time, but now it is inconvenient to have millions of political prisoners, and it makes for a much easier life simply to jail hooligans and plunderers. Thus the people who end up in the Soviet camps are mostly ordinary Soviet people, and it is quite fair to judge by them the state of our society in general.

If you want to live, learn to look sharp. Bribe the guards, swindle, steal, keep on good terms with whoever's in charge of the food. Otherwise you'll end up a stiff. Admin steals everything it can lay hands on in the camp. Bribery is universal – with a bribe you can get anything, from a visit to conditional release. They order entire suites of furniture from the factory and cart it away like offcuts from the sawmill. Not one of them ever buys firewood or building materials. They even steal the food. Between the district depot and the prisoner's bowl the food simply melts away. Admin grabs the choicest titbits before the food even gets to the camp. In the kitchens it is plundered by the cooks and trusties – the ones who are 'on the road to reform' – not only for themselves, but for their friends as well. The servers then give bigger portions to their favourites, and the simple con, who honestly believes that honest labour is the road to home, is left with slops.

Almost all of a prisoner's time is taken up looking for food. This is the axis round which camp life turns, and it defines all human relations. You help me and I'll help you. With the help of the guards, the free workers,* the drivers of the trucks that come to collect the furniture, you can buy anything you like: vodka, tea, drugs.

And if you remember that millions of people go through this meat-mincer, you involuntarily ask yourself: What does the regime want of its people? What sort of citizens is it turning them into? Judging by the established criteria for rehabilitation, the model Soviet citizen is one who is prepared to bend in whichever direction it wishes to bend him. Become an informer, do the policemen's job for them, say what you're told to say and all the time beam with pleasure.

Do the camps teach you to lead an honest life? Just the reverse: an honest man would die of hunger in a camp. They teach you to steal and not get caught. Here is a typical incident. The duty officer makes a deal with a prisoner for the latter to steal an electric drill from the work-shop toolstore. He promises to bring him ten packets of tea in exchange (that's ten roubles in camp terms). The prisoner carries out his part of the bargain – steals the drill and smuggles it out to the guardhouse without the foreman catching him. The officer carries it out through the camp checkpoint and takes it home, but doesn't bring the tea. A scandal erupts: the con demands his tea and ends up spilling the beans to admin. And what happens? The officer is reprimanded for 'acquiring a tool by impermissible means' and the con gets fifteen days in the box for 'theft'.

It is a deliberate and systematic plan to corrupt the people. And it has been continuing for sixty years. The more honest element in the people is being physically destroyed, while corruptness is encouraged. In effect, the same thing happens outside as well. Wages are beggarly, and everyone steals as much as he can. Is it that the authorities don't know? Of course they know. And they even prefer it that way. A man who steals isn't in a position to *make demands*. And if he does become so bold, he can easily be put away for theft. Everyone is guilty.

I frequently tried to explain this simple truth to my camp companions, but with no success. All of them were extremely hostile to the existing regime, and the word 'communist' was the worst insult you could fling at someone – people would immediately attack you for it. Their attitude to me, as an open opponent of the regime, was one of enormous respect. Yet they could never understand that by

* Civilian employees of the camp administration who live outside the camp and come in every day to do their work.

255

robbing the State and harming it in that way, they were none the less providing it with its greatest support. There were some who seriously regarded themselves as fighting against the regime.

One of them was even insulted when I didn't acknowledge him as one of us. He had robbed a polling station on the eve of the elections and was extremely proud of this fact. But that's the whole point. Until people learn to demand what belongs to them as a right, no revolution will liberate them. And by the time they learn, a revolution won't be necessary. No, I don't believe in revolution, I don't believe in forcible salvation.

It is easy to imagine what would happen in this country if there were a revolution: universal looting, economic collapse, internecine butchery and in every district a different band of outlaws with its own 'gang-leader' at its head. And the passive, terrorised majority would gladly submit to the first strong system of government to come along, in other words a new dictatorship.

Coercion in the camp was unbridled. We were forced to go to work almost without cease and were lucky to get one rest-day a month. Almost every Saturday they would read out an order proclaiming Sunday a working day owing to the non-fulfilment of the week's production target. Safety equipment existed only on paper, and apart from the deliberate hornswogglers there were many who lost a hand because of this. Three men had been crippled by my lathe during the preceding months and nobody wanted to work on it.

I was put on that particular lathe as a punishment to break me down. Thanks to my reputation as someone who could 'read and write', I had fairly soon started writing everybody's complaints for them. Quite unexpectedly I won a very important case for us all, namely, the right to receive visits.

Under the law, we were supposed to get two extended (up to three days) visits a year, but admin regarded this not as a right, but as a reward. In practice, the only people allowed visits were those who had 'started on the road to reform' and the rest were told they had behaved so badly that they didn't deserve visits. Having gathered together a couple of dozen such instances, I began writing all over the place – at first, of course, without success. But I managed to persuade 200 prisoners to write the same sort of complaint, and suddenly it worked: a colonel came from head office and gave instructions for visits to be allowed – but only to those who had complained. Now I had an enormous queue to contend with, and since there wasn't time to write on behalf of all of them, I simply composed a specimen text and circulated it.

On one occasion, a young fellow was beaten up by some guards in the guardhouse in the presence of a drunken officer. Fortunately there were several witnesses to this incident, and the victim himself, without them noticing, had contrived to smear some blood on the order committing him to the box. This affair took a couple of months to be resolved, but in the end the officer was punished with an official reprimand. Another prisoner was punished for not cutting his hair – he was letting it grow in anticipation of a visit from his wife. They deliberately humiliated him in front of everybody by shearing a strip of hair off right down the middle of his head. I advised him not to have the rest cut, but to leave it like that for at least a month. Sure enough, about three weeks later some official came from the regional camp administration in answer to his complaint, and seeing for himself that the complaint was justified, ordered the culprit to be punished. There was no shortage of these amazing cases passing through my hands until, at last, admin caught on to who was behind them all.

The lathe I was forced to work on as a punishment for all these complaints stood in a cold, unheated workshop. In winter you were even afraid to go near it – it seemed to exude cold, and if you touched it with your hands your fingers would instantly be glued to it by the frost and you couldn't get them off again without tearing your skin away. The exposed and unguarded blades rotated with furious speed right next to your fingers, and if you got a piece of wood that was splintered or had a knot in it, your right hand would immediately slip towards them. On top of this, the work quota had been set artificially high.

Admin's calculation was simple: if I refused to work on the lathe, they would grind me down with spells in the box for insubordination; If I did work, they'd do the same for failure to meet the norm. After trying it for about a month and seeing that I would never make it, I announced a hunger strike. Admin decided to ignore the strike and I starved for twenty-six days in all. Every day they demanded that I go to work, pretending not to know whether I was still on hunger strike or not. On the seventeenth day I was put in the box for refusal to work.

The cold was arctic at that time – it was November. The box was hardly heated and one wall was covered with ice. There were eleven of us in there; we tried to keep warm by huddling together in a bunch.

Only at night was it possible to warm up a bit, when they issued us with duckboards and our reefer jackets. There was barely room for us all to fit on the boards, lying on our sides, and we had all to turn over at once when the word was given. We were also lucky to have some tobacco. Criminals have this side of things well-organised. If you've got a friend in the box, come what may your duty is to get some smokes to him, and something to eat, too, if you can.

You had to hand it to them, they were desperate characters. The solitary was situated in the free-fire zone, enveloped in barbed wire and tripwires, yet every evening before lights out, someone would sneak out of the compound, break the barbed wire unnoticed, creep up to the window of the box and push some tobacco through the bars. If he was caught, he himself would be flung in the box and somebody else would come in his place. Later, after I had been let out, I too took part in these raids, and I must say that it was a desperately dangerous business. The guard in the watchtower might think you were trying to escape and fire on you. And to do it all without attracting attention was terribly difficult: the free-fire zone was lit up with searchlights, there were tripwires all over the place, as fine as a spider's web, and the barbed wire hooked in your clothing.

Sometimes, it's true, we managed to bribe a guard or a food-server, and then it was easier. But without tobacco it would have been very bad, especially for me after such a long hunger strike. As luck would have it I had a strong constitution and I didn't lose consciousness once or need to have the doctor called.

On the twenty-sixth day my spell in the box ended (they had given me eight days), and I went to the door, but my head spun, probably from the fresh air, everything went dark, and I crawled along the base of the wall and into the corridor, where I lay on the floor.

For a long time they argued over what to do about me. The doctor refused pointblank to take me into the hospital – I wasn't a sick man, but a hunger striker, which was no better than a self-mutilator. But the camp duty officer wouldn't accept me into the compound either – what if I dropped dead? And so they stood over me arguing. I had come to my senses again and could have got up, but resolved to stay where I was at all costs. I lay there by the door and thought: 'Let them argue. It can't be any worse for me than it is now.' And what could I do anyway? How much longer could I keep up this hunger strike? Finally, the duty officer won the argument and I was carried into the medical unit.

This officer was generally well-disposed towards me – he was amazed that I dared to do battle with the authorities. During the evenings when he was on duty, usually somewhat under the influence, he would seek me out in the compound and try to reason with me: 'Listen, Bukovsky, why do you get involved with them? Fine people to pick on! They'll simply kill you. What put it into your head to tangle with the authorities? They'll shoot you from behind a corner and that'll be that. They're bandits.'

And then he would start telling me about his experiences at the front and all the atrocities he had seen. He said all these things without the least hidden motive, not to scare me or 're-educate' me in any way, but simply out of the goodness of his heart. And out of amazement, too. I was the first political prisoner he had ever seen and he found the whole thing fascinating.

Evidently both admin and my fellow-prisoners were equally amazed. Thefts, muggings, murders – they were accustomed to that sort of thing. Or if it had been for money. But to do it just like that, for no gain, was beyond their comprehension. That's probably why they didn't make me go back to my old job again: the devil knows what this political will get up to next, he'll up and die of starvation on us. I was visited in the medical unit by the deputy camp governor and we spent a long time haggling over what work I would agree to do, and what work I wouldn't. We settled on a job in a warm workshop veneering the edges of tabletops. It was a job for 'reformed' prisoners – four hours was the most you needed to meet your norm. He hated to do it, but gave way in the end.

After that they left me alone, although I continued writing complaints as before. But towards the end of my term someone came from the camp authority to try to dissuade me. 'Pack it in, don't write any more complaints for them. Who are they to you? You're a political prisoner, they're criminals. And anyway, it won't be long before you're out of here.'

By that time I had organised a healthy criminal collective of permanent complainants – about thirty altogether. Each of them found a further ten people, sometimes more, and in round figures we saw to it that about 400 complaints left the camp every day. Gradually my friends got so carried away by this business that they learned to argue every bit as well as Volpin. They wrote virtually without any help from me.

With time we even got our rest-days back again, though not by complaining but by striking. When those days came round we simply refused to go out to work, and that was that. At first they threw us into the box and threatened to put us on trial for sabotage, but then they submitted. If we really had to work on a Sunday for some reason, they used to give us an extra day off at the end of the month.

Only the KGB didn't relax in its efforts. They weren't in the least interested in this complaints business, but did their best to catch me out on some careless statement and prolong my sentence. They were sending their agents around constantly. Most of them owned up to me and offered their co-operation, but there were others who did everything they could for their masters. About once a month a certain Nikolai Ivanovich, a KGB superintendent, used to come and summon all his agents to the guardhouse under the pretext of discussing their letters with the censor. The camp was no better than a communal kitchen in this respect, and try as you might to hide things, everybody knew everything, including the existence of the agents. 'Your friend from the KGB's here again,' they'd say to me confidingly. 'He's called in so-and-so and so-and-so.'

One day I thought I was a real goner and would never get out of it. They suddenly uncovered preparations for a regular revolt against the tyranny of the prisoners 'on the road to reform'. The camp was searched from top to bottom – all the barrack huts and the entire factory – and they found a bunch of home-made knives, metal rods and similar utensils. About fifty crooks were tossed into jail to await investigation. Nobody knew who would be named as the instigator. At this point the KGB intervened.

Early one evening I was sitting reading in the barrack hut when I was suddenly summoned to the guardhouse. Not suspecting anything amiss, I went along, and on the way ran into several groups of crooks discussing the investigation's progress. 'What, has the investigator called you in too?' they said.

'I don't know. I was told to go to the guardhouse. No, it's probably something else.'

However, it was the investigator. Two prisoners whom I had never seen before were already there. Now, looking me brazenly in the face, these two rats began giving evidence against me. The claptrap they talked! They said that I had gone to their barrack hut and they had heard me explaining the plan of the rebellion to some men who were now in jail and being investigated. According to them, I was the brains and chief organiser behind the whole plot. Insist as I might that I had never been in that barrack hut, had never known those men, and was seeing these two as well for the first time in my life, nothing was of any use. There were two of them, I was only one. And two witnesses were more than enough to consign a man to the firing squad. At the very least it meant fifteen years on special regime.

I left the investigator's office pole-axed. That was it, I was done for. It was clear that the KGB had done it. Unable to finish me off in Moscow, they would do it here. Fifteen years – my whole life – down the drain for nothing at all.

On my way back to my hut I ran into the crooks again. I told them everything that had happened and explained my theory about the KGB.

'Wait a minute, which two is that? Aha, hut number six.'

'All right now, don't you worry. We'll think of something.'

What could they possibly think of? This whole business had been a body blow. I went back to my hut and lay down on my bunk in a kind of daze. The drone of voices and the scraping of feet seemed to come to me through a dense fog. What harm had I ever done them, the swine? Never seen them in my life before. This was the last thing that flashed through my mind before I seemed to drop into a deep cellar.

I woke the next morning with a splitting headache, as if hung over. I got dressed automatically, went to rollcall, the mess-hall, work, without seeing anything around me, as if in darkness. And a cricket seemed to be chirping somewhere inside my skull.

Early that evening, on my way back from work, I ran into the crooks who had asked me about the investigator the day before. 'Hello there! What are you looking so down in the mouth about? Didn't you see your two witnesses zipping off to the guardhouse this morning to take their evidence back? Like two elks they were!'

It turned out that the crooks had caught up with them on night-shift at the factory. What they did to them, I don't know. What do you do to a man to make him scoot off at dawn to take back all the evidence he has given?

And so the affair ended without affecting me. Six months later they held a trial in the compound. Some four men were convicted – one to fourteen years, two to twelve, and one to ten, all on special regime.

About a year and a half later, soon after one of my false witnesses had been released, we heard news that he had been bumped off. That often happened. Some thoroughly 'reformed' prisoner would be released, and not long afterwards the investigator would be round to find out who his enemies were and who had been plotting revenge. But what was there to find out, if he had sold half the camp down the river? During the evening rollcall there was often an announcement: whoever knew so-and-so, go to the security office tomorrow morning. Often enough the dead man would have been killed while leaving the camp – thrown under a train or his throat cut. And if he had really done someone a bad turn, they would catch up with him at home.

My other rat was due to be released on the same day as me. What a coincidence! The nearer the day came the more miserable the looks he cast at me. He needn't have worried, I wasn't going to touch him. He had suffered enough already.

You will find it hard to surprise a Russian with drunkenness, but what goes on now can no longer be called drunkenness – it is some sort of mass alcoholism. Vodka is getting dearer all the time, and it is now normal to consume eau de cologne, methylated spirits and assorted lotions and toilet waters. Everybody is a chemistry buff, an expert at distilling hooch from every possible kind of food, but also at adding reagents and mixing, shaking or heating things to extract alcohol from brake-fluid, aircraft glue, polish, varnish, stomach medicine, toothpaste, and so on. I have even heard that soldiers in the Far East invented a method of getting drunk on boot polish. They would smear it on bread and place the bread in the sun. When the bread was saturated, they ate it, after scraping off the polish. God knows what kind of chemical was extracted from the polish, but one thing is certain – eating the bread made them high.

The State rightly perceives alcoholism as a threat: the economic losses it causes are enormous. Thousands of reservations have been built for alcoholics, where the regime is not much different from the camps – forced labour, deprivation of food as a punishment, and similar 'educational' methods, plus, of course, compulsory treatment. Naturally, the patients go to any lengths in these sanatoria to get their hands on some alcohol, whether by bribing the guards or by using 'chemistry'. In effect, bricks seem to be about the only thing you can't turn into hooch.

But all this pales beside the drunkenness in the camps. Two thousand human souls fenced in by barbed wire and confined to an area of 125 acres are crying out to get smashed. Of course, polish, varnish, paint, and so on, were endlessly filched from the stores. But these were luxuries. They used to drink acetone. It made them ill, but they drank it. They would drink unthinned paint and swallow almost any sort of pills. 'Vodka and a machine-gun are the same to us – so long as we end up flat on our backs!'

In the camps, those who smoke hash or shoot drugs occasionally obtained through the guards aren't considered to be addicts. An addict is someone who can't live without the needle. For lack of the genuine article they used to burn stomach pills, made of some horrible black substance, and shoot the resulting liquid into their veins. And these were the lucky ones. When they were really desperate they shot water or plain air. I would never have believed it if I hadn't seen it with my own eyes – that a man could inject a cubic centimetre of air into his veins and still live.

The most curious thing of all was that from the prisoners' point of view, none of this was in the least reprehensible. On the contrary, injecting and swallowing this rubbish was regarded as a daring achievement and a particular form of chic. Sometimes somebody would die of this chic, and then they would say of him admiringly: 'He died on the needle.'

The intoxicant most widely used throughout the camp was tea brewed incredibly strong and black. The illegal trade in tea in the camps had attained fantastic proportions and accounted for a significant proportion of the guards' income. The usual price was a rouble a packet (the official price was thirty-eight copecks). Ten packets at ten roubles meant six roubles twenty copecks of pure profit for one delivery. Sometimes it was more, depending upon the situation. In Vladimir prison the price was three roubles a packet – twenty-six roubles twenty copecks profit a time. What guard could resist that?

The authorities had been battling against the tea trade for thirty years. Guards caught doing it were instantly sacked and fined, and sometimes even put on trial. Prisoners caught in possession of tea were thrown into the cooler, the camp lock-up or transferred to jail, but all in vain. The very guards who solemnly escorted the column and ushered them into the prison van, train or cell, would take the first opportunity to ask: 'Need any tea?' And the bartering would begin – for money, good clothes or similar benefits.

Whether it was stealing tools or making good furniture for admin, the kickback was always the same: tea, vodka, drugs. A good camp governor, the 'boss', knew that if he needed to beat his targets or urgently repair some broken equipment – in short, if he needed some heroic effort from the cons, no compulsion, punishments or box would do the trick. The only dependable means was tea.

And where there is trade, there are special relations, dependence, blackmail. For if they get caught, the con goes to the cooler and the guard to jail. If he's brought you some tea, he'll take out a letter. In response to your letter, your family will send money to the necessary address: half to you and half to the guard.

The cons brew tea on the campfires in their logging camps, devise makeshift kettles from electric leads in their barrack huts, or even simply push a light socket into a jar of water, while the guards comfortably brew for themselves in their cosily heated duty-room. And it's the same tea. It was they who brought it to the cons and it's they who confiscate it during the searches.

There's no real difference between the criminals and their guards. Except for the uniforms. The slang is the same, the manners, concepts, psychology. It's all the same criminal world, all joined by an unbreakable chain.

'Hey, chief, let me out to have a go at those rabbits, will you?' says a crook to an escort guard in a prison train. 'I've just come out of the choky, I'm all skin and bones, and they've got some real juicy bundles there.' And the guard lets the crook out to rob the greenhorns in the next compartment, knowing that a part of the loot will come to him too.

At the furniture factory in our camp there was a whole underground production unit. Four prisoners, working on different lathes, made all sorts of oddments that were in short supply outside: chessmen, rollers for blinds, and so on, and two guards used to take them out and sell them on the black market. The cons got tea, vodka and food, and the guards got money.

And it wasn't only the guards but also the free workers – factory foremen, nurses, teachers in the camp school – all were busy with this trade.

The camp school was an amusing affair. Under Soviet law, a secondary education is obligatory, and prisoners who haven't had one, regardless of age, are compelled to study in their free time. The means of compulsion are the usual ones – the punishment cells or the banning of parcels and visits. Studying in such a school is, of course, a pure formality, the fulfilment of an obligation rather than a process of learning. Especially for the elderly, who are tired from their work and simply doze through the lessons.

The boys went to school to amuse themselves and look at the teachers, who were usually women, mainly officers' wives. Some of the boys used to masturbate during the lessons behind their desks. You never saw any other women in the camp, and it was everyone's dream to have a romance with one of the teachers. There was no chance, in camp conditions, of sleeping with them, but the lucky fellows got all the other pleasures. The tender-hearted ladies would secretly bring them tea and vodka, and send their letters off for them. They, too, found life boring, for in the cramped officers' quarters, which were usually situated next to the camp and far away from any population centres, there were no amusements, not even a cinema. Always the same old circle of friends – their husband's colleagues. Their only distraction was to start a romance with one of the young cons in the camp. Of course, the entire camp would be green with envy at the lucky fellow, and he would strut like a bantam – the cock of the village. The husbands didn't conceal their jealousy and would pursue their 'rivals' relentlessly, throwing them into the box, even beating them up.

Captain Sazonov, a typical commissar – stupid, flabby, with a red bull neck and bulging eyes – was the most jealous of all. He must have thought that a commissar's wife, like Caesar's, should be above suspicion. He personally accompanied his wife to and from school every day, looked into the classroom several times during each lesson, and in the intervals between classes would stroll importantly up and down the corridor. She – youthful, fragile, graceful – seemed not at all the right match for him, and it was strange to see the two of them walking arm-in-arm through the entire camp. It seemed that he could feel the lascivious glances of 2,000 sex-starved prisoners on his back, and he would glare about him balefully. Literally the entire camp population came spilling out of their huts to watch her go by, then, spitting on the ground, would dispatch some dirty joke after the couple. How could he stop them looking?

Sixty students signed up for Mrs Sazonov's class, all the youngest and most reckless. There wasn't enough room, they closed the list, and fighting even broke out among the disappointed aspirants. One young fellow brought a drill from the factory, crawled under the floor of the schoolroom, drilled a hole in the floor, and enjoyed the view that he got from there. Another fixed a tiny mirror to the toe of his shoe and stuck his foot into the aisle every time she walked by. She, of course, was aware of the excitement she aroused in the camp, grew embarrassed, and blushed. But there was no one she singled out particularly – until a ruddy-faced, dashing young thief by the name of Foma appeared on the scene. With bated breath, the entire camp watched their romance, while hundreds of volunteers kept an eye on Sazonov's movements and warned the lovers whenever danger approached. Everyone was waiting to see what would happen.

Of course, the inevitable 'well-wishers' tipped off Sazonov. He summoned Foma to his office, looked at him in silence for a long time with his bleary eyes, but instead of locking him in the box as everyone had expected, merely said: 'Don't ever set foot in that school again!'

And after that he began watching his wife even more closely than before.

'Foma!' the cons used to shout every time they saw the two of them arm-in-arm. 'They're taking your bride away!'

'Okay,' Foma would grin crookedly. Sazonov's neck would fill with blood and swell like a cobra's hood.

Finally he caught them. In an interval between lessons they sat quietly side-by-side, talking over a mathematics textbook. How the volunteer sentries missed him I don't know.

'I'll make you rot! I'll do for you! Three months in the box.'

Throughout the three months Sazonov went to the box every evening and glared at the man who had insulted him. He would unlock the outer door, leave the inner, barred door locked, and peer into the gloom of the cell: 'Watch out, Foma, I'll let you rot. You won't come out of here alive.'

'All the same I'll fuck your Ada. The moment I get out of here I'll fuck her,' replied Foma jauntily, although he didn't look so dashing any longer. The ruddiness had gone from his face, his cheeks were sallow and sunken, and only his voice sounded fearless. He was still alive only because his friends would creep up to the window and give him something to eat whenever they could.

He was saved by the fact that he was almost at the end of his term. They let him go. And for a long time afterwards legends continued to circulate in the camp about the dashing young Foma. Camp rumour had it that in the end he did fuck Sazonov's wife. Some even claimed to have been present.

But that was it; apart from the teachers there were no women in the camp. Homosexuality was rampant and the passive partners had female nicknames like Mashka, Lyubka, Katya. Underworld tradition in this sphere is amazingly illogical: to be an active homosexual was a mark of honour, to be a passive one was a disgrace. It was bad form to sit at the same table with the latter, and they sat together separately in the corner of the canteen. They even had their own separate dishes and God forbid that they should ever get mixed up – there was a small hole drilled in their bowls just below the rim. You weren't supposed to accept anything from their hands.

The majority of these outcasts were not voluntary homosexuals. Usually, having lost at cards, they had been obliged to pay with sex, and after that anyone who cared to could force them – they were no longer protected by camp law. How many nice boys have been crippled in that way it is difficult to say. They amounted to about ten per cent in the compound.

But homosexuality wasn't the only thing. One day a nanny goat strayed into the compound. How she got past the guardhouse was a mystery. Probably behind an entering truck. The cons dragged her into a basement of the factory and collectively abused her. Then they stuck a hunk of bread on her horn by way of payment and drove her out to the main gate. The goat's owners, a sturdy red-faced peasant, himself an old con who had settled down near the camp after his release, and his wife, caught sight of their dairy goat as the soldiers were shooing her out through the gate. Guffaws, oaths, shouts. The cons climbed on to the workshop roofs and the guards came tumbling out of their guardhouse.

'Ivan!' cried the wife to her husband in tears. 'Slaughter the goat. Look, the cons have been taking advantage of her.'

'Shut up, you old fool!' replied Ivan. 'What put that idea into your head – slaughter her. I've been fucking you for ten years now, but I'm not going to slaughter you.'

A summons from the godfather is always bad. The security officers never call you in for anything good. It's either to throw you in the box, threaten you, or try to intimidate you. Or else they're planning to stick another charge on you, with a new sentence.

'Have you any relatives abroad?' he asked when I went to his office.

I couldn't figure out what he was driving at. What did my relatives have to do with it? 'No, none. Only friends.'

'Friends? You mean the ones you cooked up anti-Soviet activity with?'

That was all I needed, political lectures from the godfather. What did he want of me? 'I wasn't charged with anti-Soviet activities.'

It turned out that the cause of my summons was a parcel for me from America. The sender was someone called Anna Denis in California. The name was completely unknown to me.

'So, do you refuse to accept the parcel?'

Not a bad way to put the question. But why should I refuse? And what was in the parcel?

'We won't show you what's in it for the moment. First tell me whether you are refusing it or not.'

'No, I'm not refusing it.'

'Ah, so that's it. All right, I'm duty-bound to hand over the parcel. But I shall be obliged to inform everyone in the camp that you are a paid agent of imperialism. Furthermore, we cannot give it to you immediately – it contains objects suitable only for use outside. It will stay in store for you until the end of your sentence. And will count as a regular one. That means you will get no more parcels during the next half-year.'

Thus did I get my first communication from the free world – warm clothing from an unknown Anna Denis. All right, so let me be an agent of imperialism, and let these things lie in the store without being used, but I couldn't insult someone who had symbolically expressed sympathy with me by refusing their gift. And the camp godfather wrote on the card: 'Parcel with non-regulation clothing from Anna Denisovna, California.'

Strictly speaking, this wasn't my first communication from the free world. I also had a radio receiver, a wonderful radio, better than any I could buy in the shops of Moscow.

Pyotr Yakovlevich was three years younger than me, but everybody in the camp respectfully called him by his name and patronymic. Before his arrest in his native Voronezh he had been known as a 'golden' pickpocket – his thieving exploits were legendary. Just in boarding a bus or simply mingling with a crowd on the street, he could judge with astonishing accuracy who had any money, approximately how much and where it was kept. And there was never a case where he was unable to lift it. But he had been caught for the first time and got four years. You'd never have taken him for a pickpocket. Unusually serious and respectable-looking, wearing thick-rimmed glasses, he had the air of a nineteenth-century intellectual. If I had met him somewhere outside, I would have taken him for a young scientist engrossed in his research. He was slow-moving and meditative, and if he ever said anything, it was his final word, carefully weighed, never off the top of his head.

Apart from his basic, pickpocketing profession, he was also a first-class radio mechanic; and after his release he was planning to devote himself wholly to this second profession. 'But what about the pockets?' said the crooks in astonishment. 'Are you really packing it in?'

'Finished, I won't do it again,' replied Pyotr Yakovlevich weightily. 'It's alright to get by on these things until your first arrest. But after that it's senseless. The cops know you, they watch you, try to pin anything they can on you, and after a couple of weeks they jail you again. It's useless.'

I had asked Pyotr Yakovlevich to make me a short-wave receiver. We were able to order all the necessary parts through one of the free workers, a 'courier' who used to bring tea into the camp. I was in a terrible hurry and kept urging Pyotr Yakovlevich to go faster, which made him frown. It wasn't his way to rush things. If a job was worth doing, it was worth doing well.

And indeed, it was a superb radio – it picked up everything: the BBC, Voice of America, Radio Liberty, Deutsche Welle, and even Radio Monte Carlo. The only station it didn't get was Moscow. How Pyotr Yakovlevich managed to exclude Moscow I will never know.

The radio was kept in one of the schoolrooms where school equipment was stored, disguised as a piece of physics apparatus. The school steward, a prisoner, used to let me into that room secretly every evening, and there I would plunge into a completely different life. I was back with my friends, deploring their arrests, accompanying them to Red Square to protest against the occupation of Czechoslovakia, writing protest letters.

1968 was the year of climax. It seemed that at any moment the regime must retreat and renounce its self-destructive obstinacy. It was getting too dangerous: like a chain reaction, their repressions were drawing more and more people into the civil-rights movement. Whole peoples threatened to move into action, and this threatened the very existence of the world's last colonial empire. For the question of whether we were citizens or subjects was decisive for the resolution of national problems, too. A citizen possesses his rights from birth. A subject is endowed with them as a dispensation from on high. But to be a Ukrainian, a Russian or a Jew was also a natural right: the State that citizens carry within them, and only that, decides what the external State will be.

The Soviet authorities had no way out. No matter how stupid, dangerous and even suicidal such obstinacy might prove to be, to acknowledge the sovereignty of those inner States in man would have signified the end of the Soviet system, just as to acknowledge the sovereignty of the separate nations would have meant the end of the empire. The authorities understood only too well that socialism with a human face was impossible. Having sent the tanks into Prague, they were in essence sending them into Kiev and Vilnius as well, and into the Caucasus and Central Asia. Yes, and even into Moscow itself.

The troops of the Warsaw Pact had been sent to destroy my castle and were defeated head-on by seven individuals in Red Square.* In

* On 25 August 1968, seven dissidents (Konstantin Babitsky, Larisa Bogoraz, Vadim Delaunay, Vladimir Dremlyuga, Victor Fainberg, Natalya Gorbanevskaya and Pavel Litvinov) demonstrated in Red Square against the invasion of Czechoslovakia. The

Execution Place, where brigands used to be beheaded, socialism was given a public execution, and I could have wept over my inability to be there with my friends. On the other hand I was delighted to hear that Vadim Delaunay was among them. So he had stood firm after our trial and mastered himself!

In the evenings, just before lights out, when I returned to the compound after listening to these broadcasts, and strolled along the barbed-wire fence, brightly illuminated by the searchlights, I was filled with a wonderful sense of freedom, ease and power.

Prime ministers and presidents maintained a cowardly silence about the invasion of Czechoslovakia, preferring their comradely dinners with Brezhnev and Husak in a friendly atmosphere. The United Nations was also disgracefully mute, paying no heed to the flood of appeals from my friends.

'They will be ground to dust,' said Pyotr Yakovlevich judiciously. 'What can they do against such power? They'd have done better to sit quietly and not be in such a hurry.'

'There you are, you see,' said the tipsy captain. 'How can you go against such a force? They'll simply murder you, you mark my words. They'll shoot you down and that's that.'

In the factories and mills, meetings of workers were organised, who unanimously approved the sending of the troops to Czechoslovakia. The newspapers printed letters from milkmaids and deer-breeders, schoolteachers and steelworkers, writers and professors. And everyone, from the President of the USA and the General Secretary of the UN to the last guard in our camp bowed their heads before brute force.

No, it wasn't I who was in the concentration camp, but they, who had voluntarily embraced their unfreedom.

The last days of my time were spent in the box. Throughout the whole of my camp term I had never once been to the political instruction sessions, and everybody had got used to this, as if it were the accepted thing. Sazonov knew this as well, but some three months before I was due to be released, he took it into his head to force me to go to them. After the affair of the parcel, he hated my guts. Most likely he simply wanted to use this as a pretext for punishing me.

I, of course, dug my heels in: what's the point of attending your church when I don't believe in your God? And in any case, political studies were not obligatory under the law.

demonstration, and the reprisals it provoked, are described in detail in *Red Square at Noon* by Natalya Gorbanevskaya (Deutsch, 1972).

And so it was box after box until I was seeing spots before my eyes.

'I'll cook your goose, even if there isn't much time,' promised Sazonov. He was right in reckoning that there was little time left and that I wouldn't possibly be able to pay him back.

At the very end he gave me fifteen days in the box, although my sentence had only seven days to run – he was mad as hell with me. And so I left owing the boss eight days. Never mind, I could finish it next time.

I had some difficulty in persuading the duty officer to allow me back into the compound even for an hour before my release, so as to get washed and bid farewell to the boys. It is the worst punishment of all to be pushed out of the camp straight from the box. The filth in the box is such that the only thing you can do when you come out is throw away your clothes – it is impossible to get them clean again. To persuade them to let you have a bath was almost always impossible. Admin absolutely hated the trouble of leading you through the entire compound, particularly as some would get away on the return journey and disappear into the barrack huts, where it was murder to find them again. People even went on hunger strikes to get a bath.

On one occasion some crooks had the bright idea of smuggling a matchbox full of lice into the box – they had collected them off the most lice-ridden character in the entire compound, an old tramp who would have been riddled with them even if you had held him in boiling water for a day. They managed to make this matchbox last a whole two months. Once a week the cry would go up: 'Send in the doctor, boss! You won't let us go to the bathhouse! We've got lice in here. Everybody's covered in lice.' And they would shove a couple of fat, indisputable lice under the officer's nose. A couple of hours of shouting, cursing and threats, and then admin would be obliged to take them all off to the bathhouse – they were mortally afraid of typhus or any of the other infectious diseases carried by lice.

My crooks brewed strong tea to see me off, and almost every one of them led me aside and said self-consciously: 'Well, er, you know, yourself. . . . If ever you need anything, everybody knows me in town. Just ask – you can always find me. If you're ever on the run. Or you politics need any guns. Or a place to lie low in. We'll do what we can.' A few of them cautiously hinted that they could even rub somebody out if I wanted. No problem.

With these messages ringing in my ears I left camp. I had not managed to convince them that criminality was a godsend to the Soviet regime. True, I had persuaded one or two of them to educate themselves, but only by using a most unorthodox argument: that an educated man could commit a crime much more efficiently than one who wasn't educated. 'Finish university first and then go thieving, if that's what you want. Then nobody will ever catch you.' This they believed. Education struck them as some sort of black magic. I even got them to read books. Dostoevsky was their particular favourite.

There's no denying it, I had grown used to them and was sad to be parting, especially from the younger ones. Who knew how many of them would ever succeed in getting out of the camps? The younger fellows were hot-tempered and fiery – at the slightest thing they'd reach for a knife. If you didn't restrain them in time, they'd have a new stretch to do. It was a shame. A lot of them were very talented fellows. I had started to teach five of them English, out of sheer boredom, while we sat in the box.

Perhaps this will strike some people as strange: criminals, thieves, murderers, tramps fallen upon hard times, drug addicts, drunkards, and all of a sudden you find it hard to part with them. Respectable people will shake their heads and the Soviet press will be overjoyed. What a find for Party propaganda! But this is our people, we have no other. And that's what they've been turned into during the past sixty years.

I slept on the same bedboards as them, under the same reefer jackets, shared a crust of bread with them and languished in the same boxes. And I crawled under the fence on my belly, pulled the barbed wire apart with my hands, tore my skin, awaited a bullet in my back at any minute, all in order to push them a packet of shag through the bars. And they did the same for me. I don't in the least regret it.

But what do *you* know of your people? What is your attitude to them? What right have you to speak in their name?

I didn't read them sermons, didn't give them political lessons, didn't create underground political parties or teach them to inform on their comrades in order to be 'reformed'. I taught them to write complaints in the hope that, having got used to the idea of invoking the protection of the law, they would learn to respect it. And it wasn't my fault that it didn't turn out that way. It was your fault. Remember what you wrote in your answers to their complaints, remember how you sprayed the rebellious inmates of the camp lock-up with firehoses on a freezing winter's morning, how you searched people in the snow after making them strip naked. Remember the ones who died on the threshold of your medical unit and the ones who cut their fingers with axes –

remember them, when the blood-maddened crowds break down your office doors, drag you out into the streets and trample you into the ground. When the wind blows tons and tons of paper – all that will remain of your empire – through the shattered, smoke-blackened streets. And you will have the benefit neither of the law, nor of a just trial.

That is what will come to pass, because you do not acknowledge the *sovereignty of the human conscience*. No one will be any the better for it afterwards. But you are leaving them no other choice.

I was frightened to think what life still held in store for them. On later prison transports I met elderly cons in the transit jails who had spent their entire lives behind bars Up to thirty or forty years. I particularly remember Lyokha Tarasov. I met him in the Serbsky Institute in 1971, waiting to go before a panel. The moment I entered the cell I noticed this man of about sixty, gaunt and toothless, like a skeleton. His whole face was hideously tattooed. On his forehead was 'LENIN – CANNIBAL', on one cheek 'DEATH TO THE CC' (Central Committee) and on the other 'SLAVE OF THE CPSU' (Communist Party of the Soviet Union.

He was younger than he seemed. In 1944, as a sixteen-year-old boy during the war, he had gone to jail for theft and had been inside ever since. In the reform colony for juvenile delinquents a rebellion had broken out, and he and his friends had stabbed eleven trusties. As a result of this he got his first labour-camp sentence. Then another one in Kolyma for attempted escape. He had long since been cured of any underworld romanticism, but still had one of his invariable twenty-five-year sentences to finish. In 1953 he had been sentenced to the firing squad for murdering a godfather, but this had been commuted to yet another 'quarter' (fifteen in a high-security jail).

Day after day he had slogged out fifteen years in Vladimir prison. Of his teeth, hair and health nothing remained. He had swallowed spoons, sewn buttons on to his body, slit his veins – anything to get into the hospital for a week. Then he had started having anti-Soviet slogans tattooed on his face. This was the quickest route to the hospital – they would cut the tattoos out at once, without an anaesthetic, out of the living flesh. And on every occasion they punctiliously extended his sentence. Later a secret decree was passed, prescribing the death sentence for anti-Soviet tattoos – for 'disorganising' the work of corrective labour establishments. There were far too many 'slaves of the CPSU' about. At that time he was in a camp, but had just been sentenced to three years in Vladimir again for some sort of offence. This was more than he could stand – after fifteen years in there he knew every stone, and he loathed the place. Therefore on the way there, on the transport where I met him, he had had new tattoos done.

'If they don't send me to the firing squad, I'll rush the escort guards. And I'll take as many as I can with me to the next world.'

He was shot in 1972, without the necessity of rushing his guards.

Knocking about the transit prisons, I sometimes heard in the evenings the sound of some boyish voice calling from the window:

'Prison, prison, give me a name!'

This was a newly converted thief, begging to be baptised for the rest of his life. On such occasions I remembered Lyokha Tarasov. His prison name was 'Prickly'.

# 8

THAT year I decided not to go to prison any more. Enough. It was 1970, I would soon be thirty, and I still hadn't lived. Hadn't lived as a normal human being. I had no profession, no family, and whenever I was introduced to someone I would wait miserably for them to ask: 'Tell me, what do you do?'

I usually spun a yarn that I was a geologist. Always away on expeditions. That was the easiest way to explain why I hadn't seen the latest film, read the latest fashionable book, or known about some everyday facts or occurrences.

'You lose touch, you know, on those expeditions. You spend all your time in the taiga.'

Being released from jail is like emigrating to a strange land. Everything strikes you as new and weird, and you are as helpless as a newborn babe. All you can do is spot ex-cons in the crowd, like fellow-countrymen abroad, by certain imperceptible signs – their walk, their gestures or the occasional familar phrase.

Enough was enough: that labour camp tedium, those endless conversations, those crazy prison transports, the swearing and the tobacco smoke.

The streets were full of people, their faces animated, not listless. They were on their way home to their families. They got by somehow. It might be difficult, but they got by. On Sundays they could go to the woods if they liked. And in spite of yourself, you found yourself secretly hating them for this – out of envy.

During my childhood a distant relative of our neighbours used to come and visit them from Siberia. He was an officer working for the Ministry of Internal Affairs – a small-time labour-camp official. He also couldn't bear to see people walking in the street. He used to get drunk. Gloomily polishing his boots in the kitchen, he would say rancorously, to no one in particular: 'Walking about smiling and laughing. Should let me have 'em a while. I'd make 'em laugh. . . .'

I feared that I, too, would come to hate everyone who hadn't done time, who didn't know what I knew. I did not dare to drink, because then all my misery and resentment would boil up inside me. But I had put in the best part of six years. It was enough.

My mother was seriously ill, and the day I was let out of the camp she was operated on. I wasn't allowed into the hospital – it was quarantined because of a flu epidemic. They passed me a note. She asked me to try to get her some Borzhomi mineral water – as usual, there was none on sale anywhere. And she also asked me to change some money into single roubles for her to pay the nurses. Every time they gave you a bedpan, changed your sheets, helped you out of your bed or fetched something for you, it cost you a rouble. Their pay was bad, they had to earn what they could on the side.

Ah, wait a minute. I know where I am now. It turns out I do have a profession after all. I was taught it by my labour-camp bosses. Why bother with shops, counters, queues? Where's the back entrance? One glance at the porter and I know he's one of us, a native from the islands of the archipelago. And so, here I am with Borzhomi water. Quarantine? Three roubles to grease the sister's palm, and I'm a young intern walking in a white coat through basements, laboratories, the mortuary, and then up the stairs. All around are my fellow-doctors, dressed just like me.

Mother forced a smile and was cheerfulness itself, and it suddenly hit me that I might have been too late to see her at all. The next time I returned from custody would definitely be too late. And there was nobody else for me to hurry home to.

No, there wouldn't be a next time. Enough. What difference was there, in fact, between here and there? The same life, the same laws. I'd get by somehow. This was my last chance to live. There would be no more time.

In February I accompanied her to a sanatorium outside Moscow. She needed fresh air and a rest. It was beautiful spring weather and we spent hours strolling in the woods, following the sledge tracks and stopping frequently to rest. While she basked in the sun, I built a snowman – a corpulent, elderly fellow, struggling to get up from his knees and holding on to the branches of a fir tree. The face came out haggard, as if he were tired of living, tired of this forest and the sun, and the eternal snow out of which he was made.

We walked on unhurriedly till we came to a clearing in the forest where the snow was covered with hare tracks, and then went back for dinner. Doubtless the hares danced here at night, in the moonlight.

In the dining room they used to look at us with curiosity – a strange pair. And in their glances I saw the accursed question: 'And what are you? You're a sculptor, aren't you?'

Fortunately no one tried to talk to us.

The sanatorium belonged to the Central Committee of the Komsomol (by chance mother had got a warrant to go there through her work), and therefore most of the convalescents were old Party or Komsomol members from the 1920s. Crossing the terrace, one would find them reclining in the sun in their chaise-longues, chatting about their youth: 'Yes, in 1922 I was in a Special Assignment Section,* had five years Party membership behind me already. What about you?' Grey, flabby Party matrons and gaffers. Never give up – still dreaming of those civil war carve-ups.

I sculpted a gleaming white skull out of snow and carefully balanced it at head height on some branches of a fir tree, in the area where they strolled during the day, waddling like ducks. Every time they saw it they trembled and looked frightened, 'What a morbid imagination you've got, how cruel you are,' said one of them when she met us on the path. I didn't reply. She, I thought, must have had a sunny imagination in 1922.

'You're not going to go back to prison, are you?' asked my mother cautiously. After a pause she added: 'You'd do better to go away from here, abroad. Here they will make life impossible for you.'

It is strange to go back to your old circle of friends after a long absence and suddenly meet new people, new faces, and hear stories of events that are completely new to you. And, in answer to your indiscreet question about one of your friends, to be met with an awkward silence.

Moscow had grown accustomed to arrests, searches, trials and interrogations – they had become the subject of jokes and society gossip, the way others talked about weddings, christenings and new clothes. A new form of social call had also appeared – attending searches.

When you are in constant contact with your friends, it is easy to know when something suspicious is going on in their flat: nobody answers the telephone even when there is a light in the window. Or

* Euphemism for revolutionary troops assigned to quell popular rebellions.

277

you make an arrangement to meet them and they don't turn up. Telephones at once ring all over Moscow – there's a search at so-and-so's! Quick, find a taxi! And guests rush in from all corners of the city. It's true, a search. Everybody is admitted, but they are not allowed to let anyone out. The flat fills up to overflowing – noise and laughter. No room to turn around. Somebody comes with a bottle of wine, somebody else with a melon. Everyone tucks in, laughing at the KGB goons. Certain papers find their way into the visitors' pockets – unwanted *samizdat*, carelessly kept letters and similar circumstantial evidence: how can they keep track of such a crowd?

The sweating goons try to drive some of the visitors away – what a hope! They're all trained: it's forbidden to let people go during a search. You have to bear with us. On the table there's a copy of the Criminal Procedure Code for everyone to consult.

'Quiet, citizens!'

'Where is it written that you mustn't make a noise while a search is in progress? Show us the article!'

Only the formal witnesses from the house management committees are horrified by this impiety.

It became a tradition to celebrate prisoners' birthdays. 'Toast number two' became *de rigueur* – for absent friends. And arrested ones – well, arrest was absolutely normal. How many had there been already?

> Oh, we'll drink and we'll drink and we'll drink up, my lads,
>   To Pashka and Natashka and Larisa Bogoraz.*

These birthday parties provided an opportunity of collecting signatures for letters of protest. In self-respecting families there would even be a desk set aside for *samizdat*. *The Chronicle of Current Events* equalled three years of jail, the Avtorkhanov book seven.†

---

* 'Pashka' – Pavel Litvinov, 'Natashka' – Natalya Gorbanevskaya. Litvinov, grandson of the former Soviet Foreign Minister, Maxim Litvinov, had earlier compiled two books, *The Demonstration in Pushkin Square* (Harvill, 1969), about the demonstration by Bukovsky and his friends and their subsequent trials, and *The Trial of the Four* (Longman, 1972), about the trial of Ginzburg, Dobrovolsky, Galanskov and Lashkova. For their parts in the demonstration in Red Square, Litvinov was sentenced to five years' internal exile and Gorbanevskaya was committed to a lunatic asylum.

The former wife of the writer, Yuli Daniel, Larisa Bogoraz assisted Anatoly Marchenko to write his dramatic exposure of the post-Stalin labour camps, *My Testimony* (Pall Mall, 1969), and subsequently became a leading figure in the human-rights movement. For her part in the Red Square demonstration, she was sentenced to four years' internal exile.

† Abdurahman Avtorkhanov was at the élite Institute of Red Professors in the Soviet Union and defected during the Second World War. He then wrote a series of

For serious talk we resorted to the 'Russian/Russian Dictionary' – in other words, writing down what we had to say and burning the paper after the conversation was over.

There were lots of chores. Families came to Moscow from all over the country on their way to Mordovia and Vladimir to visit prisoners. Everyone needed a bed for the night and the chance to buy food. They had to be met and shown around. On their way back from Mordovia they brought the news. Punishment cells, lock-ups and prison regimes were as much the small change of conversation in Moscow flats as they were in the camps.

One day it was the Ukrainians, then the Lithuanians, and then a veritable invasion by the Crimean Tartars or the Meskhetians. Whole trainloads of Tartars came up for their demonstrations. They were intercepted on the way and sent home again. And the ones who got through were hunted all over Moscow.

There had been quite an upsurge in national movements during my absence. They were extremely varied and even had different external aims. The Meskhetians and Crimean Tartars, for instance, who in Stalin's time had been forcibly deported from their homelands to Central Asia, were trying to obtain the right to return home. The Jews wanted right to go to Israel, the Volga and the Baltic Germans to Germany, the Ukrainians, the Caucasians and the Baltic peoples wanted secession, national independence and the right to a national culture. Five years before the mere mention of national independence or the right to secession would have been sufficient to guarantee fifteen years for 'high treason'. And leaving for abroad was still regarded as treason. But citizens who had resolved to submit to their conscience instead of their Party card were beginning to force their own reality upon the state.

This wasn't a political struggle, there were no heroics. It was like a 'club of the sane' in a lunatic asylum. All that was left to us was to be normal people.

'And so, whose spacemen will be the first to land on the moon?'

Here there was no right, left and middle-of-the-road. Everyone had been made equal by the Soviet concentration camps. Just as before, there were no leaders and led, no pushers and pushed, no rules and regulations – only it was easier, much easier, than five years before. There were more people, there was more publicity, and the people came from higher up the social scale: professors, academicians, writers – not to be compared with us striplings of the early 1960s. Rights

works on Soviet political institutions, of which the best known is his book *The Technology of Power* (1955–7), referred to here.

were now claimed on the spur of the moment, and yesterday's 'impossible' was a commonplace today.

How hard it once had been to get this kind of publicity! Foreign correspondents in Moscow, partly because they were afraid of being expelled and losing a good job, partly because they had been coopted and misled, were extremely shy of informing their papers of the repressions that were taking place. It was much simpler and more advantageous for them to reprint the statements of TASS and the Soviet press. There were still difficulties now – the authorities expelled anyone who got too friendly with us – but there were far more of them ready to take their chance. Interest in our problems was growing in the outside world, and whereas, before, an expelled correspondent might be regarded by his newspaper as unprofessional, expulsion was now seen as the norm and occasionally even as an honour.

Is it possible to speak of an absence of freedom of information in a country where tens of millions of people listen to Western radio, where *samizdat* exists and is regularly sent abroad, and everything said today will be public knowledge tomorrow? Of course, we had to pay a high price for making it public knowledge, but that was another matter.

An original radio game even came into being. People would come to Moscow from the farthest ends of the country in order to tell us about their troubles, then would hurry home in order to hear about them over the BBC, Radio Liberty, Deutsche Welle, etc. Raising their hands in astonishment, they would say to their neighbours: 'How do you like that? How the hell do they find out about these things in London [or Munich or Cologne]?'

This had much more effect than sending complaints to Brezhnev. A Moscow woman once stopped me in a doorway and tried to persuade me to help them get their roof repaired. 'Why don't you get the BBC to criticise them, they'll soon get their skates on then. Otherwise we won't get anywhere for the next three years at least!'

But the authorities weren't sleeping either. Hundreds of people were behind bars or had been deprived of their jobs. No matter. This was the traditional method, and if anything it increased the number of participants in the movement, for it provoked the victims' families, friends and fellow-workers to protest. For those in greatest need and for the families of political prisoners, contributions began to be collected, and a sort of home-grown Red Cross came into existence. Scientists and engineers worked as caretakers, porters and unskilled labourers. And in the camps, no matter how bad the conditions became, the campaign of resistance continued to grow – hunger strikes, protest letters, etc. After all, people did come out after they had done their terms. No, it wasn't the prospect of a camp or prison term that was frightening.

The trials in 1968–9 had been so revealing and had evoked such a resounding echo all around the world that the authorities could no longer afford to indulge in this luxury. They tried putting their victims on trial as far away from Moscow as possible, where there were no foreign correspondents or crowds of well-wishers. They deprived lawyers of their 'access permits' or drove them out of the profession altogether. And finally they started imposing sentences of internal exile under article 190, although such a measure was not stipulated by that article. In short, they did everything they could to stop the publicity. To no avail.

At this point my old friend, Daniil Romanovich Lunts, appeared on the scene again, the master case-maker. At last they had remembered him – his time had come.

It was a fact that most of the participants in the movement, with their precisely formulated civil-rights position and refusal to accept Soviet reality, were peculiarly vulnerable to psychiatric repression. I could easily imagine Lunts rubbing his hands and croaking: 'Tell me, why won't you acknowledge your guilt?'

And all the legal formulations and references to articles in the code, constitutional freedoms and the absence of intent, i.e. the entire arsenal of the citizen's rights position, devastating as it was to the investigation, would backfire on you, for it offered an irrefutable syndrome:

You don't acknowledge your guilt? Therefore you don't understand the criminal nature of your actions, therefore you cannot answer for them.

You keep talking about the constitution and the laws, but what normal man takes Soviet laws seriously? You are living in an unreal world of your own invention, you react inadequately to the world around you.

Do you put the blame for your conflict with society on society? Do you mean the whole of society is wrong? A typical madman's logic.

You had no intent? That means that you are incapable of understanding the consequences of your actions. You didn't even understand that you were certain to be arrested.

'Very well,' croaks Lunts. 'If you consider yourself to be in the right, why do you refuse to give evidence during the investigation?'

281

And again you haven't a leg to stand on – your morbid suspicion and distrustfulness are too plain.

'Why have you been doing all these things? What were you hoping to achieve?' None of us expected any practical results – that wasn't the aim of our actions – but from the point of view of commonsense, such behaviour was pure madness.

As before, this procedure worked very well with the Marxists — they had an obvious reforming mania, an overvalued idea of saving mankind. With the believers it was even simpler, as it had always been, and with the poets – a clear case of schizophrenia.

The theoretical 'scientific' base had long since been prepared. In the conditions of socialism, according to the assertions of the country's leading psychiatrists, there were no social causes of criminality; therefore, any anti-legal act was *ipso facto* a mental aberration. Under socialism there is no contradiction between society's goals and man's conscience. Existence determines consciousness, hence there is no such thing as a non-socialist consciousness.

But the psychiatric method had now been worked out in much greater detail. First of all in the form of that old, tried and true diagnosis: *paranoidal development of the personality.* (The following quotations are from Professors Pechernikov and Kosachev of the Serbsky Institute.)

'Most frequently, ideas about a "struggle for truth and justice" are formed by personalities with a paranoid structure.'

'Litigiously paranoid states come into being as a result of psychologically traumatic circumstances affecting the subject's interests and are stamped by feelings that the individual's legal rights have been infringed.'

'A characteristic feature of overvalued ideas is the patient's conviction of his own rectitude, an obsession with asserting his "trampled" rights, and the significance of these feelings for the patient's personality. They tend to exploit judicial proceedings as a platform for making speeches and appeals.'

And of course, complaints about persecution by the KGB, being searched and followed, telephone-tapping, the opening of letters and dismissal from work were pure persecution manias. The more open and public your position, the more obvious your insanity.

But here was something new as well. Snezhnevsky's school had firmly seized all the commanding heights of Soviet psychiatry. The concept of 'sluggish schizophrenia', that mystical illness that showed no symptoms and left the intellect and outward behaviour completely unimpaired, was now universally recognised and obligatory. 'Dissidence may be caused by brain disease,' wrote Professor Timofeyev, 'when the pathological process develops extremely slowly and mildly (sluggish schizophrenia), whilst in the meantime its other indications (occasionally until the committing of a criminal act) remain imperceptible.'

'In so far as the typical attributes of this age [20–29 years old] are a heightened sense of conflict, an urge towards self-affirmation, a rejection of tradition, received opinion and the norm, etc., this is a precondition for the myth that a certain number of young men, who in reality are suffering from schizophrenia, are being unjustly placed in mental hospitals, and that they are being kept there allegedly because "they don't think like all the others".'

Lunts had said to me quite frankly in the course of one of our discussions in 1966: 'It's a waste of time your friends abroad kicking up a rumpus over our diagnosis. At least a paranoidal development of the personality doesn't have to be treated. So what are you achieving? The more protests there are, the quicker everything will pass into Snezhnevsky's hands, and he's a world figure with an international reputation. Schizophrenia is schizophrenia. It calls for treatment, and intensive treatment at that. We here are fighting against the influence of the Snezhnevsky school as best we can, but you are hindering us.'

Indeed: schizophrenia might well be sluggish in its development, but the treatment was administered with alacrity in the name of saving the patient. And they started giving everybody the agonising haloperidol in doses large enough to fell a horse.

But it wasn't just a question of protests. By 1970, Lunts himself started diagnosing 'sluggish schizophrenia' all over the place.

This presented a deadly threat to our movement. Within a short space of time, dozens were proclaimed unfit to plead – usually the most obstinate and persistent. What had not been achieved by the forces of the Warsaw Pact, jails, camps, interrogations, searches, deprivation of jobs, blackmail and intimidation was now being realised with the help of psychiatry. Not everyone was prepared to risk losing his reason and sit out the rest of his life in a sadistic lunatic asylum. At the same time this method allowed the authorities to avert shameful trials – the 'unfit to plead' were tried in absentia, behind closed doors, and the facts of their cases were not examined. Thus it was almost impossible to struggle for the release of the unfit to plead. Even the most objective bystander, who is none the less unacquainted with the 'patient', retains a lingering doubt about his psychological fitness.

Who knows? Anyone can go out of his mind. And in response to all questions and petitions, the authorities would sorrowfully shrug their shoulders: 'He's sick. It's nothing to do with us. Ask the doctors.'

And the inference was clear: they are all sick, these 'dissidents'.

Meanwhile the KGB investigators openly threatened people when they refused to give testimony or didn't wish to recant: 'Do you want to go to the loony bin?' Sometimes it was sufficient simply to threaten a prisoner with being sent to have his head examined to get him to alter his behaviour.

The advantages of the psychiatric method of repression were so obvious that there was no hope of forcing the authorities to abandon it with mere petitions or protests. The prospect was of a long, stubborn struggle, with, of course, prison as one's reward – that same prison where I never wanted to go again. It seemed an absolutely hopeless undertaking. Who would risk asserting that somebody he had no personal knowledge of was sane? Especially if it meant contradicting the opinion of expert psychiatrists. There was no prospect of obtaining broad support. At the same time it was agony to see everything you had achieved at such incredible cost being annihilated before your very eyes. It was intolerable to stand by when your friends were being flung into lunatic asylums. I knew only too well what it was, this 'psychiatric hospital of a special type', this psychiatric prison.

Around the age of thirty you begin to realise that your greatest possession is your friends. You have nothing else of value. And never shall. In the last analysis, how much does the way your life turns out depend on you? Some people live long and peacefully, others have short and chaotic lives. As for hopelessness, when did we ever have any real hope? Do everything that depends upon you alone and don't hope for anything more.

I roamed around Moscow, keeping to the obscure Arbat backstreets, where the snow had still not melted and the sounds echoed clearly. Caretakers were scraping frozen snow from pavements and shovelling the tinkling ice into the gutter. It was March.

I had still not had my fill of life after the grey monotony of the camp. I soaked up the colours, sounds and hubbub of the city and would stand for ages gazing at some cornice or the fantastically patterned railings of one of the detached houses. My hair had not grown back properly yet, so I tried not to take my cap off, and my fingers, as before, were stained yellow with tobacco. It is good when the future holds at least some mystery for you – it is easier to live. But I felt that I knew it all in advance: the green Lefortovo walls, prison transports, endless arguments about generalissimos, and that foul morning muster, when, after gulping down your slops with their sticky fishbones, you stood by the main gate, shifting from leg to leg, waiting for the turnkey in his sheepskin coat to count you all off in fives.

Oh well, let's just say that I was unlucky. There would be no family for me, no profession, and when in my old age people asked who I was and what job I did, I would lie that I was a geologist: 'You lose touch, you know, on those expeditions. Always in the taiga.'

But that year I really did not want to return to jail.

In May 1970 I gave my first interview to the Associated Press correspondent, Holger Jensen. I told him about the prisons and camp. I laid most stress on a description of the mental hospitals – it was because of them, in fact, that I threw myself into the fray once again. Then I gave a long television interview to our friend Bill Cole, the CBS correspondent in Moscow, exclusively on the subject of the psychiatric repression of dissent.

This was a major operation. About twenty of us, Russians and correspondents, went off to the woods outside Moscow, together with wives and children, for a picnic. The KGB kept in the background and watched us from a distance – their main worry was not to miss the moment of our departure. Therefore it was fairly easy for Bill and me to arrange it so that the agents couldn't see him filming the interview. In fact, that was no problem – but smuggling it out was. Bill did two more interviews – with Amalrik[*] and Yakir – and I gave him a taped statement by Ginzburg that had been smuggled out of the Mordovian camps. This considerable package took three months to reach America.

There was one more incident that attracted attention to psychiatric repression, and that was the forcible hospitalisation of the well-known scientist Zhores Medvedev.[†] The Soviet academic world was up in arms – the repressions had reached their very doorstep. The most prominent scientists in the Soviet Union led the campaign for his release.

Neither Zhores Medvedev nor his brother Roy thought at that time

[*] Andrei Amalrik, author of *Involuntary Journey to Siberia* (Harvill, 1970) and *Will the Soviet Union Survive until 1984?* (Allen Lane, 1970). In 1970, Amalrik was sentenced to three years in strict-regime labour camps and in 1973 to a further three years of internal exile. In 1976, he emigrated to the West.

[†] Zhores Medvedev, a prominent Soviet biologist, was forcibly committed to a mental hospital in June 1970. As the result of a worldwide campaign of protest, he was released after nineteen days. He now lives in England.

that a noisy campaign would harm our cause – would assist the 'hawks' and hinder the 'doves' in the Soviet leadership. On the contrary, having landed in trouble, they realised only too well that nothing except wide publicity would help them. Every day, Roy Medvedev issued a news bulletin on the latest developments. Exploiting his connections in the respectable world, he persuaded people who didn't usually participate in our protests to write or sign letters in support of his brother. This event had major repercussions throughout the entire world, and although the authorities surrendered fairly quickly – after nineteen days – our statements about the psychiatric method of repression were freshly confirmed. We conceived the hope that a sufficiently energetic campaign might force the authorities to abandon the use of psychiatry for repressive purposes altogether.

It was all right for Zhores Medvedev – he was well enough known in the scientific world. But what could be done for the workman Borisov, the bricklayer Gershuni, the students Novodvorskaya and Iofe, or the stage designer Victor Kuznetsov? For them there was no prospect of academicians raising hell with the Central Committee or the world community of scientists threatening a scientific boycott. According to our information, there were hundreds of little-known individuals being held in psychiatric prisons for political reasons. Who would take up the struggle on their behalf?

I came to the conclusion that it was essential to assemble an extensive documentation, including the testimony of witnesses and the findings of the panels of doctors. The authorities' basic argument boiled down to the simple point that non-specialists could not dispute the findings of specialists. Any attempt to do so would be interpreted by them as slander. All right, I would try to find honest specialists.

Everyone contributed his bit to the documentation. The fundamental part, of course, came from our lawyers, who had defended the 'unfit to plead' and had access to their case files. Only from them could we get copies of the genuine findings of the experts. Another part of the documentation consisted of evidence given by the formerly 'unfit' – this enabled us to study the history of the question. Then came letters and testimony from prisoners still in psychiatric prisons (and from their families) about the present prison regime. To judge by their accounts, little had changed since my time, except that the 'treatment' had if anything become more intensive and more painful. We also collected evidence of the opening of new special hospitals, together with photographs of them and the names of the doctors responsible for these psychiatric abuses.

The best-known case at that time was the case of General Grigorenko. His 1969 prison diary, with its detailed description of his investigation and psychiatric examination, had already been published in the West.* But few people knew that his first examination in Tashkent, by a panel headed by Dr Detengof, not only had concluded that he was fully fit, but had emphatically recommended that no more examinations be conducted in the future. After this the KGB hastily dispatched him to the Serbsky Institute in Moscow for a second specialist examination, where it was no trouble at all for Lunts to dress up his 'sensitivity' and 'negative attitude to residing in psychiatric clinics' as paranoia, 'accompanied by reformist ideas'.

I myself knew Grigorenko very well, knew his whole family intimately. Rarely in my life have I met a man who was more cautious in his judgements or more diffident and self-critical. But the trouble was that my 'honest specialists', if ever I found them, wouldn't know Grigorenko personally. I would have to rely on the findings speaking for themselves.

There were also obvious contradictions between the opinions of different specialists in the case of Natalya Gorbanevskaya. For almost ten years she had been under psychiatric observation as an out-patient as a result of a neurotic condition in her childhood. Just before her arrest, a panel of civilian psychiatrists had examined her and recommended her discharge: 'On the basis of a study of her case history, a katamnestic analysis covering more than ten years and a medical inspection, we find no evidence of schizophrenia. At the present time she does not require committal to a mental hospital.' These findings were made on 19 November 1969, yet on 6 April 1970, Lunts and company discovered that she was suffering from schizophrenia – the same 'sluggish' variety that Lunts didn't recognise, as I knew very well. There was also an obvious, deliberate and easily demonstrable lie in the Serbsky Institute's findings. In support of their diagnosis, the Insti-

* Major-General Pyotr Grigoryevich Grigorenko, a much-decorated Red Army commander, who in 1961 began to denounce Stalinism and call for a return to Leninist principles. In 1964 he was arrested and committed to the Leningrad Special Mental Hospital where he was held for fifteen months. He became one of the unofficial leaders of the human-rights movement, and in 1969 was arrested in Tashkent, where he had gone to give evidence in the trial of some Crimean Tartars, and again committed to a mental hospital. During his investigation he wrote his prison diary, published as *The Grigorenko Papers* (Christopher Hurst, 1976). Having been declared sane by the Tashkent doctors, he was committed to the Serbsky Institute, which at once pronounced him insane. He spent the next five years in the Chernyakhovsk Special Mental Hospital until his release in 1974. In 1978, Grigorenko was allowed to visit his son in the USA and then deprived of his Soviet citizenship.

tute's specialists referred to the patient's hostile attitude to her mother and 'indifference to the fate of her children' – a symptom of emotional atrophy. Precisely during the period of her investigation and psychiatric examination, she had written her mother and children a series of letters full of concern and care, which the specialists preferred to overlook. Some of these letters we were able to obtain and attach to the Institute's findings.

As for the findings in the Riga examination of Yakhimovich, they sounded like a bad joke. The chairman of a sizeable collective farm in Latvia and a convinced communist, Yakhimovich had written an open letter to the Central Committee in 1968 expressing concern that the Moscow trials of that time were harming the cause of communism throughout the entire world. He was expelled from the Party, kicked out of his job, and barely managed to find work as a stoker; but he didn't cease protesting. From the same communist standpoint, he condemned the occupation of Czechoslovakia and was speedily arrested. The entire descriptive section of the findings in his case abounded with complimentary epithets. If it hadn't been for the heading, you would have thought you were reading the references of a man who was being recommended for a medal:

'He states that never under any circumstances will he abandon the idea of fighting for a communist system and socialism. . . . On the basis of the above, the commission finds that Yakhimovich displays paranoidal development of a psychopathic personality. The patient's condition must be equated with mental illness, and therefore, in connection with the incriminating acts that I. A. Yakhimovich has committed, he should be regarded as unfit to plead. He needs a course of compulsory treatment in a hospital of a special type.'

In short, it was a story worthy of Schweik. And it looked like an act of passive resistance on the part of the Riga doctors: 'We're producing the conclusions we've been told to, but we're describing things as they are.' Even the court was obliged to send Yakhimovich to the Serbsky Institute for a second opinion – the first was too much of a give-away. Lunts finished the case off and produced the necessary certificate.*

We only managed to collect six completely documented case histories, but each of them was unequivocal, even for a non-specialist. As for the other material: recollections, eyewitness accounts, data on the special hospitals – we ended up with a whole sackful.

The search then began for 'honest specialists', and here we ran into

* Ivan Yakhimovich was pronounced insane by the Serbsky Institute in April 1970 and released a year later after recanting.

insurmountable obstacles. Top-level psychiatrists, professors and the heads of clinics agreed with us in private that our materials left no doubt as to the criminal actions of the authorities. They even suggested certain ideas and moves to us, tipped us off about the possible mechanics of the KGB's hold over the psychiatrists, and agreed to write their own findings on the cases in question – anonymously, but they categorically refused to do it publicly.

'We don't have an Academician Sakharov among us,' they said. 'All he needs for his research is pencil and paper, but we need our clinics. If they take away our clinics, we can't be psychiatrists any more, and anyway, they would drum us all out of the profession if we said anything publicly. And that would be the least of it.'

We found young psychiatrists, of course, who were ready to make public statements, but they had no rank or title and it made no sense. What weight would their opinions have compared with the opinions of eminent professors and academicians? Particularly when their opinions were based on documents and hearsay, without a personal examination. They would simply be arrested along with me, and I didn't think that such a sacrifice was called for. (The young Kiev psychiatrist, Semyon Gluzman, nevertheless distributed his diagnosis of Grigorenko's case, and in 1972 was sentenced to seven years in the camps and three in exile.)

There was one last resort – Western psychiatrists. This seemed to offer little hope. What chance was there of breaking through all those ideological encrustations, prejudices and doctrines? I had little faith in its success, but none the less I sent the documentation to Western psychiatrists, more in the hope of attracting attention from the press. True, the English actor, David Markham, who had come to see me from Amnesty International and with whom I had discussed these questions, assured me that at least a few psychiatrists known to him in England would be prepared to study the documentation and speak out. All right, God grant that they would! A worldwide Congress of Psychiatrists was planned for the end of 1971. The prospect arose of getting our problem discussed at the Congress, and the support of each psychiatrist was worth its weight in gold. At the very least we might scare the Soviet authorities with the possibility of such a discussion. The very raising of the question at an international level would mean a great deal. At all events, it was worth a try. Perhaps there were more honest people in the world than I thought?

In my appeal to Western psychiatrists I strove for extreme restraint. I didn't want to demand political actions from anybody or draw them into politics, but simply asked for their professional help and their opinions as specialists. Deliberately confining myself to the six cases, I asked: do the said findings contain sufficient, scientifically substantiated grounds to justify, not only their conclusions about the said mental illnesses, but also the necessity of strictly isolating these people from society?

The actual idea of collecting this documentation had occurred to me almost accidentally, in early summer, in the office of the Moscow public prosecutor. The authorities had reacted nervously to my first interview with Holger Jensen about psychiatric repression. The prosecutor summoned me to his office, attempted to scare me and threatened me with jail. As if I didn't already know that I would be back inside before a year was up. Our television package was still wending its way slowly to America.

It was a stupid conversation, the usual wrangle. He maintained that everything I had said in the interview was slander, while I offered to show him the proof and call witnesses. He was unable to show in what way I had slandered anybody, but he wouldn't have anything to do with my suggested proofs and witnesses.

'You know that we can always prove your guilt.'

What *their* 'proofs' consisted of I already knew. Therefore I would have to collect my own proofs myself.

It was at this time that the question of my emigration first came up. 'Why does a man with your views live here? Go to America.'

I have known thousands of people ask, demand, beg to be allowed to leave the USSR. They were refused, driven out of their jobs and denounced as traitors. And here it was all as easy as going to the suburbs: however, even if it were easy, I wasn't planning to go anywhere.

At the same time they started pursuing Holger Jensen. He, too, was summoned to the public prosecutor's office and informed that he was a bad driver: he had braked too sharply and allegedly startled citizen Ivanov, who was now in hospital as a result. During the next two weeks someone regularly slashed his tyres, so that it was impossible for us to drive anywhere on our errands. Cars belonging to foreign correspondents usually stand in the courtyards of the special houses where they all have to live. Both the house and the yard are guarded by the policemen and no one else can get in. So who was slashing the tyres?

Early one morning, as he glanced out of his window, Holger saw their policeman walking from his sentry box towards the cars, looking cautiously from side to side. When he reached Holger's car he took out a pen-knife and carefully thrust it several times into the back tyres. Then he went to the front and did the same thing there.

A month later Holger was deprived of his driving licence for 'dangerous driving'. At the same time, as if on cue, they suddenly got worried in Washington.

'Why do we need a correspondent in Moscow if he's without a car?'

And they forbade him to send them any more articles from Moscow – as if he needed a car to do it. The Washington bosses were not pleased by our interview, either: it had worsened relations between the USSR and the USA. So what? This was nothing earth-shaking as far as I was concerned. I had never idealised that world. It stood to reason that over the decades the Soviet Union, like a chronic boil, had become encrusted with so many scabs and so much parasitic tissue around it, so many cowardly theories, doctrines and self-justifications, that the clear borderline between 'us' and 'them', 'ours' and 'theirs', had long since disappeared. In order to release the pus, therefore, it was necessary to cut through several layers of so-called 'healthy tissue'.

The KGB stayed on my heels all that year. They attached a complete operational group to me – a car with four men. Every six hours they changed the group and a new shift came on. They didn't try to hide themselves. On the contrary, part of their assignment, it seemed, was to make a show of their presence. If I walked anywhere, two of them would follow hard on my heels, while the other two drove slowly after us in their car. They had two-way radios and from time to time one of them would talk into his sleeve, making contact with the car. I started deliberately choosing routes where the car couldn't follow: against the traffic in one-way streets, or turning at cross-roads where there was no turn for cars, or walking through red lights. And then there would be panic, as on a sinking ship. I knew my fair share of these tricks, as well as the linked courtyards, house entrances with separate back doors, fire escapes.

'Go on, run! We'll break your leg!' they used to hiss in my ear. To any onlooker they must have looked ridiculous.

They had particular problems in the Metro. Three of them used to follow me underground, where I would walk very rapidly and almost run along the corridors and down the escalators. In the train I never gave them a chance to sit down – I would keep them on edge and dash out at the last moment when the doors were closing.

'Watch out, you'll run too fast one of these days. We'll push you under a train.'

They had a particularly lousy time of it if one of our men was waiting for me with a car outside the Metro station.

Every time I managed to give them the slip, they got a reprimand from their bosses. Two or three reprimands and they could be sacked. Maybe this was why they behaved with such insolence.

One day in the autumn I was on my way home and walking through a linked courtyard on Kropotkin Street when one of them caught up with me. His manner was swaggering and provocative, and he swore like a trooper, evidently trying to show that he didn't give a damn. He threatened to kill me one night in an entrance way, to shoot me when I came home late. He made great play of the fact that he wasn't like the others and wasn't going to stand by and let me get him into trouble. 'Do you think I'll suffer for it? Not a bit, they'll thank me. But why wait for nighttime? I can bump you off right here and now, and nobody'll even turn their heads. Just try giving us the slip again the way you did yesterday.'

He dragged a pistol out of his overcoat pocket. His swearing, however, wasn't up to scratch, was far too amateurish. He didn't have the labour-camp training, and just to keep the conversation going, I let him have a pile of obscenities about the size of a medium-sized New York skyscraper. At the same time I feverishly cast about in my mind for a means of cutting this milksop down to size. I wouldn't have been strong enough to get the pistol away from him – he was athletic and well-built. And a fight would have got me nowhere. Therefore, gradually slipping into the foulest and filthiest camp snarl, which would have pinned back the ears of even our old nag Yashka, who used to drag the food to the canteen, I lured him into the street and began moving slowly towards home. My calculation was simple – to run into a friend whom I could use as a witness. This donkey stayed alongside me, still hoping to impress me, while the rest of his team drove slowly in the car behind us. At that very moment my mother left the house to go shopping. They were both so surprised that they shook hands when I 'introduced' them.

'Look, Mama,' I said, 'remember this man. If anything happens to me, you'll know that he's to blame. He's been threatening to kill me. And this is their car behind us. Make a note of the number.'

I hadn't expected my mother to fly into such a rage. I was even afraid she was going to strike him. 'How dare you!' she yelled so that the whole street could hear. 'Have you been set to follow my son?'

'Yes,' said the agent listlessly.

'All right then, follow him. But your bosses will decide what to do with him. It's got nothing to do with you. That's all we need – for every scum that comes along to decide who's going to be killed and who isn't.'

'Well, he shouldn't pull any tricks,' said the agent, trying to justify himself. 'Let him walk normally like everybody else.'

A crowd of curious bystanders had begun to gather round. The agents sitting in the car were seething with rage – a reprimand was guaranteed now. My mother went on yelling: that she would go to the prosecutor's office, that she would complain to the Central Committee, that she wasn't going to leave the matter there. My presence was no longer needed and I went on my way, leaving them to argue it out. I never saw that operational group again; it was replaced by another one.

My relations with some of the other KGB groups were much better, and in the winter, when the frosts were fierce and I slipped out for some bread from the bakery on the corner, one of the agents would stand in the queue for me to pay at the cash desk and another by the counter, so as to finish quickly and get back to their warm car. On some evenings, when we had run out of cigarettes and the tobacco kiosks were closed, we used to bum them off one another and light up.

'Will you be back home soon?'

'Not long, just wait a while. I've a couple more places to go first. I'll be finished around two.'

As a matter of fact, we had got so used to them that we no longer noticed their presence. We went about our business, met foreign correspondents, collected information for the *Chronicle of Current Events* and sent *samizdat* abroad. What did we have to hide? I used to inform the correspondents of new arrests, searches and trials directly over the telephone from my home, and they used to phone me as if I was an information bureau. Sending stuff abroad, of course, was a more confidential affair and brooked no eavesdropping. We had special channels for that. The moment of maximum risk was relatively brief, and by the time the KGB had tumbled to what was going on, given the orders and had them carried out, the traces had been obliterated.

Foreigners from various Western organisations I received directly in my own home. Our apartment house was a big one, and looking at it from outside, it wasn't easy to tell where people were going. The KGB, moreover, had never expected such brazen insolence – passing *samizdat* material abroad under their very noses. As in the old days, they were still looking for special meeting places, conspiratorial pass-words and secret drops, while we did everything in the open.

Holger was recalled towards the end of 1970 and sent off to Vietnam. Bill Cole had been kicked out by the Soviet authorities even earlier, 'for activities incompatible with the status of a correspondent'. I was sorry to part with them, it was like parting with labour-camp friends – I knew I'd never see them again. Bill was glum, but put a cheerful face on it, maintaining that everything was okay. 'I didn't want to stay here anyway,' he said. 'A decent man is bound to get himself thrown out.'

Holger felt it worse. He loved Russian culture, had learned Russian and had been hoping to stay with us for about five years. He was a fanatical hunter and fisherman. Soon after he had arrived, the Novosti Press Agency had sent round some 'colleagues' and they had arranged some magnificent hunting for him in a reserve beyond the limits of the zone in which foreigners were allowed to move. They had dropped cautious hints that they could do even better than that if he behaved himself. But it all came to an end as soon as he got friendly with us. And now he was leaving for ever. As usual with Associated Press, he had to find his own replacement.

'All right, I'll find a replacement for them. I'll find you a fellow they can't scare.'

He brought along a young fellow, about three years younger than me, called Roger Leddington. It was true, Roger wasn't easily frigh-tened: they smashed his car to pieces, broke the windows, tore off the doors, left threatening notes. One day he even got into a fist-fight with the security agents when they stopped him in the hall downstairs and wouldn't let him come up to see me. The two of us used to throw them off our tracks at night thanks to the superiority of American technology; Soviet cars are unable to turn at high speed.

It was now no longer possible to meet correspondents during the day – the KGB was organising open provocations and fights. One day I arranged to meet another AP correspondent, Jim Peipert, on Kalinin Prospect in the very centre of Moscow. We had agreed to meet at half-past midnight, but I arrived five minutes early in order to have a good look round. I immediately caught sight of a group of men strolling casually up and down. 'So what,' I thought, 'let them follow us, there's nothing new in that.' Jim pulled up on the other side of the street, got out of his car and walked across to meet me. But the moment he got near me the 'bystanders' suddenly rushed us and, pretending unconvincingly to be hooligans, started lamming into us. 'What are you hanging around here for, skunk!'

I recognised one of them – he had once followed me. What worried me most was that a previously instructed police car might suddenly come along, pick us up and pin a charge of 'hooliganism' on us. There would be fat chance afterwards of proving that it was we who were attacked, and not the reverse. For that reason, so as to have at least some sort of formal evidence, I started yelling at the top of my voice and calling for help. Jim must have realised what I was up to and started yelling as well. Some people came up, and some taxi-drivers got out of their cars at a nearby rank. None of them lifted a finger, however, but simply stood there gaping. Still, that in itself was a relief – they were at least witnesses and would confirm that we had called for help.

Somehow or other we managed to tear ourselves away and run across to our car, but they caught up with us again. Jim couldn't get the key into the door lock. The situation began to turn nasty.

'Ivan Nikolayevich, go round behind!'

Some hooligans, calling each other by their name and patronymic! But there was no time to dwell on that. Two of them were twisting my arms back. A third who had jumped on me from behind was choking me and forcing my head lower, while yet another was kicking and punching me. On the other side of the car, Jim was grunting as he wrestled off the KGB men, but he still couldn't get his key into the lock. A shortish man in an astrakhan cap was running at me from the front and I realised that he was planning to take a running kick at my bent head. At the very last moment, I lunged at him, anticipating his kick, and planted my boot in his onrushing face. He keeled over. There was a moment of panic and then the other agents rushed over to him – he was evidently their boss. This pause was all we needed: Jim got the door open at last, we piled in and shot off at top speed. Out of the car window we caught sight of a policeman standing under a street lamp on the corner, no more than twenty paces away, calmly smoking a cigarette.

The authorities tried to cut off all our contacts with the outside world. For a certain time I was practically the only one left with a link, and therefore I was inundated with problems: searches, arrests, trials, loony bins, labour camps, Tartars, Jews, Meskhetians, Ukrainians, Lithuanians. Roger used to come at dead of night, or sometimes at dawn, to pick up all the information I had accumulated during the day, rush off to his office, and write up his stories. Only occasionally did someone else manage to break through, but usually it was the indispensable Roger. Happy and cheerful. He no longer had any time to write things himself – all he could do was pass on his *samizdat* haul to the others. He persuaded them that at least they needn't be afraid to write up the stories.

Pretty soon I almost never left the house. Twenty-four hours a day were taken up with appointments: who would come when, bring what, and take away what. We understood each other with half a glance: there was hardly any need to scribble messages. No one issued orders, made plans or assigned roles. Everyone knew what he could do best, where he was most useful and what was expected of him. Even complete outsiders, having once come into contact with this mass of energy, got such a charge from it that they continued for years afterwards to live at our tempo. From England David Markham, from Germany Cornelia Gerstenmaier, from Holland Henk Volsak, from France Dina Vierny. These people spent varying amounts of time with us – some a few hours, some several days.

They were very different kinds of people, but none of them could remain indifferent afterwards. And I myself, when later in jail, was able to divine from even the slightest hints from outside what was going on, what was needed, what was expected of me. It seems that we all subsequently experienced this same sense of nostalgia.

It was a nightmarish year. Towards its end the wave of human indignation evoked by the Leningrad hijackers' trial at last engulfed the Kremlin completely.* Finding themselves faced by the very real threat of total isolation, the authorities were obliged to retreat and allow emigration. For the first time ever, they recognised one of our human rights – the right to leave our country for good. The fifty-three-year-old boil had been lanced at last, because for the first time the world had found the strength within itself to demand from the Kremlin mongrels what is universally recognised the whole world over as a human right, and to demand it without making any allowances or reservations. So much for your secret diplomacy!

I will never forget the tragedy of that exodus, when elderly respectable people, loaded with ranks and regalia, suddenly lost their respectability, as if they were suddenly shedding the shell of half a century. What had happened to all their Sovietness, all the loud words pronounced at those meetings? Now they ran to farewell celebrations for

* In June 1970, twelve Soviet Jews made plans to hijack a Soviet plane and fly it to Sweden. They were caught before the attempt could be made, however, and in December 1970 given punitive sentences.

the departing, sang the long-forgotten songs of that nation whose relationship to themselves they had spent a lifetime carefully denying. They abandoned their snug jobs, their accumulated possessions and their hard-won influential connections. Whence this sudden boldness? They besieged the offices of highly placed Party officials, organised collective hunger strikes and made *demands* – perhaps for the first time in their lives. And the sullen Soviet officials satisfied their demands – also, probably, for the first time in their lives – and mentally reviewed the facts of their own parentage: who knew?

They inundated us with petitions, documents, appeals. They were being allowed to leave so fast that they hadn't had time to set up their own channels and contacts, and we willingly offered them ours. Their problem had long been our problem – one of our problems. But we had plenty of other problems, too, and when some of my departing friends informed me that in their talks with officials the latter had asked them to suggest to me that I too should leave, I could only shrug my shoulders. I still had my own problem to resolve – the one for which I was willing to return to jail.

My days were already numbered. Only one thing was unclear: would they take me before or after the Twenty-fourth Party Congress in March 1971? The most likely time was before. It was already March, full of resonant sounds, the snow dripping off the roofs, broken icicles crunching underfoot, but there was no time to roam the Arbat backstreets. In besieged, pre-Congress Moscow, neither night nor day existed any longer. Each document, each message sent during these days might be the last, yet how much more was there still to do! The last battle was being fought, when there could be no mercy shown to anything or anyone, as if everything was burned inside me. Afterwards I would be dumb.

And when at last they took me, I was filled with an enormous sense of relief, as if a great weight had been lifted from my shoulders. Long and blissful was my sleep in Lefortovo – it must have lasted at least a week. Lord, how wonderful it is when nothing depends on you any longer!

I was also pleased that I had had time to buy my family a dog – a tiny, fluffy, Caucasian sheepdog puppy. In time they would see him grow up to be shaggy and enormous.

'Wait a minute, wait a minute, I'll do the whole estimate for you. Bricks, forty roubles a thousand; the best-quality cement, thirty roubles a hundredweight. How many cubic yards of brickwork have you got? Then you have to allow for the footings. Well, we can get round that by giving the excavator driver thirty roubles – he'll do a lovely job for you. No, that won't work, it's too dear. The best thing is to buy the materials on the black market, it works out much cheaper that way. Especially if you get it from the army's construction department. They don't have any stock control, so they can trade right, left and centre.'

At this point I protested. I couldn't afford to use the black market – the KGB would be on to me like a shot. In my position I had to make sure that everything was legal and keep my nose clean.

My cell-mate, Ivan Ivanich Trofimov, former boss of the construction department and now an informer, was nostalgic for his profession. He missed all that business activity: conferences, discussing estimates, plans. He hadn't been himself since morning: first he had paced up and down the cell with his artificial leg squeaking, then he explained all about pre-stressed concrete beams. Yesterday he had spotted me drawing my castle – staircases, turrets, passages – and had asked me if he could have a look at it, and spent half the night doing calculations on a scrap of paper. He was drawing up an estimate. Now he knew his way round the castle every bit as well as I, was working out the weight the foundations would have to bear, and in the mornings we argued over what brand of cement I should buy.

'Ah, I could have the whole thing up in six months,' he said mournfully, 'maybe even quicker.'

I spent most of my time reading. Lefortovo had a wonderful library

– it looked as if all the books confiscated from the enemies of the people over half a century had ended up here. Up and down the country they had 'purged' libraries and burnt 'pernicious' books, while in here, everything was preserved as in an oasis. It had never occurred to anyone to purge the libraries of the KGB prisons – who could be holier than the Pope? Pre-revolutionary editions of Pushkin and Gogol, A. K. Tolstoy and Lermontov, Hamsun and Maeterlinck, Marcel Proust and Zamyatin. What didn't they have in here?

The books were in excellent condition, but almost all their pages were covered with rubber stamps. 'Internal prison of the GUGB NKVD' was a pre-war stamp. 'Investigation isolator of the KGB under the CM of the USSR' was a modern stamp. And in capital letters running from top to bottom of the entire page: 'Any damage done to books or marking of the text by pencil, matches, fingernails, etc., will result in the withdrawal of library privileges.'

My line during the investigation of my case had been clearcut – I refused to take any part in it. I signed no statements or certificates and spent my time writing complaints in order to give the investigators something to do. I had three of them. They summoned me rarely. Our relations were bad from the start: instead of them asking questions we simply abused one another to kill time. I particularly disliked the second investigator, Captain Korkach. He had an extraordinarily nasty mug and habits of rare repulsiveness, facts which I communicated to him in all candour each time we met. The investigators saw no need to conceal their true feelings either and were extremely cynical. It's only with novices that they try different approaches and make an attempt to persuade, flatter, intimidate or convert you for the glory of the Soviet regime. With me they could afford not to waste their time.

At the very outset I wrote a declaration in which I refused to accept the KGB as competent to conduct the investigation into my case. About three months before my arrest *Pravda* had published a long article, 'The Poverty of Anticommunism', asserting that I was engaged in anti-Soviet activities. The same thing had been declared by Tsvigun, Andropov's deputy in the KGB, in the journal *Political Self-education* in February 1971. So it emerged that the question of my guilt had been predetermined by the Party organs and the leadership of the KGB, not only before my trial, but even before my arrest. From a strictly legal point of view, not one employee of the KGB and not a single member of the Party had the right to investigate my case, as I pointed out in my endless complaints.

The situation was even worse when it came to the prosecutor supervising the investigation. This was the same prosecutor who had earlier summoned me for a talk. After leaving his office I had immediately written down the substance of our conversation and handed it to Holger, and he in turn had sent it to the *Frankfurter Rundschau*, where it was published. This publication was now part of the incriminating evidence against me, as were all my other interviews. So it would seem that strictly speaking they should have summoned the prosecutor for questioning as a witness in my case, and you can't be both prosecutor and witness in the same case.

In short, it was a juridical merry-go-round. All I needed it for was as a pretext for writing complaints. 'Never mind! I'll say my all at the trial,' I told the investigators. But that didn't suit them one bit. I also demanded they investigate the incident of the secret police sleuth threatening me with a gun. I cited my mother as a witness and gave the number of the car. All this scribbling took up two or three hours of every day. The rest of the time I read, drew my castle or listened to Ivan Ivanich holding forth on his construction problems.

At night I dreamed I was being chased. Sometimes Roger and I would speed away from the secret police and through the sleepy Moscow streets in his gleaming American car. Sometimes I was alone and running through an endless series of courtyards, attics or Metro tunnels, but whatever I tried, the KGB agents were always on my heels and I only just managed to keep ahead of them. I usually managed to dodge into a large brilliantly lit room, where I tried to explain something very important in English to the people gathered there. Every now and then they would politely and sympathetically nod and exclaim 'Aha!' as if they had just grasped the meaning of what I was saying.

But from their faces I could see that they hadn't understood a thing. I began again from the beginning and again they all said 'Aha!' but it was as though there were a glass wall between us.

By August the investigation had ground to a halt. Apart from clippings of my interviews in the Western press and copies of Bill Cole's films, the authorities had nothing to go on. They even started calling their own KGB agents in as witnesses but this didn't give them much help. Finally, Ivan Ivanich gave me a piece of news that I had long been expecting: they were going to dispatch me to the Serbsky Institute and pronounce me unfit to plead. He had been told this by my investigator, who little suspected that I would get to hear of it.

My arrest had interrupted me in the middle of my work and

deprived me of the opportunity to collect new evidence which would deliver the final blow to the psychiatric method. Now, by an irony of fate, I was faced with the prospect of becoming evidence myself – perhaps the most vivid and dramatic exhibit of all. Not long before my arrest, our psychiatric documentation had been presented at a press conference in Paris. Bill Cole's television interview was shown in six different countries. Our appeal to Western psychiatrists was published in the London *Times*, and the World Psychiatric Congress had been set for the autumn. So just let them try to proclaim me insane now, under the gaze of the entire world. We would see whether they were really so omnipotent.

Once more I sat in Lunts' office beneath the portrait of the humanist Pinel, and, just as five years before, we chatted about Bergson, Nietzsche and Freud. Only now, when our conversation was finished, Lunts no longer asked what was going to become of me.

My first month in the Serbsky Institute passed peacefully; evidently they still hadn't had time to issue Lunts his instructions. Once or twice I received a visit from the young doctor assigned to me, but our conversations were general. We simply gossiped and laughed. Lunts put in no appearances. In the middle of September the examination period expired. They hastily summoned a commission, which resolved to extend the examination period 'in view of the lack of clarity of the clinical picture'.

I could feel the change almost physically. Several of the doctors, when doing their rounds, now simply averted their eyes and walked past. Others started looking at me with that indescribable 'psychiatric' expression on their faces – that sort of semi-contemptuous sense of superiority with which humans regard ants. My doctor ceased joking and laughing.

'Why are you back in here with us again? I thought we'd never meet again,' croaked Lunts genially with his wide mouth, but behind the geniality lurked a question about the reasons for my permanent conflict with society. 'At your age, you know, it is time to settle down, start a family. Aren't you married yet? How is that?'

'Well, I didn't have time.'

'Didn't have time? Were you so busy?' Instinctively I could feel him write in his notebook: 'Indifferent to personal life. Obsession with overvalued ideas such that he "didn't have time" to start a family.' I had read so many of Lunts' findings about my friends that I felt I could write for him his findings about me.

No, Lunts never did a botched job, never took the easy way out.

He would never write the sort of thing the Leningrad specialist had written about the dissident Vladimir Borisov: 'His mental condition and conduct are characterised by . . . a disturbed sense of orientation and an incorrect interpretation of his surroundings. Thus he takes the hospital for a concentration camp and the doctors for sadists.'

Or, as Professor Nadzharov had written about Edward Kuznetsov in support of the diagnosis of 'schizophrenia': 'He asserts that there is no such thing as a communist moral code, and that the credit for its creation should go to the Bible.'

Lunts had too much self-respect and too much esteem for his reputation as a master case-maker. He would spin a web round his victim slowly, like a spider. Out of every quirk of character and twist of fate he would weave such a close-textured diagnosis that not a single commission would be able to find fault with it afterwards.

'Doctor, doctor, what a big mouth you have!'

'All the better to guzzle you with, Little Red Riding Hood.'

The piquancy of the situation lay in the fact that the subject of our conversation was to be psychiatric abuses: I was accused of slandering Soviet psychiatry. Lunts banked on finding any number of symptoms. In the first place, over-estimation of my own personality – a non-specialist was taking it upon himself to refute the specialists; secondly, chronic suspicion and hostility towards psychiatrists – very typical of a paranoiac; and then there was my interview, with its description of a special hospital – the distorted impressions, of course, of a mentally deranged individual. In short, he had a limitless field of action.

He deliberately underlined my ignorance, my incompetence in the field of psychiatry, hoping thereby to catch me on the raw and provoke an emotional reaction. But I was ready for that. 'That's as may be, but I appealed to other specialists, to Western psychiatrists. I sent them your findings and other documents.'

Strangely enough, this was news to him – he hadn't known which findings and documents I had sent. We argued at length over individual cases, but I was careful not to get heated and didn't make any assertions. Only in the case of Gorbanevskaya did I pin him to the wall. Priority in psychiatry goes to those doctors who have observed the patient first, when the illness is acute, and who have done so over a longer period. The doctors who had had Gorbanevskaya under observation for ten years had failed to detect any schizophrenia in her. Lunts, however, had found it. And the main thing was that Lunts had never recognised sluggish schizophrenia before.

'So, you still think you're a better judge than the specialists, do you?' he said defensively.

'No, no, not at all. I am turning to you, the specialist, for an explanation.'

'By the way, why in fact did you appeal to Western psychiatrists and not to Soviet ones?'

'I did appeal to them. Some said that there was no Academician Sakharov among them. Many, however, abused you in private and disputed your findings.'

'What did they say?' said Lunts eagerly.

'That you are a poor clinician, that you've never observed the dynamics of illness, and that your diagnoses are pure guesswork.'

'Oh, did they!' said Lunts, offended. 'And who told you that?'

I only laughed in reply. He was wounded. No matter how much I insulted him, nothing could hurt as much as the opinion of colleagues with whom he had sat for so many years in the same symposia and conferences. Evidently this was not the first time he had had to defend himself against accusations, because he at once pulled out some psychiatric 'samizdat' of his own and with an aggrieved air began demonstrating to me how people had been slandering psychiatry over a very long period. As early as the nineteenth century, one of the fathers of Russian psychiatry had publicly denounced insinuations against psychiatrists, and said the fact was that psychiatrists had never ever abused their profession.

'But what about Chaadayev?' I said in astonishment.

'There, you see,' he jumped in, 'off you go again, taking it upon yourself to judge things you know nothing about. Chaadayev was never examined by a psychiatrist. He was just looked at by the court doctor. There weren't any psychiatrists at that time.'

And it was true, Chaadayev was lucky. There weren't any psychiatrists, special hospitals, sulphazine, haloperidol or 'roll-ups' in those days. Nor did Tsar Nicholas I have his own Lunts at court. But you and I now know that Chaadayev was suffering from real schizophrenia – of the sluggish variety, of course.

I knew that this time they wouldn't let me leave the special hospital alive – the whole gang of them were furious with me. Or at the very best I would leave as an idiot, a warning to all. But then, I wouldn't wait for that to happen.

They kept me apart, in a special isolation cell downstairs. They didn't want me to mix with all the other patients being examined, in case I was talked about afterwards. Also, they were afraid lest I found a way of communicating with the outside world – I had been here too often, I knew all the sisters, nurses and guards, and was on friendly terms with them.

To keep me company, they put another fellow destined for oblivion in my ward with me, Andrei Kozlov, a chap of about twenty-two who was a worker from one of the big Leningrad factories. One day he had had an argument with his friends in the factory hostel about whether he could hit a bull's eye with a small-bore rifle at a distance of 100 yards. They had a rifle in the hostel, and he really did hit a lamp in the factory compound at a distance of about 100 yards from their window – the hostel was next door to the factory, with a fence running between them.

'That's nothing,' boasted Andrei. 'I can hit a target even further away. Take that path to the director's office over there. I could hit the director when he goes to work in the morning.' Their director was a really big wheel, a deputy of the Supreme Soviet and even a member of the Central Committee, if I'm not mistaken.

Several days later they were all arrested. And try as Andrei might to prove that he wasn't intending to assassinate the director but had merely been joking and boasting about his accuracy, it was all to no avail. In the lamp they found traces of the bullet, the rifle was confiscated after a search, the evidence was there for all to see. Conspiracy to commit a terrorist act. And the investigators dug out the fact that some time previously Andrei had written to Moscow to complain about this director for not paying him some overtime he was due. So the motive was personal hostility.

'Damn and blast it!' said Andrei with pent-up frustration. 'If I'd known this would happen, I'd have killed the so-and-so long ago! I might just as well have done it if I've got to go to jail for it.'

The investigator looked at him heavily and strangely for a moment, as if having just noticed something special about him, and merely said: 'You will never see him again.'

Andrei didn't understand what he meant. Were they going to shoot him or something?

I didn't try to explain – I felt too sick at heart myself. Instead I spun him all sorts of yarns about the camps and escapes, and entertained him as best I could. By some miracle or other we got hold of a map of the world. It was a small map, true, but big enough to travel on.

To begin with, of course, we went to Italy, to Venice, to ride in the gondolas. Then to Naples via Rome. The weather was wonderful the whole time, we took good care of that. We drank cheap wine in the trattorias along the road and nibbled on goat cheese and onions. We talked to bronzed peasants about the grape harvest. In Rome I showed him all sorts of monuments: the Colosseum, the Baths, St Peter's, but he soon tired of that.

We argued over whether to go to Spain or not. After all, Franco was there. Andrei didn't want to go: the devil knew, maybe he'd fling us into jail. We were from Russia, after all, and we didn't know the language.

So we went to Greece and from there to Israel. We had to have a look after all the fuss there'd been. And then on farther, to India, Singapore (what a beautiful name), Hong Kong and Japan, where all the streets were festooned with hieroglyphs like garlands of flowers. We ended up in California.

Sometimes he was overcome with anxiety: what did the investigator have in mind? 'Damn and blast that director! What did I need him for? If I'd known what was going to happen, I could have bumped him off long ago!' And he looked guardedly in my direction – maybe I didn't believe him either?

'Oh yes, that's what you tell us now,' I said with make-believe suspicion, 'but who's going to believe you?' He laughed with relief. I had managed to sound just like his investigator.

At night I still kept dreaming about the brilliantly lit room, with me trying to explain in English about our *method*, the one we'd had in the Leningrad Special Hospital. The people nodded their heads sympathetically and exclaimed: 'Aha!' as if they had just grasped it at last, but I knew they understood nothing at all.

I never told Andrei about our *method* – I just couldn't get my tongue round it.


To this very day I don't really know what happened at the beginning of October 1971. Of course, my friends were writing protests – but they were always writing them and it never helped. I heard vague rumours about some sort of expensive porcelain dish broken in Paris by Mrs Brezhnev, and Mme Pompidou's exploitation of the moment to request my release, but I don't believe it. There was also talk of widespread indignation in the West, but I don't put much faith in that either. The most they could have done was say their eternal: 'Aha!'

One day my doctor came galloping in and literally dragged me upstairs to the big room where the commissions usually sat. Before opening the door I heard snatches of some sort of argument or quarrel: 'Don't you understand what this will mean? Have you thought of that? Do you realise what you're doing?'

There were just two of them sitting at the table: a hunched-up, ashen-faced Lunts, with quivering jowls, and an equally quivering Morozov, grey-faced with fear.

Hardly bothering to look in my direction, as if continuing a conversation that had been in progress for some time, Morozov said to me venomously: 'What's all this about being too busy to get married?'

I wasn't even sure that it was me he was talking to.

'Well, I studied, was about to get into the university, then made some money by doing English translations, worked as a secretary to the writer Maximov, and I did think about marrying after that – love, as you know, sometimes takes a while . . . doesn't always work out as quickly as you'd like it to. . . . Well, somehow I just didn't get round to it.'

I was lying through my teeth, amazed by my own effrontery. I instinctively guessed what it was Morozov wanted to hear.

'There, you see!' he said acidly, turning to Lunts. Then back to me: 'And what were you thinking? Didn't you realise you'd be arrested?'

'Didn't realise? I said in my very first interview, in May 1970, that I'd be arrested within the year.'

My case file lay on the table, crumpled and disarranged. But they didn't bother to consult it. 'There, you see!' said Morozov to Lunts again.

But it didn't sound like a boss bawling out one of his subordinates. They looked, rather, like two conspirators caught in the act, and wrangled without being in the least embarrassed by my presence.

Suddenly, as if remembering himself, Morozov gestured in my direction, for all the world as if brushing a crumb off the table, and my doctor hauled me back downstairs again, to my isolation cell.

'What have you been up to now? You've really put Dr Lunts on the spot!' he said on the way down, but I had no idea what I was supposed to have done. 'But mind you – this wasn't a commission,' he said when we got to the bottom of the stairs, 'in case you send out more rubbish about us.'

Again I failed to understand. For some reason he kept putting everything down to my intrigues.

At the beginning of November a real commission was indeed convened. Specialists from the Serbsky Institute were merely in attendance, the members proper were Professors Melekhov, Lukomsky and Zhari-kov, who had never been involved with forensic psychiatry before. I doubt whether they had the faintest idea of what was going on, be-cause the Serbsky doctors were falling over themselves to show that I was sane and that they themselves had never doubted it.

This business of making me sane again had begun immediately after my interview with Morozov. Doctors who earlier averted their eyes were now all smiles; others regarded me with unconcealed hatred but at least hated me as a human being. I was transferred upstairs to join the other patients awaiting examination – the blockade was over. Just before the commission met, my doctor came to see me and frankly asked me to instruct him on how to explain some of the more com-plicated episodes in my tangled biography, so that I could be made to look completely sane. He was a young man, and regarded the task of reporting on my case to the commission as a sort of oral examination. After all, he would be speaking before some of the most prominent psychiatrists in the Soviet Union.

This must have been the funniest commission meeting I have ever attended. Everyone was shooting into the same goal. It was hard to tell who was kidding whom. You might have thought that the Serbsky Institute doctors were defending me against the commission. What had become of all their doctrines, symptoms, criteria? When the com-mission members timidly asked why it was that I felt obliged to risk my freedom for people I didn't know (that time-honoured question about the reasons for your conflict with society), the Serbsky specialists all chorused as one: 'But they are his friends! He knows every one of them!' As if this had ever been a sufficient explanation for them!

Lunts sat well off to one side, looking old and depressed, and took no part in the debate. In fact, there wasn't any debate to speak of, and there would have been nothing to argue about had it not been for Professor Zharikov, sole representative there of the Snezhnevsky school. Neither one side nor the other now questioned my fitness to plead, but there was still the nature of the illness to determine, the noso-logical roots. Zharikov had to argue that in both 1963 and 1965 I had shown symptoms of schizophrenia – sluggish, of course – but the Serbsky Institute men stood four-square for paranoidal psychopathy. It was a pitched battle between two mafias for key posts, the manage-ment of clinics, dissertations, fat salaries, titles, private motor cars and personal pensions. The ultimate judges in this conflict were the Party authorities, who controlled the distribution of life's limited blessings; whoever was best at dressing the Party's will up in scholarly clothing would come out on top. So it made no difference what the orders were – to pronounce me fit or not, as the case might be.

They all appeared to tremble before Melekhov, who had come here evidently to put them to rout.* But there turned out to be nobody to rout and he was somewhat discouraged. He couldn't understand why I didn't dispute my 1963 diagnosis, why I was so willing to express 'criticism' of my former 'sickness', and above all why the Serbsky specialists were behaving so strangely. I feared that he formed a low opinion of me and generally regretted having got involved in this affair. But towards the end it seemed that he had begun to guess what was going on, because when I left, he stood up and ostentatiously shook my hand, which meant that the other specialists were obliged to do the same. Damn it! If only I could have met this Melekhov before my arrest – maybe there was a Sakharov among the psychiatrists after all.

As soon as the professors left, Lunts summoned me to his office.

'It isn't usually done to inform patients under examination of commission results. But to forestall false rumours, I will make an exception in your case.' They still seemed to think that I had a secret link with outside and still feared 'false rumours'! 'But by the way, what do you think yourself?'

'I think that *we* lost,' I replied.

But he didn't seem to catch the ambiguity of my words, because he gazed absentmindedly out of the window and croaked into space: 'He thinks he lost. . . . Mm – yes. Well, you were pronounced to be of completely sound mind and responsible for your actions.'

'And how did they resolve the question of the 1963 episode? The nosological roots?'

'They found that it was an attack of a schizophrenic character without further development.'

'But that cannot be, Daniil Romanovich! You yourself know there are only two possibilities: if it's schizophrenia, there has to be a development; otherwise it's not schizophrenia. It can't happen any other way.'

'Yes,' agreed Lunts, making a gesture of helplessness, 'it can't happen. It was a compromise.'

I never saw him again.

The KGB nad counted heavily on my unfitness to plead. In deciding my fate and making their moves for political reasons of their own choosing,

* Professor T. D. Melekhov is head of the Diagnostics Department of the Psychiatric Institute of the Ministry of Health in the USSR, and a well-known and respected psychiatrist. He has never been associated with the use of psychiatry for punitive purposes.

the Party chiefs hadn't bothered about the question of how the investigators were going to extricate themselves from a mess like this. The poor secret policemen – they had little thought they would ever see me again, let alone have to prepare a case against me. But it was too late to recover the situation – the investigation period was due to expire by the end of November and the KGB had about three weeks in which to put my case together.

In an investigation, as in chess, one can sometimes wriggle out of a tight corner when one's opponent gets himself into 'time troubles'.* My investigators had done just this with their attempt to dump me in a loony bin. Still, they didn't bother too much about it, they simply amalgamated all the papers that had accumulated over this period. 'Never mind, it'll do. It's come out even better than we expected,' smirked Captain Korkach sardonically. These boys were hard to disconcert. But I had a plan that would take even them by surprise.

Over the previous years the authorities had been refusing 'access permits' to just about all honest lawyers who took our cases. Once a defence counsel had requested an acquittal for his defendant in a political trial, he was automatically crossed off the list of those with 'access'. Not a single law mentioned these 'access permits'; as always in such cases, the authorities invented a secret regulation that no one had ever actually seen. It was even impossible to protest, since to do that you needed some sort of document where the 'access permit' was at least mentioned.

The situation was complicated by the fact that when they came up against these insuperable difficulties, prisoners and their families tended to yield and hire another lawyer from the list offered to them – it struck them as too risky to remain without one. Anyway, what difference did it make? They'd give you seven years regardless of whether your lawyer was an honest one or a 'permitted' one.

The lawyers themselves seemed unable to overcome this calamity.

There remained only one chance to pierce this wall: a prisoner should refuse pointblank to accept one of the 'permitted' lawyers and insist on his own 'unpermitted' representative. What could the authorities do then? According to the law, the court had no right to refuse such a demand. At all events, it would set a precedent and provide a basis on which to protest. 'The first one of us to be arrested should try it out,' we had joked.

* A chess term. It is used in games when a time-limit is in force and a player dallies over his earlier moves, leaving himself with insufficient time in which to plan his later moves properly.

I had had every reason to suppose that I would be the first. Dina Kaminskaya, my defence lawyer in the demonstration case in 1967, had long since been deprived of her 'access permit'. There could be no better candidate for the job. She wasn't difficult to track down and I had talked to her about it. I needed to be sure that she wouldn't refuse, that she wouldn't submit to pressure, that, come what may, even if she were at death's door, she would announce publicly that she was prepared to defend me. Just in case, however, I had the names of two other lawyers who had been deprived of their 'permits' – Kallistratova and Shveisky.

Now I was able to put our plan into practice.

My investigator didn't have the slightest premonition of trouble when I entered a plea to have the advocate Kaminskaya nominated as my defence counsel. But the following day he came running back looking extremely perturbed. He carried an answer from the presidium of the Moscow City College of Advocates, signed by the chairman, Apraxin: 'The Advocate Kaminskaya cannot be assigned to the defence since she does not possess a permit giving her access to secret records.'

This was what I needed, a document with a reference to the 'permit'. After that it was plain sailing. 'What permit? What secret records?' I said indignantly. 'Never heard of them. They're not stipulated by law.' And I launched a battery of complaints in all directions: the Central Committee, the Ministry of Justice, the Council of Ministers, and so on. The term for the investigation was expiring, it was time for me to have the whole case read to me and sign that this had been done, but I wouldn't hear of it: according to the law I had the right to have the case read to me in the presence of a lawyer.

The investigator had no way out: if a case isn't closed by the end of the investigation term, the prisoner has the right to be released from custody. But he chose another way out. He resorted to forgery and wrote in the investigation record that I had simply refused to have the case read to me. Not a word about defence counsel.

At this point I announced a hunger strike. In fact I was quite satisfied with the present situation: a forged accusation, no charges read and no defence lawyer provided. All right, you can carry me starving into the courtroom, if you like, on a stretcher. It will be as good as a play! I'll prepare a hundred identical applications for the advocate Kaminskaya to be summoned and every five minutes will hand one to the judge without a word.

Now the trouble began. The authorities always turn savage when you get them into a corner. But that is precisely the moment to break their backs.

I was put in an isolation cell and they confiscated my books, paper, pencils and smokes. No newspapers, no exercise, not even a bath. Not even an aspirin for a headache. The assistant prison governor, Stepanov, came to see me and announced in his comical provincial accent that no medical treatment was available to hunger strikers.

'You are in the position of a suicide,' he said. 'Suicides are not allowed to have medical treatment. Stop your hunger strike.'

That same day they started force-feeding me – through the nostrils! About a dozen guards led me from my cell to the medical unit. There they straitjacketed me, tied me down to a bed, and sat on my legs so that I wouldn't jerk. The others held my shoulders and my head. My nose is bent a bit to one side – I used to be a boxer as a boy and damaged it. The feeding pipe was thick – thicker than my nostril – and wouldn't go in for love or money. Blood came gushing out of my nose and tears down my cheeks. I must say a nose is incredibly sensitive – I can think of only one other organ that equals it. But they kept pushing until the cartilages cracked and something burst – enough to make you howl like a wolf. But fat chance there was of howling when the pipe was in your throat and you could breathe neither in or out. I wheezed like a drowning man – my lungs were ready to burst. The doctor watching me also seemed ready to burst into tears, but she kept on shoving the pipe farther and farther down. Then she poured some sort of slops through a funnel into the pipe – you'd choke if it came back up. They held me down for another half-hour so that the liquid was absorbed by the stomach and couldn't be vomited back, and then began to pull the pipe out bit by bit. As they say in the Soviet Union – like a razor across your balls . . .

There had just been time for everything to heal during the night and the blood to stop flowing when the brutes came back and did it all over again. Every day they found it harder and harder. Everything swelled up until it was agony to touch. And always the terrible smell of raw meat. And so on every day.

Round about the tenth day, the guards could stand it no longer. As it happened it was a Sunday and no bosses were around. They surrounded the doctor: 'Hey listen, let him drink it straight from the bowl, let him sip it. It'll be quicker for you too, you silly old fool.'

She almost threw a fit. 'If I do that he'll never end his blasted hunger strike. Do you think I want to go to jail because of you lot? From tomorrow I'll feed him twice a day.'

311

The only consolation I had was that I knew my mother was due to bring a parcel any day now. Without my signature they couldn't accept the parcel, and mother would be bound to guess what was going on. And then the boys would think of something to do.

For twelve days they tore at my nostrils, and I too was growing quite savage. I could think of nothing in the world except my naso-pharynx. I would pace up and down my cell all day, gurgling through my nose. I had lived my whole life and never suspected that there was a link between my nose and the Moscow College of Advocates.

On the evening of the twelfth day the authorities surrendered. I received a visit from Deputy General Prosecutor Ilyukhin. 'I just happened to drop in – by chance you know – and suddenly I heard you're on hunger strike! What "permits", who told you such rubbish? There are no such things, I guarantee you.'

'And what about Kaminskaya?' I said with a pronounced French accent. The sounds wouldn't go through my nose, only bubbles.

'Well, what about Kaminskaya, what about her?' said the prosecutor fussily. 'A good lawyer. I know her personally, we've met in court. We have nothing against her. But that's a bit tricky now, you know. As a matter of interest, why are you making such an issue of Kaminskaya? The world's large enough, we have plenty of excellent lawyers.'

'I wasn't making an issue of it. Anyway, take your choice: Kaminskaya, Kallistratova, Shveisky. Any lawyer who's had his permit taken away will do for me.'

'Oh, there you go again with those permits!'

It was a long wrangle before we settled on Shveisky.

'What the hell,' shrugged the prosecutor. 'Let it be Shveisky. At least he's a Party member.'

Shveisky had defended Amalrik before me, and the Ministry of Justice had already taken a decision to have him struck off the register.

My trial took place on 5 January 1972 – or rather, the judicial spectacle took place on that day. Even the sentence was known to me in advance. At our last meeting, my investigator, Captain Korkach, had said with a satisfied air: 'Oh well, that's it. We'll be rid of you for the next twelve years.'

For the trial they chose a remote district of Moscow, where it was easier to cordon off the building and keep out my friends and foreign correspondents. The body of the court, as usual, was filled with KGB employees and party functionaries, portraying an 'open trial'.

The whole thing was done in a fantastic hurry – for some reason they were determined to finish the thing off in a day. The charges had been drafted so vaguely that not even the Party officials in court had any idea what was going on. I had 'systematically sent slanderous, anti-Soviet fabrications abroad'; the Western newspapers in which these 'fabrications' had been published were listed. The judge extracted the newspaper cuttings from a file, held each of them aloft in turn and then neatly placed them back in the file again. It was the same with Bill Cole's film: they showed it right there in the courtroom, using the back wall for a screen. The film was shown in English, and no one in court, not even the judge or the prosecuting counsel, could understand its contents.

I entered nine pleas. I asked for the charges to be made more specific, for the precise nature of the slander to be indicated, for the text of my interviews to be read in Russian, for them to summon ten witnesses who could substantiate the truth of the facts I had quoted in my interviews, for my friends to be admitted into the court, and so on.

They were all refused. The court was interested in only one thing: had I or had I not given the interviews and had I been in contact with correspondents and with foreigners in general? The content of my interviews didn't interest them in the least. When I myself tried to describe their contents, I was cut short.

'Defendant Bukovsky, there is no need to go into such detail. Do you admit that you gave an interview to the Associated Press correspondent, Holger Jensen?'

'Yes, I do.'

'Is that you who appears in the film? Did you know that your statements would be published in the West and the film shown on television?'

'Yes, I did.'

'And you didn't object to that?'

'No, I didn't object. I even asked them to do it.'

They were determined to keep away from any discussion of the heart of the matter, and I was equally determined to bring them back to it. They wanted to keep their hands clean, wanted not to hear about all the insults, murders, blood and filth. What did it have to do with them? After all, they weren't killing anyone themselves, weren't suffocating people in 'roll-ups', breaking spines or trampling people with their boots. All they ever did was shuffle papers, sign them and rubber-stamp them. And the end result of it was none of their business. They had comfortable positions and slept soundly at nights. Never mind, you're going to sit and listen to it all from me now! And into that hushed and hate-filled courtroom I emptied all the stench of a Special Hospital, all the sickening details of its tortures. Let them suffocate, even if only for a moment. The judge's face was contorted.

'Have you had medical training?' floundered the prosecuting counsel, as if you needed to be an academician to grow indignant when a man was crippled before your very eyes.

Naturally they refused to call my witnesses, pronouncing the lot of them unfit and incapable of giving testimony. I had foreseen this eventuality and had therefore included in my list people who had never been seen by a psychiatrist, including the wives of General Grigorenko and Victor Fainberg. But the judges were in such a hurry to refuse my request that they didn't notice this. I also included Sergei Petrovich Pisarev, who had once got his diagnosis reversed, but he too was pronounced mad on this occasion.

The prosecution trotted out its own 'witnesses': a KGB officer whom they had once tried to plant on me in Moscow, a terrified young fellow whom I had seen two or three times in my life, plus two young soldiers whom I had accidentally met in a café and whom I had advised, after discussing the Polish workers' strike in Stettin, never to fire upon unarmed people.

What could they say? That I was dissatisfied with the existing system? That I had complained about the absence of democracy in the USSR? It all sounded a bit thin. Suddenly the prosecuting counsel asked: 'You said earlier that an absolute condition of getting a discharge from a special hospital was that the patient should renounce his views. Did you also renounce your views when you were discharged?'

She thought she had nailed me with that question. If I hadn't recanted, I was guilty of slander, because that meant that you could get out of the loony bin without recanting. If I had recanted, even better: how can you believe a man who is prepared to renounce his views when the going gets tough?

How could I explain to those people how fantastically lucky I had been not to have to recant? How could I explain about the many hundreds of people who would never now be able to tell the world about the psychiatric crimes they had suffered? That was the way they worked: some did the torturing, forcing repentance out of people, while others dressed themselves up as moralists and asked underhand questions. And everyone kept quiet. Those who recanted had lost the right to speak out, while those who didn't were doomed to eternal silence. Samsonov, whom they had tortured for eight years, couldn't be there – he had died of a heart attack. Fainberg, Borisov and Grigor-enko couldn't come, for it was unlikely that they'd ever be let out alive. Anyway, why should the people who couldn't hold out be ashamed? The shame belonged to the torturers.

'Yes,' I said firmly, 'I was obliged to recant before they would release me. Otherwise I wouldn't be standing before you now.'

The audience shifted in their seats and fidgeted, and a gloating murmur rippled through their ranks: aha, so he did recant and repent. But I didn't feel any shame for my lie or my imaginary repentance. All I could feel was the pain of others.

And so it came about that I was consigned once again to my prison transports and transit jails, quarrelling with the officer in charge and listening to those endless prison arguments. They sentenced me tc twelve years – twelve years of camp musters, searches, icy punishment cells, and that gnawing hunger that after a time, like a toothache, ceases to be felt, so that your chief discomfort was that your bones stuck out and prevented you from sleeping.

I didn't regret what had happened. I merely regretted that I had achieved too little in the one year, two months and three days, that I had been at liberty. That's what I told them in court, in my 'final word'.

Usually when you depart for *there*, you take with you the last echoes, voices and impressions of the world you have left behind. At one moment your mother's face appears to you, with a host of scenes it evokes, then it's snow-covered Moscow and the crooked Arbat back-streets, or simply snatches of some melody, and you can't for the life of you recall where you heard it or in what connection.

You invariably remember the trial, with their questions and your answers. You run these pictures through your mind afterwards hundreds of times, and every time you find something you could have said better.

My lawyer, Shveisky, was very frightened. They were about to drum him out of the City College of Advocates, the question had already been settled, and now suddenly, everything had been changed again. Not only was he not expelled, but they even gave him back his permit. He had come to see me the day after I ended my hunger strike and sat there for a very long time, looking meaningfully at the wall. He must have suffered from a nervous tic, because from time to time he made a strange movement with his head, as if his tie was choking him or an invisible noose was tightening round his neck. 'As a

Party member, I do not approve of your actions,' he said, looking at the wall.

It cost me a great deal of effort to get him to settle for a position of strict legality.

At the trial, however, he was in good spirits. And although the invisible noose kept tugging at his neck, he demanded a verdict of not guilty. And that was all I needed from him.

The idea of a defence lawyer is that he should act, as it were, as his client's mouthpiece. He should say everything that the defendant is unable to say. In our political trials, everything was reversed. The position was that we defended our lawyers, rather than they us.

This time I made my final word shorter and more energetic, going over all the violations of the law committed by the KGB in my case: 'What was the reason for all these provocations and flagrant illegalities, this flood of slanders and unsubstantiated false accusations? What was the reason for this trial? Was it all to deprive one single individual of his liberty?

'No, there's a "principle" at work here, a "philosophy" of a kind. Behind the stated charges lies another, unstated charge. This trial is designed to say: "Don't wash our dirty linen in public." Their aim is to conceal their own crimes – the psychiatric repressions of dissidents and their prisons and camps. They are trying to shut the mouths of those who have been telling the world about these crimes, so that they can stand forth in the global arena as the irreproachable champions of the oppressed. But they are too late.

'Our society is still sick. It is sick with the fear that we have inherited from the Stalin era. But the process of our spiritual emancipation has already begun, and no repressions will be sufficient to halt it now. Society now understands that the criminal is not he who "washes the dirty linen in public" but he who dirties the linen in the first place.'

Of course, I could have said it better – you always think of better ways of saying it afterwards. But that wasn't my main concern. 'Had all this been worth the twelve years – or rather, the rest of my life?' I asked myself. And by 'all this', I meant not the trial and not my speech, but that process that was now unstoppable. As I saw it, it had. At least, I never came to regret what had happened.

Day and night, without respite, the transports roll east. The transit prisons are packed to overflowing, sixty to eighty men in a cell. Sleeping on bunks, under the bunks, simply in rows on the floor, and even on the table. Hardly any air. The trains are packed so full that they can't even close the doors – the escort guards have to ram them shut with their boots. Mothers with infants at the breast, toothless old women, adolescents, invalids, surly peasants, devil-may-care young men. And for everybody there was a 'case' in a brown envelope. With a photograph pasted on the outside, and a biography. How else could the escort guards cope?

'Surname?'

'Name and patronymic?'

'Article?'

'Term? Move along!'

'Surname?'

'Name and patronymic?'

'Article?'

'Term?'

Your brain reels after the monotony of prison. As if the entire country were on the move. Brothers! Is there anybody at all left at liberty, or have they rounded up the whole bloody lot of us? Shouts, curses, the stamping of feet, a baby's heart-rending cries, and somewhere a fight has broken out.

'Faster, faster,' says the guard.

Some with bundles, some with sacks, some with shabby suitcases, and some with just a regulation-issue herring sticking out of their pocket and a hunk of bread in their hand. 'We're off!'

'Where to–o–o?' bawls a locomotive plaintively.

'To the e–e–e–ast!' plaintively replies another.

Don't turn up your nose at that herring, brother. It might be rotten and it might stink, but it's the only one you'll get. You've got a long way to go – you'll eat it all right. In forty-eight hours everything around you will become saturated with that lousy herring, it will get on to everything. And you won't get any water afterwards – how do you expect the guards to bring water for a mob of this size? You'll end up in an agony of thirst and totally hoarse. And even if you do get any water to drink, they won't let you go to the toilet afterwards. Nevertheless hang on to it, stick it in your pocket. Mark the words of an old con. Towards evening time, when everything settles into place, when the baby has fallen asleep, the chorus of curses has died down, and the women in the next compartment strike up a melancholy song, you will guzzle that herring as if your life depended on it, bones and all. To hell with the fact that it makes you sticky all over. At least you've got something in your belly. Maybe you can even manage forty winks.

You can pick out an old con straightaway. While you were sorting yourself out and hesitating in the doorway, he has already occupied the best place – the middle shelf on the right, from where you even get a glimpse of the free world outside if you can persuade the guard commander to open the corridor window a crack. And his bundle is small, as if he were only on his way to the bathhouse, though there's everything that he needs for the road in there. A good shirt or a sweater to flog to the guards for a packet of tea, a bite to eat and some smokes. Somewhere he's got a small knife, a decorative cigarette-holder, made in the camps – also for flogging off to some uniformed aboriginal. There's a clean mug in there: even if they do keep the TB's apart, there's only one mug for the rest of you. And he's got some cash, though you'd never find it in a month of Sundays, no matter how often you frisked him.

You won't lure him down now for anything in the world, or disturb him – where's the sense in empty conversation? Except with the offer of some tea. And while the younger men gather round to brew this tea over a lighted towel rolled into a cylinder, and others stand by the doors to shield them from the guards, he will unhurriedly tell you a tale or two. But listen hard. The best stories are still to come, when the mug begins to circulate.

Sometimes you can't figure out what he's driving at. He'll dream up a whole novella or treatise for you, and then at the most exciting moment say quite unexpectedly: 'Give us a smoke, brother.'

There is a set of signs by which you can infallibly recognise a genuine con. In the first place, he's always in for nothing. Or because he was sloppy – pinched a cow and left the calf. Secondly, he's always suffering from some chronic, incurable ailment. A hernia, for instance. It's a good ailment, worth a fortune, and a clever con nurtures his ailment and keeps it in reserve, for the time when things get so bad that he's ready to try a breakaway. The silly ones break an arm or cut off a finger, but the thrifty ones go straight into the medical unit.

'Well, it's like this you see, sir. I've got a hernia and I can't work.'

Sometimes a week's malingering is worth a whole year of life.

A respectable con is absolutely bound to have some longstanding claim against admin – some unpaid money, unissued boots or an unreturned parcel. For years he will write endless, tedious complaints, going higher and higher up the Party ladder. His claim will accumulate documents, decisions, recommendations, until it ends up with no one remembering what it was all about in the first place. But it only needs his boss to tighten the screw a bit and he's up in arms again! No beginning or end, no commas and no punctuation at all – the entire complaint in a single unbroken sentence: he's been inside for nothing at all for the last seventeen years, he's seriously ill and admin won't treat him, they assign him to dangerous work, and his boots haven't been returned. The easiest way of all to tell a genuine con is when he's suddenly crossed. Never in your life will you again hear such a virtuoso performance of fabulous cursing, with modulations, flourishes and a host of whimsical figures. Everyone stops talking and cocks an ear respectfully – the greenhorns with envy, the connoisseurs with approval. Listening to this melody, a knowledgeable man can at once determine his entire camp biography. 'You're from Kolyma, brother, aren't you?'

If you're very lucky and have managed to bribe the escort guards for some vodka or eau de cologne, you won't even want to go to sleep. You'll hear stories of quite a different sort, and the only thing you'll regret is that you can't write them down. Your prison term begins to seem not too long after all, and life is grand, and they did the right thing by slinging you in jail.

The wheels clack, the carriage jolts over the points, the women sing sorrowfully, while the guards walk up and down the corridor, peering in at the cons.

'To the e–e–e–east,' wails the locomotive.

Where are they shipping us? To Komi, Tyumen, Kirov or Perm? What difference does it make?

The trains going west are empty. There is no point in taking us west.

It was strange suddenly to find myself among people I had long known at one remove. As if I'd gone to the next world. In Moscow all sorts of information about arrests, trials and the circumstances of different cases had passed through my hands, and, later, I had received news from inside the camps – protests, statements, hunger strikes. The only thing was that we had never managed actually to see these people, and now I examined them with great interest.

Here were the 'hijackers', sentenced in the Leningrad hijacking trial. My God, how long ago that was! That crazy, cruel December of 1970, when the authorities completely cut off all contact with Leningrad, closed down the telephone lines and took people off the trains, and only Volodya Telnikov managed to break through to Moscow with the text of the sentences and a transcript of the trial. And the crazy chase through Moscow: linked courtyards, doorways, the Metro, cars.

In the end we threw them off and somewhere in the vicinity of Pushkin Square, in the flat of one of my friends, feverishly copied the texts. Later that night I still had to break through to the correspondents. 30 December was my birthday – the first time for many years that I had celebrated it at liberty. We spent it hanging around outside the Supreme Court, waiting for the results of the hijackers' appeals. It was late at night before Sakharov came out and told us that the death sentences had been commuted.

'It was all right for you!' I said cheerfully to the hi-jackers. 'Fouled the whole thing up with your plane and been lolling around here ever since. But think of all the trouble you caused us!'

The Ukrainians – Svetlichny, Antonyuk and Kalynets – were jailed after me, but I knew them from *samizdat*.

And who was this skinny fellow, looking like a survivor from Auschwitz? Iosif Meshener? Of course I remembered him. Suslensky and Meshener were two schoolteachers from Moldavia: seven and six years for protesting against the invasion of Czechoslovakia.

Pavlenkov – that was for the Gorky case, university *samizdat*. Gavrilov was the Baltic Fleet submarine officers' case, also in *samizdat*. Why, here was a living *Chronicle of Current Events*!

'Hey, brothers, does anyone drink tea in this compound?'

'You bet!'

'Okay, let's have a brew-up.'


Up till the early 1970s, all the Soviet Union's political camps were situated in Mordovia. There have been political camps there since the very beginning of the Soviet regime. Practically all of Mordovia was criss-crossed with barbed wire. Even according to the official census, there were more men than women in Mordovia, whereas in most of the country the situation is the reverse.

First there was Tyomniki, then Dubrovlag, and now Yavas, Potma, Barashevo. The number of people who have died there is incalculable, and when they dig in the ground, they invariably turn up human bones. They used to say that one survivor had been in the camps from the first years to the last, a participant in the Kronstadt rising. An old, old man, taciturn and ailing, he used to walk about the compound with a pronounced roll, as if on the deck of a cruiser in a storm.

Naturally, such prolonged proximity to the camps had not been without consequences for the local inhabitants. Several generations of them had worked as camp guards, handing down the job from father to son. They had become accustomed to regarding the camps as their provider. For a captured fugitive they got a sack of flour. 'Daddy, did you frisk anyone today?' asks the little boy of his father. 'Have you brought me anything?'

As time passed, commercial relations between the cons and guards went so far that you could get literally anything done for money. Protests, declarations, announcements of hunger strikes freely travelled out to the outside world. In 1970, we had even received a tape recording of a statement by Ginzburg.

The authorities grew alarmed and in 1972, dispatched a special transport of the more 'dangerous' political prisoners to Perm province, which was much further from Moscow. This operation was shrouded in the strictest secrecy. To prevent the prisoners from somehow smuggling out news of their route, the train windows were completely blocked off and battened down. There was an incredible heatwave in the summer of 1972, when forests burned and peatbogs spontaneously caught fire: a suffocating pall of smoke hung over Russia. The metal train-carriages turned into veritable ovens. The men inside them choked and lost consciousness and one prisoner died.

In Perm province they built two new camps – numbers 35 and 36 (later came number 37). Total isolation, especially selected guards who were at once promoted to ensigns to make them more loyal, and a harsh, northern climate.

I was sent straight to camp 35, near the station of Vsesvyatskaya. I had spent the first year after my trial in Vladimir prison – my sentence had decreed two years in jail, five in the camps, and five years' internal exile. By the spring of 1973, when I was due to be sent to a camp, the 'Perm experiment' had been completed and I never saw Mordovia.

Our camp was a small one – about 300–350 people – and the majority of its population, as in the other political camps, consisted of 'veterans' – Ukrainians and Lithuanians who had participated in the national liberation struggles of the 1940s. Many of these prisoners had never experienced normal life in the Soviet Union, because ever since they took to arms in their youth when their lands were invaded by Soviet troops, they had been languishing in the labour camps. These were the remnants of a generation that had been completely shattered. In Lithuania alone, the 'liberators' had repressed 350,000 of the population; in the Ukraine, the total ran into millions. They had been jailed for treason to their motherland. Which motherland Stalin's military tribunal had in mind it is difficult to say. Their views on life, their traditions and customs had been preserved from former times and no longer existed in their homelands. It was amazing to see the way they worked – even in the camps to earn a mere bread ration – diligently, hard, with utter dedication – like the peasants had once worked on their own land. One sensed in them an obstinate belief in the value of human labour, despite everything. Nobody outside worked like that any more; the Soviet regime had taught them differently. We used to joke that any one of these old men would make up for three machines if a fuse were to blow.

Camp somehow preserves a man. His hair turns grey, his teeth fall out, his face is wrinkled, but inwardly he grows no older or more sedate. It was weird to watch these fifty-five-year-old men gambolling together like adolescents, pummelling one another in the ribs; only lack of strength prevented them from playing tag. Their lives had come to a halt when they were about twenty. Simple peasant lads who had never been able to become the fathers of families.

On summer Sundays they would crawl out into the sun with their accordions and play tunes that had long since been forgotten in their native lands. Truly, it was like having entered a country beyond the grave.

They found it hard to understand us or to grasp the meaning of our actions. They were still living with the guerrilla psychology of the 1940s. If even such a large number of armed men hadn't been able to win freedom, what was the point of writing all these bits of paper? For many of them, the very idea of addressing appeals to the authorities was unacceptable, since they didn't acknowledge the legitimacy of those authorities.

From among the Lithuanians I became friendliest with Ionas Matuzevichus. He himself had joined the 'forest brethren' at the beginning of the 1950s, when everything was already lost and the struggle was hopeless. Perhaps this was why he understood us better. When captured, he had kept shooting till the last, intending not to be taken alive. They had dragged his bullet-sliced body away and literally pieced him together again – they needed him alive in order to torture him. I was amazed at how, after all this, plus twenty-five years in the camps, he had retained an astonishing *joie de vivre*, with a sense of humour and a sort of inner purity. I don't know what to call it, but I suppose that that is the way monks ought to be. It probably had something to do with his absolute unrelieved pessimism. We were issued ten days' worth of sugar at a time in little packets, and everyone used to dole it out as carefully as possible to make it last. But Ionas used to put the whole lot in his mouth at once and with a grimace of pleasure, swallow it in one gulp.

'Ionas,' they used to say to him reproachfully, 'what are you doing? That's supposed to last you for ten days!'

'To hell with that!' said Ionas. 'What if I kick the bucket tomorrow? At least the enemy won't get it.'

One day as we were cleaning the boiler-house we came across an old, crumpled, leathercloth boot – there were plenty of them lying around. I went to the men who were mixing cement and poured the boot full of it. When the cement had set, we carefully cut the boot away with a knife. The result was a perfect cement cast. We found a large round stone, a piece of barbed wire, and made a monument to the leather-cloth boot. Everyone took an active part in this enterprise. Someone traced a rough map of the world on the stone with mortar. One end of the barbed wire was stuck under the boot, and the other wound round the leg. When the whole thing was set, we decided to hold a solemn opening ceremony for our monument – each of us was to make humorously pompous speeches. After all, the boot could have belonged to a guard, a sentry or a soldier, but might equally well have been a prisoner's. We invited the Ukrainians, the Lithuanians and anybody who wanted to come to the 'private view'. But it didn't work, there was no fun in it. Somehow nobody could bring himself to open his mouth. We stood around the boot in sorrowful silence and then dispersed. Later the guards found it and spent a long time smashing it up – it was nice and hard by then.

None of these people had ever actually seen their sentences or read them. They were simply told at the time: twenty-five years. And that was that.

As a matter of fact, they rarely give you a copy of your sentence to keep even now. They usually hand it to you to read and then take it away again. The sentence is regarded as 'secret', although once more this is nowhere laid down by the law. (In practice, the only people to be given copies of their sentences were those whose cases had been fairly widely covered in *samizdat* or the foreign press.) Therefore, one of our tasks in the camp was to obtain and send out copies of these sentences.

Until my last arrest, I had been somewhat misinformed. I thought that in our time there were virtually no more 'accidental' political cases, that is to say where the convicted man didn't even suspect before his arrest that his activities might land him in jail. Nowadays, I thought, political repressions are directed only at participants in the human-rights movement or at the members of various national and religious movements – that is, at people who, although they have committed no crime, are aware that in conditions of arbitrary, tyrannical rule they can be arrested at any moment. But I was wrong. The percentage of 'accidental' cases is quite high.

In the first place they include the writers of anonymous letters and complaints. It often happens that a man who has been outraged by some act of injustice decides to write a complaint to some high Party officials, sincerely thinking that in this way he can correct the evil. As the answers coming back grow more and more insolent, the man gradually begins to generalise the results and his complaints take on the character of indictments. He is then called in by the KGB, and if at this point he doesn't allow himself to be intimidated, he is arrested.

In 1976, for example, I was in Vladimir prison with the dentist Airapetov, from Baku, a forty-seven-year-old Armenian. Having discovered that embezzlement and bribery were going on where he worked, he started writing to the Central Committee, but getting no satisfaction, gradually came to the conclusion that the Central Committee was deliberately covering up the corruption. He wrote to Brezhnev several times, denouncing the machinations of the high authorities in Azerbaijan, and in the end was arrested. He refused to repent under KGB pressure and was sentenced to three years in prison and four in the labour camps, for anti-Soviet agitation. But he couldn't for the life of him figure out why he was guilty.

'Whom did I agitate?' he asked at his trial. 'Brezhnev?'

'You know,' they said, 'Brezhnev has lots of secretaries, assistants and consultants, and it was them you agitated'

Other people, realising that they might have difficulties at work and friction with their bosses if they complained, wrote anonymous letters instead. But they, too, were always surprised to be arrested.

An interesting category is made up of people sentenced for writing messages on their ballot papers. Balloting is secret by law, and no one has the right to know who voted which way or put which paper in the ballot box. Furthermore, there is a special article in the Criminal Code stipulating detention for officials who violate the secrecy of the ballot box. But this doesn't prevent the KGB from imprisoning people who write on their ballot papers.

One such case was Chekalin, whom I met in Vladimir and who was released in May 1976, at the end of his five-year term. He had gone almost completely deaf during the time of his imprisonment, since he suffered from a severe and progressive ear infection, and of course was never given any treatment for it.

The case of V. Bogdanov, whom I met in the Perm camp, read just like a joke. He had been a worker in the small town of Electrostal outside Moscow, where he had worked in a secret factory for the enrichment of uranium ore. For several years he huddled in one lousy room with his mother and wife, went round all the party bureaux, wore out everybody's doormats, but got nowhere about being given a flat. Embittered by all this, he lifted a secret, radioactive part from his place of work – judging by his description, it was some sort of plutonium rod from a uranium furnace. He was expecting the security guards to notice the loss, raise a terrific hullabaloo, and then he would offer to return the rod in exchange for getting a flat. But nobody batted an eyelid, as if nothing at all was missing. For three months the rod lay under his bed at home. Then, after drinking with some friends one day, he decided to take the rod straight to the Minister of Medium Engineering.

They rode from one end of Moscow to the other, with the rod stuffed under their overcoats. On the way there they had some more to drink, so that by the time they arrived at the Ministry they were half sloshed. The sentries wouldn't allow them inside. And despite the great racket they made, they couldn't get in to see a single Ministry official. Upset and confused, they called at a shop to top themselves up, then topped up again. Several times they lost their plutonium rod – first they forgot it on a bench in a public garden, then in a shop. In the end they decided to try and sell it to some foreigner – after all, it was a secret part. In the eyes of Soviet man, every foreigner is a spy, and a spy's whole purpose in life is to find out about Soviet secrets. They spent a long time scouring the centre for a suitable foreigner, and at last stumbled across an American in the vicinity of the Hotel Metropole. How they communicated with this American, Bogdanov no longer remembered – he was thoroughly drunk at the time. All he remembered was that the American had been scared out of his wits and had immediately taken to his heels, and they had pursued him until they lost him in the crowd. After that, in despair, they had tried to palm the secret rod off on some Pole. They didn't ask much for it – only a bottle – but the Pole declined. After that they drank beer and got really pissed. The price of the rod was now down to a pint. What happened after that was an absolute mystery to Bogdanov – how they got back to Electrostal, how they found their way home and, above all, what became of that confounded rod. His memory was a total blank.

The friends, however, were hardly awake the next morning when they ran off to the KGB. It was with enormous difficulty, in Lefortovo and under investigation, that he recalled where he had put the blasted rod and owned up to the investigator. In 1968 Bogdanov got ten years for treason. And he remains inside till this day.

The 'accidental' cases should also probably include the case of Nikolai Alexandrovich Budulak-Sharygin. As a fifteen-year-old lad at the beginning of the war, he was shipped from the Ukraine to Germany by the German troops, went to school there, got a job, and when Germany itself was occupied by the allies, found himself in the British zone. He moved to England, lived there for twenty years, completed his education, married, and worked as a salesman for a big electronic-equipment firm. One day on business for his firm, he was sent to Moscow to conclude some trade agreements. He conducted the negotiations with the Committee for the Coordination of Science and Technology attached to the Council of Ministers, and with the Ministry of Electronic Industry, but all of a sudden, at the height of the talks, he was arrested. The KGB spent a long time trying to persuade him to become a spy for them, alternately threatening him and promising him the earth, but Sharygin didn't succumb. The case had taken a nasty turn – how could they let him out now? News of this strange arrest had already appeared in the British press. Yet there was nothing to jail him for. According to Sharygin, the matter was resolved by Andropov personally, in his presence. After examining his passport and papers at great length, Andropov said to his aides, poking a finger at the passport: 'Why do you keep going on and on about him being an Englishman? He was born here, in the Soviet Union. Don't worry, the English queen's not going to declare war on us for his sake.'

Sharygin was sentenced in that same year of 1968 to a term of ten years on a charge of treason – because he hadn't returned home after the war. They didn't give him a copy of his sentence – it was 'secret'.

But we came across an even more fantastic case in 1974 in Vladimir prison. They brought in a real genuine Chinaman by the name of Ma Hun. Intimidated, frightened of everyone, he knew hardly a word of Russian, but he was a sharp and thrifty young fellow. In a strange country, in a new place and in jail, he'd already managed, on his very first day, to swipe an extra mattress cover. And that's how he arrived in our cell, with two mattress covers. With us he felt a bit more at home and melted a bit. The boys used to ask him:

'Well now, Ma Hun, how do you like it here?'

'Velly good,' he would say. 'Velly, velly good.'

'What do you mean, good? This is prison, starvation.'

'What starvation?' Ma Hun looked astonished and pointed at the flies flying about the cell. As if to say, if there had been real starvation, this wild life would long since have disappeared. The boys got a fit of the shivers – what do the poor sods call starvation back in China?

In time Ma Hun was able to tell us about the starvation in China, when they ate all the leaves off the trees and all the grass. For fifty miles around you couldn't find even a dung beetle.

His real name wasn't Ma Hun, but Yui Shi-lin. He had been born in 1941 in the province of An-Hui, the son of a civil servant. Some years later, when the communist army advanced, his father had fled to Taiwan. The family was left destitute. Furthermore, they were constantly persecuted for their non-proletarian origins. The more he told us about China, the more it reminded us of our own 1920s and 30s, under so-called 'Stalinism'. But if anything, it was worse in China: more cruelty, cynicism and hypocrisy. They didn't need any concentration camps there, they simply killed their undesirables off. For instance, all the Chinese volunteers who had been captured in Korea and returned by the Americans were simply wiped out, to the last man. But they were far from being the only ones. There were the 'class aliens', the 'wreckers' and the 'opportunists'. And above all, of course, the intelligentsia. The rest were herded into state farms and communes to be re-educated by work.

They refused to take him into the army – his background was unsuitable. And it seems that without serving in the army, you couldn't finish your studies or get a decent job. Even to get a job as a tractor-driver, you had to have been in the army first. He himself was chased into a militarised State farm near the Soviet border, where he worked as a shepherd. His mother died, but he wasn't even allowed to attend the funeral: you can't travel anywhere in China without a special permit. There was one younger brother left, but he had no idea of his whereabouts.

At the height of the 'cultural revolution' there was a moment when many like him thought they'd have a chance to settle accounts with the regime. But it didn't last long. The army was brought in. In 1968, to escape certain death, he fled across the border into the USSR. He brought with him his only possession, a radio receiver. This was a great treasure in China.

Here in the Soviet Union he was at first arrested and was to be charged with illegally crossing the border. But that was just a formality. In actual fact, they threatened to send him back to China unless he agreed to become a Soviet spy. There had been many of these cases, and the Chinese border guards invariably shot fugitives on the spot as soon as they were handed over. There was no choice. If you agree, we'll send you back to China as a spy. If not, we'll hand you over. It meant certain death either way. He refused.

After they had failed to make a spy out of him, they gave him one last chance: he could enter a secret organisation of Chinese refugees on Soviet territory. Evidently the KGB regarded this as the embryo of a future Chinese 'people's liberation army'. And it was now that he became Ma Hun – they made him change his name.

He was given a residence permit and got a job in a factory as a metal-worker. As an individual without citizenship, he was not allowed to move about the country, but Soviet life still seemed like paradise to him: you were paid money for your work, which you could use to buy food and clothing without restriction. Not like in China, where you got nine yards of cloth per person per year. As for the hypocrisy, he was used to it. Soviet hypocrisy struck him as child's play compared with the Chinese variety.

Once in his early childhood he had been taught to play the violin, and throughout his life he had looked back on that time as on a fairy tale. The violin for him was a symbol of happiness. Not surprisingly, he now bought one. Sometimes he played it, but more often he listened to his radio. He could get Japan, Taiwan and even Australia on it.

One day he heard an announcement during one of the broadcasts from Australia. It said that there was a centre which helped Chinese people to locate their lost relations, and Ma Hun wrote to them and asked if they could help him find his father in Taiwan. At this moment he was arrested.

The investigation lasted for almost two years. Ma Hun was accused of espionage. As if he had come to the Soviet Union for that purpose on an assignment from Chinese intelligence. Several times they examined his radio receiver to see if there was a transmitter inside it. They took it apart screw by screw, but found nothing. Then they started on the violin. What was a Chinaman doing with a violin? Highly suspicious, they smashed it to little pieces, but still didn't find anything. Then they started on Ma Hun himself.

'If you own up, you'll get five years. If you don't – ten.'

There were many in the Alma-Ata investigation prison who had 'owned up' in this way. Some of them had got only two to three years for espionage, and were now working as trusties. It was from among them that the investigation picked its witnesses against Ma Hun. These testified that they had seen Ma Hun in their intelligence schools and that he had been a high official there.

On 30 November 1973 a military tribunal of the Central Asian Military Command sentenced him to fifteen years (five years each in prison, labour camps and exile) and to the confiscation of all his property for 'attempted espionage'. He never did admit his guilt.

We all got very attached to Ma Hun, helped him to learn Russian and questioned him about China. The entire prison knew him and even the crooks, on their way past our door to the exercise yard, used to peer through the peephole and say:

'Hey, where's your Chinaman?'

Ma Hun studied with great determination, from reveille to lights out, and in six months spoke Russian very decently. The only thing he could never get used to was our consonants – he couldn't manage the 'b', the 'g' or the 'd', and he always said 'to work' instead of simply 'work'. Life had so trained him that he couldn't imagine the word without the preposition.

He went on hunger strikes with us and took reduced rations. For New Year, he and I made a Christmas tree from the green bindings of some exercise books, cutting the boughs out with a needle. He also made a tiny Chinese lantern – he wove the framework out of pieces of broom and stuck paper over it. Only it turned out that in China they don't call this lantern 'Chinese'.

Ma Hun told us that the inhabitants of the various Chinese provinces all had their distinctive traits. In one province they were all trouble-makers, bullies and bandits, in another traders, in a third such villains that nobody wanted to have anything to do with them.

'But what about your province?' we asked. 'What's that famous for?'

For a long time he wriggled, evaded the question, blushed, and then at length owned up:

'Stubbornness.'

Evidently the KGB hadn't known these subtleties, otherwise they would never have tangled with him. This, probably, was what made him friendly with us. We were all to a certain extent from the province of An-Hui.

Our best complaints specialist, Mikhail Yanovich Makarenko, wrote him a complaint against his sentence, and Ma Hun spent from morning till night copying it out. Instead of practising his Russian. For six months or more he sent it out to everybody at all levels of the Party. Simultaneously we threatened the KGB that we'd make Ma Hun's case public if his sentence wasn't annulled.

At last something gave and Ma Hun was taken away for investigation. The Chinese witnesses admitted that they had testified under pressure from the KGB. But it was a whole year later before they released him, on 9 August 1976. It is easy to throw people into jail, but much, much harder to get them out again.

There has been no shortage of 'accidental' cases over the years! The only 'non-accidental' cases were those against *polizei*, the war criminals and collaborators with the Nazis. They had been carefully planned.

In the early post-war years the section for combating war criminals was virtually the major one in the KGB. Half the country was then numbered as war criminals: everyone who had been captured or occupied. Sometimes it included whole nations. But thirty years went by. Almost everyone who'd seen a living German soldier had died, and this section was on the brink of extinction – it was due to be closed at any moment as redundant. It was now that the *polizei* came in handy. The KGB was in no hurry to arrest them, but simply registered their existence and let them live peacefully for the time being. Now and again they would summon one to the KGB for a chat, then let him go. His turn hadn't come yet. Show trials of war criminals occurred regularly at the rate of about one a year. A lot was written about them in the newspapers, the details were savoured, one or two would be given the death penalty and the rest fifteen years apiece. Each time, of course, the KGB made out that only now, as a result of superhuman efforts, had it been able to catch the villain.

This method suited the Party authorities, too. After all, these trials were needed for patriotic and military propaganda purposes. The war criminals themselves submissively awaited their turn, working away, beating their targets, taking part in socialist competitions. In fact, they were perfectly ordinary Soviet people, accustomed to bend in whichever direction they were bent. During the war, many of them had fought several times with Stalin and several times with Hitler, won medals and promotions from both, and often enough had ended up the war with the Russian occupation of Berlin. After the war they had become superintendents and collective-farm chairmen. One or two of them had even entered the ranks of local deputies.

In the camps, as if by magic, they all ended up in positions of authority: brigade-leaders, activists, members of the collective council, trusties – in short, prisoners on the road to reform, the hope and support of the camp godfather. Sometimes you barely had a chance to open your mouth before one of them was on his way to the guard-house to inform on you.

It was interesting, however, to listen in on a summer's evening when a group of these world-war veterans would get together to reminisce and boast about their youth.

'So we were on one side of the river beyond the bridge. And they came charging up from the other side, not expecting us, you see. Boy, did we make it hot for them!'

'Who were you with then, grandad,' you interrupt in all innocence. 'Was it the Reds or the Germans?'

'The Germans, no, the Soviets. Wait a minute. I think it really was the Germans after all. . . . Oh shut up, don't interrupt! Let me finish what I was saying.'

I didn't stay in Camp 35 for long – a little under a year. From the very first day they were after me: Why don't you stand up when an officer comes in? Why don't you take off your cap? Why don't you stand there, sit here, go over there? Someone else might be doing the same, but he goes scotfree, while you get punishment after punishment: no shop privileges, no visits, the box, and so on.

Before shipping me from Vladimir to the camps in the spring of 1973, they brought me back to Moscow again, to Lefortovo. Officially it was to question me as a witness in the Yakir case, but in fact it was to persuade me to recant. My trial and the denunciation of psychiatric abuses had had a considerable resonance throughout the world – not sufficient, unfortunately, to put an end to the psychiatric punishments and oblige the authorities to release me (the World Psychiatric Congress in Mexico had cravenly declined to discuss our documentation), but still sufficient to force them to look for a way out. As usual, they banked on being able to extricate themselves at the victim's expense. The KGB officials now admitted in conversation with me that they had tried me unjustly – I should never have been tried at all – and they were now prepared to correct their mistake and release me. But naturally I had to help them, by repenting in writing and requesting a pardon. It was quite comic really: we're to blame, so you beg our pardon.

When they had established that such a solution was unacceptable to me, they lowered their demands. As they put it, it would be sufficient for me to renounce all public activity in the future – leaving my past and my views to one side – and there would be no need for me to return to the camp.

'All right, if you don't like the word "pardon", write "I ask you to release me".'

And then they began hinting that they wouldn't stand in my way if I were to go abroad. And there I could do what I liked.

I again refused. I had decided this question for myself once and for all in 1970, and didn't wish to return to it any more.

At this point they lost patience.

'What the hell do you want? Do you really find it so enjoyable sitting in jail?'

I explained that the present situation suited me fine. I was snug in my cell, reading my books, while they were being inundated with protests, demonstrations and resolutions. To tell the truth, I said, I strongly doubted whether I could cause them half as much trouble at liberty as by remaining in jail. 'Note that it wasn't I who asked for these negotiations. You have a greater interest in freeing me than I have in being freed. However, I am prepared to accept your proposals both for ceasing my activities and for going abroad – but first you must totally renounce your psychiatric persecution of the dissidents, publicly condemn this method, release the people in the loony bins and punish the guilty men. In effect, all my so-called "activities" have come down basically to fighting these psychiatric abuses. If you now renounce them, I will truly have nothing more to do. And I don't need your pardon. Appeal for my sentence to be quashed as is laid down by the law.'

This declaration aroused them to extreme indignation. 'Do you think you're going to dictate to us? Speak to us "from a position of strength"? It won't work! Watch your step – you'll come begging to us later. The way to a pardon is always open to you. Think about it carefully. And we'll see to it that you don't forget our proposal.'

With these words ringing in my ears I had gone off to the camps. The last phrase had had an ominous ring to it and held out little prospect of a pleasant life.

Even without this, the situation in the camp was pretty tense. The real masters were the officers of the KGB, and admin merely carried out their orders. It was totally isolated, with no channels to the outside world, and there was the harsh climate of the northern Urals. Add to this a policy of unconcealed coercion and the absence of any medical facilities and you will understand what was the meaning of this 'Perm experiment'.

Among the old men brought here from Mordovia, many were already seriously ill and living out their last days. And even the health of the younger ones was not that good. In short, they had brought all the most unrepentant of us here in order to finish us off without fuss.

Soon after my arrival a special 'doctors' commission from Perm examined almost all the prisoners and pronounced them healthy and fit for work. Even men who had had invalid status from birth were deprived of it now: the hunchback Vasily Pidgorodetsky and two one-legged men were all pronounced capable of working, and the same went without saying for the men with stomach ulcers, weak hearts and TB.

The results were not slow in showing themselves, and in August a twenty-five-year-term prisoner named Kurkis died of a perforated ulcer. After being deprived of his invalid status, he had been sent to do heavy work and within a couple of weeks he was finished. For twenty-four hours he lay in the hospital adjoining the camp, bleeding profusely. The hospital possessed neither blood supplies nor the necessary equipment, nor even a surgeon. By pure chance we managed to get this information out extremely swiftly, so that within three days our friends in Moscow knew all about it. At the same time we launched a campaign of protest. We had to hurry, for on our speed and efficiency would depend the number of people who could avoid a similar death. But this was only the beginning.

The year 1973 was in a certain sense a decisive one for our movement as a whole. Having achieved a certain amount of success with the Yakir–Krasin trial, the authorities moved quickly to paralyse the entire movement.* Dozens of people were subjected to open blackmail. They were threatened with the arrest, not of themselves but of their families and friends if they didn't put a stop to their human-rights activities. The *Chronicle of Current Events* came to a temporary halt: the KGB promised to meet each new number with fresh arrests. It was a system of taking hostages. Simultaneously, they unleashed a frenzied campaign of persecution against Solzhenitsyn and Sakharov, following their familiar recipe – from academicians to deer-breeders to milk-maids.

It is always like that. It is sufficient for one to weaken and the pressure increases on all. Ten men surrendering to blackmail can sow panic among tens of thousands. Camp life is like a barometer, and at such moments the regime is savagely tightened, achievements won by years of hunger strikes are suddenly lost again, and everyone finds

* Yakir and Krasin's public confessions in 1973 were used by the KGB to discredit the entire human-rights movement.

himself on the edge of oblivion. A superhuman effort is required to preserve your life and your rights.

We were the first to beat the enemy back, and by the end of the year the camp medical system had been smashed. Not a day went by without commissions coming to see us. Important generals strode about the compound with their retinues, smart colonels in trousers with a stripe down the side, and some sort of civilians who had the whole of admin bowing and scraping. On special instructions from Moscow, a surgeon was sent from Perm to take over the running of our hospital. Invalid status was returned, the sick were prescribed treatment, and we even managed to get one seriously sick man transferred from the box to the hospital, a thing that had never happened before.

Outside, the turning point came later, with the deportation of Solzhenitsyn in January 1974. This event rocked everybody, and, as happens at moments of real disaster, strengthened their resolution. The *Chronicle of Current Events* started appearing again, but the authorities no longer risked using the system of hostages, and the promised arrests never took place. The blackmail ended as soon as people ceased to submit to it. But we faced a long and uphill struggle to get back everything we had lost during that time.

Of course, the authorities had not overlooked my role in the breaking of the 'Perm blockade', and the time had come anyway for them to carry out their promise – to remind me of our Lefortovo discussion about a pardon.

The camp governor, Major Pimenov, didn't conceal from me that the decision had come from above, independently of his will. He didn't care for the KGB, they made his rule a fiction, and he took every available opportunity to play them some dirty trick. He wanted to be a real 'boss', the sole ruler of his tiny world, and whenever he was obliged to carry out the instructions of the KGB he always tried to do it in such a way as to underline the stupidity of the instructions.

Had he been ordered to give me fifteen days? By all means. And he put me inside for allegedly being absent from my place of work on 3 February, which was a Sunday, when nobody worked anyway.

'Next comes three months in the penal isolator and after that you yourself know what it will be,' he said to me on parting. Vladimir prison was what he had in mind.

I immediately refused to go to work. Working was all I needed if I was to be in the box on bread and water. Anyway, the work quotas were deliberately set too high: cut a thread by hand on 120 bolts per day, when you didn't even have the strength to cut one.

ORDER of the MOI, USSR, no. 0225, dated 25 April 1972

Confirmed by the Public Prosecutor's Office of the USSR and the Council of Ministers of the USSR.

Convicted prisoners committed to the Penal Isolator with or without the requirement to work, but maliciously refusing to work or intentionally failing to meet the production quotas are to be maintained on norm 9b, with the issue of hot food every other day. On days when hot food is not provided, they are to receive 13·5 ounces of bread, salt and hot water.

### DAILY FOOD NORM 9b

| | | | |
|---|---|---|---|
| Rye bread | 13·5 oz. | Potatoes | 7·5 oz. |
| Fish | 1·8 oz. | Vegetables | 6·0 oz. |
| Flour | 0·3 oz. | Groats (wheat, oats) | 1·5 oz. |
| Fat | 0·18 oz. | Salt | 0·6 oz. |

So whether you worked or not, if you couldn't reach your quota you would still get fed only every other day.

For three months and fifteen days those were my rations. And I was regularly flung in the box for refusing to go to work. This would have been enough to kill even a healthy man off, and I had just developed a stomach ulcer. In short, they had it all worked out. And if I didn't actually kick the bucket, it was due exclusively to stubbornness. I was determined not to give them the pleasure.

'All right, today you get no hot food,' the turnkey would inform me gaily, putting my bread ration on the food flap. 'Will you take some hot water?'

My God, will I! Hot water's my only hope. It takes the place of broth.

'Give me my salt. I'm due point six of an ounce.' What do I need it for, this salt? I can't eat it anyway. But you have to insist on it, it's the principle of the thing. Give me my due.

Thirteen-and-a-half ounces of bread – is that a lot or a little? You can eat it all at one go if you like. Then it's a lot. Or you can divide it in three: breakfast, lunch, supper. Then it's little. Or else you can leave it altogether, so as not to tantalise yourself for nothing.

After a couple of weeks you have to get up slowly in the mornings, for your head begins to spin. After a month, the skin begins to peel from your arms and legs. After two months you find it impossible to read; you just can't take anything in.

Of course, the authorities didn't forget me. One or two important officials came to have a look at me and pinch my flesh.

'Why don't you stand up when an officer enters?'

'I'm conserving my energy.'

For this I got seven days in the box.

'Why don't you want to go to work?'

'You can't get much done on thirteen ounces of bread.'

'You don't say! During the war, during the German blockade, the Leningraders used to get six ounces a day, but they still worked!'

It was they who compared themselves with the Nazis.

In April the snow began to melt, and suddenly revealed a multitude of mouse-tracks – the mice had been having a fine old time all winter under the snow. Now they had to be extra careful before dashing out of one hole and into another. The sun's rays were getting so warm that it was possible to sun myself by the window. Steam rose from the raked strip in the free-fire zone. I wasn't expecting to see the grass that spring.

'Today you get no hot food,' said the guard with springlike cheerfulness. 'Take your bread.'

At the end of April my lawyer, Shveisky, came to visit me. He had changed little and still jerked his head as if an invisible noose were tightening round his throat. Glancing meaningfully round the walls he said: 'Believe me, I'm not speaking on anyone's instructions, no one has asked me to do it, but you know, you need to find some sort of compromise. You can't go on like this. It seems to me for some reason that if you were to plead for a pardon. . . .'

I also hadn't been asked by anyone, no one had given me any instructions, but I knew that when one weakened, it got much worse for the rest. If it came to that, the Leningraders in the blockade had managed on only six ounces a day.

Of course, the fellows were doing everything they could, and in Moscow they had long known of my position. By this time our links with the outside world had been organised so neatly that we were able to send out letters, statements, copies of sentences, verse anthologies. We even started sending out our own 'Chronicle' – the *Chronicle of the Gulag Archipelago*. In May there was a three-day hunger strike – as a warning. Admin saw that serious events were gathering head. The campaign in our support was rapidly growing – only later did I learn its true scale. The authorities could no longer keep me in the camp lock-up. On the morning of 9 May, Pimenov came to see me. Squinting craftily, he looked round my cell and said: 'Mm – yes. This lock-up's wrongly equipped, it doesn't meet with regulations. We shall have to tear it apart and rebuild it.'

For greater verisimilitude in this cover story they sent some cons over from the building brigade, who demolished the bunks. And so I was 'amnestied' eleven days early, although they weren't supposed to release cons from the lock-up until their time was done.

But the same force which had swept me out of the lock-up despite all the regulations was irresistibly carrying us further, and now it was our turn to strike. The screw they had been tightening for several months had at last slipped its thread, and we all realised that if we didn't now put a stop to the coercion and get back the ground we had lost, we would never be able to do it.

Three days later, forty men went on hunger strike, and those who couldn't manage it proclaimed a normal strike. The local garrison was put on the alert. The sentries in the watchtowers were doubled. Admin tried persuasion, intimidation, blackmail, but nothing helped.

They summoned the Ukrainians: 'Why have you got yourselves mixed up with those Yids and lousy Russians?' They summoned the Jews: 'Why have you got yourselves mixed up with those anti-semites? You want to go to Israel, don't you?!'

The hunger strike lasted a month. Whoever couldn't hold out – lost consciousness after a heart attack, or the aggravation of other complaints – was carried off to the hospital. Having got their strength back, they joined the hunger strike again. Even the old men with the twenty-five-year terms took part.

'An interesting time is beginning,' said one of them to me, a Ukrainian. 'I shall even be sorry to be let out.' He had only a few months to go until his release.

Soon after us, the neighbouring camp, no. 36, also went on strike. The demand everywhere was the same – put an end to coercion. The authorities didn't know what to do next. They started flinging the hunger strikers in the box – so then we refused to go out to roll-call. A grey-faced, enraged Pimenov came running up. 'Do you understand what this means? Are you aware of the consequences? I order you all to go out for rollcall!'

Nobody moved an inch. The other, non-striking half of the camp waited in silence out on the road.

'Don't break ranks!' commanded Pimenov. 'You can all wait for the rest of them!' But it began to drizzle with rain and everybody, including the stool-pigeons, wandered off to their barrack huts. The authorities' campaign had collapsed in ruins. More and more men came to join the strike. Some for a day, some for a week, depending upon their health. Others simply dispatched protests.

Admin was in total confusion. The political commissar yelled that he would bring troops into the compound. The security officer threatened to have everyone charged with sabotaging the work of the camp. At the same time, they called the cons in one by one and promised them parcels from home or even an extra visit if they would put an end to the hunger strike. Nothing helped. There was no more room in the lock-ups. There was nowhere to jail anyone any more. In great haste they summoned the so-called collective council, consisting of former *polizei*. But even they refused to condemn us. This was the last straw.

Meanwhile, all the radio stations beamed at the Soviet Union were broadcasting our *Chronicle of a Hunger Strike* and *Chronicle of the Gulag Archipelago*. And the guards, those handpicked guards who had been given their ensigns' epaulettes for maintaining secrets, whispered to us what was being said in the broadcasts.

'How on earth do they find out about it all?' they wondered.

The Perm experiment had collapsed.

I didn't see the end of this epic. On 27 May, on the fifteenth day of our hunger strike, I was shipped off to Vladimir. I never did get to eat my fill that spring – what with the box, then the hunger strike, and then a month on reduced rations in Vladimir. To hell with it! Just make sure the bones are there, the flesh will grow on its own.

# 10

THE days dragged by in Vladimir with the constant war over the strict regime, the hunger strikes, the box, and all those endless ounces, degrees and inches that an outside observer never will be able to understand. A monotonous, unchanging sinking to the bottom, from which you could save yourself only by concentrated daily study.

The news from outside was not very cheerful. What the authorities had failed to achieve with arrests, blackmail, the taking of hostages and even the psychiatric prisons was being done by emigration. People with whom my entire life had been bound up were disappearing for ever. Some left Russia of their own accord, having lost all patience. Others were kicked out. But the result was the same. Moscow was growing empty. They were taking parts of my life with them to the West, and I myself was hard put to it now to say where I was.

Captain Doinikov used to come and see me, talking his endless twaddle. But more and more often and ever more insistently he would bring the conversation round to 'abroad'. He felt awkward playing this role. After all, I shared the cell with men whom he was obliged to 'educate' in quite a different spirit, demonstrating how wonderful it was to live on Soviet territory. He would shift from one leg to the other in embarrassment, contradict himself and at times talk himself into completely anti-Soviet utterances. My cell-mates could only gape with astonishment.

No, I didn't want to leave. The Jews were going to Israel, the Germans to Germany. That was their right; it is the right of every man to go wherever he wants. But where were we to go, we Russians? There was no other Russia. And why, when you came to think of it, should we be the ones to leave? Let Brezhnev and company emigrate.

That was why, you might say, my future life was mapped out. I would have time for two more spells of liberty, and then I would be back in prison in time to die.

*I didn't even notice how the night had passed. My cell-mates were asleep, having covered themselves with their overcoats on top of their blankets. The cell was filled with dense blue smoke – I had been chain-smoking the whole night long. Why was I being such a fool as to worry?*

*Just think, they'd brought me to Lefortovo and given me a suit. So what? In a while they'd probably start questioning me, and I hadn't slept a wink, like an idiot. Maybe there was still time to get an hour's shut-eye? But as if he'd been listening to my thoughts, the guard opened the food flap: 'Wake up!'*

*In winter it's hard to tell the difference between night and morning. It was still dark outside. While we washed and had our breakfast, it began to get a bit lighter.*

*'Get ready for your exercise!'*

*They were taking us out rather on the early side, weren't they? It never used to be like that. My cell-mates were yawning, they hadn't properly woken up yet. 'You go if you want,' they said. 'We're not going. It's better to go back to sleep.'*

*I wouldn't have minded half an hour's kip – who knew what was ahead of me? But the door was already open.*

*'Ready? Come on out!'*

*'I could do with some sort of overcoat,' I said. 'They've taken my reefer jacket away. I'll freeze outside in just a suit.'*

*'Right away, right away,' fussed the block guard. 'Come with me, we'll find you an overcoat.' He led me through the baths and in the direction of the frisking boxes again. 'Here's an overcoat.'*

*On a table in one of the boxes lay a brand new overcoat, a hat and something else I couldn't quite make out. The block guard was fussing round me and seemed incredibly nervous, with an unpleasantly unctuous smile on his face. Why was he so obsequious?*

*I had just put on my overcoat and not yet had time to button it when – click! Mother of God, handcuffs! He had handcuffed my hands behind me, instead of in front. Were they going to beat me, or something? Instinctively I jerked away and jumped back so that he couldn't hit me. That was what the guards always did when they were going to beat you. They would put American handcuffs on you, which tightened automatically at the least movement of the wrists, and then take a running kick at them, so that they tightened up to the limit. It was such agony that you screamed in protest. But a man's absolutely helpless to resist afterwards and you can do what you like with him.*

'Easy, easy . . . don't worry, its nothing, it just has to be done that way.'

An amazingly vile face! But with an ingratiating smile, he stuck a hat and tie on me and buttoned up my overcoat.

If it hadn't been for the handcuffs I would never have let him dress me up in this revolting rubbish, which I had never worn in my life.

Yesterday's minibus stood by the porch. Its windows were shuttered. Just off to one side was a police car. The same KGB agents as yesterday got in and surrounded me. We drove for about an hour and a half. Again a police car with a flashing light cleared the way ahead of us. And now I hadn't the least clue where they were taking me, especially when we left the outskirts of Moscow.

'Are the handcuffs hurting you?' asked one of the KGB men from time to time. 'If they tighten up, let us know.'

It is awfully uncomfortable to sit with your arms behind your back.

At last we seemed to have arrived somewhere. We stopped. It was quite light now; it must have been around nine o'clock. The KGB men kept getting out of the car and then coming back in again to warm up. We were waiting for somebody. Cars came and went. I could hear voices and then the roar of engines. An airport?

'Yes. In a minute we're going to put you on a plane. Your mother, sister and nephew will be going with you.'

Strange, this news left me completely unmoved. As if in the depths of my soul I had long since known that this would happen. I had known it and yet kept it from myself – I didn't want to be disappointed. But in actual fact, how else could it all have ended? Wasn't this what they had wanted all the time? The only strange thing was that there were no documents, and they'd said nothing about a decree. I was a prisoner and still had something like six years ahead of me.

It seems odd, after prison, to be able to look to the side. To look over your shoulder and see something new. But you don't remember anything of it, your eyes have got out of the habit. With some difficulty I scrambled up the steps into the plane – it's an extremely awkward thing to do when you've got your arms behind your back. I looked down – cars, a copse, a snow-covered field. An unfamiliar airport, definitely not Sheremetyevo. Later I learned it was an airforce base.

The plane was empty except for me and the KGB men. And again it seemed like a kind of prison, this time with wings.

'Can you maybe take these handcuffs off now?'

'Not yet.'

Their chief officer reminded me of a borzoi. The same slightly bulging brown eyes. He was chain-smoking.

'Well, loosen them for a minute, then. I need a cigarette.'

'Give him a cigarette.'

One of the KGB men stuck a cigarette between my teeth and then took it out from time to time to shake off the ash.

'We're just going to take you to the door to show you to your mother and prove that you're already here. Otherwise she refuses to get into the plane.'

Again I glimpsed the copse, a group of cars, some people, my mother among them. And back again. They carried Mishka, my nephew, aboard on a stretcher. I hardly recognised him – it was six years since I'd seen him. The lad had grown.

How uncomfortable it is to sit with your arms behind your back. The hand-cuffs had tightened and were squeezing my wrists. It would be a lot easier if they had handcuffed me at the front. The guard on my right was entertaining me with stories about planes. He told me how many crashes there were a year, and on which airlines. He attentively fastened my safety belt. But I was look-ing out of the window over the shoulder of another agent, who was as silent as a sphinx. Perhaps I was seeing Russia for the last time in my life? Should I be glad or sorry?

Here in Russia they had done their level best, from my childhood on, to remake me and change me, as if the State had no other care in life. Just think of the prisons and camps they had flung me in, the ways they had found to pillory me! The strange thing was that escaping now from this eternal persecution, I felt neither bitterness nor hatred.

No matter where I went or lived subsequently, my recollections would be unavoidably tied to this land, and such is the nature of memory that it holds no dark, but retains only the bright pictures. So I ought to be sad, oughtn't I? But no matter how intensely I gazed at the departing, snow-covered earth, I couldn't force myself to be sad.

Of course, I would miss my friends who remained behind, and probably the Arbat backstreets and the familiar Russian speech to which my ear was attuned. But I had felt the same about my friends who had already left. And hadn't the dream of my whole life been to visit London? No, none of this was connected for me with the concept of Motherland.

But shouldn't I, at least, be experiencing a sense of joy? The joy of victory? No matter which way you looked at it, we had conducted a desperate war against this regime of utter scum. We were a handful of unarmed men facing a mighty State in possession of the most monstrous machinery of oppression in the entire world. And we had won. The State had been obliged to retreat. Even in jail we had proved too dangerous for it.

Finally, shouldn't I be experiencing the joy of liberation?

I didn't feel any joy either, only an incredible fatigue. That's the way it *always was with me before a release. I wanted nothing but peace and solitude – and that had been precisely what I never got. And wouldn't be getting now.*

*My mother kicked up a hell of a fuss with the* KGB *demanding to talk to me. Somehow or other she had discovered that I was handcuffed. The chief officer with the borzoi eyes appeared and reluctantly permitted a meeting.*

*Mother was in an absolute rage. 'You are criminals, you are absolute scoundrels!' she cried. 'Even here in the plane you go on tormenting him. As if you haven't tormented him enough all these years!'*

*The* KGB *chief frowned in vexation. 'Nina Ivanovna, calm yourself, please.'*

*All these years my mother had been waging a desperate war against the authorities. She had inundated them with protests, sent open letters to the West, and hadn't given them a moment's respite. Towards the end, in fact, she had been doing everything that I had once done.*

*Only now, from her, did I learn that I was being exchanged for the Chilean communist, Luis Corvalan. What a strange, unprecedented deal! It had happened in the past that two hostile countries had exchanged foreign spies they had caught or prisoners-of-war. But to exchange your own citizens – I had never heard of that before.*

*Well, what of it? That made two political prisoners less in the world. It was amusing to think that in the eyes of the world the Soviet regime was equated with that of Pinochet. This was a symbol of our times.*

*As for the handcuffs, shouting would never get them off: violence was not the way to obtain freedom. No matter how much you wriggle in handcuffs, you only make them tighter.*

*And was it really the cowardly officials who had put the handcuffs on us? We simply hadn't learned to live without them yet. We didn't understand that the handcuffs didn't exist any more.*

*I stared intently into the canine eyes of the chief officer and he quickly looked away. Dogs and secret policemen can't endure a straight look – I have verified that on many occasions. What did he fear most of all in this world? His immediate superior in the service.*

*'But why, actually, are you keeping me in handcuffs?'*

*'Well, all right, I'll tell you.' He fidgeted and looked away. 'You're still a prisoner.'*

*'Ah, so that's it! And what will you do when we cross the Soviet frontier? That should happen in about twenty minutes. Over Austria, for instance, will I still be a prisoner?'*

*He didn't know what to answer. And the thing that bothered him was not the truth, not international law, but the possibility of a reprimand from his boss. He went into the cockpit to make contact with Moscow, to get his instructions.*

'Take the handcuffs off him,' he said on his return. And, turning to me: 'Only please behave yourself properly.'

What was he trying to say? That I shouldn't try to jump out of the plane? At last I could chafe my wrists and light a cigarette properly. That was better.

'The handcuffs are American, by the way,' said the agent who took them off, and he showed me the trademark. As if I didn't know without his help that almost from the very beginning of this regime, the West had been supplying us with handcuffs. Did he think he was disillusioning me? I had never entertained any illusions about the West. Hundreds of desperate petitions addressed, for example, to the United Nations, had never been answered. Wasn't this sufficient indication? Even from Soviet institutions you got an answer – maybe senseless, but it came. But over there the ground just swallowed them up.

As for the so-called 'policy of détente' – the Helsinki agreements and so on – we could feel on our backs in Vladimir prison who gained from those. It wasn't the first time that the West's 'friendly relations' with the Soviet Union had been built on our bones. The most repulsive thing of all was that the West tried to justify itself with all sorts of intricate doctrines and theories. Just as Soviet man has created a countless multitude of self-justifications to facilitate his collusion with total violence, so the West, too, likes to soothe its conscience. Sometimes these self-justifications are the same. But violence relentlessly revenges itself on those who support it. Those who think that the frontier between freedom and unfreedom corresponds with the State frontiers of the Soviet Union are cruelly mistaken.

The KGB chief came back again.

'We have crossed the Soviet border and it is my duty to inform you officially that you have been expelled from the territory of the USSR.'

'Do you have some sort of decree or order?'

'No, nothing.'

'And what about my sentence? Has it been quashed?'

'No, it remains in force.'

'So, I'm sort of a prisoner on holiday, on vacation?'

'Sort of.' He grinned crookedly. 'You will receive a Soviet passport, valid for five years. You are not deprived of your citizenship.'

A strange decision, flying in the face of all Soviet legislation. And they insist that their laws should be taken seriously! They don't even know either how to jail or release you properly. A jolly country, never a dull moment!

The plane commenced its final run in to land, and the secret policemen looked down at Switzerland with interest. 'They've got fewer forests than we have.'

'But look at how many fields they've got. They're all private here.'

'Everybody here has his own house and his own plot.' It's good when there's an 'abroad' in the world, and returning from some service assignment, you can bring the wife some foreign trinkets. Isn't that the highest blessing?

The closer we came to this 'abroad', the more noticeable was the change in the men. That KGB impenetrability and enigmatic reserve melted away. What was left was Soviet man. There was a certain envy in the looks they gave me – before their very eyes I was turning into a foreigner.

We taxied up to the airport buildings. Suddenly some armoured troop-carriers rolled out on to the runway and soldiers jumped out of them. They cordoned off our plane. 'Mm – yes,' said one of the KGB men sadly. 'That's that. They won't even let us into the airport now.'

Now it was they who were in prison, under armed guard.

An ambulance drove up and took Mishka off to hospital. Then they let mother and me out. We got into a Soviet embassy car. An American car drew up, belonging to Ambassador Davis, and we were transferred to it. And that was the entire ceremony of the exchange. We never did see Corvalan or see him get into the Soviet plane.

No search, no checking of documents. A miracle! All my gear, my priceless prison treasures, were lying here too, still in the prison mattress cover, just as I had gathered them up in my cell. Books, notebooks, hidden knives and razor-blades, ballpoint pens, refills. Many weeks of life for someone. But none of it had any value any more: in a single instant accustomed values had been turned on their head.

As we drove to the airport terminal, I couldn't rid myself of a strange sensation – as if, thanks to a blunder by the KGB, I had carried out something very precious and important, something forbidden, that should never have been let out of the country. Something no search could ever discover.

# Index

Abramov, Colonel, 232
access permits, for lawyers, 234, 309–10
Akhmatova, Anna, 114
alcoholism, drunkenness, 262
All-Russian Social–Christian Union for the Liberation of the People, 98
Amalrik, Andrei, 285
aminazine, 161, 162–3, 164, 165
amnesties, 239–40, 253
Amnesty International, 216, 289
Andropov, Yuri, 146, 326
anti-semitism, 81–2
Antonyuk, Zinovy, 320
Arkus, Dr, 202
artists, exhibitions of nonconformist, 122–3, 132, 181
*Assembly* (magazine), 121n.
Associated Press, 285, 294; *see also* Jensen, Holger; Leddington, Roger; Peipert, Jim
Astaurov, B. L., 219
Avtorkhanov, Abdurahman, 278n.

Babitsky, Konstantin, 269n.
Bakstein, Ilya, 125, 131
Bashkiria, B. born in, 70
Belebei, B. born at, 70
Belyayev, Anatoly, 165
Beria, Lavrenti, P., 185
bitches, Polish thieves, 245–6
Bogdanov, V., 325–6
Bogoraz, Larisa, 241, 269n., 278
Bologov, Dr, 211
Bolsheviks, 97–8
books, in prison, 28–30, 299
*Boomerang* (verse collection), 117
Borisov, Vladimir, 302, 315
Bor (camp), B. in, 240, 246–51, 256–61, 267–9, 270–3

box, *see* punishment cell
Brezhnev, Leonid, 152, 154, 192
Budulak-Sharygin, Nikolai Alexandro-vich, 326
Bukovsky, Konstantin (father of B.), 70, 73, 85, 103, 106, 129, 131
Bukovsky, Nina (mother of B.)
  and arrest of B., 136
  and birth/childhood of B., 70, 73
  complains to authorities, 212, 213
  and discharge of B. from Leningrad Hospital, 176
  illness of, 276–7
  KGB agents abused by, 292–3
  leaves Russia with B., 342, 343
  at trial of B., 239
  and visits, to B. in prison, 28, 159, 162, 167, 311–12

CBS, *see* Cole, Bill
Camp 35, B. in, 248, 252, 321–3, 331, 332–8
camps, corrective labour
  coercion in, 256; *see also* work, *below*
  criminals and political prisoners to share same, 218
  drugs, drug-taking, in, 262–3
  drunkenness in, 262
  food in, 254–5, 335
  four types of, 32n.
  guards in, 65, 263–4
  injury, self-inflicted, in, 250–1
  inquiries into, *see under* commission of inquiry
  location of, 252, 320, 321
  medical treatment in, 251, 258, 332–3
  punishment cell in, 257–8
  'reformed' prisoners in, 248–9
  school in, 264–6

camps, corrective labour—*continued*
 sex in, 245, 264–7
 visits in, 256
 work, forced labour, in, 247–8, 249–51, 252, 256
capitalism, underground, 151–3
cards, playing, 242–3
castle, Bukovsky's fantasy of, 22–4, 46, 139, 198, 298
Chekalin, Alexander, 324–5
*Chronicle of Current Events*, 241, 278, 333, 334
*Chronicle of the Gulag Archipelago*, 336, 338
church, the, 62–3, 155–6, 156
citizen, concept of a, 189, 192, 198
City Psychiatric Hospital No. 13, Moscow, 201–2, 206
civil rights movement, 131, 217, 269, 281
*Cocktail* (verse collection), 117
Cole, Bill, 285, 294, 300, 301
commission of inquiry
 into camps, 334
 into mental hospitals, 174, 175, 306–8
 into prisons, 31–2, 36
Communist Party
 B. and Moscow City Committee, 104–7
 dissidents attacked by, 120–1, 130–1
 inner-party democracy, 84, 128
 22nd Congress of, 125, 126, 130
 youth organisations of, 79; *see also* Komsomol; Young Pioneers
complaints, by prisoners, 30, 33–7, 48–9, 230, 231, 232, 256–7, 259–60, 299–300, 310, 324
convicts, crooks, non-political prisoners, 32–3, 41, 317–19
 political prisoners, relations with, 41, 42, 243, 271–2
constitution, Soviet, 190; *see also* law
Constitution Day demonstrations, 130n.
corrective labour camps, *see* camps
correspondents, foreign, 280, 285, 293; *see also* Cole, Bill; Jensen, Holger; Leddington, Roger; Peipert, Jim
Corvalan, Luis, 343, 345
Criminal Code, amendments to, 217–19
Czechoslovakia, invasion of, 269n., 270

Daniel, Yuli, 278n.; *see also* Sinyavsky, Andrei, and Daniel, Yuli
Delaunay, Vadim, 223, 224, 232, 236, 239(2), 269n., 270
demonstrations
 in Pushkin Square (5 December 1965), demanding trial for Sinyavsky and Daniel, 198–9, 202–4
 suppression of, by amendments to Criminal Code (1966), 217–19
 in Pushkin Square (5 December 1966), 219
 in Pushkin Square (22 January 1967), protesting against arrests, 220–3, 229–30, 235–6
Detengof, Dr, 287
détente, policy of, 344
diamond thieves, trial of, 149–50
Djilas, Milovan, his book copied by B., 136–9
Dobrovolsky, Alexei, 119n., 220, 240
doctors' plot, 81, 186
Doinikov, Captain, 10–11, 47, 48, 65, 339
Dostoevsky, Fyodor, 272
Dremlyuga, Vladimir, 269n.
drugs, drug-taking, in camps, 262–3
drugs, in psychiatric abuse, 164; *see also* aminazine; haloperidol; sulphazine

economy, Soviet, 150–4
education, 75–6, 87, 100–1, 125
Eisenhower, President Dwight D., 133
Ellman, Michael, 216
emigration, from Russia, 296–7, 339
Engelhardt, V. A., 219
English
 B. studies, 8, 28, 167
 in prison communication, 44–5
Eurocommunism, 89
evening institute, B. at, 107

factory, work lessons at, 101–2
farms, state
 experiment at, 152–3
 work lessons at, 102–3
Fainberg, Victor, 269n, 315
force-feeding, 311–12
forced labour
 in camps, 249–51, 252, 256
 in prison, 33
Fyodorkov (prisoner), 98

Gabai, Ilya, 223, 224, 229, 232, 235, 241
Gagarin, Yuri, 121
Galanskov, Yuri, 117n., 119, 119–20, 128, 129–30, 182, 203, 220, 240–1
Galich, Alexander, 89n., 116
gambling, in prison, 242–3
Gavrilin (prisoner, nicknamed Savage), 39
Gavrilov, Gennady, 320
Gerstenmaier, Cornelia, 296
Ginzburg, Alexander, 117, 119n, 220, 240, 285, 321
Gluzman, Semyon, 289
godfather (prison security officer), 23–4, 143, 247, 267
gold, hoarded, *see* 'millionaires'
Gorbanevskaya, Natalya, 269n., 278n., 287–8, 302

Gosplan, 253
Grigorenko, Pyotr, 287, 289, 315
Gritsai, Anatoly, 148–9
guards, in prisons/camps, 39–40, 48, 65, 263–4
Gubanov, Leonid, 203
Gumilyov, Nikolai, 114

haloperidol, 283
Helsinki agreements, 344
hijackers, Leningrad, 296, 319–20
homosexuality, in prisons/camps, 245, 266–7
Hungary, Hungarian revolution, 89–90
hunger strikes, 28, 30, 310–12, 337

Ilyukhin (Deputy General Prosecutor), 312
informers, in prison, 142–9
insulin shock treatment, 165
investigation, of political crime, 224–9
Ivanov, Colonel, 137
Ivanov, Mikhail ('Mishka'; B.'s nephew) 342, 345
*Izvestia*, 204

Jensen, Holger, 285, 290, 290–1, 294, 300
Jews, anti-semitism, 81–2
jokes, political, 53, 61, 114–15

KGB (Committee of State Security)
    and B., 78, 122–3, 126–7, 128–30, 132, 136–9, 148, 199–200, 260–1, 285, 291–4, 294–5, 299, 308–9, 331–2, 341–5
    and financial trials, 143–6, 150
    investigation, methods of, 156–7, 224–9
    jokes about, 115
    and Khrushchev thaw, 109–10
    and Mayakovsky Square readings, 120, 122, 122–3, 125–6, 127–8
    and police, 122, 200
    prison security officer of, *see* godfather
    and psychiatry, 49n., 156–7, 284
    and war criminals, 330
    mentioned, 27n., 146, 219
Kalinin, Lieutenant-Colonel Leonid Alexeyevich, 169–71, 176
Kallistratova, Sophia, 234, 235, 310
Kalugin, Victor, 119
Kalynets, Igor, 320
Kaminskaya, Dina Isakovna, 234(2), 235, 310, 312
Kaplan, Mikhail, 119
Karaulov (mental patient), 167–8
Kashchenko Hospital, 194
Kashirov, Sanya, 207–8, 209
Kaverin, Veniamin, 219
Kazakhstan, state farm experiment in, 152–3

Khaustov, Victor, 119, 129–30, 220, 221, 222–3, 232, 234, 236–7, 240
Khrushchev, Nikita, 111–13
    assassination of, alleged plot concerning, 127
    and dissidence as mental illness, 155–6
    removed from power, 192
    and Stalin, 83–4
    on stealing, 150
    and Tarsis, 194
Khrushchev thaw, 108–11
Khudenko, Ivan Nikiforovich, 152–3
Kiselev, Major, 39
Klempert, Iosif Lvovich, 145–6
Klimov, Sergei, 158–9, 160
Komsomol, 79, 80–1, 114, 120, 122, 122–3, 124, 128, 204
Korkach, Captain Vladimir, 299, 309, 312
Kosygin, A. N., 150, 192
Kovalsky (psychiatrist), 157–8
Kovshin, Vladimir, 119
Koslov, Andrei, 304–5
Krasin, Victor, 113n., 333
Kurkis (prisoner), 333
Kushev, Yevgeny, 223, 232, 236, 239
Kuznetsov, Edward, 119, 128, 131, 132, 302
Kuznetsov, Victor, 286

labour camps, *see* camps
*Lamp, The* (magazine), 117n.
Lashkova, Vera, 119n., 220, 240
Lavrov (murderer), 176
law, legal rights, 130, 131, 187, 189–91
    Soviet man's ignorance of, 226–8
lawyers
    and access permits, 234, 309–10
    dissidents aided by, 234–5, 286, 309–10
    role of, in political cases, 228
Leddington, Roger, 294, 295–6
Lefortovo prison, 140–1, 154, 298–9
    B. in, 66–9, 138–42, 154, 159–60, 224, 297, 298, 331–2, 340
Lenin, Vladimir Ilyich, 85–6, 109, 186
Leningrad hijackers, 296, 319–20
Leningrad Special Mental Hospital, 155, 163
    B. in, 160–77
Leontovich, M. A., 219
*Literary Gazette*, B. attacked in, 46–7
Lithuania, Lithuanian prisoners, 321, 322
Litvinov, Pavel, 241, 269n., 278n.
Lubyanka prison, B. in, 127, 128, 136–8
Lukomsky, Professor, 307
Lunts, Daniil Romanovich, 213–15, 281, 287(2), 288, 301–3, 306, 307, 308

MVD, 27n.
    security officer of, *see* godfather

349

Ma Hun, 326–30
magazine, at B.'s school, 100, 103–6
Makarenko, Mikhail Yanovich, 329
Malenkov, Georgi, 83
Malyarov (Assistant Public Prosecutor), 144, 233
Mandelshtam, Osip, 114
*Manifesto of Man* (Galanskov), 119–20
Marchenko, Anatoly, 278n.
Markham, David, 289, 296
Matuzevicius, Ionas, 322–3
Mayakovsky Square, poetry readings in, 116–22, 122–3, 124, 125–6, 128, 130–132, 195
Medvedev, Roy and Zhores, 285–6
Melekhov, Professor T. D., 307, 308
Meshener, Iosif, 320
'millionaires', hoarders of gold and valuables, 143–6, 150, 153–4
Mishka (B.'s nephew), *see* Ivanov, Mikhail
Mordovia, camps in, 320
Morozov, Dr Georgi V., 215, 216, 306
Moscow Human Rights Committee, 130n.
Moscow University, B. at, 107–8, 123–5

Nadzharov, Professor, 302
Naritsa, Mikhail Alexandrovich, 173, 193–4
Nikiforov, Captain Vladimir, 126–7, 136

Obrubov, Captain Nikolai, 40
Okudzhava, Bulat, 115–16
organisations, secret, 96–7
  at school, 90–6, 98–9
Osipov, Vladimir, 117n., 119, 121, 131

Pasternak, Boris, 114, 193
Pavlenkov, Vladlen, 320
Pechernikov, Professor, 282
Peipert, Jim, 294–5
Perepelitsyn, General, 194
Perm province, Perm experiment, 252, 321–3, 332–8
Petrenko, Colonel Alexander, 139–40, 231, 231–2, 239
*Phoenix* (1961), 117; (1966), 119n., 220
Pidgorodetsky, Vasily, 333
Pimenov, Major, 334, 336, 337
Pintan (would-be emigrant), 172
Pisarev, Sergei Petrovich, 184–6, 314
Podgorny, Nikolai, 192
political instructor, 24, 47–8
  at Vladimir, *see* Doinikov
political prisoners
  'accidental' cases, 323–30
  criminals, relations with, 41, 42, 243, 271–2
  number of, 30

types of, in mental hospital, 171–3
and Western press, 31, 196–7; *see also* correspondents, foreign; *and under* West
and work, in prison, 33–9
*polizei* (collaborators), 248, 330
Pozdnyakov, Dr, 209
*Pravda*, 299
Prisakaru, Nikolai Georgievich, 172–3
prison
  books in, 28–30, 299
  communication in, 42–5
  deterrent function of, 25–6
  exercise in, 43–4
  food, hunger, in, 8, 17–18, 26, 27; *see also* hunger strikes
  four types of, 32n.
  guards in, 39–40, 48, 65
  informers, stool-pigeons, in, 142–9
  inquiries into, *see under* commission of inquiry
  life in, 16–19
  medical treatment in, 38–9
  punishment cell in, 19–23, 27
  useful objects, smuggled into, 9
  work in, 33
  *see also* Lefortovo; Lubyanka; Vladimir
Prisovsky, Yuri, 146
pseudonyms, writers' use of, 193–4, 196
psychiatric abuse, 155–76, 209–10, 281–4, 285–90, 301–3
psychiatrists, 200–1
  western, 289–90, 301, 303
psychiatry, Moscow and Leningrad schools of, 169, 171, 211–12
punishment cell (box)
  in camps, 257–8
  in prisons, 19–23, 27

Radzievsky, Paul, 220, 235
re-education, socialist, 87, 89
  forced labour as, 249
Rode, Gunnar, 38, 66–7
Roifman (prisoner), 144
'roll-up' (punishment), 164
Romm, Mikhail, 219
Rotstein, Professor, 215
Russell, Bertrand, 152

Sakharov, Andrei, 130n., 219, 320, 333
*samizdat*, 89n., 115, 116, 117, 119n., 120, 195, 218, 241, 278
Samsonov, Nikolai Nikolayevich, 164 314–15
Sapronovich (mental patient), 166
Sazonov, Captain, 265–6, 270–1
schizophrenia, 169, 302, 308; 'sluggish', 171, 215, 282–4, 302, 307–8
searches, in Moscow, 277–8